Propaganda and counter-terrorism

Manchester University Press

Propaganda and counter-terrorism

Strategies for global change

Emma Louise Briant

Manchester University Press

Published by Manchester University Press
Altrincham Street, Manchester M1 7JA, UK
www.manchesteruniversitypress.co.uk

British Library Cataloguing-in-Publication Data
A catalogue record for this book is available from the British Library

Library of Congress Cataloging-in-Publication Data applied for

ISBN 978 1 5261 0729 9 paperback

First published by Manchester University Press in hardback 2015

This edition first published 2016

Typeset
by Action Publishing Technology Ltd, Gloucester
Printed in Great Britain
by Lightning Source

Contents

List of figures   *page* vii

Acknowledgements   ix

List of abbreviations   xi

1 Introduction   1

2 Propaganda 'boundaries' and the extended apparatus   35

3 Formal propaganda (mis-)coordination   94

4 Domestic planners, initiative and propaganda   126

5 Anglo-American relations in the counter-terrorism propaganda war   185

6 Iraq War case study   223

7 Countering terror, denying dissent   244

References   254

Index   281

Figures

1.1 Levels of PSYOP – adapted from Joint Chiefs of Staff, 2003: ix,
x, 1–4   *page* 13
6.1 Personnel inside the palace at CPA Baghdad, from presentation
by Ian Tunnicliffe, Baghdad, 2003.   226
6.2 Ian Tunnicliffe inside the palace at CPA Baghdad,
from presentation by Ian Tunnicliffe, Baghdad, 2003.   226
6.3 Slide from presentation by Ian Tunnicliffe, Baghdad, 2003.   229
6.4 Slide contrasting US/Arab media images, from presentation
by Ian Tunnicliffe, Baghdad, 2003.   230
6.5 Slide contrasting US/Arab media images, from presentation by Ian
Tunnicliffe, Baghdad, 2003.   230
6.6 The 'Green Room' – Office of Strategic Communication,
CPA Baghdad, from presentation by Ian Tunnicliffe, Baghdad, 2003.   237

Note: All images in Chapter 6 were taken in Baghdad, 2003, and shown in a presentation by Ian Tunnicliffe in 2004.

Acknowledgements

I want to give my utmost gratitude to my doctoral supervisory team, Prof. Greg Philo and Prof. Sarah Oates for all their help, guidance and perpetually positive outlook even when I felt things a struggle. I consider being a member of Glasgow Media Group a great privilege, and I would like to extend my thanks to all those there who helped and supported me. Particular thanks go to Daniela Latina and Keirstan Pawson, the dedicated and meticulous research assistants who assisted me with my transcription, and Alex Cox and Giuliana Tiripelli, who were kind enough to do some proofreading. Thanks to Prof. John Eldridge who was always there with smile, a wise word and an excellent book. I am particularly indebted to Prof. Bridget Fowler and Greg, both of whom helped me secure funding for the research, as well as the ESRC for that funding. I wish to thank all my interviewees whose agreement, support and contributions formed the basis of the research, particularly Joel Harding and Angus Taverner for helping greatly with contacts. I would like to thank all the people who assisted me during my time in Washington, DC, particularly Verenda Smith Camire and John Stanton. I am also grateful to all my friends and family who gave me their patience and encouragement throughout. Lastly but importantly I would like to give my gratitude to Tony Mason and the excellent staff at Manchester University Press.

Abbreviations

CIA	Central Intelligence Agency (US)
CIC	Coalition Information Centre
CENTCOM	United States Central Command
CJPOTF	Combined Joint Psychological Operations Task Force
COIN	Counter-insurgency
CPA	Coalition Provisional Authority
DIA	Defense Intelligence Agency (US)
DOD	Department of Defense (US)
DTIO	Director(ate) of Targeting and Information Operations (UK)
FCO	Foreign & Commonwealth Office (UK)
GICS	Government Information and Communications Service (UK)
IIA	Interactive Internet Activities (US)
IO	Information Operations
IRD	Information Research Department (UK)
MoD	Ministry of Defence (UK)
MI5	(Domestic) Security Service (UK)
MI6/SIS	(International) Secret Intelligence Service (UK)
MISO	Military Information Support Operations (US)
NCO	Non-Commissioned Officer
NCTC	National Counterterrorism Center (US)
NDAA	National Defense Authorization Act
NSA	National Security Advisor (US)
NSC	National Security Council (US)
OSI	Office of Strategic Influence (US)
PA	Public Affairs
PD	Public Diplomacy
PR	Public Relations
PSYOP(S)	Psychological Operations
SIS/MI6	(International) Secret Intelligence Service (UK)
TAA	Target Audience Analysis
USIA	United States Information Agency

1

Introduction

Following the September 11th 2001 terrorist attacks, the so-called 'psychological terrain' was seen as the crucial counter-terrorism 'battleground' where compliance might be created or conflict influenced in Afghanistan and Iraq. Much has been written about the 'hearts and minds' campaigns of the governments of the United States and United Kingdom. Yet this book will illuminate an unseen story, that of the planning behind the propaganda, from the mouths of the key planners themselves. It traces their efforts to adapt propaganda systems that were seen as 'outdated' within a rapidly changing global media environment that defied geographical boundaries and muddied traditional 'targeting'. The book will argue that these counter-terrorism adaptations resulted in initiatives that gave propaganda wider reach and challenged existing structures, 'rules' and practices. Change was not an uncomplicated process, however, and this book examines Anglo-American adaptation and explains how, why, and to what extent the countries were 'successful' in adapting. Documenting changing ideas about propaganda in both countries during this transitional period, the book will point to the active mediation of propaganda strategies into the culture and practices of government departments and military organisations.

Where the operation and systems of propaganda are often discussed as if they were a systematic or unproblematic 'machine', this book demonstrates that the systems of this machine do not always function as governments hope and, like any large bureaucracy, they can struggle to adapt. They are of course formed of people, and propaganda planning can become a site of active struggle, dependent on evolving informal structures founded in relationships and culture. The Anglo-American relationship emerged in this struggle as one element that could sometimes be engaged in the process of propaganda adaptation and exchange. Ultimately the book will show how a structural development of the propaganda apparatus and gradual culture change, particularly in the US, brought a (more permissive) re-definition of 'legitimate' propaganda function, developments that were seen as necessary to shift out old ideas and solidify the changes necessary for operational effectiveness.

The rest of this introduction will provide an entry point into the specialist area covered by the book including debates about security and ethics. It will begin with a short history of propaganda theories, including important definitions and concepts from academic perspectives as well as those dominant in contemporary defence policy. This section will be followed by a brief history of Anglo-American relations and propaganda use to provide valuable context to the contemporary relationship. This will lead into a discussion of how 'security' and 'threats' were defined and constructed for the 'War on Terror'. There will finally be a brief note on method.

Theoretical and ethical debates on propaganda

Although this research focuses on the use of propaganda by two particular modern liberal democracies, the use and indeed the study of propaganda is ancient and global. From the early democracies of ancient Greece until the early twentieth century the term most commonly used to refer to what we now think of as propaganda was 'rhetoric'. Its morality was debated from the first. Although he was generally unhappy about rhetoric's use, Plato regarded the *motives* of the propagandist to be of great importance. In *Phaedrus* he argues that rhetoric should not be used unless the rhetorician has good motives and a solid knowledge of the 'truth'. Aristotle appeared to judge the act of using rhetoric by the *ends* to which it is directed, its context and methods, with much being acceptable if done with good intentions (Aristotle, 1984; Triadafilopoulos, 1999). Machiavelli famously claimed in *The Prince* that ends justify means and that deception was acceptable as a means for retaining power, and his description of the Prince reflects an understanding of the need for a leader to occasionally appear to be what he is not (1961: 55–56).

Ethical debates regarding 'truths', 'ends' and 'motives' have continued to be central to the study of rhetoric and propaganda. The prescience of the study of political tools like rhetoric and propaganda has become increasingly apparent into modernity and it is important to understand where the 'rules' governing persuasion stem from, since they are integral to societal values and a debate rooted in the very origins of Western democratic culture. Representative democracy raises particular issues regarding the relation between public opinion and policy, and it may be that propaganda is simply irreconcilable with democratic values. Responding to the British government's lies during the First World War, Lord Ponsonby declared propaganda 'The defilement of the human soul' and 'worse than the destruction of the human body' (1928, quoted in Taylor, 2003: 1). Robert Goodin echoes this, saying propaganda is 'the evil core of power' (1980: 23), which by 'deceptively subverting' the recipients' 'powers of reasoning' becomes more objectionable even than force (1980: 21–22). If a person is suffering oppression, coercion or terror they are aware of this and may be able to take steps to reassert their will. However, the art of propaganda does not allow for this possibility. It attempts to gain willing compliance often unconsciously.

Throughout the early twentieth century, public opinion was seen as essentially unpredictable and susceptible to the influence of external propaganda and marginal interests. Harold Lasswell (1934), for example, saw public opinion as irrational, inconsistent and in need of leadership. Likewise, Walter Lippmann argued that public opinion is not sovereign, nor should it be, for this would create tyranny or failure of government. For him the public are 'outsiders' who should fulfil the role for which they have been prepared and not try and delve into politics when they lack expertise (1954: 51–53). Should we reject such elitism, the model of rational ignorance tells us that, as the public are unable to know everything, they must to some extent trust in information presented to them (Goodin, 1980: 38). A negative conception of public opinion would hold that it cannot be the basis of stable, responsible government. Since democratic government cannot operate outside the pressure of the electorate and public opinion must be seen to be expressed in policy, by such reasoning attempts to adjust opinion to correspond to government policy lose their perception of illegitimacy. This was significant in Edward Bernays' early 'public relations' work, inspired by Lippmann, which used the psychology behind persuasion both to engineer consent to govern and fight wars through propaganda, and to aid consumerism (2004).

As the mass media flourished in the post-war period, propaganda was increasingly viewed as a key characteristic of modern democracy. There developed a highly influential school of thought drawing insight from behavioural psychology and applying this to propaganda. Lasswell, Doob and others saw propaganda largely as a tool that could be manipulated in order to produce desired responses in the audience (Robins, Webster and Pickering, 1987: 3). The study of propaganda revolved around 'audience effects', including experimental studies which have since been denounced (Ellul, 1973: Ch. 4, App. 1). Such theories saw the audience as passively absorbing information, as if injected by a hypodermic syringe. Theorists have since rejected such notions in favour of more sophisticated understandings that account for the wider context through which information is organised, filtered and interpreted. While many still looked at the mechanical aspects of propaganda, thought gradually moved towards the consideration of power and social relations reacting against the less optimistic ideas of public opinion. The mass persuasion and propaganda of Goebbels for Hitler also drove post-war fears of the implications should government fall into the wrong hands. The political and social elements of the use of propaganda came into focus, as well as more sophisticated psychological approaches. Discussion stemmed from the emerging work of the Chicago

School, which saw public opinion as essentially rational and requiring a public sphere characterised by lively debate (drawing on Enlightenment ideas such as those of J.S. Mill) (Robins, Webster and Pickering, 1987: 16). If we are to believe that public opinion is rational (or at least no less so than elite opinion) and the only basis for responsible and legitimate government, then propaganda can surely never be justified? Habermas, for example, was critical of propaganda, which he feared was leading to the destruction of the public sphere, the means whereby public opinion is formed (Webster, 1995: 101–134). This book will return to this debate in Chapter 4.

In the US, while fears about propaganda remained, it was seen as a priority to ensure engagement in influencing global perceptions and debate, and permissions as well as restrictions were established during the Cold War period (see below). While the term 'propaganda' was commonly associated with dictatorships and totalitarian regimes (conceived as 'what the enemy said'), its methods were increasingly recognised as a standard tool of democratic government. Qualter, for example, saw propaganda as acceptable as long as there was the 'greatest possible degree of free competition between propagandists' (1962: 148). Fraser stressed that 'propaganda as such is morally neutral', and it is the surrounding circumstances or the methods applied that are evil or good (Ellul, 1973: 242). He emphasised that although these methods can be abused, this should not be extended to an ultimate judgement of the use of propaganda (Fraser 1957: 12). Merton (1995) also made a distinction between propaganda that provides facts and that which denies such information, rooting his arguments on morality around this distinction. Even Ellul, despite his highly critical stance towards propaganda (he articulates concern over pollution of our shared knowledge-base, saying that propaganda corrupts those who use it), concedes that it is an inevitable part of any democracy (1973: 242–243; see also Burnell and Reeve, 1984).

Some contend that it is the growth of democracy and mass communication that has confirmed the place of propaganda in politics. Democratic governments must live with a political reality that their citizens have some level of political awareness and come up with a strategy to deal with this. According to Ellul, 'propaganda is needed in the exercise of power for the simple reason that the masses have come to participate in political affairs' (1973: 121). The emphasis has gradually changed from the techniques and practices themselves and refocused on those employing them, and social theorists have attempted to scrape away the rhetoric and illuminate and challenge the roles propagandists play within wider social power relations. A great debt is owed here to Gramsci's work on cultural hegemony, as he developed Marx's concept of the 'superstructure' in his *Prison Notebooks*. Hegemony, for Gramsci, emerged through various competing ideologies, some of which are theories created by academics or political activists, others of which are more 'organic', emerging within the common people's lived experience and articulated through religion, education, family and the media. These were 'functionaries' of a structure, yet 'mediated' by their relation to the rest of society (Gramsci, 1971: 12). Gramsci saw some scope for resistance and 'will' in these 'organic intellectuals' (1971: 129), but this exists alongside their tendency to shape perceptions of institutions and wider society towards the dominant culture. Essentially, for Gramsci, this tension was necessary for the coordination of 'the dominant group' with 'the general interests of the subordinate groups' so that the state could modify any 'unstable equilibria' of interests (1971: 182). This underpinned the illusion that dominant interests were also those of society, and government was 'based on the consent of the majority' as it is expressed through the media (Gramsci, 1971: 80).

Gramsci thus articulated a theory of how the dominant group are able to manufacture consent and consensus in society, while allowing conflicts to be resolved or absorbed. Much of his theory is helpful in considering the way that democracies work today and how the dominance of neoliberal ideologies is maintained through propaganda, both within the state and in its relation to civil society and the public. For Gramsci, more traditional intellectuals and the 'party' reproduced the dominant order most closely; having survived a transition in the mode of production, they falsely retained beliefs that their thought somehow *transcended* social class and had 'independence' (1971: 129). Gramsci described how intellectuals can 'exercise such a power of attraction that [they subjugate] intellectuals of the other social groups; they thereby create a system of solidarity', engineering consensus through psychological and social bonds (1971: 182). McLellan argues this can form an all-pervasive notion of 'common sense' (something we will see illustrated in later accounts in this book); he points to how, devoid of 'feudal' engagement with a peasantry, America's ruling class were still able to exercise a strong hegemony of capitalist values (1998: 203).

Contemporary arguments often still incorporate an ends–means analysis; for instance, Philip Taylor argued that what was needed was 'to redirect any moral judgement away from the propaganda process itself and more to the intentions and goals of those employing propaganda' (2003: 8). Generally, if a strategy successfully achieves a desirable goal the methods employed are quickly overlooked; it is usually when the plan backfires that criticism flows – if, of course, this becomes public knowledge. But too much focus on 'ends' may be dangerous. Ellul points out that the 'truth' about actors and outcomes as we understand them is elucidated through history, and that history is made by the powerful and successful. He highlights a conflict between the principles of democracy and the need for and processes of propaganda (Ellul, 1973: 232–238). Taylor stressed the importance of remaining within the boundaries of certain 'democratic' principles, which he argued evolved during the events of the twentieth century. This led him, after 9/11, to argue for an enhanced US propaganda effort during peacetime to attempt to counter rumour, hostility and misunderstanding in the international arena (Taylor, 2002: 438). However, the history of democracies' propaganda campaigns during the twentieth century does not support Taylor's idealistic notion that a 'strategy of truth' evolved during this era that can be reasserted now (2002: 438). From Vietnam to Korea, Granada to the Falklands, the US and Britain (as well as other democracies) have utilised extensive propaganda campaigns that have bypassed such principles to support foreign policy goals. The conduct of the democracies of Britain and America today should not be seen as exceptional. They are a reflection of a perception of heightened tension and a perceived 'need' to address this. Political actors were no more ethical in the past, yet today the scale of access to information and therefore the growth in its status as a powerful commodity has increased the visibility of propaganda efforts, requiring us to prioritise this debate.

Taylor also argued that US and UK governments' use of propaganda 'is not incompatible with toleration of minorities, acceptance of the "other" or respect for law and order' and that what is important in the debate over propaganda is '*how* this should be done' (2002: 439). Both he and US academic and former USIA official Nancy Snow (2003) claim that the pursuit of an 'ethical' propaganda is possible. A 'democratic propaganda' would be essentially truthful and restrained, with respect for the individual. Democracy recognises that there may be other truths (allowing 'competing propagandas', as Snow (2003) advocates). Ellul concludes that debate renders democracies' propaganda ineffective; respect for the individual denies the propagandist sufficient monopoly over the mind (1973: 238–242) and the search for an *effective* propaganda is therefore an essentially corrupting force. Fraser argues that, although propaganda is not necessarily lies, those who do lie may sometimes win over the truth. This means that a liberal democracy must on occasion choose between upholding its moral principles and winning a propaganda war (1957: 12–13). This goal was seen as justification enough for British and American Second World War activities (explored further below). R.K. Merton observes that a propagandist might be driven to cynicism or desperate attempts to justify their actions by the outcome of such a dilemma (1995: 270). Where covert propaganda is used it is difficult to imagine how any individual might secure true freedom of thought.

The dominant position inhabited by those in power ensures that propaganda seems incompatible with a truly democratic culture. Herman and Chomsky's 'Manufacturing Consent' (1988) and their later work has been highly regarded both popularly and in academic circles. It is critical work that struggles against the mainstream. Noam Chomsky, recognising the key role of propaganda in modern democracies, has provided a consistent stream of work that has inspired many to take a more questioning stance towards contemporary propaganda. Chomsky rejects the idea of the irrationality of public opinion, which is used to justify propaganda, as a myth propagated by the elite to serve its interest (1991: 17–19). Chomsky gives us a convincing account of how, in democracies, corporate power and the state influence the media and therefore the nation. He famously stated that 'propaganda is to a democracy what the bludgeon is to a totalitarian state' (2002: 23). He has argued that the model of media organisation that is natural in an advanced capitalist democracy is a 'corporate oligopoly' (1991: 21), in which the public have a minimal level of democratic participation and where participation is marginalised to areas such as community radio. Debate is encouraged, but only within the boundaries defined by the elite (1991: 59). Anything that might spread dangerous ideas among the people excluded from political participation is censored. The development of this system, Chomsky argues, coincides with increasing individualism and private enterprise, the decline of political parties and the elimination of unions (1991: 21).

A similarly critical analysis is presented by another contemporary academic, David Miller, much of whose work looks at counter-terrorism propaganda the UK context (e.g. Miller and Sabir, 2012). He recognises the importance of the US and UK working to achieve 'interoperability' in propaganda, and the present book provides additional evidence to support this idea. Some of Miller's writing draws attention to the tensions and cultures within propaganda systems; on these dynamic elements his work on Northern Ireland is particularly strong (1996).

Censorship and media freedom

Debates around the ethics of propaganda are inextricably linked to discussions about democracy and its foundations in open debate. Classical liberal arguments underpinning media freedom in democratic culture include those of Jeremy Bentham (1843) who considered accountability and openness to be of the utmost importance and wrote at length about the benefits of publicity, which he felt would prevent the abuse of power. John Stuart Mill, similarly, argued that

> complete liberty of contradicting and disproving our opinion is the very condition which justifies us in assuming its truth for the purposes of action: and on no other terms can a being with human faculties have any rational assurance of being right. (1989: 23)

Herman and Chomsky (1988) and others have pointed to the contradictions of a capitalist democracy as corrupting this freedom. For example, Robert W. McChesney's significant work argues that the US corporate media system prevents true democracy, limiting debate around the interests of corporate power (2000). Keane's work also illustrates an inherent contradiction between economic and political liberalism through what he calls 'market censorship', a tendency for economic liberalisation to lead to the restriction of the circulation of information, a claim also made by James Curran (Curran and Seaton, 1988; Keane, 1991).

Censorship has historically been considered crucial in any propaganda system. It enables a propagandist to ensure that an audience's critical assessment of propaganda is undermined by a lack of contesting perspectives. It thereby increases audience vulnerability to persuasion. The British government has a long-held reputation for secrecy of this kind. On the grounds of 'national interest' this policy is underpinned by the Official Secrets Act of 1911. Section 2 contained a 'public interest' defence, which was repealed in 1989. This Act allows an official request – a 'Defence Advisory Notice' – to be made by the government to oblige newspaper editors not to publish certain information. Recent UK legislation has included the Terrorism Act in 2000, which made it an offence to possess information likely to be of use to a terrorist, and in 2006 a far-reaching law made it illegal to 'glorify' terrorism. Goodin warns how secrecy can corrupt and argues that usually when censorship is justified in the name of 'national security' this is to cover up personal advantage (1980: 51).

Over-classification can also act as censorship, as Arendt warned; the dangers of over-classification find those with top clearance ignorant of many important facts as they neither have the time nor will to seek them out, while those who would benefit most from this information remain ignorant of it (Goodin, 1980: 21–22). Goodin warns of 'co-optation', as those privy to certain sources of information can begin to bend their own ethics or moderate their demands in order to retain this privilege (1980: 52–56). Information overload can have the same effect as secrecy and certainly in the short term and for democracies today it might be considered more effective. This is the practice whereby the audience is flooded with so much information that it is unable and/or unwilling to digest it independently to form criticism. Today governments make a wealth of information available to the public online – through Freedom of Information releases for instance – although few people, even journalists, sift through everything. Governments simultaneously produce press releases that detail those facts they consider most 'important' for the public to know – a framework for interpreting the data. This conforms to their own preferences and downplays or frames any negative aspects of the information from the government perspective. Anomalies later discovered by the audience are often put down to personal error, a process that shifts responsibility away from the propagandist or their organisation. However, the propagandist can end up viewing the world through their own interpretive framework (Goodin, 1980: 60). In this case it is questionable whether, despite 'informational advantage', they are any more able to make 'objective' or 'rational' national security decisions than the audience they manipulate.

Defining propaganda

The definition of propaganda has been contested by many and often given a politically weighted slant. Some prefer a neutral definition, others a more loaded one, some define more broadly and some narrowly. Some even consider the concept so complex and contested that it is somehow beyond definition, or too difficult to define (Ellul, 1973; Fraser, 1957: 14). Lasswell defined propaganda broadly, as 'the technique of influencing human action by the manipulation of representations' which can take 'spoken, written, pictorial or musical form' (1934: 13). Doob defined propaganda as 'the attempt to affect the personalities and to control the behaviours of individuals towards ends considered unscientific or of doubtful value in a society at a particular time' (1949: 240). It has generally come to be accepted that, although propaganda can involve lies, it can also be based on fact or 'truth'; indeed the most effective and persuasive propaganda is based largely, or wholly, on fact. Even the Pentagon accepts that enemy propaganda may contain truth: 'These propagandists attempt to mix truth and lies in a way that is imperceptible to the listener' (US Army, 2003: 11–3). More recently, government propaganda has come to be popularly referred to as 'spin'; this negatively denotes political information, and the term 'spin doctor' has also developed to refer to those advisers who attempt to present information in a favourable light. Although other authors have used many different terms in speaking of these kinds of communication, here the term 'propaganda' will be applied, as it is the most accurate and appropriate term for the very specific type of communication discussed. For the purposes of this book, propaganda will be defined as *the deliberate manipulation of representations (including text, pictures, video, speech etc.) with the intention of producing any effect in the audience (e.g. action or inaction; reinforcement or transformation of feelings, ideas, attitudes or behaviours) that is desired by the propagandist.*

Categories of propaganda

Different classifications of propaganda have been used to aid theoretical analysis and such categories can be helpful to further distinguish between forms and styles of propaganda use.

White, black and grey propaganda

The first classification drawn on here is that between white, black and grey propaganda. White propaganda is that where the use of the propaganda is overt, its source being known to the audience and the information being largely accurate. Black propaganda is often lies; it is covert and it may be attributed to a false source. Grey propaganda encompasses the majority of propaganda and occupies the territory between these two extremes. It is characterised by uncertainty regarding either the source of the information or its accuracy (Jowett and O'Donnell, 1992: 11–15).

Internal and external propaganda

Internal propaganda is that used within a group upon its members or by a country upon its citizens and is normally used for the purposes of integration or to build morale. External propaganda, on the other hand, is directed outside of the group or country being examined. This would include propaganda used by Britain against the citizens or administration of another country such as Afghanistan.

Vertical and horizontal propaganda

Vertical propaganda is made by a propagandist in a superior position or a position of authority who wishes to influence an audience below; for example, propaganda produced by a government and used to target its own people or the people of another country, or even those in a parallel position in another country who might be placed at a lower level by a lack of knowledge of the propagandist's subject matter. Horizontal propaganda, on the other hand, occurs between a propagandist and another person on the same level. Ellul only observed this as occurring between members of a group, for example members of a political party or organs of government which all promote their own activities (Ellul, 1973: 79–84). This form of propaganda is clearly important in building the psychological adherence of the propagandist to the information being distributed and the goals he or she is pursuing as part of a collective.

Horizontal propaganda is useful in an analytical sense as a theoretical ideal type, where we can distinguish activities as having horizontal characteristics. Promotional material within a government agency such as the MoD directed internally to staff to positively reinforce the work undertaken might be an example of this. It may be instigated from the top of a hierarchy, but the knowledge levels of the target audience and production team are sufficient to qualify this as having horizontal elements.

Propaganda understood by the state

In an attempt to make the discussion of propaganda more acceptable, euphemisms are often used by governments with reference to these practices, including 'information' and 'communication'. These are very broad umbrella terms that could encompass a wide spectrum of activities, which is one of the benefits of using them. This language is also being employed increasingly in academia, but as Taylor suggests, euphemisms merely obscure the reality of propaganda and are a result of the confusion that has developed over what propaganda really is (2002: 437). The acceptance or rejection of state-centric definitions of security means that there has been a disparity between how propaganda has been studied within political and social theory, and how it has been considered operationally and by academics with a background in defence. David Miller and Tom Mills (2010) argue that since 9/11 increasing numbers of what they call 'terrorologists' have emerged in Britain: a community of security 'experts' or academics who lack independence and have connections to government or contracting. This community has strengthened state-centric definitions of security, terrorism and propaganda. For clarity, in discussion of specific policies/documents/departments, this book will use the 'official' terminology explained in this section, but otherwise euphemisms, for reasons of academic rigour, have been avoided in analysis.

The Pentagon defines propaganda as 'intentionally incorrect or misleading information directed against an adversary or potential adversary to disrupt or influence any sphere of national power – informational, political, military, or economic' (US Army, 2003: 11–3). The definition specifies that it is *what others do*: 'This information is normally directed at the United States, U.S. allies, and key audiences in the [Joint Operations Area] or [Area of Responsibility]' (US Army, 2003: 11–3). In the past, commentators with professional ties have distinguished their own propaganda and censorship as activities within the wider area of *information warfare* (or an 'information campaign' when speaking more specifically about actions within a particular conflict or time frame). The definition offered by the Institute for the Advanced Study of Information Warfare is

> the offensive and defensive use of information and information systems to exploit, corrupt, or destroy an adversary's information and information systems, while protecting one's own. Such actions are designed to achieve advantages over military or business adversaries. (Goldberg, 2004)

Information warfare reaches out more widely to include interception and re-broadcasting of messages across existing enemy radio stations as well as activities involving infiltration of enemy computer systems and censorship (Tatham, 2006: 7; Interview: Taverner, 18th July 2004).[1] The term has been largely replaced by Information Operations (IO). Also an umbrella term, IO is used to encompass a number of activities, including Psychological Operations (PSYOP) and electronic warfare, computer network operations and deception. During the 1990s IO transformed from being largely focused on 'state-sponsored hackers' to a 'full-spectrum' joint doctrine fully utilising the information component. Former IO Officer Joel Harding described a range of possible activities in IO:[2]

honestly ... the objective of what you are trying to do, is limited by your imagination and special forces tends to think a little differently ... Information can be used to terrorise somebody, or create conditions where someone doesn't wanna do something, or all kinds of things ... Information Operations is supposed to be a military operation ... 'Is my idea to create your combat force to be combat ineffective?' 'Is it to create chaos?' 'Or ... discontent where you don't trust your leaders?' ... there's a million things that you could do to get a military force to stop fighting. (Interview: Harding, 15th January 2013)

Media Operations (in Britain) or Public Affairs (PA) (in the US) and Public Diplomacy (PD) – targeting domestic or international propaganda audiences largely through mass media – are distinguished from PSYOP – propaganda used for an international, largely enemy audience during military operations or in peacetime. A defining characteristic of military categories of propaganda is the continually evolving terminology used in an attempt to escape negative connotations. For example, in late 2010 in the US, PSYOP was renamed Military Information Support Operations, or MISO. Joel Harding stated that both terms are used: 'They're still within the Psychological Operations branch in the military, but the units themselves are called MISO' (Interview: 15th January 2013). Rear Adm. McCreary argued that 'it is a disingenuous term to start getting the word PSYOPS out of the taxonomy ... because of the negative connotation' (Interview: 15th October 2013).[3]

Ministry of Defence doctrine defined Media Operations as

> That line of activity developed to ensure timely, accurate, and effective provision of Public Information (P/Info) and implementation of Public Relations (PR) policy within the operational environment, whilst maintaining Operational Security (OPSEC). (MoD, 2002: Glossary-5)

PSYOP is designed to support military action in the theatre of war. It is defined, within British military doctrine, as 'Planned psychological activities designed to influence attitudes and behaviour affecting the achievement of political and military objectives' (MoD, 2002: Glossary-5). Col. Ralph Arundell clarifies that, for the UK, 'Media Operations is delivered by *overt* means *via* a communications channel to an audience. IO is delivered by *non-attributable* means *direct* to an audience' (Interview: 18th April 2013; original emphasis). Recently he noted

> As social media evolves at an exponential rate it is increasingly important to be able to communicate direct to audiences and the information age makes that faster and more flexible thereby blowing the edges off traditional distinctions. (Interview: 20th February 2014)

US Department of Defense (DOD) doctrine defines PSYOP more specifically, as

> Planned operations to convey selected information and indicators to foreign audiences to influence their emotions, motives, objective reasoning, and

ultimately the behavior of foreign governments, organizations, groups, and individuals. (Joint Chiefs of Staff, 2003: 10)

This is the strongest propaganda form and its diverse methods include 'psychological manipulation and direct threats' (DOD, 30th October 2003). As with all such propaganda, 'the purpose of psychological operations is to induce or reinforce foreign attitudes and behavior favorable to the originator's objectives' (DOD, 8th November 2010). As regards scope of use, PSYOP is targeted towards affecting foreign political, economic and social structures as well as military targets (Whitley, 2000: 6). The three ordinarily applied 'levels' of PSYOP shown in Figure 1.1, drawn from US doctrine, are also applied readily within British PSYOP.

America defines Public Diplomacy as 'engaging, informing, and influencing key international audiences' but it 'is practiced in harmony with public affairs (outreach to Americans) and traditional diplomacy' (US Department of State, 2004).

The scope of this book includes strategy in both countries concerning all activities defined within the realm of Public Diplomacy, Public Affairs and PSYOP, yet it recognises that such concepts are institutionally defined and politically motivated. IO, as state propaganda, must be examined as an element of the wider goals of the foreign policy and defence strategy of the country, to which it acts as a force multiplier and political tool. As such the book examines propaganda strategy through an analysis informed by interview data and insights drawn from debates in the traditions of propaganda theory discussed above.

Strategic Level PSYOP (Long-term goals)	Conducted both during conflict and in peacetime by government agencies to influence foreign attitudes, perceptions, and behaviour in favour of strategic goals and objectives.
Operational PSYOP (Intermediate goals)	Campaigns conducted both in peace and war within a geographically defined operational area across the range of military operations to support the campaigns and strategies of the responsible commander.
Tactical PSYOP (Near-term goals)	Conducted within an area assigned to a commander across the range of military operations to support tactical missions against opposing forces. This form of PSYOP is conducted on the battlefield to attain tactical objectives to support the campaign.

Figure 1.1 Levels of PSYOP.

The morality of the use of persuasion in foreign policy, counter-terrorism and conflict is not black and white. Persuasion is an innate communicative element of human nature. It could be argued to be inevitable and indeed is not necessarily negative in society (we may be persuaded to eat more healthily, to try and alleviate the poverty of others, to act on environmental concerns and so on). Attitudinal and behavioural change – the ultimate aims of propaganda – can become problematic in the hands of power and, particularly, when conflicts of interest exist. This book does not claim to be the ultimate arbiter of the morality of the use of persuasion during times of conflict, or even in the context of the conflicts discussed here, but merely encourages the debate.

Within the theoretical perspectives above, these techniques are usually evaluated in relation to the context in which they are used; how and why they are used and whether or not the particular conflict or purpose is considered a 'just' cause. Popular understandings often take a negative view of *all* military attempts to persuade, regardless of context. Ralph Arundell explained his own views on Information Operations which he felt had

> [a pejorative tone] attached to it in people's minds. Propaganda. Psychological Operations. People have this image of a bunch of guys sat in darkened rooms. You know. Messing with people's heads. Psychological Operations. They're not. They were influence activities for all very noble intentions. You know, to get people to understand, to educate, to shift perception, shift behaviour, build confidence. And ultimately, a lot of the activity that we were conducting in my time, particularly in Afghanistan, was about building Afghan self-belief. (Interview: 18th April 2013)

The academic and consultant Dr Lee Rowland (from British contractor Behavioural Dynamics Institute) here explains a point of view that my research found most practitioners share, referring to his colleague:

> [Nigel Oakes] wholeheartedly believes that using information/communication/ psyops is a better way to resolve conflict than is murdering people. He thinks the moral arguments are nonsense. It is Machiavellian in the sense that the end justifies the means – yet he would argue that the means must be favourable ones, for all concerned. (Email: 7th May 2013)

Similarly, UK former Commanding Officer 15th Army PSYOP Group Steve Tatham stated that 'the UK should use whatever technology it can to avoid the horror of conflict wherever possible' (Email: 11th February 2013). It is not an unreasonable argument that, in the context of war, persuasion might save lives, is preferable to taking lives, and may determine the outcome of the conflict. Increasingly, propaganda is recognised as a powerful tool of 'limited' war.[4] This claim seems increasingly dominant in justifying approaches that weaken restrictions to coordination between propaganda forms. For example, Adm. William Fallon spoke of 'influence' as one positive way to 'save yourself incredible waste of human life and treasure' (i.e. resources) (Interview: 21st July 2009). Conversely, Graham Wright observed a popular and alarming military perception that discussing Abu Ghraib might 'inflame' criticism and 'put soldiers at risk on the ground' (Interview: 1st June 2009).

Col. Ralph Arundell warned that this claim (the moral argument that IO limits the human cost of/need for war) can be overplayed by those who believe that somehow

> if you increase your emphasis on soft power somehow that will offset the requirement to have hard power. I'm afraid there is a harsh reality in some areas of activity that ultimate force is the only option and no amount of clever activity is going to get them to behave a certain way.

However, he said that asymmetric warfare requires this element and 'no amount of guns, bombs, planes and tanks is going to stop some of that asymmetric threat'. In his opinion 'most sane, right-minded human beings in Britain would go "well I'm bloody glad we're doing stuff like that, I'd be a bit worried if we weren't"' (Interview: 18th April 2013). Furthermore, Arundell said, 'Everybody does it. Advertising.' He pointed to the public's imbalanced response to military activities and commercial advertising:

> I think generally speaking if the public realised the levels to which PR agencies, advertising agencies … the lengths to which they will go to sell a product to you, they would be astonished. But if you explained it in the terms that are attached to equivalent military activity … Psychological Operations … black this, grey that, people would just be up in arms about it. But they're quite prepared to accept product placement and adverts in television programmes, or films – in whatever it may be. All of it at the end of the day is subliminal messaging and that's what we're in the business of doing. Is that sort of messaging to people to effect change. (Interview: 18th April 2013)

The moral debate must engage with the reasons *behind* the conflict, and if these are questionable, any action, violent or otherwise, is unjust.

The harsh reality of 'ultimate force' in warfare, of course, includes, in recent history, global assassination policies, pre-emptive detentions and torture. It is important to remember the 'hard power' context in which 'soft power' is used. The justifications too are invariably subject to propaganda, as occurred in relation to Iraq. Of course, the very nature of propaganda is such that to be effective it must be hidden – it is essentially secretive or obfuscational at best, which makes enquiry in this area problematic but not impossible. At the very least, any rules *governing* propaganda use should, in a democratic society, be transparent and subject to enquiry. Whether or not a democratic society will ultimately support the propaganda use domestically or externally, it is imperative that such issues as the rules which govern it (when, how, if and where it is used) are debated, particularly at times when they are being rewritten to respond to the changing nature of contemporary conflict and the changing media environment, as we shall see in subsequent chapters.

The ethical position of propaganda and press freedom is often treated as long ago decided. We are complacent about the protections in place, assuming that the matter is resolved in our existing laws and traditions, and seeing these for the most part as reliable (save for a few isolated incidents where the powerful overstepped their authority). It is true that Western democracies enjoy a large amount of freedom of debate. But our freedoms are not decided. Our rapidly evolving media environment bypasses territorial borders, leading to a increasingly globalised culture, a connected world. This in turn is changing the way in which modern warfare is conducted, the way 'threats' are dealt with. And with rapid transformation such debates need to be revisited. To do so, both individuals and governments must understand the historical conditions in which our current traditions have been cultivated. We must take from the past that which will inform this current debate, recognising the significance of evolving historical contexts upon political thought. The following section therefore gives a short introduction to recent US and UK history, including the origins and power politics of a relationship in which propaganda played no small part.

Anglo-American relations and propaganda histories

Propaganda is often neglected in the large body of work on the Anglo-American relationship; its role in the defence, intelligence and diplomatic relationship has not previously been singled out for systematic academic research.[5] The Anglo-American propaganda relationship often emerges in a piecemeal way in propaganda texts in relation to government agencies, studies of particular conflicts, or as an aside in books on propaganda generally.[6] Propaganda was part of the engineering of Anglo-American relations across two world wars. The balance of power between the US and Britain is also important in understanding how this operates; by comparison with other strong US ties, the relationship may be weakening today. Yet it is certainly notable in the fact that it has been maintained, despite Britain's decline as a world power, and propaganda has played an intriguing role from the start. The relationship emerged amid a historical US 'Anglophobia' (Moser, 2002: 55–65) and, beyond the oft-cited economic and defence relationship, was crafted through a persistent British propaganda campaign, which sought to shift American elite neutrality towards intervention in the First World War (Snow, 2003: 33–34). Cultural transfer has been bound up with propaganda and both countries helped secure the cultural bonds that have maintained this tie.

From earliest US history, a preference for isolationism in foreign policy was deeply rooted in ideology. George Washington's farewell address laid the foundation for this tradition, declaring European interests to be 'foreign to our concerns'. He also considered it 'unwise' to 'implicate ourselves' through 'artificial ties' in European politics (in De Toqueville, 1839: 21). President Thomas Jefferson further entrenched these ideas in his inaugural address, stressing 'peace, commerce, and honest friendship' internationally and 'entangling alliances with none' (in Fromkin, 1970). Woodrow Wilson made a first challenge to the dominance of this thinking, and after securing presidential re-election with the slogan 'He kept us out of war', he promptly, though reluctantly, intervened in the First World War (Conlin, 2008: 612). This has been attributed largely to the effects of British diplomacy and propaganda. Peterson argues that Wilson, 'like most other articulate Americans of that time, believed so many of the British propaganda arguments that he would have regarded himself "pro-German" if he had not acted as he did' (1939: 180). But it was still seen as a threat to US sovereignty to have foreign policy decisions taken in alliance with other states, and the US Congress rejected Wilson's commitment to enter into the 1920 League of Nations (the predecessor to the UN).

Early British propaganda bodies, including the Milner Group[7] (a loose, though powerful network) stepped up efforts, targeting the media and intellectual debate (Quigley, 1981: 3–14). America began using the 'Creel Committee'[8] and feeding its emergent PR industry. This continued between the wars during a comparative lull in British efforts (Snow, 2002: 36–38). Walter Lippmann, along with the 'father of public relations' Edward Bernays, both worked together on the 'Creel Committee'. President Roosevelt was sympathetic to British concerns, but Congress fought US involvement in any potential war, passing the 1936/1937 Neutrality Acts. America's economic crash in 1929 had led to a public climate of resistance to foreign political concerns and a focus on domestic American needs. Gallup polls in 1939 revealed that 94 per cent of the public favoured isolationist responses to war (Gross, 1990: 20).

Isolationism was only really challenged as a policy as a result of the Second World War. The British Embassy, the Ministry of Information and the Milner Group, building on existing Anglo-American ties, helped bring America into the war (Cull, 1994; Kirby, 2000: 390; Quigley, 1981). Peterson argues that 'American newspapers of those years should be viewed not as a mirror reflecting American reactions to the war, but as the principal medium through which the British influenced Americans' (1939: 159). According to the head of the Associated Press, Kent Cooper, because the British controlled Reuters during the war they were able to control news about the US *internationally*: 'Reuters sent only the news the British wanted us to read, and sent to the rest of the world only the news about us that the British wanted others to read' (1944). As Britain and France declared war on Germany, Roosevelt recognised this as he warned: 'Passionately though we may desire detachment, we are forced to realize that *every word that comes through the air*, every ship that sails the sea, every battle that is fought, does affect the American future' (Roosevelt, 1939; emphasis added). Once France fell, Britain was the only remaining democracy between Germany and the US. America was divided between isolationists and interventionists who feared German invasion (or coexistence with a fascist European bloc). Economic fears remained, so despite a Foreign Relations Committee dominated by isolationists, Roosevelt established a compromise through which the US could be seen as economically benefiting while staying politically noncommittal (Adler, 1957: 282). Building economic ties with the British and French (through a fourth Neutrality Act in 1939 and the Lend-Lease Act of 1941), on which the US economy now depended, established an American position alongside the Allies in their fight against Nazi Germany. These first contracts also established a US military industrial complex that eventually became a powerful and independent political force with an interest in extended interventionism. In December 1941, with the Japanese attack on Pearl Harbor, intervention became unquestionable policy; fear dominated American public opinion and focused it on the defence of America's Pacific interests.

The intelligence-sharing that began during the First World War deepened during the Second World War, and cemented the foundations for a long history of Anglo-American propaganda. The 1943 BRUSA Agreement facilitated cooperation between the US War Department and the Code and Cypher School at Britain's Bletchley Park. Smith claims that 'Never before had sovereign states revealed their vital intelligence methods and results even to their closest allies' (1992: vii). Britain's Special Operations Executive (SOE) (thought superior to the Secret Intelligence Service (SIS) or MI6), and its sister propaganda body the Political Warfare Executive (PWE) (from 1941), worked closely with the American Office of Strategic Services (OSS) during the war on propaganda activities (Foot, 2002). Bradley Smith argues that as British intelligence was far more advanced than American systems, 'along with acquiring valuable secret information, and learning many tricks of the trade ... the American intelligence partners ... had the benefit of being deeply immersed in a professional and traditional intelligence system and culture for the first time' (1995: 62). The professional culture of the organisations thus has similar roots, which gave a long-established precedent for cooperation despite their structural dissimilarity. Reynolds (2000) documents extensive concern to ensure a harmonious relationship and facilitate US activities in Europe. Cooperative propaganda by both countries worked to this end, particularly as the war intensified, to ensure that the influx of American GIs in Britain from 1942 produced agreeable perceptions on both sides. An Anglo-American organisation, the Psychological Warfare Division, was established to manage propaganda during and after D-Day, headed by US propagandist Brigadier-General Robert McClure and bringing together staff from the PWE, OSS and SOE (Paddock, 1982).[9]

The Second World War also made close economic ties with America seem indispensable to Britain, and confirmed the latter as no longer a rival to the US.

The Lend-Lease agreement, crucial to Britain's success in the war, ensured continued British military commitment to America and American leverage in all post-war global planning. After the war, as the varied resources it had taken from its empire and commonwealth declined, so did Britain's world role and the power of the Milner Group (Nicholas, 1963; Quigley, 1981). Finally, on 28th July 1945 the Senate formally approved US membership of the UN. President Harry Truman argued that 'It must be the policy of the United States to support free peoples who are resisting attempted subjugation by armed minorities or by outside pressures' (Truman, 1947). Mainland United States had been left undamaged by war and became the premier industrial and military power. The post-war period also saw US concerns about expansionism by the Soviet Union ensure Britain's continued importance. While some in London feared that US interventionism would provoke conflict with Russia, others feared US isolationism and withdrawal (Aldrich, 2002: 65) – so much so, Anstey notes, that 'British officials had been advised by their US counterparts to persuade Americans that the way of life in which they placed so much faith was in all fundamental aspects "much the same as the British way of life"' (in Kirby, 2000: 396). Successive UK governments sought to retain a global position which could only be envisioned alongside the United States. Britain's world role was renegotiated over subsequent decades, mediated within the ideology, culture and propaganda of a relationship that was now perceived by both countries to be in their mutual interest.

After the war, the SOE was absorbed into the SIS, under the Foreign Office, in part inspired by America's centralised wartime OSS (a prized facility by this time), so that these capabilities came to the core of British foreign policy (Aldrich, 2002: 74, 86). British intelligence was not subject to such severe post-war austerity measures as defence; in 1947 the Cabinet Defence Committee stated that 'the smaller the armed forces the greater the need for developing our intelligence services in peace' to provide 'adequate and timely warning' (in Aldrich, 2002: 74, 67). The Americans dismantled the OSS in 1945, with a few key facilities (including a London office) relocated temporarily to other departments. Relations continued with difficulty, and in 1946 they were formalised in Signals Intelligence for the Cold War through a secret treaty – the UKUSA Agreement. While FBI founder J. Edgar Hoover saw the SIS as 'basking in the self-generated light of their own brilliance' and 'basically unsuccessful', his attempt to contest it as a model for the new Central Intelligence Agency failed (Tamm, 1945). Jimmy Byrnes, US Secretary of State, believed that 'the British Intelligence Service was the best in the business' (Byrnes, 1945) so the new CIA in 1947 forged strong ties with the SIS that remain today (Jeffrey, 2010: 720–721). The Anglo-American relationship would always be a public mask for differences in policy, and an agreeable framework within which each state saw that their national interests could either be guided invisibly, or negotiated quietly. Kirby cites many examples where the image of the relationship was cooperatively constructed during the early Cold War years to allay fears and create favourable attitudes and approaches on either side of the Atlantic (2000: 391). Meanwhile the relationship acted externally as important propaganda to suit joint interests. The ability to manage opinions about the alliance externally, and within the alliance (both domestically and by the partner), has been crucial to the relationship's stability from its inception.

The Marshall Plan and the development of NATO in 1947, in a defensive gesture based on the fear of Russian communism, formally committed America to a role in European and world affairs across subsequent decades. However, the form of intervention was subject to some debate. Truman rejected pressure from Kent Cooper to make it a requirement for Marshall Plan aid that recipients establish a free press (Truman, 1945). An outcome of debate about the US global propaganda role and the appropriate degree of foreign intervention was the Smith-Mundt Act (1948) which enabled the State Department to take a stronger role in promoting America's image internationally. The US Information Agency (USIA) was then established in 1953.

During the following period of virulent US anti-communism, it is notable that domestic fear and political events led to domestic US propaganda 'rules' becoming more codified in a way that they were not in the UK. This shifted the US to more 'indirect' forms of propaganda such as PR and enhanced the role that commercial media, advertising and film played in constructing the American image at home and abroad. From the 1960s McCarthyism, urban unrest, the Vietnam War and Watergate built greater distrust of government in the US and contributed to concerns about propaganda. Some members of Congress fought for curbs to be placed on propaganda for 'domestic use' in the Smith-Mundt Act:

> In 1972, Sen Fulbright, who was known at the time as The Dissenter, virulent in his opposition to what he viewed as constant USG [US government] misinformation and lies, changed the definition of S-M, both its legal construction and in the minds of anti-Gov / can't trust Gov folks ... (Email: Armstrong, 16th June 2013a)

What came after, Matt Armstrong argued, was that the 1980s became more about selling US material interests than idealism and promoting values: 'the 1980s was more about convincing people [that Pershing missiles] were good for Europe than the truth about the western political system and aspirations and the communist system and goals' (Email: Armstrong, 16th June 2013b). Senator Zorinsky in 1985 pushed this further, and was successful in securing domestic curbs on Smith-Mundt.[10] Some today see the 1980s as a 'golden age' of Public Diplomacy. Others, like Armstrong, were very critical of this period; he argued that during this period the US shifted from 'what do we do that people will support?' to 'this is what we want, give them a nice story'. We were supporting anyone against the soviets regardless of what the leader did at home. The idealism of [Kent] Cooper and Truman were long gone. We were not projecting our values by our foreign policy so our messaging changed accordingly. (Email: 17th June 2013)

Coordination of each country's image and that of the relationship can be evidenced by the relations of Britain and America throughout the Cold War, despite occasional policy differences (Indo-China/Vietnam for example: see Page, 1996; Parsons, 2002). British intelligence remained hugely prized by America, and was one means by which Britain held on to relative power as its military capability and economic strength reduced. Exchanging intelligence was an acceptable way of 'spying upon each other, as much as upon common enemies', giving each an understanding of the other (Aldrich, 2002: 84). This 'insight' was subject to propaganda, since both countries doctored documents intended for the other's eyes, especially at the top levels, to create the right perception. Aldrich describes how the Cold War brought an 'intelligence gathering revolution' and expansion of 'covert action' and propaganda in both countries, which enabled them 'to maintain the liberal fiction that democratic states did not commit aggression against other democratic or popular' states (2002: 641).[11] Weiner documents some key examples of the ongoing collaboration, including a 1957 CIA/SIS campaign to make Syria 'appear as the sponsor of plots, sabotage and violence directed against neighbouring governments' (2008: 159). Stonor-Saunders also gives an illuminating account of CIA activities in Europe through the Congress for Cultural Freedom, which included a sometimes antagonistic relationship with the SIS (2000). According to Aldrich, this often-romanticised relationship was kept going after the war 'based on carefully calculated realism rather than mawkish sentiment' and could be 'prickly' especially when policies clashed (2002: 81). In the UK anti-communism was not nearly as strong as in the US, but it was balanced by the need to maintain this key ally. The British Information Research Department (IRD) work during the Korean War in particular helped to build the relationship between London and Washington; it is clear from this the extent to which it became a relationship with accepted internal parameters and a negotiated external image. For example, when the issue of whether to use nuclear weapons arose, Britain required that it be consulted first. Due to domestic concerns the countries cooperated directly and agreed that the American public statement would be worded strategically to discourage the perception of any threat to US sovereignty. It was *publicly* pledged that Britain would only be 'informed', but this was for propaganda purposes only – the unwritten understanding was that full consultation would occur (Parsons, 2002: 105). Likewise, during serious animosity over Suez, strong Anglo-American exchange/cooperation continued in intelligence and propaganda (Lucas and Morey, 2000).

Responding to its broadening security interests, America adopted massive global interventionism. The Thatcher–Reagan era and the birth of neoliberalism defined one of the strongest periods of the Anglo-American relationship, before, according to Dumbrell, 'the end of the Cold War removed much of the security underpinning' (2001: 224). After the 1980s dedicated 'media relations' and informational capabilities were seen as a necessity for all government departments in both the US and Britain, and an important role was being played by PR industries (Miller and Dinan, 2008). From the 1990s the explosion in global media meant that ensuring the consistency of the propaganda message became a huge area of activity, particularly for the US. By 1999 the sheer scale of bureaucracy and the global reach of each agency of US government led to a belief that one body, the USIA, could not perform the propaganda function. 'Cross-government' integration and the increasing recourse to the private sector allowed the propaganda apparatus to become a normalised part of government bodies. As Britain's Graham Wright (former Ministry of Defence Director of Targeting and Information Operations) pointed out, having a centralised propaganda entity also 'makes it sound sort-of suspicious' (Interview: 1st June 2009).

Security concerns consolidated Anglo-American relations following 9/11. As Riddell points out, committing troops 'in such crises has been at the heart of Britain's relationship with America' since 1950 (2004: 291). Today Britain still has a permanent seat at the UN Security Council and provides reliable support to the US. It also provides the US with secure military bases and key sites for intelligence-gathering. It was over this intense period of time that the important changes that are at the heart of this book occurred. A closeness persists today between America's National Security Agency (NSA) and the British Government Communications Headquarters (GCHQ). The UKUSA community is still the central structure of collaboration, with facilities in Australia and Canada forming ECHELON, a global intelligence-gathering system (Bomford, 1999). Johnson argues that this enables members to request that a partner spy on their domestic population, where this would otherwise be prohibited (2004: 165). The CIA has targeted US citizens repeatedly during its history. The recent revelations from Edward Snowden demonstrate reciprocal spying (Hopkins and Ackerman, 2013), but these were preceded by domestic activities under Kennedy, Johnson, Nixon and George W. Bush (see Weiner, 2008: 223). UK intelligence officials are particularly driven by concern over the implications should there be an attack on the US by British citizens. Bruce Riedel, a former CIA officer now leading Barack Obama's Afghan strategy, has stated that 'The 800,000 or so British citizens of Pakistani origin are regarded by the American intelligence community as perhaps the single biggest threat environment that they have to worry about' (in Shipman, 2009). Therefore, while UKUSA members are prohibited from spying on each other without agreement, permission is often given (Bower, 1996: 90). While US concerns about Britain meant some tension, they also rejuvenated the relationship as a crucial security – and propaganda – concern for America. According to Grey, since the Second World War 'the [CIA] London chief and his staff ... serve on some of Whitehall's key intelligence committees' and are granted an advisory role in the British Joint Intelligence Committee. And Grey suggests that Britain's own exclusive broad access to US intelligence is given 'in return for preserving the special relationship' (2003). Ultimately, for the alliance to be seen as credible, both countries must be perceived internationally, and within the alliance, as being committed to cooperation. This means that the communication of the alliance and its propaganda is in both governments' interests.

To give an idea of the imbalance between the two countries, US defence spending in 2001 was $385,142m compared to the UK's $46,099m (SIPRI, 2010). Despite this, some point to the UK's diplomatic weight in a globalised world: Dobbs (2003) argued that in Iraq, 'Britain remains the indispensable ally for it provides international cover' for an otherwise all-American operation. While the decision to invade Iraq was widely opposed, many others besides Tony Blair held a misplaced belief in the merits of the invasion (Azubuike, 2005: 124; Riddell, 2004: 291–292). This reflected not only a faith in the general superiority of Anglo-American intelligence, decisions and assumptions that is characteristic of the relationship, but also a commitment to 'sticking together', which has important cultural underpinnings. A romantic notion of the 'special relationship' has long been an aspect of shared culture that remains within horizontal propaganda, as sugar-coating on bitter economic imperatives. This propagandised history and culture enabled the Anglo-American relationship to survive and even thrive, as other powerful states rose to take positions important to US interests and as economic and security concerns have brought disagreements.

While many in the UK argue that a material imbalance with America cripples British autonomy in foreign policy, Blair saw Britain as a bridge between America and Europe. The former British Foreign Secretary Robin Cook sarcastically noted that 'a bridge cannot make choices' (2003: 133). The United States is the UK's largest single export market, buying $57 billion worth of British goods in 2007. Within any examination of Anglo-American relations, the effect of an imbalance of power must be considered. Kimball notes that 'common histories, common institutions and ideologies, a common language, and a common enemy can facilitate cooperation, but nations continue to pursue their interests even within a close partnership' (1994: 117). Through the lens of a realist analysis, in close relationships 'when an imbalance occurs, one nation sees opportunities while the other worries more and more about protecting its interests', and Kimball notes that 'rough equality' in Anglo-American relations occurred 'only in the early stages of World War 2' (1994: 117). McKercher notes how dominance began to move from British to American hands, when America began to contribute greater assets to the final stages of the Second World War (1999: 343). Lundestad agrees that 'Anglo-American relations became "special" only when, after 1945, Britain became so clearly inferior' (2005: 28). While heightened British insecurity regarding its global position is undoubtedly an element which has impacted greatly on both countries' conduct of the relationship, a 'relative gains' analysis as suggested by Kimball fails to fully account for the continued importance, longevity and depth of this tie. While some said Blair was Bush's 'poodle', obediently pandering to the patronage of a stronger power, others conceded that Britain can be the 'brains' to guide US brawn (Sharp, 2003; Whitaker, 2003). The 'poodle' theory is certainly an oversimplification, but, according to Riddell, opposition to the Iraq War such as that of the French (and as demanded by British public opinion) was 'inconceivable' given the Anglo-American ties (2004: 290). It would involve the reversal of a culture in foreign policy-making built on '60-year-old foundations', and Britain's nuclear power status is also dependent on privileged access to US technology and intelligence (Riddell, 2004: 290; see also Baylis, 1984; Dumbrell, 2001). This also benefits the United States of course, since that is where Trident's missile delivery systems are manufactured and maintained. The British–US trade relationship is strong in defence: arms exports from the US to the UK between 2001 and 2012 were £4,498m; US exports to the UK were worth $2,445m (SIPRI 2013).

Certainly, Britain could not have 'become a "reliable" partner of the United States until it was no longer powerful enough to be a serious rival' (Skidelsky, 2004). But its long history and traditions, combined with commonalities in culture and language, means the Anglo-American relationship is sustained beyond hard power politics through an expectation of permanence. Since the Second World War, through the participation of successive elites, a supporting concept of the relationship developed over time to solidify and institutionalise a privileged 'community' that could be engaged as required. Chapters 5 and 6 will return to this, showing how it accompanied planning for campaigns in Afghanistan and Iraq and could be drawn on by governmental cultures for planning in propaganda and beyond. The relationship is therefore still a reliable tool for propaganda, both externally in communicating alliance, and in terms of propaganda cooperation to achieve limited national and shared goals within the alliance's power constraints. 'Threats' and evaluations of security are also defined not just in relation to external actors but within the ideological framework of this community.

Security threats during the Anglo-American 'War on Terror'

As the preceding sections demonstrate, it is important to study propaganda use in its context. The 'war on terror' propaganda context must consider the state-defined concept of 'security', and how 'threats' and the range of 'solutions' are defined in relation to this. After 9/11 some commentators claimed a rise in 'anti-Americanism' or hostility towards Western policies and some pointed to 'ineffective' propaganda post-USIA (Cull, 2012; Datta, 2014; Nye, 2004; Parmar, 2008; Pilon, 2007). Taylor, for instance, linked increases in hostility in the Middle East and a worsening terrorist threat to a perceived down-grading of the US propaganda apparatus (2002: 439). A brief examination of US and UK governments' use of the term 'terrorism' during the conflicts in Iraq and Afghanistan suggests that terrorism was assumed to be an uncontroversial and homogeneous concept.[12] US Secretary of State Colin Powell's former Chief of Staff, Lawrence Wilkerson, referring to a Cold War Western audience, described how he and Powell often discussed how much easier it was when there was a 'distinct "other"' (Interview: 23rd June 2009). He said:

> you always need an enemy, you need an 'other' ... we've always had ... within our own minds, Western minds ... in both our countries, we've always had the majority with a very distinct impression of the 'other' and it was easy to manipulate ... propagandise and so forth. (Interview: 23rd June 2009)

State-defined threats were now diffuse and often asymmetric – heterogeneous networks with loose ties that no longer corresponded to territorial boundaries or traditional organisational structures. As Kevin McCarty (former National Security Council Director for Global Outreach)[13] observed:

> the bad guys in our mind were Al Qaeda, which is a very loose term for a whole bunch of bad guys doing different things. I mean, there wasn't really an Al Qaeda, there just were a lot of different bad guys. Some of them used the name, some didn't. (Interview: 13th March 2013)

Publicly there was a need to demonstrate a homogeneous 'other' as a threat to unite the public against and to declare 'war' on, so in 2001 President Bush made his battle-cry 'either you are with us or you are with the terrorists' (in Kean and Hamilton, 2004).

The difficulty associated with defining terrorism has resulted in flexibility in the term's usage, and thus its being represented as 'surging' or 'falling' according to political motive (Deutch, 1997: 10). Kibbe (2004) notes the change in Bush's rhetoric during the early days in Afghanistan which can be attributed to the conceptual and structural changes in the country's approach to its foreign policy. Initially, following 9/11, Bush referred to the attacks in criminal terms, reflecting existing precedent in dealing with acts of terrorism by non-state actors. However, he quickly began referring to acts of war. Bush first stated in his address to Congress on 20th September 2001 that 'Our War on Terror begins with al-Qaida, but it does not end there. It will not end until every terrorist group of global reach has been found, stopped, and defeated' (Reynolds, 2007). Through analysis of discourse, van Dijk demonstrates how this term 'terrorist' has become synonymous with the Arab as 'other' through positive and negative evaluations of 'us' and 'them' (2000: 39). The broader 'war on terror' rhetoric accompanied efforts to authorise measures such as covert action by the military.[14] Governments can use a crisis such as a war to create a symbolic threat, respond such that they are perceived as acting to defuse the threat, and then declare a symbolic victory (Chermak, 2003: 12). The 'war on terror' depicted in the media bore no relation to the reality of the threat; rather, Lewis suggests that media coverage *responded* to an increase in political rhetoric. A massive increase in coverage occurred during a period when, despite occasional peaks, the number of terrorist attacks was the lowest in twenty years (2004: 19). Yet from 2005 (the time of the London bombings), it has been observed that BBC coverage has largely 'avoided the dialogue of fear' still common in the US and in much political rhetoric (Oates, 2007). By 2007 Tony Blair was trying to move away from Bush's expression 'war on terror', a move later shadowed by Obama (Reynolds, 2007). However, this phrase has now so saturated discourse that it persistently threads through global understanding of twenty-first-century American, and Anglo-American, foreign policy.

The British government definition of terrorism is contained within Section 1 of the Terrorism Act 2000; it encompasses the use or threat of 'action' (violence or endangerment, serious damage to property, or serious interference with an electronic system). This, combined with 'use of firearms or explosives', is sufficient to constitute terrorism. Otherwise, this 'action' must be intended 'to influence the government or an international governmental organisation or to intimidate the public or a section of the public ... for the purpose of advancing a political, religious or ideological cause' (Lord Carlile, 2007). As Philo argues, 'ideology and the struggle for legitimacy go hand in hand' (2007: 178). Terrorism is, by this official definition, what others do; it has often been defined thus. Since it was first used by the Jacobins to describe the French 'reign of terror', the use of the term 'terrorism' has always been relative, and politically motivated. All this means that terrorism has been popularly misunderstood. According to Held, terrorism itself 'is not always or necessarily more morally unjustifiable than war' (2004: 59). It seems appropriate that instead 'debate should focus on the justifiability or lack of it or the aims sought' (Held, 2004: 59). This approach is obviously a helpful guide in our approach to the truly horrific terrorist attacks prompted by Islamic fundamentalism on the American mainland and internationally. However, it should likewise be extended to methods of 'countering' terrorism or insurgency being employed globally, the doctrine of 'pre-emptive war' in Iraq[15] and indeed the propaganda systems used to generate support.

At the start of this period *state* concepts of security and responses were often still formulated in terms of global competition between sovereign states. These foundations, on which security was traditionally understood, have become seen as problematic in the absence of a clearly definable enemy. With a diffuse multitude of 'global' insurgent targets, traditional military solutions were seen as inadequate, and through their failures and collaborative efforts, Britain and the US began to seek out 'more tools' (Interview: Armitage, 21st July 2009). As Nagl points out, 'if the only tool in your toolbox is a hammer, all problems begin to resemble nails' (2005: 203). Counter-insurgency (COIN) or counter-terrorism was seen as a solution that would bring together force and coercion with propaganda to change behaviour and counter global perceptions of the West. Sir Robert Thompson's book *Defeating Communist Insurgency* (1966) drew on his experiences of fighting the 'Malayan Emergency' (a British colonial war to oppose the Malayan independence movement), and has defined subsequent British and American doctrine. It distinguishes five 'principles of counter-insurgency' which identified the political nature of this form of conflict with propaganda as a key component.

1   The government must have a clear political aim: to establish and maintain a free, independent and united country which is politically and economically stable and viable.
2   The government must function in accordance with law.
3   The government must have an overall plan.
4   The government must give priority to defeating the political subversion, not the guerrillas.
5   In the guerrilla phase of an insurgency, a government must secure its base areas first. (Thompson, 1972: 50–60)

Thompson's fourth 'principle' has helped enshrine propaganda as a form of political warfare, and an important tool for counter-insurgency operations and planning, though he was far from the first to propose this. The increasing prominence of terrorism within contemporary foreign policy has led to an emphasis in defence on asymmetric warfare. And the ideological component of this struggle brought corresponding calls to consider what Joseph Nye and others said the US had neglected (2004). Galula's classic text argues that

> The insurgent, having no responsibility, is free to use any trick [and] is not obliged to prove; he is judged by his promises, not what he does. Consequently propaganda is a powerful weapon for him. With no positive policy but with good propaganda, the insurgent may still win. (2006: 9)

Crucially, Galula's 'first law' of counter-insurgency is therefore that 'the support of the population is as necessary for the counterinsurgent as for the insurgent' (2006: 52). Propaganda has thus been incorporated into contemporary US and British counter-insurgency doctrine and the US army's recent counter-insurgency handbook also states that

> Counterinsurgency (COIN) Operations require synchronized application of military, paramilitary, political, economic, psychological and civic actions [as] the political issues at stake are often rooted in culture, ideology, social tensions and injustice. (DOD, 2007: 5–1)

Defined and organised in relation to governments' accepted definition of terrorism, rhetorically insurgents and terrorists become one and the same. In contrast, Kilcullen's definition sees terrorism as a *tool* that can be used by governments or insurgents; the use of 'politically motivated violence against civilians ... conducted with the intention to coerce through fear' (2004: 15). He pointed to this frequent conflation of the terms, arguing that 'the current campaign is actually a campaign to counter a globalised Islamist insurgency'; he argued that insurgency is 'a popular movement that seeks to change the *status quo* through violence and subversion' whereas 'terrorism is one of its key tactics' (Kilcullen, 2004: 15). Counter-insurgency (and all components thereof) is thus, *by definition*, conservative, in that it seeks to ensure the integrity of existing social structures, preventing challenges to these as well as preventing the violence and 'terror' that insurgents might bring (see also Miller and Sabir, 2012).

Rarely were the Western economic and foreign policies that were attracting such hostility interrogated; the problem was necessarily located outside the West or in its ineffective propaganda. Notably, former CENTCOM Commander Adm. Fallon related security to economics and growing awareness of inequality through images of the West being seen in economically disadvantaged areas of the world. He argued that

> in Iraq, the economics they know is 'I have a camel that gives milk and people buy it' ... most people know 'I want' and it's very difficult I've found in ... developing countries, to proselytise for ... the long term – 'you gotta save', and they look around and they ... see particularly the TV and cinema version of things – 'All we can see is you guys have *everything*, this material stuff and if you can have it why can't we?' (original emphasis)

Security is necessarily defined by material, and often locally defined, human realities when survival is at stake. Fallon's response was that the local population's reaction represented 'huge disconnects' in understanding, and it all goes 'back to messaging. It's all back to information, and assumptions, and perceptions.' Fallon's response clearly shows us that 'huge disconnects' in understanding do exist, but in the *West's* assumption that discontent stemming from material inequalities can be countered through changing 'perceptions' (Interview: 21st July 2009).

While the media has gone global, people's *concerns* have often stayed local, including in the US: Fallon argued that the American media has sparse content and 'the only reason people look at these things is to find out about local stuff and advertisements'. With increasing commercialism comes change in focus. Fallon argued that in the West, during the Cold War, public awareness of threat

> became part of the culture ... the mind-set was it [the threat] could come ... at any time. That's all gone now. Our young people have no clue ... One full generation has no experience along these lines. They don't know. So security is related to ipods ... things now that are very, very important to people. They're all related to economics.

Economic issues, while dominant in security concerns, are still not seen as an acceptable motive for war, and economic pacification is the only permissible answer within the institutionalised capitalist ideology of the West. Yet images of Western opulence cannot be confined. As Fallon notes, 'You have to play to multiple audiences. You can't just focus on one' (Interview: 21st July 2009).

Beyond its physical effects, terrorism demonstrates the conditional nature of the sovereign state and interrogates perceptions of its legitimacy, particularly in the eyes of those who have genuine grievances about material inequalities. Terror is defined and fought in the name of 'national security', a concept treated as fixed by governments, yet which is essentially contested. State security goes beyond the traditional notion of 'anarchy' within the state system that has dominated the field of international relations; beyond this it is the fear of the unknown future and the unknown populace, the embodiment of which is public opinion. Rear Adm. Frank Thorp identified a general US military fear that 'if we talk about it the enemy will take advantage of it' – a Vietnam-era prejudice that has proved persistent among US personnel (Interview: 24th August 2009). In writings that have been hugely significant in influencing planners from President Barack Obama to Former Defense Secretary Robert Gates and Former Deputy Secretary of State Richard Armitage, Joseph Nye has emphasised the relative power of media compared with government information sources:

> Editors, filters, and cue givers become more in demand, and this is a source of power for those who can tell us where to focus our attention. Power does not necessarily flow to those who can produce or withhold information. Unlike asymmetrical interdependence in trade, where power goes to those who can afford to hold back or break trade ties, power in information flows goes to those who can edit and authoritatively validate information, sorting out what is both correct and important. (2002b)

Such analyses define the national security 'threat' of media and unfettered public debate. They underscore the sense of threat and common identity within the defence apparatus, marking out within ideological and institutional structures of government both a territory of conflict and one of containment. It is this contested cultural framework through which propaganda is legitimated within many of the accounts discussed below.

A note on method

The research on which this book draws analysed the evolving Anglo-American counter-terror propaganda strategies that spanned the wars in Afghanistan and Iraq, as well as reconstruction, between 2001 and 2008. The book offers insights into the transformation beyond this period, tracking many key developments as much as possible up to the time of writing (2013) and providing a retrospective on the 'war on terror'. Using empirical data located within multiple spheres (military, commercial, cultural, political, strategic), the book draws on sociology, political science and international relations, developing an interdisciplinary analysis of political communication in the international system that brings a crucial contribution to literature in this area.

The primary method for data gathering was exploratory elite face-to-face and telephone interviews, of which 66 were conducted with Public Relations professionals, journalists, and foreign policy, defence and intelligence personnel. Where interviews were not possible information was obtained by email correspondence (45 emails contribute to the book). The 75 US and British participants included 40 UK participants (37 UK interviews and 8 UK emails) and 35 US participants (28 interviews and 36 emails including 1 Iraqi-American and 1 Egyptian-American). I also included one Australian email participant who worked closely with UK/US personnel. In addition to these, several high-profile interviews were also conducted which were off the record. These examined how domestic dynamics, and the current state of diplomatic and defence relations between the US and the UK, shaped the nature and development of British and American information strategies and their planning in a shared theatre of war. Finally, I also carried out a detailed analysis of a large number of British and American documentary sources.

As Croft observes, the construction of a 'war on terror' narrative 'was an elite project' involving not just government but 'many other social institutions, in the media and in popular culture' (2006: 2). It is thus important to note that this is not a study of media production, media coverage or the content of propaganda output in either country. Rather it is a study of the interstate and domestic dynamics involved in decision-making and planning of propaganda strategy.

For methodological reasons the scope of the research is drawn quite broadly. The difficulties of gaining access to elite sources and in obtaining information freely once in interview has meant the selection of appropriate examples was inevitably influenced by opportunity. While it was initially intended to focus on 'defence' propaganda in a limited way, in restricting scope to the military alone it quickly became apparent that the nature of how the information war was being fought (seeking cross-governmental solutions) rendered this an artificial distinction. Initial research findings also demonstrated that globalisation was making the 'target audience' an increasingly arbitrary and meaningless distinction. The erosion and maintenance of these understandings of propaganda distinctions became an important element of the analysis. They prompted a critical rethinking of:

a) how the structure of government ensures propaganda concepts retain the strength of their analytical stature; and
b) how they can come to be conceptually and institutionally shaped through the agency of those involved in its processes.

The scope of the research was ultimately focused on demonstrating the often 'messy' informal mechanisms and relationships through which the Anglo-American propaganda 'structures' – those involved in planning and shaping – operated or faltered. By way of clarification, the term 'Anglo-American relations', as used frequently here, encompasses many forms of interaction ranging among the interpersonal, structural and bureaucratic relationships. It includes relations operating informally in friendships, or relationships formally laid down in protocol; even these are often sustained despite the formal divergence of often varied careers. It potentially included all forms of interaction across each country's structural hierarchy involved in the cross-government organisation and implementation of the propaganda war. The interviewees were approached about their own experiences of working alongside colleagues from across the Atlantic, and asked for their observations of policy and practice from an 'insider' perspective during campaigns. These interviews built a picture of the more informal and indirect ways that Anglo-American relations and propaganda policy development occurred.

Conclusion

This introduction has presented some of the numerous perspectives and histories that offer essential context for the discussions of Anglo-American propaganda that follow. Debates about ends, means and motives, the balance of Anglo-American power, democracy, and the nature of public opinion will be developed throughout the book. It has introduced both academics' and practitioners' approaches to propaganda and considered both ethical arguments and those of utility and necessity (particularly in war), before problematising the notion of a 'democratic' use of propaganda and defining the term. Through examples, Chapter 2 will show how rapidly evolving media technologies presented legal, structural and cultural problems for what were seen as rigid propaganda systems defined by their emergence in an old media system of sovereign states with stable target audiences. It will detail the adaptations and initiatives that gave propaganda wider reach and challenged the existing structures, rules and practices. Subsequent chapters will demonstrate the planning involved: they show how these changes in response to the new environment were less a reliable product of a well-oiled propaganda machine than a happy accident for these governments, delivered by proactive elements within them. Chapter 3 will describe how the formal structures failed to coordinate effectively amid government urgency to impose strategic control on a sprawling apparatus. Propaganda successes and advances were an inconsistent by-product both of malfunction and of relationships, cultures and rivalries, both domestically (as argued in Chapter 4) and between the partners (as argued in Chapter 5). The differing social relations of planners and propagandists to wider society create tensions within the 'machine', however leaders may want it to function. The book will demonstrate that the 'messy' nature of bureaucracy and international systems as well as the increasingly fluid media environment are all important in shaping what actually happens. In a context of initial failures in *formal* coordination, the book will stress the importance of informal relationships to planners in the propaganda war. This situated Britain in an important yet precarious position within the Anglo-American propaganda effort, particularly in Iraq, which is the focus of Chapter 6.

Notes

1 Interviewees' full titles are given in the list of interviews on pp. 254–258.
2 Harding claimed to have been a central part of this movement, '*My* contribution was the fact I was pushing within the Pentagon, pushing for IO to be full-spectrum. And not based fully on computer network operations *or* electronic warfare *or* whatever, and now it's finally progressed' (Interview: 15th January 2013). Miller utilises a concept of 'information dominance' in explaining US and British propaganda strategy in Iraq as part of a greater US strategy to achieve the 'total spectrum dominance' (2004a). Former Executive Director of the US Advisory Commission on Public Diplomacy, now Chairman of the US Broadcasting Board of Governors, Matt Armstrong noted that a more fluid media environment necessitated a change in approach for those in government: 'The terms [information] superiority, dominance, etc reflect dated and/or obsolete and/or naive views of the communication environment ... the heyday of [Public Diplomacy] as people today look back, was marked by the ability to control narratives. (Interview: 29th April 2013). It is important not to assume when we use such concepts that propagandists have a naive, deterministic understanding of persuasion and audience reception: this is not always the case.

3 According to one angry US PSYOP operative who commented on a *Small Wars Journal* blog about the recent terminology change to neutralise PSYOP into Military Information Support Operations (MISO): 'some of us joined Psychological Operations because it sounded awesome' and the 'intimidation factor brought on by the words alone are what attracts many recruits' (Anonymous, 2011).

4 This is the notion that, in a nuclear age, belligerent states may demonstrate through international agreements that they will refrain from using the full extent of their weapons capabilities, in order to preserve those systems or in order not to escalate conflict to a point deemed unwinnable or otherwise unacceptable.

5 For instance, Scott questions why scholars examining the intelligence agencies largely focus on comparatively well-researched 'information gathering', rather than 'clandestine diplomacy' and the 'secret intervention' function that is crucial to exposing hidden political agendas. This is very true of the literature discussing the Anglo-American relationship (2004: 322).

6 For instance, see the work of Kirby (2000), Miller (2004b) or Peterson (1939).

7 What has become known as the Milner Group was an informal elite network including Cecil Rhodes and Lord Milner, and every editor of *The Times* was a member from 1897 to 1945 with only three years' exception (1919–22) (Quigley, 1981: Ch. 1). Members often held senior government positions and worked behind the scenes to enhance the interests of the British Empire, including building support for the Boer War. It had influence in both Liberal and Conservative Parties (Quigley, 1981).

8 The Committee on Public Information, also known as the Creel Committee after its chairman George Creel, was an agency of the US government set up by President Woodrow Wilson to influence domestic public opinion regarding participation in the First World War.

9 Some personnel from the Anglo-American collaboration took the skills developed through Second World War forecasting and propaganda and moved on, Peter Zellner and Dr John Dollard among them. Dollard's ideas and skills came to the attention of the DuPont corporation, and then Jody Moxham at advertising firm PhaseOne (which later became a 'war on terror' propaganda contractor). Moxham brought Zellner's expertise in to establish PhaseOne, and also worked with DuPont on developing the 'Dollard System' (Interview: Stelloh, 23rd June 2009).

10 In the UK historically there has been less distinction made between the foreign and domestic audience; the world was always more 'connected' for the British through empire, whereas US imperialism through capitalist expansion was kept more at arm's length from the US public.

11 Recent US history, however, proves this to be a shallow claim: Public Diplomacy was modelled on CIA covert propaganda under the lead of William J. Casey and Walter Raymond Jr within Reagan's National Security Council. Staffed by CIA and Pentagon propagandists, it was used to target *domestic* American perceptions during the Iran-Contra affair (Parry and Kornbluh, 1988). It was headed by Otto Reich; he and Richard Armitage (interviewed here) were among several of those implicated in the Iran-Contra scandal who were returned to government by George Bush (Roff and Chapin, 2001).

12 This unity was demonstrated by the support of Israel against Palestine (Held, 2004: 59).

13 According to the website of 'Sherpa Analytics' for whom McCarty is a Chief Strategy Officer, 'Prior to the National Security Council, Kevin served in the Intelligence Community where he created and stood up new capabilities and programs to assist in

counterterrorist efforts' (www.sherpaanalytics.com/kevin-d-mccarty/).
14 See Chapter 3.
15 This policy of preventive war came to be embraced in the media's flexible use of the term the 'Bush doctrine', which had more widely included a belief in America's right to secure itself against foreign regimes that support terrorist groups; see Krauthammer (2008).

2

Propaganda 'boundaries' and the extended apparatus

Introduction

This chapter will argue that the course of the propaganda 'war on terror' fuelled a domestic rethink of the propaganda apparatus in Britain and the US, and resulted in far-reaching changes to combat the vaguely defined and globally dispersed enemy. These pressures of systemic change ultimately placed great strain on strategic control mechanisms. This chapter shows how government agencies adapted to the demands of a fluid media environment. The globalised media was seen as precluding any capacity to target different audiences with different messages while remaining credible and convincing. Prompted by this, during the period of study, each country's propaganda apparatus underwent three main transitions:

a) The propaganda apparatus was restructured to adapt it to new conflicts and a transformed media environment.
b) Previous distinctions between the propaganda forms (e.g. Psychological Operations, Public Affairs etc.) were restructured or gradually eroded.
c) The audience targeting 'boundaries' previously held to be important in legitimating propaganda forms came to be seen as obstructive within institutional cultures.

These changes will be shown in later chapters to have differed somewhat in the US and UK, but for both countries were driven by informal in-agency, inter-agency and inter-country relationships that shaped the entire propaganda effort.

Propaganda audiences

Historically, there are two reasons why both Britain and America have divided their propaganda capabilities according to audience. The first relates to ethics and legitimacy. As explained in the introduction, a natural conflict exists between the principles of openness in a democracy and the need for (effective) propaganda to be so complete it goes unnoticed.

Therefore while both countries' external propaganda permitted more aggressive persuasion (particularly where it was directed toward enemies), the perception that the media must provide a check on government secured more scope for debate domestically. The reason often cited for this conceptual divide is transparency (domestically and between allies) and ensuring domestic propaganda remains 'uncontaminated' by messages intended for the enemy. As former National Security Council Director Franklin Miller put it, 'first and foremost the US government cannot, does not and should not propagandise its own people', a rule he quickly qualified, saying 'as an administration it is perfectly proper to put your message out' (Interview: 3rd August 2009). This claim has long been considered essential in order to present propaganda as justifiable and necessary within a democracy, and organisational division has been essential to maintaining its plausibility. Structural divisions have also served to conceptually sequester domestic propaganda from its foreign equivalents in the cultures of the Public Affairs personnel. Organisational structures, cultures and doctrine presented internal/domestic propaganda as merely 'honest facts', distinguishing it from external propaganda.

While the organisational specialisations and conceptual constructs are related to the use of black, white and grey propaganda (see Chapter 1), the audience divide has been reflected structurally in both countries' military and bureaucracy (e.g. PSYOP and Public Affairs (PA) in wartime are the responsibility of separate US military entities; and the US Department of State, like its UK equivalent the Foreign & Commonwealth Office (FCO), has responsibility for Public Diplomacy (PD)). Propaganda has been functionally distributed across government and normalised as departmental 'communication', rather than being visibly concentrated in a Ministry of Information. US and British practitioners argue for the practices to be considered as separate and very different.[1] In contrast to the image of openness traditionally used to justify propaganda domestically, an undeclared function of the conceptual and structural division and broader distribution of propaganda ensures it is less visible as an entity in the apparatus of government. As former DTIO Graham Wright acknowledged, this nullifies the 'suspicious' connotations that a centralised entity can have (Interview: 1st June 2009). Ellul's analysis from 1973 still applies here; a 'combination of covert and overt propaganda is increasingly conducted so that white propaganda becomes a cover and mask for black propaganda' (1973: 16).

Practitioners refer often to claims of truthfulness, particularly with respect to the media. Both this and the degree of psychological 'persuasiveness' are of course important. But the issue does not rest simply with telling truth. Even with Media Operations – 'white' propaganda – there remains the crucial issue of allowing room for a complete media debate on an issue. Even if a propaganda message has 'truth', its structurally institutionalised production means it necessarily endeavours to restrict and narrow public debate to serve powerful interests. It has been recognised that 'transparency is of tremendous value' in building credibility (Interview: Thorp, 24th August 2009). With a focus on transmission, Graham Wright observed, 'It's not about lying, it's about – how is this going to come across better?' (Interview: 1st June 2009). Issues of morality, communication and persuasion actually cannot be reduced to a question of truth: 'a selection of the truth' would be a better phrase. The notion of truth is not necessarily incompatible with either of Adm. Fallon's statements:

> influencing people to do the things that I'd like them to do, assuming that they're in our own best interests for mankind, is the way we ought to be going

or:

> you've gotta start figuring out how you're gonna get in the people's heads to get them to do what you want them to do. (Interview: 21st July 2009)

These are examined below. It's the passivity of the audience that is problematic.

The second reason often given for these audience targeting differences is, as former Department of State Chief of Staff Lawrence Wilkerson puts it, the propaganda message 'can't be the same for the Indian Muslims, as it is for the Indonesian Muslims, as it is for the Malaysian Muslims'. Equally, 'you can't send the same signals to the 1.5bn Muslims, as you're sending to your own people to Ra-Ra them up for the conflict' (Interview: Wilkerson, 23rd June 2009). There is another, *operational,* reason which underpins these audience rules: the traditional approach to propaganda results in multiple messages being refined for separate audiences due to different persuasion objectives for those audiences, and different behavioural outcomes being sought. If messages aren't honed for an audience, they are ineffective.

It is now impossible for practitioners to isolate and monopolise audiences and there followed a drive to coordinate to avoid contradictory messages flowing across borders. What the transformation in global media and global conflict did was to present *operational* reasons for practitioners to change audience-targeting norms, putting these in tension with the 'ethical' justifications discussed above. Practitioners' understandings of rules and 'boundaries' are important, given that many of the propaganda solutions and responses we will discuss in this and subsequent chapters were driven forward by the initiative of these government employees. Subsequent chapters will also indicate the extent to which this tension was resolved in favour of prioritising operational concerns and will discuss ways in which arising debates over audiences and ethics played out.

Interestingly, interviewees' perceptions frequently presented the other country as being less open and their propaganda as less well regulated, with real or imagined differences sometimes condensing into stereotypes.

British perceptions of US/UK rules

Echoing the traditional narratives in propaganda, some British officers seemed to perceive the United States as having weaker traditional boundaries and stressed the purity of UK PSYOP activities. Britain's former Assistant Director of Media Operations Policy, Col. Paul Brook, giving evidence for the Third Defence Select Committee Report in 2004, insisted that 'we are quite clear to separate out media operations from, if you like, information and deception type of work', insisting on the importance of being 'accurate and credible'. Col. Brook added that it is an 'American doctrine that tends to see the world as a global whole' (2004: s498). But practitioners have come to question the absolute boundaries they see as having prevented the necessary coordination. Arundell said that culturally in the military it was almost an urban myth:

> We all go: 'Go separate out IO and media' . . . and you then turn to somebody and go 'Where's it actually written down that we've got to do that?' And everybody goes: 'Do you know, I've no idea. We just – we just don't do it do we?' Now, there are very sensible reasons why you would maintain a degree of separation but ulti- mately both sides have got to work to a common information strategy. I think we're getting to a much better place in terms of ensuring that IO and media are joined up. There needs to be a degree of separation but then, so long as you are delivering clear straight factual information, I see absolutely no problem with coordinating it. (Interview: 18th April 2013)

In interview, British PSYOP personnel suggested that many of the practices which are routinely carried out by US personnel would violate the principles under which British troops operate to ensure 'ethical' PSYOP practices (Inter- views: 15th Army PSYOP Group, 22nd November 2005). Former UK Director Plans in the Office of Strategic Communication CPA, Baghdad, Ian Tunnicliffe, stated that 'their idea of legality was completely separate from ours ... They seemed to be able to operate in ways that we couldn't' (Interview: 8th July 2013). British PSYOP evolved, however, through colonial policing and civil operations in Ireland. And Dorril has observed how

> One of the things that's come out of the Bloody Sunday Enquiry[2] is the fact that the British ... establishment hates the idea of Psychological Operations. That term. Because it suggests that it involves domestic operations, and they're very,

very careful to be seen not to be involved in domestic ... Psychological Operations.

He argues that the attempts by operators in Northern Ireland to deny that Psychological Operations took place domestically there is 'fairly absurd'. He said, 'they fear being found out if they're involved in domestic stuff. So they're very careful about it' (Interview: Dorril, 20th July 2010).

Both countries' personnel sometimes voiced traditional narratives regarding propaganda audience protections. The DTIO during the Iraq invasion (2003–4), AVM Mike Heath, has insisted that, under directions of the Secretary of State, Information Operations must be 'truthful at all times' with the 'very specific exception of *that bit where we would try and lie and dissuade or persuade* military commanders' (Heath, 2004: s498; emphasis added). Heath was Senior British Military Advisor to US Central Command, Qatar, from 2003 until his death in 2007. Stephen Jolly, who has published widely on the history of British black propaganda, was the choice in 2012 for MoD Director of Media and Communications, which might be considered an odd choice. The former Senior Media Relations Officer Angus Taverner stressed that the MoD only do white, truthful Psychological Operations: 'British doctrine for Information Operations is all white. To the best of my knowledge we have not done black propaganda *in the British military* for many, many a long year' (Interview: 23rd January 2013; emphasis added).

It is of course possible to mislead, or influence, without recourse to lies and it is often more effective to do so utilising truthful information. Black propaganda also tends to be commonly designated to covert or clandestine activity and knowledge of it would be restricted.

Caution is exercised by UK personnel in engaging with the media, as Taverner reported:

> Good Media Operations revolves around trust and ... when I used to train people I used to try and persuade people you had to go probably about 50 per cent of the way down the street. You must never fall into the ... pothole of trusting a journalist implicitly because if you do, you're almost guaranteed to be let down. But equally, if you treat all of them as being equally dreadful and a bunch of lying thieving scum then you're not gonna achieve much [unclear] either.

Taverner observed 'Well, I can present my side of the story, the media are perfectly at liberty to go and talk to the other side and see what the other side of the story is' (Interview: 23rd January 2013). But there is also the question of whether the media seek alternative information and sources, or whether these are available to them.

Taverner said of the Americans that, unlike UK personnel, 'their Public Affairs people ... absolutely massive great concrete wall between them and what the dark arts of PSYOPS are up to' (Interview: 23rd January 2013). Indeed,

Graham Wright, the former UK DTIO, said that 'those boundaries were created ... by our American colleagues' (Interview: 1st June 2009). MoD Assistant Head Defence Media and Communications Operations Plans, Col. Ralph Arundell, further clarified this, stating that:

> The Americans are not allowed to conduct non-attributable information activity and have some very strict constitutional rules. The other area where they are extremely limited in what they can do is particularly with the internet ... the Americans can't conduct activity that could potentially play back against the US audience. (Interview: 18th April 2013)

Although, compared to America, UK budget and resources for propaganda are small, the number of personnel 'in the loop' is further restricted on some sensitive activities. This limited circle is also partly to protect individual operations from public exposure – it ensures their effectiveness where the credibility of a message might be affected if the source were known. According to Arundell, 'people that have been involved in this area you could probably count on the fingers of two hands at most, at the higher level anyway, probably not even that many', in line with this security restriction. Additionally, Col. Arundell confirmed that in the UK 'there is a big difference between the sort of activity conducted at the tactical level and all that sort of stuff ... and what has then been subsequently conducted at the strategic level' (Interview: 18th April 2013).

American perceptions of US/UK rules

It was also the *American* perception that UK rules were less restrictive. In PD, former National Security Council (NSC) Director for Global Outreach Kevin McCarty compared the US with the UK: 'Whereas like, in the UK ... the government *does* things like this [operate or sponsor broadcasts to its own people]. I mean, there is no foreign–domestic line like there is in the United States' (Interview: 13th March 2013; original emphasis). He pointed to the example of the BBC, stating that the US is not permitted to allow a public diplomacy broadcaster such as Voice of America to broadcast to and potentially influence Americans, no matter how it might be operated. The opinion that 'boundaries' are more restrictive for the Americans is strong. But when asked specifically about this claim, legal expert Dr Thomas Wingfield said:

> I think that your interviewees may have been right when they said that the US has more legal restrictions than the UK, BUT: the common core of both systems is much greater than the differences; there are slightly more restrictions; and the impact of these additional restrictions has little operational significance – they are much more about domestic approval chains, rather than flat-out prohibitions of this or that. (Email: 1st May 2013)

So the 'restrictiveness' may be more about the US military's formal hierarchical approval structures being cumbersome. There is no UK equivalent to the Smith-Mundt Act (1948) or US Code (1956) prohibitions, however, which will be detailed below.

Legalities and points of confusion

Some of the beliefs about the US's propaganda 'boundaries' are based on confusion over the legal position. The 1947 National Security Act restructured US national security and intelligence after the Second World War, and restrictions were created in reaction to what had been witnessed of Goebbels' propaganda efforts in Germany. This was intended to curb any ability to monopolise information supply to the country's domestic audience, whilst also enabling government engagement. The Act's authority was superseded by Title 10 (in military operations) and Title 50 (for covert action) of the US Code in 1956. Title 10 reserves the American military's use of PSYOP, its most aggressive form of propaganda, for special forces.

In the US, the foreign–domestic line is usually explained with reference to the Smith-Mundt Act 1948. It actually *enabled* PD within parts of the State Department but never applied to the DOD, or other parts of government. It restricted the State Department from 'monopoly' in the 'production or sponsorship' of information, however, and propaganda had to be attributable. But Congress originally did not specify that output should *only* be directed abroad. That amendment wasn't passed until 1985. Content had previously been targeted across the western hemisphere, but the department itself requested insertion of the phrase 'disseminate abroad', as it sought broader abilities internationally during peacetime. But this meant the Act ultimately restricted Public Diplomacy campaigns like Voice of America from being broadcast domestically (Armstrong, 5th June 2012; Smith-Mundt Act, 1948). Finally, in 2012 an amendment was passed to 'authorize the domestic dissemination of information and material about the United States intended primarily for foreign audiences, and for other purposes' (Smith-Mundt Act, 2012). Former Director of the US Advisory Commission for Public Diplomacy Matt Armstrong argues that it 'eliminates an artificial handicap to U.S. global engagement' and sees it as ensuring domestic accountability for Public Diplomacy (Armstrong, 2012). Though it is popularly understood as the 'anti-propaganda' law in US government, Smith-Mundt was conceived as an *enabling* law and not restrictive (Email: Armstrong, 30th April 2013). Its rules don't actually apply to the DOD, or agencies other than a part of the State Department and the Broadcasting Board of Governors, which is a point of frequent confusion both within government organisations and the wider media.

Often, the restrictions in the Smith-Mundt Act are erroneously thought to have been intended to apply more generally across defence. For example, this was stated on Wikipedia when checked by this author on 30th April 2013. Joel Harding also stated, in one of his emails:

> until only recently [Broadcasting Board of Governors and U/S of State for Public Diplomacy and Public Affairs] products were prevented from 'import' into the United States by the Smith-Mundt Act, which was finally overturned by the latest NDAA (I believe in December 2012). In a way it is ironic that *the same act which prevents the military from using propaganda inside the United States* actually allowed propaganda intended for external audiences back into the US. (Email: 30th April 2013a; emphasis added).

Matt Armstrong referred to 'the made-up world surrounding Smith-Mundt'. He stated that

> much of what is known about S-M is based on myth and not research. A casual review of the literature reveals circular references (Bob wrote something and cited Jane ... Jane's source is Joe who cited Bob ...) or unsubstantiated statements. (Email: 30th April 2013)

This confusion leads to what some practitioners see as an 'over-cautious' attitude among their colleagues. As Kevin McCarty described it, 'in the strategic communication, influence world, you start walking into a lot of lines that are really fuzzy and people are afraid to go there'. There was a strong belief that the existing audience rules are outdated. McCarty expressed the concern that 'every Department, Agency or Office including that of the President, have limitations around what they can and can't do. And none of them were written for the world we live in now' (Interview: 13th March 2013). In a climate in which many believe the US is more restricted than it actually is, it was stressed by some that Britain's services were prized, partly as Britain could help 'navigate' the restrictions US officials found outdated (see Chapter 5).

Dr Thomas Wingfield was Civilian Rule of Law Advisor to Gen. Stanley A. McChrystal's Counterinsurgency Advisory and Assistance Team (October 2009–February 2010). Legally speaking, Wingfield said,

> Title 10 of the US Code does prohibit publicity and propaganda by DoD within the US, but the exception, unless 'otherwise specifically authorized by law' allows Congress to permit DoD broad authorities (in Defense Authorization Acts, etc.) for public affairs, recruiting, etc. These prohibitions are much more about coordination and transparency in authorization than they are about preventing the activities themselves. (Email: 1st May 2013)

The reality has often been that rule-breaking and rule-bending occurs. For example, prior to Bush's presidency, in 2000, a programme was exposed and greatly criticised where the US PSYOP Unit had placed 'interns' into CNN and NPR (NPR, 2000).

For US military and CIA covert PSYOP (where the US source is hidden – the message may or may not be 'true') target audience rules are designated by two Executive Orders. Executive Order S-12333 governs intelligence and also 'covert action' more generally, including by the military. It states:

> No covert action may be conducted which is intended to influence United States political processes, public opinion, policies, or media. (Executive Order S-12333, 2008: 14)

Dr Wingfield stated that, for these activities,

> the procedural safeguards on these [operations] don't even need to mention the word 'propaganda'. (Email: 1st May 2013)

So, non-attributable PSYOP is, in fact, permitted for both the US military and CIA for foreign audiences. In addition, DOD Directive S-3321.1 governs *overt* PSYOP during peacetime, and again specifies 'foreign countries' (DOD Directive S-3321.1, 1984).[3] For this reason, a 2005 PSYOP Field Manual states that 'U.S. PSYOP forces will not target U.S. citizens at any time, in any location globally, or under any circumstances' (US Army, 2005a). But externally, the US has a fairly free rein. Joel Harding said that 'the restrictions only apply within the borders of the United States, outside the US it is basically a free-fire zone, only the restrictions by the Ambassador or a military commander prevail' (Email: 30th April 2013a). Wingfield confirmed this, stating that 'PSYOP may be used whenever they are not specifically prohibited'. He said the CIA

> isn't big on publishing or on doctrine, but they can do almost anything that is 1.) authorized in a presidential finding, 2.) not targeted against a US person, and 3.) not a violation of a jus cogens norm. (Email: 1st May 2013)

All UK operations are governed by the law of armed conflict, which states that 'Ruses of war are not prohibited. Such ruses are acts which are intended to mislead an adversary or to induce him to act recklessly.' They cannot breach international law or deceive the enemy into believing they have surrendered, nor violate international agreements, but 'mock operations and misinformation' are permitted (Chiefs of Staff, 2004). For the British military, 'There is a system of checks and balances in UK Information Operations operated through Central Legal Services within the MoD' (Interview: Anonymous UK Official, 2013).

The scope of each country's intelligence agency activities is different. The CIA component responsible for propaganda is the National Clandestine Service (NCS) which former CIA Station Chief Stelloh stated was responsible for selective engagement in activities which are designed to influence an outcome. That ain't collection. That's influence. And by definition, because the Agency does it, it's covert influence. (Interview: 23rd June 2009)

US covert action can 'try to manipulate policies by influencing popular thinking about an issue or it can focus on a single key official or on a few key individuals' (Le Gallo, 2005: 38). Stelloh recalled the CIA being called in when 'the President determines, "well we can't invade the country but we still wanna ... keep it boiling around the edges, so we oughta engage in non-attributable activities..."' (Interview: 23rd June 2009). Allies can also be helpful; Richard Norton-Taylor revealed CIA activities involving powerful influence with hundreds of Britons in business and media (see Nugent, 2008).

CIA resource dwarfs that of MI6, but the relative import of both countries' intelligence agency contributions to the propaganda war cannot be seen as equal to this resource differential. While small, Britain has always been good at keeping secrets; MI6's strategic Information Operations ('I/OPS') remit goes beyond propaganda in its attempts to influence international and external events toward an outcome that suits British interests. Efforts in Britain are also broad and political; and by comparison, even CIA propaganda activities are subject to open debate. MI6 I/OPS potentially has more scope in what it is allowed to do than its US equivalent, as it doesn't require ministerial sanction in the same way the CIA needs congressional approval. But (as in MI6) 'because it's a covert organisation [the CIA also] can do things in other countries under the banner of Information Operations which other [agencies of US government] couldn't do' (Interview: Wright, 1st June 2009).

In the UK, MI6's I/OPS, according to Richard Tomlinson, 'looks after media contacts' and provides 'cover facilities' (2001: 73). Dorril believed in 2010 that they had 'about 25 officers employed in their information section, which is a lot', but all dedicated to 'media relations'. It seems MI6 see *their* activities in terms of political warfare, distinguishing that from the CIA's PSYOP-oriented approach.[4] Dorril didn't think this facility was 'involved in what would be called traditional Psychological Operations' like the CIA are, probably due to their comparatively small budget (Interview: 20th July 2010). They use the UK domestic media: for example Richard Keeble cited numerous cases, contemporary and historical, of journalists 'on the payroll' of MI5 or MI6. He argues that the impact of British Intelligence in shaping media 'from the limited evidence ... looks to be enormous' (Keeble, 2008). Gordon Thomas describes how former MI5 Director-General Eliza Manningham-Buller would 'dine a carefully chosen National Newspaper Editor or the BBC Security Correspondent' giving them 'just enough detail to give a favourable spin' to an operation (2009: 75). Dorril claimed this is rarely revealed with the foreign correspondents, 'I mean it must've happened but there aren't many [public revelations]'. By contrast more come to light with 'the domestic stuff, Con Coughlin on the Telegraph or whatever'. Dorril argued that 'it's just become a bit more difficult to identify foreign correspondents in the field', though 'a fair number who've gone to Afghanistan' are likely to have had 'contacts' (Interview: 20th July 2010). It is likely that MI6 activities in Iraq and Afghanistan involved the setting up of newspapers, radio stations and other media. They probably also recruited Iraqi and Afghan journalists and photographers. Dorril reports that

> before postings and missions abroad, officers receive a briefing from the Informa-tion Operations (I/OPs) unit, which provides them with a list of sympathetic journalists who can be trusted to give them help and information. (Dorril and Anonymous, 2004)

One such journalist, David Rose, may not have been sympathetic enough. He claims he was cut off for being critical, and that editors in particular are courted, to ensure 'every national paper and broadcasting outlet has one – and usually, only one – reporter to whom each agency will speak, provided they observe the niceties' (Rose, 2007). MI5 and MI6 in this way ensure a channel for information that permits 'plausible deniability' were the content of the briefings to arouse debate or provoke questions. Former Weapons Inspector Scott Ritter also claims to have been recruited, in 1997, for the MI6 propaganda campaign 'Operation Mass Appeal' to plant stories in the media regarding WMD in Iraq. Ritter was asked to provide 'information on Iraq that could be planted in newspapers in India, Poland and South Africa from where it would "feed back" to Britain and America' (Rufford, 2003). Placing false stories in the media is referred to by the agencies as 'playback', 'spillover' or 'feed back', especially where the intention is that it will make its way back home. MI6 confirmed that this campaign existed and Ritter recounts being told by MI6 black propaganda specialists:

> We have some outlets in Foreign Newspapers – some editors and writers who work with us from time to time – where we can spread some material. We just need to be informed on what you are doing and when, so we can time the press releases accordingly. (Ritter, 2005: 281)

This appears to provide a distant, and deniable, route to leach propaganda into Western media.

Not within our borders . . .

Deliberate targeting of a US domestic audience would be unlawful and it is required that the 'intent' be to target a foreign audience. The Information Oper-ations Roadmap stated that 'the distinction between foreign and domestic audiences becomes more a question of [US government] intent rather than information dissemination practices' (DOD, 2003).

With overt operations, in terms of liability, the assurance that deliberate domestic targeting will not occur rests on compliance with directives and 'chain of command, for military MISO ops [formerly PSYOP], with legal review at the brigade level and higher' (Email: Wingfield, 10th May 2013). As Wingfield states:

> as long as you had the right target, got the right authorizations, and took the right precautions, then it doesn't matter what kind of spillover happens – there's nothing blameworthy in your op. Stuff happens, especially in this line of work. (Email: 21st May 2013)

Regarding US PSYOP flowing into the US media, in overt or covert activity, there is little to prevent this *accidentally* happening, however.

Proving a state of mind such as 'intent' is difficult. To ensure commanders comply, Wingfield stated that in *covert* PSYOP, 'The process requires the President to take personal responsibility (in writing) for each covert op' and legal opinion will be obtained (Email: 29th May 2013). Wingfield said that the value of this is in 'making the president think twice about ops that will eventually be briefed to congress post hoc, and the legal/political/budgetary problems doing the wrong thing may cause' (Email: 22nd May 2013). The lawyer would need to take into account proportionality, considering whether the risk of the PSYOP output entering US domestic media is outweighed by the value of the operation. There is also post-operation oversight by Congress, but they have 'no role in prior approval' (Email: Wingfield, 22nd May 2013). Ren Stelloh explained congressional oversights for the CIA through four principal committees. The Senate Appropriations Committee and House Appropriations Committee, who say 'OK, we're gonna give you a hundred million dollars to go and do that'. Then the House Permanent Select and Senate Select Committees on Intelligence. But these are 'not full committees, it's the covert action staff ... has the ability to be intrusive and ask questions' (Interview: 23rd June 2009). Wingfield stated that:

> I think Congress is looking out for English-language covert PSYOP that could have an effect on the US public if inappropriately released through our media – although, in their case, almost always after the fact. (Email: 29th May 2013)

He said Congress and the President 'both have an institutional interest in keeping an eye on sloppy PSYOP that might leak to domestic media' (Email: 29th May 2013).

But in reality there is also little active effort to weigh whether risk of US PSYOP flowing into the US media is proportional. Regarding the 'proportionality' of covert operations, concern is more focused on 'kinetic' covert action, where lives are at risk. There is considered to be little risk of 'harm' where the fall-out is informational – 'psyops almost never produce the kind of physical damage required for a full-on law of war analysis with distinction and proportionality evaluations' (Email: Wingfield, 21st May 2013). So any operation that spilled back into US media would still probably be considered 'proportionate', despite the difficulty of proving any 'benefit' or impact of a propaganda campaign in shaping battlefield outcomes, or in proving it changed the behaviour of the targeted in-theatre audience. When asked about this, Wingfield stated that:

> You're right that there can never be absolute certainty about the ultimate effect of any military operation, but the concern is somewhat reduced if it is a cyber or psyop intel activity that, even in a worst-case scenario, wouldn't kill anybody. Some leakage to US audiences is probably inevitable, but as long as the intent is not there to target the US, and all reasonable precautions have been taken, then a well-designed operation has a very small chance of blowing back and becoming a US media sensation. (Email: 29th May 2013)

If the lawyer, Congress or whoever is weighing a campaign's downsides against its positive impact, the assessment of proportionality is dependent on measures of effect. I asked Wingfield: Even if it doesn't become a damaging 'media sensation' in the US, if you can't prove the operation was effective in theatre, how can *any* leakage to the US be proportionate? His reply was that

> Measuring the effectiveness of psyops is a whole other problem, if they are targeted at a public and not a few identifiable decision-makers. The proportionality thing is only a legal requirement if you're killing people and blowing things up – otherwise, it's just a good idea. (Email: 8th June 2013)

Another issue that has implications for the audience norms is how the global counter-terrorism campaign has expanded the range of DOD activities. As Scott observes of bureaucracy, often 'the relationship between organisation and function varies over time' (2004: 332). In America it is the NSC who 'are ... supposed to oversee that interagency piece to ensure that the right departments are tasked with the right things' (Interview: Wright, 1st June 2009). For instance covert strategic propaganda operations would traditionally be the responsibility of the CIA, not the Defense Department. Title 10 requires that military PSYOP be associated with a specific *military mission* and Silverberg and Heimann state that,

> labelling the ongoing effort a 'global war' or even a 'worldwide irregular campaign' greatly expands the range of activities that can be justified as a 'military mission.' (2009: 79)

During preparations for Iraq, and before the war, Ian Tunnicliffe described a US/UK legal disagreement of this kind:

> the no-fly zones ... had been previously defined as areas in which we could operate ... whereas outside of them it was still Iraqi sovereign territory ... An effort to broadcast into that was technically an aggressive act ... when they [the

US] were gonna do a leaflet drop from aircraft from Diego Garcia, that was technically us [the UK] aiding and abetting under a legal sense. I never actually heard what happened about that.

For Britain it meant, 'In the run-up ... you didn't get any active IO ... there was covert stuff ... not run out of MoD ... other agencies might've been doing things' (Interview: 8th July 2013).

The end of the USIA was intended to end the dominance of one 'propaganda body' and communications became a cross-government activity, but investment in capabilities at the Pentagon was so great as to dwarf other efforts. Wilson argued that 'especially after 9/11 ... what had been already an imbalanced allocation of resources between the military and non-military parts of foreign engagement became significantly so' (Interview: 10th May 2013). The range of DOD involvement extended into activities usually undertaken by the poorly funded State Department, for example utilising a website in a location where conflict is not actually taking place. This expanded Pentagon reach to new audiences. Silverberg and Heimann have also claimed that the DOD is widening its remit (particularly with reference to interactive internet activities):

> communication activities are increasingly separated in time and space from a kinetic mission; are directed at broad, cross-regional audiences; and, on their face, appear more like a public diplomacy campaign than a military program. (2009: 78)

They raise the problem that the personnel engaged in these activities may not have the necessary training or oversight and warn that 'if an agency's mission is viewed as indistinct ... the need for funds becomes open-ended' (Silverberg and Heimann, 2009: 84, 90). They further state that

> When one eliminates the need for a nexus between communication activities and a specific military mission ... then PSYOP theoretically can be conducted anywhere, for the broadest of purposes. And that is where DOD is now. (Silverberg and Heimann, 2009: 81)

Doug Wilson criticised the blending of PSYOP and PD, saying, 'I don't think they can be blended, I think they can be used in tandem'. He said in that in the DOD, 'This middle kind of plant that grew up ... some called it MISO, some called it strategic communications' – it was 'this middle area that caused everybody such heartburn'. For him, it was 'a glaring example of how little on the non-military side of Public Diplomacy was working effectively' (Interview: Wilson, 10th May 2013). Similarly, regarding Strategic Communication in the UK, Ralph Arundell said, 'my own feeling is that what has happened is that we've run the risk of turning it into a black art instead of what it really is which is about synchronisation of effect, activity and communications' (Interview: 18th April 2013). He thought Strategic Communication runs the risk of becoming 'a sort of fairy dust that you magically sprinkled on things [that] made all bad things good' and around it developed 'a cottage industry that develops its own policy and doctrine and whole range of staff that do it' (Interview: 18th April 2013). More recently, Arundell noted that 'huge strides have been made in recent months both to achieve far greater coherence and to mainstream Strategic Communication' (Interview: 20th February 2014).

Adm. McCreary felt MISO 'clearly is' encroachment of PSYOP into Public Affairs:

> What you've created with [MISO] is they believe their effort is to go into foreign audiences and convince everybody that only the United States' way is right ... There is no such thing as strategic PSYOPS, PSYOPS is an operational function, and it was originally designed to convince people to do or not do something on the battlefield to give you operational advantage. And, well, they say that's what we're trying to do but at the strategic level ... They're trying to define the ... battlespace as the globe and everything's a battle. (Interview: 15th October 2013)

Investment in PD, reported at $1.2bn in 2003 (including Department of State, Broadcasting Board of Governors and Middle East Partnership Initiative), was seen to be inadequate and one report stressed that the US 'lacks the capabilities in public diplomacy to meet the national security threat emanating from political instability, economic deprivation, and extremism, especially in the Arab and Muslim world' (Djerejian, 2003: 26, 13). Wilson believed that PD had been marginalised since the closure of the USIA; the military ended up de facto implementing many of those functions on the battlefield. 'Military Information Support Teams' were deployed to US embassies and according to Donald Rumsfeld's biographer, their working alongside special forces led to 'the military becoming much more assertive and dominant ... overshadowing our diplomatic efforts' (Interview: Graham, 24th July 2009). In 2014 PD spending in the US was approximately $1.831bn (combined figures from Office of the Spokesperson, 2013 and Broadcasting Board of Governers, 2013). In 2012 $54m was spent on the MISO budget (not including other streams such as Public Affairs) and there are 7,000 army personnel, although much of course is contracted out (GAO, 2013: 1). Since 2001 there has been a rapid expansion in defence communications: Vanden Brook (2012) reports that the US military Information Operations spend rose rapidly to a peak in 2009 of $580m, though it may be more.[5]

However, the perceived audience boundaries have shaped internal cultures and enable the cognitive separation that propagates the belief that *openness* and *legitimacy* can exist alongside a belief in the *necessity of propaganda* without conflict for civil servants and propagandists. People and systems both 'compartmentalise' propaganda from belief in public debate, in order to allow for effective operations. Horizontal propaganda and institutional and societal cultures confirm faith in the processes to which an individual contributes and dissenting views are systemically managed (see Chapter 4).

A global 'challenge' to targeting propaganda

If an operation is deemed necessary, government can form a response. Indeed it becomes increasingly difficult to see any substance in claims that domestic media debate is secure, as the pressures of the contemporary information environment increasingly prompt a *global* response. The increasing immediacy of communication and the globalised media environment mean a full monopoly over audiences is now difficult. Today government messages mingle in the melting pot of the mass media and according to Lawrence Wilkerson, who was Colin Powell's Chief of Staff, emerge as the soup of something 'absolutely non-effective' (Interview: 23rd June 2009). Col. Arundell stated that the big question for planners became 'how do you conduct an operation for effect, for an informational effect against a constantly fluid enemy that has no tangible borders?' (Interview: 18th April 2013). Agencies of government cannot be seen to contradict each other; the lack of a consistent message destroys credibility. This means audiences cannot be treated as distinct, and targeted accordingly with differing messages. The Information Operations Roadmap, a secret 74-page directive produced in 2003 by US Defense Secretary Rumsfeld, argued that the global media age meant PSYOP/covertly planted stories were increasingly re-entering the US indirectly through its domestic media (Department of Defense, 2003). Similarly, in 2005, Col. Jeffrey Jones, former Director for Strategic Communications and Information on the NSC, concluded that 'traditional dividing lines between public affairs, public diplomacy, and military information operations are blurred' because of the internet and global media (2005: 109). A subsequent NSC Director for Global Communications, Kevin McCarty, challenged the organisational structures that respond, saying that 'Our government agencies are divided by borders and rules that don't exist anymore' (Interview: 13th March 2013).

In 2013 McCarty described the pressures that faced practitioners in a changing media environment that, as the conflicts progressed, made old approaches to influence seem outdated. Attempts to get America's message out were inconsistent, and Franklin Miller complained that they were not addressing audiences through a medium they actually used:

there was so very little being done down range ... it was contracted out to some group of Americans who were trying to broadcast from Jordan as I recall. And it just didn't work very well at all. They finally set up Al Arabiya as a TV station, but for the longest time Al Jazeera was what people were watching in Iraq. (Interview: 3rd August 2009)

There was conflict and strong opposition from many in the US who were opposed to engaging with Arab media (Tatham, 2006). In a 2005 article Dorrance Smith, who was media advisor to Coalition Provisional Authority Ambassador Bremer, declared Al Jazeera 'The Enemy on our Airways' (US Senate, 2006). In interview he stated they:

> were complicit with the insurgency on certain events with IEDs and explosives that cost American lives. [Their] cameras would be there because they had been told to be at a certain corner at a certain time, *that* was complicit in the event. [They also] maintained a relationship in terms of cooperation with all the media networks in the United States so that any video ... would go right from Al Jazeera onto the air in the United States. (Interview: 10th September 2013)

But many practitioners saw it increasingly as not enough to establish a large propaganda organisation or broadcaster and get it pumping out information; its messages would get lost among the numerous other competing voices and rival, respected, news organisations. McCarty observed that 'It's become a very pull environment' and argued that the highly segmented audiences require a different approach for governments (Interview: 13th March 2013). He contended that, instead, the message needs to be carried on a medium already being 'pulled' by the target audience – a source that is already credible and widely accessed. Angus Taverner, former British Media Operations and Plans at the MoD, also recognised this, and argued that it was necessary for the MoD to take an active role in communicating its perspective in the existing media:

> The Americans were ... slightly simplistic sometimes about things. They'd take the [unclear] idea and throw enormous amounts of money at it. The Bell Pottinger contract was worth millions and millions and millions of pounds and you ended up thinking why are we spending our tax-payers' money on this? But I think cause they do things like they started up Al Hurra ... and they would say 'Right, we'll set up a radio station'. The trouble is, you've got to persuade people to listen to the radio station. Surely it's better not to chuck Al Jazeera out of Iraq as the CPA [Coalition Provisional Authority] did in 2004 but actually engage with Al Jazeera? Because, after all ... that's what people listen to. (Interview: 23rd January 2013)

Ralph Arundell described how those credible sources are brought in:

> we want to communicate subject x to audience y. Who do we want to do that through? Senior Correspondent so and so. How are we going to do this? Get him a background briefing with the Foreign Secretary then get him to my team in Brize

Norton, stick him on the back of a C130, fly him to Afghanistan ... and we'll then deliver a set of packages that we've worked up in conjunction with British Embassy Kabul that is: What are the stories we want to tell in country? What does the correspondent or his editorial supervision want to *see*? That's their point here and here's our point here. Let's find what matches in between and deliver it from there to get the best result for both parties. (Interview: 18th April 2013; original emphasis)

In the US, McCarty argued that,

there's so many voices out there, so many media channels ... the old model of building a BBC or ... your own website ... there's already a thousand of them out there, you build one more ... how much of an impact is it going to have? So the infrastructure approach of making communications work, to me is an old model that doesn't work. It has to be about *how do you affect the information flow*. How do you insert into that, get it to grow. (Interview: 13th March 2013; original emphasis)

Former Director of the IO Institute Joel Harding argued that credible sources need to be nurtured in Information Operations too and that these can include the established PD outlets:

Now one of the biggest IO initiatives and the same thing for Public Diplomacy is to establish credible sources of information for the audiences far in advance of any crisis that might appear. So there are all sorts of websites that are informally or even covertly being funded by Information Operations and Public Diplomacy efforts ... And I've talked to the editors of Voice of America, Radio Free Europe and Radio [unclear] and all this, and they ... have reiterated a million times to me they say our idea is to present fair and objective news and if we were to give you something that even remotely smells like propaganda that we're trying to sell you, the audience will ignore us ... That's the idea of the Public Diplomacy arm of the government. Now, there's a very important nuance when it comes to Information Operations. At one point I said, 'It's to give you truthful news.' And an IO operator at the time came back to me and said, 'No, don't use the word truthful ... It has to be based on truth, but it doesn't have to be totally true, right?' And their answer to me was, 'Don't limit us.' So I said 'O-kay ... You might as well say you're lying a little bit.'

But the idea is far in advance of a crisis or war, you have to establish these websites as a credible place for honest and fair reporting. Credible information that can be believed. (Interview: 15th January 2013)

He stated that the PD platforms like Voice of America present fair and objective news that establishes them as a credible source ahead of when the government may need to use them. Then, during a crisis situation or war they would be used by IO people too as a credible channel for their IO output, which may be more persuasive or influence-based than usual Public Diplomacy content (Email: Harding, 27th May 2013).

While, in contrast to the US, UK global reach has diminished, Britain also invested in defence communications and its informational efforts have been dispersed across government for reasons of flexibility, cost and deniability. Cross-government integration is perhaps a logical consequence of the increasing scale of the propaganda operation; it appeared to provide a more responsive solution honed to departmental requirements. The evolution of propaganda into a cross-government activity seemed to be accepted as inevitable and necessary across the interviews conducted for this book, with military and public servants in both countries. Moving away from a notion of defence propaganda as being an activity of just the military, the 'message' is being more overtly woven into the actions of other government bodies, with the focus increasingly on a wide, cross-government objective.

In defence, the nature of the new enemy without borders brought a new focus on fighting insurgency, and a new approach to warfare that prioritised flexible responses in an expanded theatre of war. It of course meant corresponding changes to the defence infrastructure of both countries, both in the narrow military sense and in broadening how war was fought. America's Vietnam experiences preceded it: Nagl (2005) points to a historic resistance to change in American warfighting and observed the US military's inability to learn as an institution. Contemporary counter-terrorism is argued here to be characterised by pragmatic attempts to overcome this systemic inertia. The MoD's military was historically better prepared and it entered Iraq with a strategy it hoped would address the causes of problems like global terrorism through 'non-operational' international activities intended to 'stabilise' the region (see MoD, 2003b). This greater primacy given to 'peace' support, counter-terrorism and stabilisation had implications for strategic propaganda.

The following does not represent one coherent strategic plan for either country or the coalition (as the next chapter will show, this did not materialise).[6] However, the examples seek to show how through the responses of the propaganda apparatus to the changing conditions, propaganda evolved, and within this evolution found ways to navigate traditional 'outdated' propaganda practices.

Military solutions: effects-based approaches

The big problem was that violent action was often contradicted by peaceful messages of democracy, leading to charges of hypocrisy. A lack of 'coordination' was seen as driving cleavages between what was communicated by policy and military action, and messages sent out on the ground. Early on, in America and then Britain, planning began to evolve toward what is known as 'effects-based' planning. According to Ian Tunnicliffe, 'DTIO was in fact established [in 2001] using the concept of effects-based operations and the idea was to bring the hard, kinetic, the targeting piece of the thing, marry it with the ... softer communications piece ... and therefore target things based on ... effects you needed to achieve' (Interview: 8th July 2013). It was 'a much broader remit of what was being done at the time ... essentially a national security activity rather than purely traditional notion of defence' (Interview: Arundell, 18th April 2013). Effects-based planning was a whole-of-military approach that was intended to deal with this. In propaganda, it moved to integrate information warfare into policy and military planning processes to ensure all planning was directed toward a particular outcome, an effects-driven approach. It responded to the failures of a rigid formal military apparatus that determined a division of capabilities in an environment where these were no longer seen as helpful.

Former US Navy Head of Media Frank Thorp described one such problem:

> the United States [and the United Kingdom] has said that we want to eliminate civilian casualties on the battlefield ... The problem though with that message is, that's an *internal message*, for ourselves ... But when you're in combat in war, there will be civilian casualties. And the enemy is able to take advantage of what we're saying there, in order to use it against us. (Interview: 24th August 2009)

Thorp argued that the effects-based approach was a solution because the end goal shapes all policy so that 'both actions and words communicate the same thing in order to create the desired effect'. Effects-based approaches prioritised a need for systems to be flexible, with responses tailored to specific outcomes. They placed an enhanced emphasis on media and Information Operations in an effort to produce a more consistent holistic image, and, ultimately, a more effective outcome. In an effects-based approach 'the idea of truth is more than just not telling a lie, [it is] ensuring [the message] is consistent with the actions and the policies of the commander'. This effects-based approach propaganda would 'put the heat of these civilian casualties on the Taliban' and emphasise that 'we are ridding the country of this disease of the Taliban' (Interview: Thorp, 24th August 2009). Thorp took this approach rather than stating an aim to reduce casualties, as while these aims were true, he said they might not be achieved.

The approach formalised early steps toward coordinating communications and IO into planning. In so doing it began to introduce changes needed to ensure consistent operational outcomes and reinforced a focus on ends. But Ian Tunnicliffe, who was MoD Iraq Desk Officer during the invasion, said, conceptually, effects-based operations 'sounded great, but never really worked ... what you actually married was a quite mature ... well-structured targeting process ... with an immature, partially-fuzzy system' under the DTIO, who usually has 'the most kinetic background you could possibly get in the military' (Interview: 8th July 2013).

Military solutions: coordinating PSYOP and Public Affairs – the US impasse

The internet and other new technologies completely challenged the way information warfare was handled within each country's military. It is perhaps arguable that it was the greatest challenge for the US, a country whose restrictions have been more formalised, with a large bureaucracy and greater global reach. Traditionally then, in both countries PSYOP (for foreign audiences) was distinguished from PA and PD to ensure the perceived 'purity' of those messages. Where efforts to change the apparatus have been publicly discussed they have generated hostility, even within the military's propaganda 'streams' where some personnel resisted change to the preference for separation. Public Affairs personnel involved strongly defended these divisions, and didn't want their work to be 'tainted'. Yet boundaries and functions were renegotiated within defence during this period. This was done to increase consistency between what was said by covert and overt PSYOP, PD and PA. The divisions between these were consistently massaged and coordination of all of these components increasingly accepted as necessary and crucial to ensuring a consistent campaign. Torie Clarke stated that 'the coordination at the time, before, during the start of and the first several months of the Iraq War, it worked pretty well, so some of those problems [between PA and PSYOP] may have reared their heads more after I left' (Interview: 4th December 2013). The changes formalised after 2005 around a 'Strategic Communication' approach to coordinate all propaganda activities with other functions across government. This section will show that traditional conceptual labels and divisions were nominally retained but the implied conceptual differences, and actual functional differentiations of propaganda structures, were being eclipsed during this period as propagandists did what they could to produce an effective and consistent message. However, this was not a uniform policy delivered from the top: the process was messy, and was not seen as necessary throughout every department. Critics within the administration fought what they saw as both encroachment on their discipline and unethical activities that threatened media freedom.

Rumsfeld's biographer described how many of the Pentagon's internal struggles were 'rooted in a fundamental clash ... of views about what was the proper' mission 'for US military' particularly in 'the grey area ... countering Al Qaeda in friendly regions ... and the internet' because 'you can't isolate operations anymore' (Interview: Graham, 24th July 2009). An early project that blurred lines was Rumsfeld's Office of Strategic Influence (OSI) established in late October 2001. Now popularly derided among most government personnel, the OSI was disbanded in February 2002 due to fatal public exposure of its use of covert black and grey propaganda for targeting 'free' global media. This 'damaged the reputation and effectiveness of the office' (CRS Report for Congress, 19th July 2004). A Pentagon review found no evidence of plans to use disinformation; the media reported some activities, and speculated about contractors involved, but little detail was really made public.

Now dismissed as an early short-lived 'mistake', I would argue that the OSI remains of interest. Director of contracted think-tank The Potomac Institute for Policy Studies,[7] Dennis McBride, a contractor from the OSI's short life, stated that 'the President himself ordered that a special office be created within the [Office of] Secretary of Defense' and then Karen Hughes, 'a very close ally of President Bush', established it.[8] He described how 'the original idea [was] that [stories] would be written by locals but picked up and published by *us* or publishing houses and redistributed' (original emphasis). After 'tearing walls down at the Pentagon, ordering experts in', McBride argues that Public Affairs began stirring (Interview: 5th June 2009). According to Franklin Miller, the source of resistance, supported by the Office of the Secretary of Defense's Public Affairs team, was 'the Chairman's Public Affairs people ... and I think it was a one-star'.[9] Miller claimed Gen. Myers took a 'very firm stand based on the advice of staff' (Interview: 3rd August 2009). The PA 'one-star' under Gen. Myers at this time was Frank Thorp who 'wrote every single statement he ever made to the press' and 'prepared him for every interview he ever did'. Thorp acted as a powerful gatekeeper controlling the message and said he ensured there was 'never ever a Psychological Operations input in anything he said'. Thorp succeeded Rear Adm. Terry 'T' McCreary in this position and as Chief of Information, and both were extremely sensitive and vocal in the impasse with IO and against the OSI; according to Frank Thorp ultimately Rumsfeld 'killed it' (Interview: 24th August 2009).

McBride said that the project Potomac were hired for developed along an 'interesting administrative trajectory' (Interview: 5th June 2009). By July, the OSI was publicly replaced with the more acceptable face of the Office of Global Communications, an office centralised at the White House, responsible for distributing 'truthful and accurate messages' (The White House, 2003). As a visible entity this dealt with the short-term news cycle rather than long-term goals of persuasion as the OSI had. Some say the OSI was not disbanded. Rumsfeld (2002) stated in a press briefing that 'You can have the name, but I'm gonna keep doing every single thing that needs to be done and I have'. Some reports suggested it was absorbed deep in the Pentagon into the Information Operation Task Force, others that it actually was replaced quietly with a Tampa-based 'Joint Psyop Support Element' (see US News, 2005). Some interviews supported the notion that it relocated and when questioned about this, the former State Department Chief of Staff Lawrence Wilkerson laughed:

> Rumsfeld never stopped anything when someone told him to ... I was told by the person he'd put in charge of it, who was an old friend of mine, I was told 'We took the name off the door and the door was just blank!' ... He had a placard made up

for his door. He said, 'I was told by Rumsfeld to take it off, but to keep doing what I was doing'. (Interview: 23rd June 2009)

McBride confirmed that work was relocated within the Defense Department, but, crucially, told how when 'Karen Hughes ... showed up again as number two under Secretary Rice' in the State Department, Potomac were hired back. They were working on a project to target women with propaganda and exploit their informal power within the family. This time, though, Potomac were contracted to the State Department to work on the same project. They did the preparatory work, and although they stated that this was the limit of their involvement in the ongoing project, McBride said it was 'pursuing the same idea ... and I think what happened is that the idea has merits ... targeting the female networks is just ideal'. McBride said Potomac had particular expertise in exploiting 'female networks' (Interview: 5th June 2009).[10]

Anecdotal evidence suggests that political 'sponsorship' of media by domestic political parties is common practice in Iraq (Interview: Anonymous, 2010) and it is viewed as 'working the system' of that country to US planners. It clearly was not McBride's project of planting stories in the press that the administration took exception to, it was the OSI's visibility: once it became public this damaged credibility. The State Department's primary remit, Public Diplomacy, is meant to be guarded and distanced from military PSYOP to retain its credibility. But as Joel Harding stated above, this does not stop them working together with IO when needed. But the Potomac project's 'interesting administrative trajectory' demonstrates propaganda activities being redistributed across government, and the institutional functions of the State Department adopting the same programme.

Rumsfeld's biographer, Bradley Graham, identified early 2002 as the height of the 'impasse' between IO and PA, saying Rumsfeld's 'Information Operations Roadmap' which came in 2003 was 'a first stab at this problem' (Interview: 24th July 2009). But the Pentagon had already drafted an amendment to Directive 3600.1 which guides military IO. This changed audience targeting, revising PSYOP targeting from 'adversary' targets to 'foreign' targets (DOD, 2001). Though it is not widely known, friendly and neutral countries are targeted by PSYOP overtly through the Overt Peacetime Psychological Operations Program (discussed in Chapter 4). This early amendment allowed PSYOP funds to be extended to covert operations to 'influence public opinion in friendly and neutral countries' and 'publish stories favourable to American policies, or hire outside contractors without obvious ties to the Pentagon to organise rallies in support of Administration policies' (CRS Report for Congress, 2004).

It acknowledged that media fluidity means PSYOP and covertly planted stories increasingly leach into US media. The Pentagon accepted that territorial boundaries were no longer realistic. This doctrine, to coordinate international propaganda, was publicly exposed (Shanker and Schmitt, 2002) shortly after the revelations that the OSI had been breaching the Pentagon's traditional claim to separate 'PSYOP' from 'Public Affairs'. The OSI had paid journalists to provide stories 'and possibly false ones' to foreign journalists and 'influence public sentiment abroad' (CRS Report for Congress, 2004). The Pentagon distanced itself from criticism and closed the OSI following a *New York Times* article and other media exposure (Shanker and Schmitt, 2002).

The Information Operations Roadmap did not remain an authority for long though. Matt Armstrong stated:

> nobody references that document. It is not 'in force' as it were. Nobody really cares, except for academics ... and pundits who find it online. After all, it has never been replaced or declared obsolete. So, in effect, it is still 'current'. (Email: 30th April 2013)

It's possible its significance may also have been over-played at the time. Armstrong stated elsewhere: 'My observation has been that no one seriously considered the IO Roadmap as guidance' (Email: 13th May 2013). But while doctrine quickly moved on from the Roadmap, the problems of dealing with targeting different audiences remained. Actual practice is more fluid than doctrine. As Armstrong notes,

> it depended on the individuals, because the *doctrine* is not there. And the other thing, they keep calling it the doctrine, and this is really important and I have even seen the DOD Inspector General *screw* this up. Doctrine is guidance for mid-level officers, it's *not* the rule of law. It is *not* the instruction manual, it is *guidance*. (Interview: 6th March 2013; original emphasis).

Former Senior Director for Defense Policy and Arms Control on the NSC, Franklin Miller, expressed frustration that, in the US,

> when we try to get somebody in the Pentagon to look at making sure that overt and covert work together, the Public Affairs people in General Myers' Office said, 'Oh no... those are lines we can't cross.' The people who do whiteworld stuff cannot talk to the people who do blackworld stuff because then they'll be corrupted. And so, it always proved impossible to get unity of effort. (Interview: 3rd August 2009)

Matt Armstrong points out that PSYOP personnel 'are not necessarily black, they may not even be grey, they may be completely white but they are treated as grey or black' because they are responsible for the black activities and so kept separate from Public Affairs (Interview: 6th March 2013).

From 2004–6 America's Deputy Chief of Staff for Strategic Effects and Coalition Iraq Spokesman, Gen. Caldwell, was also fighting to rewrite official IO doctrine to lessen this boundary. When David Petraeus was Commanding General of the Combined Arms Center Fort Leavenworth (2005–7), he helped transform the structures responsible for the 'information' sphere. Glenn Ayers described how under him:

> The army has split up. There used to be five pillars of IO: [Electronic Warfare], Computer Network Operations, [Operations Security], Military Deception, Psychological Operations ... that's all gone away. So right now, all they have in IO is ... 'coordination of Public Affairs and Psychological Operations'.

He said, 'they are supposed to help Public Affairs *talk* to Psychological Operations officers – well, thank you very much, I don't need someone to help me talk to a PA officer' (Interview: Ayers, 17th May 2013; original emphasis).[11]

During this time concern had continued to come from PA who objected to the way they were being urged to coordinate with PSYOP. That there was a need for change and 'coordination' of some sort was, by 2005, accepted. After Gen. Myers retired, former Head of Media at Central Command Rear Adm. Thorp sought to facilitate a shift in the American military the 'Public Affairs' way. He said he recognised the audience conflict and looked for a 'Public Affairs driven' solution. He said 'the Public Affairs folks saw what the Psychological Operations folks were doing on the battlefield in Iraq' and formed the 'perception that, hey – they're saying one thing, the Public Affairs people are saying another thing and the United States is looking pretty silly' (Interview: 24th August 2009). He regarded the *total* separation of Public Affairs from PSYOP as counterproductive but felt PA should be controlling the message. Thorp looked to the UK as an example of a successful balance of coordination. The propaganda 'Roadmap' this time was Strategic Communication (Deputy Secretary of Defense, 2006), and Thorp authored the first doctrine on this. Thorp described his approach, rooted in his background in PA:

> There were folks in the Psychological Operations world could not understand why in a million years we would talk about ... for instance investigations ... the whole Abu Ghraib thing. There were those who said 'Why should we even talk about that publicly?' – because if we talk about it the enemy will take advantage of it. Well that's true, but the issue is not *not to talk about it* the issue is *not to do it*. It will become public one way or another. (Interview: 24th August 2009; emphasis added)

Thorp's approach differed greatly from what others saw as necessary for Strategic Communication.

Many in government thought Thorp did not go far enough or was obstructive to coodination; he opposed certain changes Information Operations personnel wanted to make. Some interviews indicated that his 'doctrine' reflected the fact that Thorp was 'a hard-core Public Affairs person' which is 'not Strategic Communication'. The strategy, according to Matt Armstrong, reflected a view that 'Public Affairs is the centre of the universe and everything else is mischievous, and full of lies and obfuscations' (Interview: 6th March 2013). Indeed

Thorp located PA as the lead within this, something that derived from his own position which, from the other interviews, did not reflect the views and actions of the DOD IO personnel. Some could be very derisive; Glenn Ayers mocked Public Affairs' lack of engagement with in-theatre audiences and cultures:

> I'm gonna stand behind this podium with ... and I'm gonna talk to you in *English*, and if you don't understand I'm gonna talk to you *louder* in English ... just so I can get out the *Public Affairs* note. (Interview: 17th May 2013; original emphasis)

Armstrong points out that Public Affairs don't just 'throw unadulterated information over the wall ... the funny thing is it's always adulterated'. Thorp's approach, according to Armstrong, is, 'I inform, I do not influence ... It is the general PA doctrine'.[12] But Armstrong made the argument that, though the word is never applied, PA actually *does* influence people:

> OK, you're the Public Affairs Officer for Fort Bragg. The main gate is going to close for construction so you need to inform the community ... cause it's going to disrupt traffic. So you're actually going to suggest alternative routes ... why are you doing that? You're doing that because you wanna show the community that the army cares ... and by the way did you realise you're changing their behaviour? Not only that, not just influence, but you're changing their behaviour! 'Changing behaviour' was one of the key components of *PSYOP*. (Interview: 6th March 2013; original emphasis)

Thorp insisted, however, that for an information campaign to be strategically coordinated, there needs to be 'one set of rules' and it is necessary to decide 'whether the Public Affairs rules are right, the Psychological Operations rules are right or we need a new set of rules' for guiding propaganda. This necessarily applies both to the cross-government information war and a campaign where operations are conducted jointly. Having dedicated his career to it, Thorp saw PA as the lead in this (Interview: 24th August 2009).

Eventually, though, the systems and cultures that support it at the DOD began changing:

> for a long time in the period you're looking in, PA was viewed as the white horse and everything else was dark and simply being in the same room tainted PA and so they couldn't even be there. But you have that concept breaking down at the personal level. You have some folks in the field working very well together and properly integrating the activities. (Interview: Armstrong, 6th March 2013)

A US Army field manual appears to prioritise PSYOP over other elements of the IO campaign:

> The ideal counterpropaganda plan incorporates a loose network of organizations with common themes and objectives. All elements of IO can and will support the counterpropaganda plan, but the focal point for such operations should remain with the PSYOP forces. (US Army, 2003)

Matt Armstrong gave an example of where he saw IO take the lead:

> this senior officer ... was IO, and smart, and the junior officer was PA, and the PA deferred to the IO guy ... and he led the initiative. He was essentially in charge of the communication synchronisation.

But he confirmed that this could be inconsistent and depended on the initiative of the Commander; it 'really varied', and sometimes, 'you had the ... Commanding Officer ... only want his PA person in the room and figured IO was something to be brought in later and sprinkled onto a project.' This was seen as a problem because, 'Of course the PA guy's not thinking *locally* [in theatre], the PA guy is thinking back in US primarily to the US public, congress and the Pentagon – the *IO* guy tends to be focused locally and regionally ...' (Interview: Matt Armstrong, 6th March 2013; original emphasis). However, this does appear to have been changing since Col. Jim Treadwell commanded 5th PSYOP Group in Iraq in 2003. He stated that

> From my vantage point it appears that most PA officers working in the field are more focused on supporting their operational commanders than they were 20 years ago. By that I mean they are still informing the public, but they are doing so under-standing that the information they provide will have an influence. Perhaps you could say they are informing with a purpose. (Email: Treadwell, 6th May 2013).

This impasse of course concerned differences in how to deal with the implica-tions of a fluid media environment; the internet era had transformed the landscape. At least in part due to these arguments, DOD policy on internet activities did not emerge until 2007. Prior to this, internet activities were governed by PSYOP regulations, legislated at a time before the internet was anticipated. The form in which it did then emerge served to further blur the functions of Public Affairs Officers (PAOs) and PSYOP personnel. The regula-tions introduced by the Deputy Secretary of Defense were the 'Policy for DOD Interactive Internet Activities' (IIA) which enabled two-way communications using blogs, emailing, chat-rooms etc (8th June 2007), and 'Policy for Combatant Command Websites Tailored to Foreign Audiences' (only non-interactive websites) (3rd August 2007).

IIA applies to online PA activities and 'programs, products and actions that shape emotions, motives, reasoning, and behaviours of selected foreign entities' (Deputy Secretary of Defense, 2007). It is of particular note as legal opinion from Silverberg and Heimann argues that it 'might be viewed as fusing PSYOP and Public Affairs into a generic communication effort', since it applies to both PSYOP personnel and PAOs and does not specify different activities for each (2009: 82). It also has a similar definition to PSYOP, the only difference being the words 'shape' and 'influence'. PAOs target media/journalists, but their *activ-ities* are not defined differently or distinguished from PSYOP. It is possible they could be tasked with influence since they are permitted to 'shape'; this term is vague and open to interpretation as it is not defined. But Col. Glenn Ayers, who got the document passed, stated that a policy document 'wouldn't go into that detail'; this would be for the doctrine to specify (Interview: 17th May 2013).

Furthermore, Silverberg and Heimann state, 'contrary to two decades of practice, the delegation empowers commanders to conduct information operations at their discretion' where 'previously they had to have senior-level Departmental approval' (2009: 82). Ayers was significant in pushing this through and he said:

> Those commanders ... in the area ... knew the environment better than anybody else ... so if they *had* ... a [non-commissioned officer], school-trained ... from a PSYOP unit ... or an officer, and it worked through the proper procedures, they could approve at an O-6 level [that of naval captains or colonels in the other services]. (Interview: 17th May 2013; original emphasis).

Silverberg and Heimann argue that if different personnel are used, the oversight, training and authorities that applied to PSYOP activities are lost (Silverberg and Heimann, 2009: 84).

There is a requirement for IIA to be 'true in fact and intent' but while 'attribution' is specified there is broad scope for the commander to navigate this due to 'operational considerations' (Deputy Secretary of Defense, 8th June 2007; Silverberg and Heimann, 2009: 85–86). This was a point of contest for PAOs, Ayers said, because of a kind of turf war:

> that was the first time ... in that [IIA] *document*, that we had *articulated* the different types of attribution and who could use them. And specifically it says in there that P.A. can only work in the realm of attributable information. Psychological Operations could work in all three of them [US attribution; concurring partner nation attribution; non-attribution]. PA does not like that.[13] (Original emphasis.)

This was because it excluded them from influencing the other messaging, which then might re-enter the domestic audience and 'when it blows up in their faces, and they're standing on a podium, they look at it from that standpoint' (Interview: Ayers, 17th May 2013).

Silverberg and Heimann state that the policy 'establishes a hybrid PSYOP-Public Affairs model' (Silverberg and Heimann, 2009: 86) and steps into the territory of State Department Public Diplomacy, which of course further establishes the changes in the role of PA mentioned in the previous section. The DOD is where the money is, however, and Matt Armstrong argued that in overreaching its usual territory into Public Diplomacy, the DOD 'was a very unwilling ... participant, they were ... forced into it because somebody had to do it. They didn't want to, they ... were, really not very good at it' (Interview: 6th March 2013).

Military solutions: coordinating PSYOP and Media Ops – the UK impasse

While its military was not so dominant, due to the same problems raised by the changing communications environment similar tensions emerged in Britain. Politicians' focus on the domestic media fed political pressure to bend the 'boundaries' of IO by encouraging personnel to dabble in media issues. Former Director of Targeting and Information Operations Graham Wright recalled how politicians 'look to the IO guys sometimes' with *media* problems: 'I'm like "no, no ... this is nothing to do with me"' (Interview: 1st June 2009; original emphasis).

But Mackay and Tatham saw the resistance of Media Operations to coordinating with PSYOP as evidence that the Ministry of Defence has been 'stovepiped' internally by bureaucratically insular divisions – separating IO, 'psychological operations, media operations, consent-winning activities, profile and posture activities' which they saw as 'key enablers of what is effectively one and the same thing' – influence (2009: 16). Tensions surrounding the conceptual division between PSYOP and Media Operations can be seen as a challenge to the traditional view mentioned above by Wright, Brook and Taverner. The Director of Targeting and Information Operations during the Iraq invasion (2003–4), AVM Mike Heath, had actually advocated the breakdown of such barriers as essential to effective campaigns (Heath, 2004: s498).

The UK too has had 'old school Public Affairs people' who wanted to keep a very strong distinction and separation between activities directed at the media and IO/PSYOP. And Taverner stated that:

> the Civil Servant GCN [Government Communication Network] ... GICS [Government Information and Communication Service] as it was then called ... took a very firm view that they were in the sort of public information business ... I think they ... felt within their own core ... set of beliefs that dealing with the dark side of what they saw as propaganda was not to go. (Interview: 23rd January 2013)

The Phyllis Report in 2004 called for the GICS to be disbanded due to what it called 'a narrow view of communications which is often limited to media handling, rather than an ability to communicate effectively with many different audiences, which is an integral part of modern government' (Phyllis, 2004: 8). The GICS was replaced with the GCN as a result, which extended the centralisation of communications, and encouraged strategic long-term planning and cross-government coordination. But even recently, Taverner observed that at a study day he

> found very strong resistance amongst old school Public Information people who just think that supping with PSYOPS, and Info Ops, and everything else around, is absolutely for the devil and is utterly wrong. And I think the military have moved on from there and GCN have moved on from there. There is still as sort of philosophical resistance in some places.

Angus Taverner commented on the gradual change, saying that 'I'm not going to lie to the media, but at the same time ... you do have to know what the other ... the Information Operations guys are doing.' Further he said, 'today there are people who utterly understand and buy into the fact that Information Operations in a way is just another branch of what we're talking about and it's not a dark art, the idea is that you're trying to influence the other side in an operation' (Interview: 23rd January 2013).

Cross-government and military solutions: from 'winning hearts and minds' to behavioural 'influence'

The British military, particularly in recent years, has evolved from its effects-based approach, toward coordinated IO where PSYOP and Media Operations unite behind a holistic effort to achieve clearly defined objectives. This stems from the belief that changing attitudes through information is not enough. It gives increased emphasis on the *ends* over *means* and is sharpening the military's focus on the outcome of *behavioural change*. It goes beyond propaganda products including other activities, and doctrine increasingly refers conceptually to 'influence' activities more broadly. The focus is still on 'effects' but some influence now reaches beyond propaganda's distribution of persuasive information to combine this with deliberate manipulation of *the circumstances or environment in which people act and make decisions*. It is no longer about winning hearts or minds, as 'whether an Afghan likes ISAF soldiers is irrelevant ... to the influence campaign which simply seeks to change behaviour not opinion' (Rowland and Tatham, 2010: 2).[14] This focus on 'attitudes' in the US was recognised as a concern by some US interviewees too. Matt Armstrong (who speaks highly of Tatham) stated a preference for the phrase a 'struggle for minds and wills' since it is the will to act which is important: 'I don't care if the person likes me or not, that's not the purpose, I'm here to change their behaviour' (Interview: 6th March 2006). One of the key thinkers in this area is Nigel Oakes, who said 'there has been a behavioural revolution insofar as the military now understand that changing people's behaviour is now the end goal'. He advocated 'introducing influence and behavioural change into ... the government because up until now they've only understood ... attitudinal change [and] in such crass ways' (Interview: 24th October 2013).

Concern developed that influence was not central to the planning process. For example, a British PSYOP officer noted to me in 2006 that 'Information Operations needs to be in the planning process and it can even *drive* the planning process. And in somewhere like Iraq in the current situation it needs to' (Interview: Corcoran, 8th June 2006; original emphasis). A paternalistic 'behavioural' approach developed out of Brig. Mackay's Command in Helmand, Afghanistan. This was developed in the book *Behavioural Conflict*

(2009) and Mackay was the architect of Britain's counter-insurgency doctrine. A behavioural approach might potentially engage a wide range of informational and other activities superficially unrelated to the desired outcome in order to create behavioural changes in the target population. It involves an assessment of 'in what circumstances behaviour will change' and then influences activities to trigger those circumstances. The desired behaviour change may not be obviously clear from the activities themselves, and this might obscure the intentions of the process from observers, as well as withholding informed decision-making from the target population. It is justified by the claim that the West knows what is best for that population and that these behaviours will ensure security. Actions may, of course, potentially have unexpected outcomes. Mackay sought to create a situation whereby the target of persuasion makes the 'right' decision without being aware it was desired by the propagandist, who has changed behaviour, not opinion, without debate even being raised (Rowland and Tatham, 2010: 2).

The changes are based on the premise that traditional marketing approaches are flawed. Behavioural approaches necessitate a greater level of flexibility and enhanced knowledge of the localised audience; they require greater focus on 'Target Audience Analysis' and 'Measures of Effectiveness'. US IO expert Joel Harding explained through example why he thought the approach was superior:

> the UK approach I believe is correct in that the question is asked, under what conditions will such a behaviour change ... And the example that has been used and ... Nigel Oakes of the Strategic Communication Laboratories ... says if you have Ahmed ... a bomb-maker in ... Iraq and ... he loves the US, and he's setting up money so he can move his family to the US but there are no jobs available and the only way that he has to make money is to build bombs that kill Americans... and he feels bad but that's the only way ... so the conditions under which the behaviour will change is that you give him another job ... He doesn't care if it's making shoes or sweeping the sidewalk ... it's a job that earns him money ... And so the answer is to make jobs. And therefore you can change the behaviour and do away with a lot of the bomb-makers. So the Americans wouldn't look at that, they'd say well he likes America so we'll bombard him with pro-American commercials ... Our approach is totally different and not effective. (Interview: 15th January 2013)

Mackay and Tatham said back in 2009 that 'not only are Whitehall messages a diluted and distant memory by the time they reach the tactical level but they might actually have no relevance at ground level anyway' (2009: 15). Graham Wright stated that as a quick decision is sometimes required many companies were flattening command chains to empower lower ranks (Interview: 1st June 2009). Mackay and Tatham argued that messages must be 'tuned to local events, local perceptions' while also complementary to the wider operational and strategic context (2009). In order to achieve really 'dynamic influence' like this, Mackay's Brigade prioritised 'delegating to the lowest levels' and Mackay and Tatham argue that the British military must 'empower' its people, delegating influence below the commander 'to as low as possible' to gain further flexibility (2009: 17). Of course, this means extending capabilities of lower level personnel, putting propaganda and 'influence' activities in more hands, as personnel operate in a continually changing environment in which the emphasis is on use of cultural understanding to create responsive and immediate campaigns for strong behavioural effect among a very culturally different local population.

Behavioural approaches are being adopted in other parts of government too. A new unit at No. 10 known as the Behavioural Insight Team – or 'nudge unit' – is doing behaviour change work for different departments. According to the outgoing Downing Street Head of News it is seen as very successful and an area in which Britain is selling its expertise:

> we're now attracting interest from overseas, who want to share those similar skills. It's that successful ... Australians. Yeah, yeah, it's a matter of public record that we are now looking to sell our services to other governments. (Interview: Sheriff, 18th April 2013)

Cross-government and military solutions: civil society and private sector

During Bush's first term (2001 to 2004) the annual PR budget averaged $62.5 million; a figure which increased until just seven federal departments spent on average $78.8 million on private PR firms per year between 2003 and 2005 (Farsetta, 2006). The slimming down of bureaucracy and growth of private contracts also reflects a general dislike of 'big government' in the US, a trend that has been more cautiously adopted in the UK drive to privatisation throughout the 1990s and through Public Private Partnerships and Private Finance Initiatives. While contracting is not a new phenomenon, it became increasingly central to conventional warfare and the propaganda war.

Britain's Foreign Office has also made efforts beyond contracting to coordinate private sector work and seek solutions outside government, extending outreach to voices that carry British influence (Carter, 2005: 30–31). The UK's ten-year Public Diplomacy Strategy in May 2003 involved increasing private sector and civil society engagement with 'people outside Government – parliamentarians, business, the media, trades unions, NGOs and interest groups' (Foreign & Commonwealth Office, 2004: 146–147). Torie Clarke, similarly, talked about how domestically and internationally Public Affairs in the US Defense Department couldn't 'depend on the conventional news media' so beyond conventional communication plans, we had people meeting with endless, endless groups from all sorts of quarters in the United States and elsewhere [including] the educational community ... the religious community ... the business community ... There were literally hundreds of people in different departments that ... had relationships with different elements of the business community say, or the religious community, and they worked with them on an ongoing basis ... A relatively decentralised plan. (Interview: 4th December 2013)

There was a drive to bring in 'outside experts', often with poor results. The approach also increased the merging and overlap between PSYOP and Public Affairs. The State Department pulled in private sector expertise in October 2001 with the appointment of Charlotte Beers, an advertising executive, as Under-Secretary for Public Diplomacy and Public Affairs. PhaseOne were contracted to do impact analysis on her branding campaign 'Shared Values'; they concluded that the content was inappropriate. Then Company President Ren Stelloh stated that

Part of the problem was those were public service announcements done by committee, lawyers had a big role in it, and I think ... they kinda already knew that they had blown it. When you can't even broadcast that in [Asian Muslim Action Network]! The friendly King, he says no, no, no ... you've gone an' crossed the line! That's a wake-up call. They had $15m allocated to that effort. They spent 10, they were gonna go to a second stage, but, I believe in part due to our analysis it was ... stopped. (Interview: 23rd June 2009)

On resigning in 2003 Beers admitted that 'the gap between who we are and how we wish to be seen, and how we are in fact seen, is frighteningly wide' (Beers, 2003). But, undeterred, a 2003 government accountability report recommended that the Secretary of State develop a strategy to bring private sector PR techniques into integrating its Public Diplomacy efforts. The State Department, of course, agreed – in line with a growing trend in US propaganda strategy which is also now significant within British policy.

Thorp thought that 'there's clearly a role for contract support', something he strove to increase in both PA and PSYOP. He said, 'as the Chief of Public Affairs, that's where I took the navy ... we had not used contract support in the past. But I changed it' (Interview: 24th August 2009). Contracting this way allows the military to scale down the investment in infrastructure and cutting-edge resources required to run a competitive modern propaganda war. As contracting extends the propaganda apparatus, each individual process will also attract less criticism among the media cacophony and where one activity becomes visible it serves to distract critical attention away from the rest. Efforts to decentralise to outside contracting are also intended to speed up process and bring in area specialists.

From a military point of view the UK's former DTIO Graham Wright saw contracting as 'a good thing'. Wright argued that contractors like John Rendon ('Rendon Group') provided 'continuity and experience' lacking in a British military where people are reposted every two and a half years. Wright saw it as logical since '98 per cent of the occupation of the information space is civilian anyway' and there was 'expertise ... we should capitalise on rather than trying to grow it ourselves'. But, he said, 'there wasn't enough money available in Defence for me to do all of the things I would like to contract' (Interview: 1st June 2009). Arundell pointed out that contracting isn't new: 'What did we do in the first and second world wars? If we wanted to conduct deception operations, we brought in people from the theatre, people from the movie business. You know, you take the skill sets that are out there to achieve the effect you're after. The difference was you could mobilise them for the national effort. Now you have to buy it in' (Interview: 18th April 2013).

This appraisal was echoed by American interviewees including former CENTCOM Commander, Adm. Fallon, who argued that it was cheaper and easier to contract in this kind of expertise: 'Rumsfeld actually *got this!* It's money. Rumsfeld said ... I wanna pay big money to have an army that's trained for military, I want 'em to do military things ... [not] these other things' (Interview: 21st July 2009; original emphasis). The Contractor Sean K. Fitzpatrick agreed: the military's job 'should be to break things and I think it is a major, major mistake on our part to put our services to work on building things', including culturally (Interview: 30th June 2009). The propaganda streams are a career path in the US, but career progression is limited and personnel move on into the private sector.

Since the 1980s the CIA has also begun outsourcing much of its propaganda work to private contractors. George Tenet (Director of Central Intelligence after 9/11) and Bush agreed that CIA funds would be distributed to 'establish relationships and demonstrate seriousness'; propagating the general view that support could and would be bought – it would speak the US message among other nations (Woodward, 2004: 117). Jeffrey Jones in 2005 argued that propaganda resources were still inadequate 'by a factor of ten', reflecting a tendency by the US of injecting money into attempts to solve problems primarily rooted in strategic planning and organisation (2005: 109).

PhaseOne, a commercial company once tasked with marketing dog food, were drawn into government contracting by the CIA shortly after 9/11. PhaseOne forecast the psychological persuasiveness of communications and made subsequent recommendations for content, for both the Defense Department and the CIA. Former CIA Station Chief Ren Stelloh recounted how after 9/11,

> within a few weeks, ... our then [Deputy Director of Operations] Jim Pavitt sent a back-channel to the Domestic Chiefs asking that we redouble and if we hadn't

started, start right now, scrubbing the commercial world ... for tools that we could bring to bear on the War on Terrorism.

Stelloh recalled asking a friend for advice – Jeff Baxter, a key government advisor to Members of Congress on Ballistic Missile Defense, perhaps better known as a former member of Steeley Dan. He is son to the late Loy Baxter, once Senior Vice-President to J. Walter Thompson and the first President of PhaseOne. Stelloh contacted them in his CIA capacity and saw a good fit for them 'in the phase that involved the hearts and minds, attitudes and behaviours' (Interview: 23rd June 2009).

Rendon Group, another major contractor, also secured a $100,000-a-month contract with the CIA and enjoy an extraordinary level of security clearance. They helped set up the Coalition Information Centers, advised the Office of the Secretary of Defense, and worked with the Pentagon Offices of the Joint Chiefs of Staff and Special Operations/Low Intensity Conflict who approve PSYOP plans there. John Rendon describes their activities as 'helping foreign governments to correct things that are bad or wrong in the news cycle, and amplify those things that are not bad' (Hedges, 2005). Rendon remains a consistent but secretive force in this area: he held five defence contracts with the Pentagon in 2005. These included a $6.4m contract to track media coverage in Iraq; contracts advising Afghan Prime Minister Hamid Karsai; and the Afghan Interior Ministry counter-narcotics campaign (Hedges, 2005). This last campaign was previously British operated (Interview: Reeve, 20th April 2006). Graham Wright confirmed that Rendon used to 'pop in and see me every month or so' when in the UK but refused to discuss him specifically (Interview: 1st June 2009). My own attempts to secure an interview were futile, but he has claimed contract experience in ninety-one countries, in nearly every war since the US operation in Panama (Bamford, 2005). Rendon claims an experiential edge – 'nobody else has done this' (Hedges, 2005). Wright emphasises that this makes contractors valuable to a military who must identify 'niche capabilities that there is no point you paying for full-time, when a company can do it better' (Interview: 1st June 2009).

Some would argue, however, that contractors' 'niche capabilities' are securing profit, and whether this produces propaganda campaigns that are by anyone's evaluation 'better' is highly questionable. It leaves a financial imperative driving the campaign and favours short-term, measurable effects. As McBride argued, the 'use of contractors makes a lot of sense because you can ... incentivise' (Interview: 5th June 2009). Former Deputy Secretary of State Richard Armitage argued that in both Britain and the US 'We depend more on contractors ... there's no question ... unless we dramatically increase the size of our own forces, we're gonna have to depend' on them (Interview: 21st July 2009). These companies, with access to a full range of capabilities used in the commercial sector, are profit-driven and ultimately accountable to shareholders, not to the public. Contractors and academics extend their capabilities to government entities and form an extension of the apparatus and its work beyond accountable parties and public visibility.

Rendon, for example, was apparently contracted to the Office of Strategic Influence before it was scrapped. The latter's Director Pete Worden stated in 2005 that another contractor, Science Applications International Corp, did most of Rendon's work (Hedges, 2005). However, Rendon has since denied involvement in the controversial planting of stories in foreign media which Potomac stated the OSI were engaged in. In June 2004, Special Operations Command in Tampa (where US News and World Report asserts that the Office of Strategic Influence's former activities were transplanted) awarded another contractor, the Lincoln Group,[15] and two other companies a huge contract for PSYOP, including prepared newsreels for media use (Gerth and Shane, 2005). Again there was a media backlash against OSI-style revelations in 2005; Lincoln paid Iraqi newspapers to publish stories written by US military officials, designed to look Iraqi-originated and authentic (Londoño, 2009). One such article read 'Western press and frequently those self-styled "objective" observers of Iraq are often critics of how we, the people of Iraq are proceeding down the path in determining what is best for our nation' – it quoted the Prophet Mohammad and pleaded non-violence (Gerth and Shane, 2005). While some articles were marked as advertising, the original source was not revealed to be American. Pentagon officials argued that these campaigns are necessary to tackle insurgent groups, who they said were making the media their key battleground, and an overtly US-attributed source would not be credible.

Of course, Chairman of the Joint Chiefs of Staff, Gen. Pace, and Pentagon officials retrospectively expressed concern that this media manipulation could have happened. Lincoln was justified by explaining that 'the Public Affairs people don't know anything about it' – they had not been 'tainted' by the programme (Interview: Thorp, 24th August 2009). It did not halt the practice of coordinating PSYOP and PA – instead, PAOs concluded the opposite: that they needed to be apprised of future activities, to be able to coordinate and prevent contradictions. Rumsfeld began calling for a 'meeting of the minds of the different communities in the department' (Interview: Graham, 24th July 2009). Thorp thought the Lincoln incident was a catalyst for seeking a more coordinated strategy. He briefed the Joint Chiefs and emphasised the importance of adopting an effects-based approach with more coordination. He said Public Affairs had realised that, 'you can't have one set of rules in the military for Public Affairs folks and another set of rules for everybody else' but were firm believers that they would need to be the ones determining those rules (Interview: Thorp, 24th August 2009).

Contracting, of course, added to the multitude of 'voices' and possible messages feeding into the propaganda war. As mentioned above, the internet complicates targeting; it seems to have produced a 'grey area' which potentially allows online propaganda much liberty. Contractor Ren Stelloh mused on his own experiences at PhaseOne, describing how even among foreign audiences, 'the lingua franca of the internet is English', so this means

> the lawyers will ... say obviously you're targeting English speakers ... and we say 'Well, yeah ... but they're not Americans!' ... well how can you ensure that? ... so you go through things ... to try to make that case.

This clearly leaves a wide berth for subjectivity and interpretation and Stelloh's account demonstrates the nonchalant response of Congress to occurrences of 'feed-back':

> There is a requirement however that, if anything spilled ... there is always a foreign focus ... whatever activities undertaken should never be *designed* to influence an internal audience ... and if there is inadvertent spill-over, say the *New York Times* picks it up and replays it and you, 'Oh shit.' We go tell Congress and say ... And, nine times out of ten, they say ... '*OK!*' (Interview: 23rd June 2009; original emphasis).

Rear Adm. McCreary stated that, 'In PSYOPS, I tell you now, we wanna influence people. Well that's counter to a democracy.' He argued, 'Once you get everything into English it really becomes an international device and should be ... open, honest, truthful, trustful, transparent ... to provide an understanding so people can make informed choices' (Interview: 15th October 2013).

Wilkerson was critical of the close relationship contractors foster with Congress. He said they 'come back in, create their congressional lobby group you know, contribute a little money ... and suddenly you've got Mitch McCall on your side ... or whomever' (Interview: 23rd June 2009). All of this discredits the claim that the DOD gives good oversight. A further issue raised by contracting out is effective oversight and its distancing propaganda from accountability. Silverberg and Heimann argue that with military internet activities, 'The blurring of the lines of authority becomes even more acute' (2009: 84). They highlight 'the practical difficulties of providing "oversight" to instantaneous interactive communications such as text messaging and blogging' and criticise how this 'injects a third group into the mix [with PSYOP and PA] by authorizing nonmilitary, nongovernmental personnel to engage with foreign audiences' (Silverberg and Heimann, 2009: 84).

Former CENTCOM Commander from the Gulf War Gen. Zinni argued that the Pentagon understand 'how to do monitoring' and their extensive experience made them 'excellent contractors' (Interview: 2nd June 2009). Zinni was more critical of the State Department's contracting, arguing that they were 'overwhelmed with the number of contracts' they took. He thought good contracting lay in a well-drawn contract but that the State Department 'write poor contracts ... don't manage them well' and even 'get victimised by some contractors' which may impact on governance (Interview: 2nd June 2009).

Adm. Fallon considered contracting to have worked during his tenure as CENTCOM Commander (2007–8). He closely positioned contractors amongst his uniformed personnel as they would be 'uniformed people doing things that had little to do with guns' ensuring 'they looked like very competent security personnel' but could deliver the message and 'all of it was designed to engender support from the people' (Interview: 21st July 2009). Former State Department Chief of Staff Lawrence Wilkerson said that Rumsfeld was overextending and taking on too much 'and essentially doing it through outsourcing ... Rendon, Lincoln ... different people like that. And no real oversight of what they were doing. Just a release of them to do it' (Interview: 23rd June 2009). Miles Pennett, a media contractor himself, was critical of how much corruption he encountered in Iraq contracting:

> A lot of people subcontracted beyond belief, say for example, when you pay a security guard, you put in the initial quote $1,000 a day ... then someone would go 'cool', they then employ someone for $600 a day, *they'd* employ someone for $400 a day and at the end of the day you have ... it happened out there ... you'd get South Africans'd come out to work on a contract and they're on a $150 a day as a security guard, but you know three chains up they're getting a grand. (Interview: 15th February 2011; original emphasis)

Pentagon military personnel may be particularly sought-after targets for contractors. Kambrod, in his 'how to' guide to defence contracting, suggests lobbying young majors and lieutenant colonels whom he sees as driven by promotion and receptive to technology (2007: 18). Kambrod argues in contrast that Pentagon civilians may not have the 'fire in their belly' for developing combat systems (2007: 18). He states that civilians with long tenure are the 'hardest people with whom to do business' arguing that greater 'job security' means efficiency is not their overriding priority (Kambrod, 2007: 18). It is not unusual to find a close relationship with defence contractors: Vice President Cheney and Haliburton is just one example. Apparently 'after leaving the government in 2005, Jeff [Jones, the NSC Director of Communications] continued to be involved in developing concepts and approaches for strategic communications as a Senior Associate at the consulting firm Booz Allen Hamilton' (Armstrong, 2010).

Former Deputy Secretary of State Richard Armitage was on the board of MANTECH International, who 'do a lot of work for Defense Department, for NSA, for CIA, etc ... so, Justice ... FBI ... We're in forty-seven countries including Iraq' (Interview: 21st July 2009). The extent of this closeness of government personnel with contracting can be seen in the account of Ren

Stelloh, who, while still a CIA Station Chief, became increasingly involved with the work of PhaseOne, a propaganda contractor who keep a very low profile. Their CEO, Jody Moxham,

> asked me a question in February 2002 saying well, what comes next for you? ... Well, she said, you got it quicker than anybody else we've talked to. I can see you playing a role in the growth of the company – so I said that's really interesting let me take that on board ... and we started this kabooky dance and all of a sudden I said oh shit, oh dear, I need to call the Office of General Council – the ethics guys – have I crossed the line from an ethics perspective? ... and they said you're in a position to influence the ... potential contract? I said 'No, I ain't gonna write a contract, I'm just a field rep, the senior guy in the field' and they say, well, as long as you relegate your behaviour, sort of, in that channel, facilitate communication between the headquarters elements and this company, you're OK.

These 'limits' of course allow a wide remit for private contractors to develop privileged interests with particular high-placed and well-connected government employees. For Stelloh this was profitable: 'Long story short, June 3rd 2003 ... I retired and June 4th I started working for PhaseOne' (Interview: 23rd June 2009). He became their Chief Operating Officer and President. The Rendon Group have also built their powerful connections with US government through drawing staff from its ranks. Linda Flohr, for example, left the CIA after working on Iraqi Clandestine Operations supporting the Iraqi National Congress, to join the Rendon Group in 1994. She returned to government as Director of Security for the Office of Homeland Security and Director of Counter-Terrorism for the NSC in 2002.

There are still further financial incentives; Armitage emphasised 'hidden costs' in the DOD running its own capabilities, explaining that if you take an 'actuarial approach to a soldier coming in the army these days during a war, you find the cost of adding a soldier is astronomical compared to adding a contractor'. Armitage argued this is because there are 'health benefits, there are veterans if they get hurt, benefits' and contractors might

> work for KBR ... or Haliburton or whatever ... for a set period of time ... but the health benefits, the 41Ks ... you know, all these kinda ESOP, Employee stock option plans, are not part of their contract. So in the longer run it's cheaper for everybody.

Apart from the costs to the contractor's employees, perhaps, in terms of their benefits. Of course, Armitage said, 'a contract to go to war is always gonna want a lot of money. My brother's there now, and he gets paid very well' (Interview: 21st July 2009).

One key issue here is the role that these contractors play and which functions should only be performed by military personnel or bureaucrats. Opinions on this varied. Former CENTCOM commander Adm. Fallon had a liberal approach: 'contractors can help in anything ... there isn't any specific, they do this and I do that. Whoever can help, I don't care, I'm not biased. I'll take anybody that has a brain who can help me' (Interview: 21st July 2009). Former UK DTIO Graham Wright argued that the responsibility of the military should be 'military planning ... what are the objectives we are trying to achieve, and then you outsource, you go to where the pools of expertise are to do things' – pools that might include 'media analysis, cultural understanding ... polling, all sorts of stuff in that sort of open domain' (Interview: 1st June 2009).

Despite the problems some contractors have posed, often those at the top did not see a need to pull back, preferring to call it the responsibility of the contractors to ensure better management. Armitage assured me,

> Where it got out of control ... I think were some of these like CACI[16] and others, who got involved in interrogations ... previously I was on the board of CACI, years ago, and I couldn't understand what they were doing so far afield from their field of expertise!

He argued for contractors sticking to their 'core competencies' (Interview: 21st July 2009). Yet of course often the commercial drive is to do just the opposite; for companies to find new ways to expand and adapt to changes in markets and demand.

Thorp, referring to Lincoln Group, did suggest still stricter limits were needed. For him,

> there is a role for them to create product not content. Public Service Announcements things like that, leaflets and websites ... But when it comes to content, that is an area that is strictly the purview of [uniformed personnel] or government civilians. (Interview: 24th August 2009)

Yet this was not happening. Manufacturing the message itself is precisely where PhaseOne's 'niche capabilities' lay. Stelloh described how,

> demographically, and more importantly psychographically, we can determine based on what we know from all of the social sciences and the hard science what that group's hopes, fears, aspirations, wants, desires [are] so that when you focus a particular communication to them – *will it resonate? Or not? And if not, what do you do to fix it?* (Interview: 23rd June 2009; emphasis added)

Multiple bilingual researchers perform a complex form of discourse analysis applied across all forms of communication to work out 'how do you influence, how do you create value', factoring in 'the demographics and the psychographics of your target audience'. They claim to be able to do this even if it is not possible to visit the target population. Stelloh explains:

> Let's say that we have a client that isn't able to talk to the inhabitants of Waziristan ... Let's say the tribe are remote and they're not a friendly lot to begin with! What

you can do is use surrogates that allow you to establish a reliable psychological profile. We will buy whatever research is available, we will talk to cultural experts ... So you look at the education and how are they taught to think. You look at the system of justice and morality...

Ultimately they were asking 'what makes a character believable? What are the behaviours that you see that allow you to suspend disbelief?' While Stelloh initially implied that this was a 'theoretical example', saying 'let's say ...' it quickly became clear that PhaseOne had worked there. Stelloh went on to say, 'The Waziristan example is a really interesting model. Some of our research indicated the issue of honor and how honor is perceived' (Interview: 23rd June 2009).

Yet, impressive as their 'niche capabilities' sound, despite having been working abroad commercially with AT&T and other companies since 1987, PhaseOne were cutting their teeth with this project. Stelloh explains,

> when the government gave us an assignment and we said 'OK, where's your market research, where's your demographic, psychographic data that allows us to calibrate tools that have a fidelity, validity?', they said, 'We don't have it – you go figure it out' ... So that's when we did the reverse engineering of the analytical process. The education, the morality, values, justice system, the ... what makes the character.

They were of course instructed to do this to *create messages*, not just manufacture products. As Stelloh recounts,

> once you have that understanding it allows you to develop ... an informed strategy and ... that's the backbone ... for the development of ... communications and activities, designed to influence that group ... to move them toward a behavior or an attitude ... You disseminate your messaging and then the important piece is you track and monitor ... And then it's this continuous loop. (Interview: 23rd June 2009)

There certainly does not seem to be any reduction of interest in PhaseOne's 'niche capabilities' and in 2012 it was bought out by another larger contractor. Their profiling and forecasting techniques initially were developed by MI6 and the CIA during the Second World War then perfected in commercial and academic applications afterwards.[17] These capabilities were also contracted to the DOD, and in this way contracting is bringing intelligence-originated capabilities into the DOD.

That PhaseOne were permitted to tread new ground the way they were, not only in creating messages but in developing their technique for targeting groups remotely, indicates how desperate the CIA and the DOD had become. Thorp argues that it is problematic when somebody develops themes and messages ... in isolation of the policymakers, isolation of the people who are planning the military mission ... they're not true, even if they intend to be true, they are developed in isolation of the policy or the plan and they've become what an individual thinks people want to hear as opposed to what the truth is. And that's a problem.

Thorp was Chief of Public Affairs and also coordinated with PSYOP; he said that when he brought contracting to the navy he ensured it was 'for product, not content' (Interview: 24th August 2009). Similarly, Adm. Fallon stated that he cautioned staff that

you better be doing your own thinking. You can hire people to get information for you and to help you, but ... you have the responsibility for making decisions, you better make 'em.

But Fallon's experience told him '*that*, unfortunately, isn't the way it works, particularly round Washington, there's far too much stuff that's handed off to somebody else'. He later acknowledged, 'There are trade-offs, frankly' (Interview: 21st July 2009; original emphasis). A friend of Ren Stelloh and fellow contractor, Sean Fitzpatrick, argued that contractors need to be creating the messages, as they have expertise in the media, that to expect the military to be able to design them is unrealistic:

if they could tell [contractors] what to *do* then they wouldn't have to hire 'em ... people in the military and the intelligence community don't really have that ability. (Interview: 30th June 2009; original emphasis).

An American advertising executive (now retired), Fitzpatrick gained experience in Northern Ireland working for the UK 'to run their counter-IRA advertising campaign'. Apparently, it was imperative the anti-IRA message got 'a life of its own' and continued beyond the campaign in a self-sustaining way. Following a belief that women are 'very good at communicating' Fitzpatrick chose to exploit female networks, targeting commercials at women; 'his objective was to get to a tipping point where it was not only OK to snitch, it was your duty ... even if it was your brother'. McBride, who later worked with him at the Washington-based Potomac Institute, commented 'you couldn't have a more successful campaign' than Fitzpatrick's anti-IRA campaign (Interview: 5th June 2009). Fitzpatrick has been engaged in a number of contracts across US government:[18] the DOD is listed on his website. Fitzpatrick stated:

Trying to persuade Islamic militants to do anything ... is probably a fruitless exercise. But, there are segments of that society, and sub-segments that *can* be spoken to. The first would be youth and the second would be women. Because they exist ... outside the corridors of power. But those outside influences ... accumulate. (Interview: 30th June 2009; original emphasis).

While Fitzpatrick declined to comment on non-commercial projects himself, McBride confirmed that they worked together at Potomac on a contract with the OSI, describing Fitzpatrick as 'the world's best artist in the world of persuasion'. They began looking at whether 'the UK approach [would] work for the US and UK in another part of the world' and with an 'Arab-Muslim' population; and apparently the State Department continued to explore this after the OSI was terminated (Interview: 5th June 2009).

The State Department's Office of Private Sector Outreach for Public Diplomacy and Public Affairs opened in 2007, tasked to 'develop and coordinate innovative ways for the State Department to engage the private sector in our public diplomacy initiatives' (DoS, 2007). It began by conducting the first ever US Marketing College organised jointly with top US private-sector marketing professionals. Hosted by the Foreign Service Institute, it 'equipped officials from across the interagency with relevant marketing strategies to employ in the war of ideas and for other public diplomacy programs', according to organisers (Midura, 2008).

In each quarter of 2008 the Bush administration held four Round Tables, quizzing 'leading personalities in philanthropy, academics, IT [unclear] from the silicon valley, and CEOs' about what should be done in the war of ideas. This bridged the Bush and Obama administrations, and PhaseOne's CEO Jody Moxham put a fifth group together with 'global marketing organisers from some of the biggest corporations around'. Stelloh recounted how,

> it was very interesting talking to some of the leading figures ... briefing some of the leading personalities from ODNI [Office of the Director of National Intelligence], DOD, State Department ... on how the private sector does it. (Interview: 23rd June 2009)

He told me that it encouraged belief that the government can learn from the commercial world. Sean Fitzpatrick had also been taking 'groups of majors and lieutenant colonels to study at advertising agencies and banks and investment firms' (Interview: 30th June 2009). This trend continued; the Defense Department in 2008 gave contracts worth $300 million over three years to private contractors (SOSi, Lincoln Group, MPRI and Leonie Industries) producing content for the Iraqi media including news stories, entertainment and public service adverts in support of US objectives and the Iraqi government (DeYoung and Pincus, 2008).

Contracting does not always seem to have close governance and this is now affecting the industry. By 2010, some American defence contractors began 'turning their backs on the "soft power" market' and becoming 'fearful' of the 'political backlash against the expanding presence of wartime contractors'. But it is the high-profile firms like Lockheed Martin, 'top defense contractors that obsessively protect their corporate image', that shy away; their 'CEOs don't want to risk ending up on the witness stand on Capitol Hill or being grilled in the media' like Blackwater (Erwin, August 2010). Contracting is not disappearing: in the six years after Ren Stelloh joined in 2003, low-profile government contractor PhaseOne had quadrupled its expert staff, 'and we're hiring like nobody's business . . . simply because the demand is there' (Interview: 23rd June 2009).

The larger defence contractors that dominate the area of Information Operations in the US can be highly conservative; they are often not the ones driving innovation. Large contractors have resource and experience to conduct traditional operations on a large scale, and are often quick to embrace technologies – gimmicks that sell. But McCarty notes,

> you have a huge existing business base of people who do traditional media research, you know, they put together lists, they make expert opinions, they do polls, they do surveys and you know, they're very resistant to any sort of change because that probably means they'll lose money in business . . . they don't want change because that scares them. (Interview: 13th March 2013)

And they don't need to change if they are still securing contracts and have good connections, so compared to smaller or emerging 'niche' companies, many are a conservative force doing what they have always done, in the ways described above.

Angus Taverner, formerly of MoD Media Operations and Plans, stated his belief that there is a

> symbiotic relationship [between the military and contractors] because the military needs the equipment and the other side needs the military to *buy* the equipment. And of course, it's not like being able to go to Tesco's and being able to find everything you want on the shelf and having to go to Sainsbury's to find it instead. There is really only one supplier of tanks. And so it tends to become a slightly incestuous and perhaps overly close relationship . . . I know there are conspiracy theories out there that suggest that contractors actually start wars . . . you end up having to raise an eyebrow or two when the Vice-President of the United States of America becomes the President of Haliburton and two years later we're in Iraq and guess which company gets this massive shed-load of contracts! . . . I'm not sure I'm completely with the conspiracy theorists but I do think that there is sometimes an unhealthy relationship . . . because it has to be so close, it is almost inevitably *too* close. It's a little bit like, you know . . . being forever locked in with the same plumber . . . you can't change plumber! But he needs you to go on having problems with your plumbing otherwise he's not gonna have any work, so you know . . . As a result you do get companies like SAIC . . . and . . . you know, Bell Pottinger became very dependent upon both DOD and the MoD to give them large amounts of money. And that's never healthy. (Interview: 23rd January 2013; original emphasis)

As Gulf War General Tony Zinni put it, 'I think that the problem with contractors is the whole business of contracting exploded too fast. So nobody understood it' (Interview: 2nd June 2009). Britain's Col. Arundell saw large contractors as the future: 'Companies that can deliver a range of activity: behavioural understanding, target audience analysis, proven media output across multi-platform media. And who can measure it … Or somebody that can pull together those various strands as a range of subcontractors.' But he recognised that 'the risk is of course it ends up sounding as though they're marking their own homework' (Interview: 18th April 2013).

While some high-profile contractors are in the midst of PR recoil, it seems unlikely that the industry will be allowed to collapse. In 2009 the Ministry of Defence was reported 'to be considering a large increase in the number of support contracts it outsources to industry' (Defense Management, 2009). The maintenance of an open international economy is a crucial element of the 'whole of government' plan (Armitage and Nye, 2008: 3). The drive to SMART power[19] identifies a clear goal of creating a 'free trade' core in the WTO and demands the Obama administration 'lock in a minimum measure of global trade liberalisation' (Armitage and Nye, 2008: 10). One function of this will be to strengthen government relationships with 'nonofficial generators of soft power', which according to Nye and Armitage include 'everything from Hollywood to the Bill and Melinda Gates Foundation', a private actor they describe as having 'the throw-weight of a government' (Armitage and Nye, 2008: 4). Many of these ideas receive bipartisan endorsement; everyone from Hillary Clinton and Madeleine Albright, to military leaders such as Gen. Zinni, Adm. Smith and Gen. Abizaid voiced their support (Armitage and Nye, 2008: 6).

The same large US companies keep getting contracts and are heavily relied upon. It was seen as an easy solution and big-spend solutions were embraced. Richard Armitage noted that 'no one's got a handle on how much [contractors] do' and warned that any move away from this would need to be 'carefully done' (Interview: 21st July 2009). The efforts to innovate noted later in the book, by individuals within the bureaucracy and military, were forced, prompted by necessity, and often in reaction to a perception of large-scale failures by the cabal of large contractors. In the private sector there is considered to be more scope for new approaches and innovations. Those leaving the government seem often to enjoy the freedom of the private sector where they feel they don't face the same bureaucracy and constraints. McCarty stated that 'Strategic Communication to me, it's not something free governments are ever going to do well. There's other ways to make it happen and that's the kind of stuff I get into now … Pushing the boundaries in the field is what you want.'

One example of the emergent approaches can be seen in Obama's election campaign; he had 'a secret little cave of people' employing more sophisticated behavioural psychology methodologies and focused on motivation and emotional issues.[20] The group, known as the Consortium of Behavioral Scientists, were unpaid. During the campaign a lot of 'private donors' and 'advocacy groups' come forward to help candidates get elected but the government cannot access this support. Services must be paid for. Apparently, 'Obama the candidate could do different things to what Obama the President could do'. Part of the problem is expertise: 'there's money out there but ... military officers in general are not Strategic Communication and audience, understanding experts. That's not why they joined' (Interview: McCarty, 13th March 2013). This means that, with their powerful political connections, and lack of expertise within the establishment, the traditional contractors continue to siphon away government money, securing the large contracts.

As the military evolves and educates itself in this area, however, it is evident from my interviews that the focus on seeking 'attitude change' is being replaced by focus on 'behaviour change' and recognition of a need for greater audience understanding. This may slowly be shaping the contracting work sought by the military. Steve Tatham stated that 'it is an area of on-going discussion. The US remains very wedded to marketing and advertising techniques but I sense there is a slow but perceptible change' (Email: 11th February 2013). Joel Harding also praised behavioural approaches, referring to the work of UK organisations SCL and BDI; he spent a week with Nigel Oakes and Lee Rowland in summer 2011, and said he had introduced Oakes to Pentagon officials. He described how the two companies were related, saying that Lee Rowland 'works for BDI ... and that's inside the Royal College of Defence Sciences [in Shrivenham] – that is their *non-commercial* ... branch. So Lee can stay honest and write all the academic articles but SCL runs all the commercial services' (Interview: Harding, 15th January 2013; original emphasis). BDI was established in 1990 by Nigel Oakes and original members included Adrian Furnham at UCL, Barrie Gunter, Bruce Dakowski and David Fellowes; Phil Taylor and Nancy Snow have also worked with them (Interview: Rowland, 5th July 2013).

The Defense Science Board recommended in a report on strategic communications that more use be made of the private sector, claiming it had 'a built-in agility, credibility and even deniability' (Defense Science Board, quoted in Gerth and Shane, 2005). This means surrendering some of the centralised grip that the government once enjoyed over propaganda, and brings in a powerful tool which distances by process the policy-makers from implementation and audience effects. The pragmatic commercial desire to secure future contracts could result in favouring particular immediate ends over wider strategic concerns, ethical foreign policy and long-term effectiveness. Apparent 'rule-breaking' resulting from delegated planning and decision-making may be being conducted with the tacit approval of those at the top, who are now able to look away; distancing, and delegating authority to profit-based entities. In his classic theory originally applied to the Holocaust, Bauman argues that physical/psychic distancing between an act and its consequences 'quashes the moral significance of the act and thereby preempts all conflict between personal standards of moral decency and immorality of the social consequences of the act' (1988: 484). Bauman's observations were of modernity, and help our understanding, even in a contemporary democracy, of how 'nice' people might enable systems responsible for odious acts.[21] Meanwhile the British government has put forward proposals to allow self-regulation of security contractors (Norton-Taylor, 2009).

Thorp recognised a key issue regarding the sanctity of the message. He said, 'if I'm paying somebody and I'm measuring their ability to change somebody's mind then truth might not become a limiting factor'. Thorp agreed that distancing sometimes occurs but stressed the answer was ensuring that in PSYOP or Public Affairs 'content has to be pure' – derived from those accountable (not contractors) – and essentially truth. Thorp himself argued that he was communicating the 'good, bad and the ugly' (Interview: 24th August 2009). Even if a propaganda message has truth, whether the message formulation is mediated by commercial practice or by well-meaning bureaucrats, its structurally institutionalised production means it necessarily endeavours to restrict and narrow public debate to serve powerful interests.[22] The issue is not simply about truth, it's about complete debate.

Military solutions: co-opting 'covert action'[23]

In the conflicts in Afghanistan and Iraq, traditional 'boundaries' between what once were CIA responsibilities and those of the DOD began to blur as Rumsfeld sought to integrate covert action capabilities within his Pentagon. The credibility of the propaganda message often requires the relative invisibility of campaigns within the global media environment. Former Chief of Staff to the Secretary of State, Lawrence Wilkerson, argued that the problem of credibility and how to deal with the conflicting messages flowing through our media increased reliance on 'the secret message' (Interview: 23rd June 2009). Concerned to expand the capabilities available to the DOD in dealing with the propaganda war, Donald Rumsfeld began looking to utilise activities that were previously under the CIA. Military practices evolved to give an enhanced role to 'covert action', a trend that enhanced animosity between the CIA and the DOD. In US law covert action is activity meant to 'influence political, economic, or military conditions abroad, where it is intended that the role of the United States Government will not be apparent or acknowledged publicly' (National Security Act, 1947). Rumsfeld's reinterpretation of Title 10 of the US Code for Iraq set a new precedent in US defence; Rumsfeld significantly increased the authority of Special Operations Command, bringing them to the forefront of his 'War on Terror'.

Covert action by the military's Special Forces, traditionally a CIA activity or one conducted jointly with the CIA, became Rumsfeld's preferred option in Afghanistan. These military covert actions are predominantly kinetic, yet also include PSYOP. Special Operations Command was key to Rumsfeld's more flexible military, honed to increase expertise in asymmetric and global warfare. Rumsfeld rejected the US war-planning bible, the 'tip-fiddle' (Time-phased-forces-deployment list – TPFDL), and insisted that he, not the Joint Staff, would control timing and flow of troops.[24] Rumsfeld's staff changes further strengthened the presence of Special Operations officers in a military crafted to be loyal to Rumsfeld. He joked that the Clinton-appointed generals had the 'slows', wanting 'too big' an operation; they were swiftly replaced in a move that divided the military (Hersh, 2004: 251–252). To head Central Command (CENTCOM) Rumsfeld brought in Gen. Franks, according to Seymour Hersh's account a commander who it was claimed 'will do what he's told', along with Gen. Myers as Chairman of the Joint Chiefs (2004: 253).

Alongside this military trend, advocates of 'covert action', like former CIA National Intelligence Officer for Counterterrorism Andre Le Gallo, sought to bring propaganda further into the activities of the private sector, civil society and other government agencies which would increase deniability. In 2005 Le Gallo argued that the strategic, long-range needs of the US, in battling the root causes of radical Islam, could be met through *offensive* covert action, particularly within the media and education. He sees America's challenge as

> reversing beliefs apparently accepted by mostly young, underemployed populations that their problems are of 'foreign', mostly American and capitalist (dating back to Cold War propaganda), origins and by an allegedly continuing Christian crusade against Islam.

He argued that such beliefs might render the American message 'dead on arrival' and Al-Hurra TV and Radio Sawa lost credibility by being overtly US sponsored. For him, even beyond the CIA, 'covertly sponsoring private media outlets to reflect the voice of moderate mainstream Islam should not be out of the question' (Le Gallo, 2005: 39).

Seymour Hersh quotes a former advisor who claimed that, as Iraq brought increased demands for troops (something needing public justification in the global media), 'so you invent a force that won't be counted' (2004: 284). Thus Special Operations allowed Rumsfeld to distance the reality from a reassuring public image of low troop numbers. Special Operations Command, once a 'supported command', and only able to contribute to other combatant commands' missions, now became a 'supporting command', enabling it to plan and execute its own operations, reporting directly to Rumsfeld.

The DOD sought to reduce the proof required to justify covert operations. A Pentagon memo moved away from what it said was a 'paralysing' reliance on 'actionable intelligence', choosing instead to 'be willing to accept the risks associated with a smaller footprint'– clandestine activities would be only loosely controlled, to enhance agility (Hersh, 2004: 267). As the former Deputy

Assistant Secretary of Defense for Special Operations & Low Intensity Conflict put it, to 'recalibrate our expectations for what was actionable intelligence ... lower that threshold' and increase 'tolerance for pain in the event we miscalculate or things go wrong' (Billingslea, 2003 quoted in Kibbe, 2004). The number of people reviewing and checking missions was reduced (Kibbe, 2004: 110). This raises serious potential for corruption and abuse when combined with a pre-emptive military strategy and increased emphasis on propaganda to facilitate and legitimise actions. The changes were to enable Special Forces like 'Gray Fox' to be used as part of an assassinations policy and, according to Scahill, were part of an existing neo-conservative project that was foreshadowed in Bush's campaign speeches back in 1999 (2013, see Ch. 1). This continued, as assassinations and secret prisons were not challenged under Obama and 'targeted killing' greatly increased, particularly through the use of drones (see Scahill, 2013, esp. Chs 31, 32). According to O'Connell (2012), 'over 2,200 persons are estimated to have been killed in the three years of the Obama administration in Pakistan alone'.

Expansion of the military's role in covert operations was generally opposed by both the CIA and Special Operations Operatives. One operative told Hersh in 2002 that 'the perception of a global vigilante force knocking off the enemies of the United States cannot be controlled by any strategic deception plan' (2004: 261). But Rumsfeld almost doubled the budget of Special Operations Command in two years; among other things, this was to enable the 'establishment of a unit to coordinate trans-regional PSYOP activities' (Billingslea, 2003: 12). It realised plans for new regional PSYOP and Civil Affairs units during 2004 and set aside funds to pay foreign agents (Gellman, 2005).

While the Pentagon wields more intelligence resources than the CIA, the CIA is seen by some as less bureaucratic, more flexible and more accountable than the military. One of the main problems is the different ways the CIA and military plan covert missions. According to Jennifer Kibbe from the Brookings Institution, 'because its primary mission is combat, [the DOD] has full authority to make its own operational decisions with no outside input or oversight' (2004). Steven Aftergood, Director for the Federation of American Scientists Project on Government Secrecy, argues that ultimately 'there may be a temptation to opt for a purely military action to take advantage of the loophole in congressional notification requirements' (quoted in Alexandrovna, 2007).

There are some indications that while the CIA operated its 'pro-democracy' propaganda campaign in Iran, the Pentagon took care of more aggressive black operations there in a campaign that began with the Iraq War and therefore is deemed an extension of a military campaign. The Pentagon can conduct covert operations abroad without congressional oversight or recourse, during wartime or if military action is 'anticipated' (Kibbe, 2004). This allows great scope for interpretation, particularly in an open-ended 'War on Terror', and the Pentagon resists attempts to tighten the law. Senate Joint Resolution 23 authorised the use of 'all necessary and appropriate force ... in order to prevent any further acts of international terrorism against the United States' (Senate Joint Resolution 23, 2001). Some legal experts argued that it grants 'the president virtually unlimited authority as long as he "determines" that a particular target has some connection to Al Qaeda' (Kibbe, 2004).

This process was begun by Rumsfeld but fully realised under Obama. Dorril argued that Obama has 'let the military off the leash' in covert operations. Where normally,

> the CIA carry out this kind of operations, the military do clandestine, militarised things [now]. Obama signed this order that had allowed the military to expand, at a massive rate, its covert activities. And so a lot of stuff is going on in the military rather than CIA. (Interview: Dorril, 20th July 2010)

With this, Obama established a US Cyber Command in 2009 to 'conduct full-spectrum military cyberspace operations': this would enable warfare across the information spectrum. It would 'ensure US/Allied freedom of action in cyberspace and deny the same to our adversaries' (US Strategic Command, 2010). Obama's defence plans are an attempt to stay 'in the game' using the military for crossing borders with military action and information warfare as 'terrorists' and other non-state actors do. Bush's former speechwriter, Marc Thiessen, now at conservative think tank the American Enterprise Institute, has suggested that this could be used to control Wikileaks (2010). If this were possible, through the globalised potential of their structural censorship it would threaten other states' sovereignty (allies and enemies alike) at a level crucial to the maintenance of trust and credibility. Although, of course, these states may not find out.

The planting of stories to feed back into the domestic press, plausible deniability and the payment of 'agents' in the press are tactics used by intelligence agency propaganda, and are being used by the Pentagon. It is certainly clear that the US government target covert 'perception management' campaigns at the international media, not just in theatre. Former Deputy Secretary of State Richard Armitage told me that

> we cannot do perception management here in the United States, that's against our law, but if we were going to do perception management in Europe this would be a covert operation where we'd insert ... certain stories in certain newspapers that would try and affect, for instance, the thinking of Saddam Hussein. (Interview: 21st July 2009)

Covert actions hinge on deniability, hence they are hidden from the public even after action has occurred. This gives the military an ability to act even where actions may be publicly unacceptable, and limits the scope for prior debate.

A very recent development during the raid on Osama bin Laden's compound saw military Special Operations troops put under CIA control, bypassing the military command structure. There were suggestions that this approach would be used in Afghanistan after draw-down in 2014, as this would allow Afghan and US officials to deny US troops were in the country, maintaining this public appearance. But it effectively removes combatant immunity for the troops according to Berger: 'combatant immunity necessitates prisoner of war status ... that status requires a military chain of command. Replacing the Secretary of Defense with the CIA director eviscerates this' (2012).

Enhancing the role for 'Special Forces' covert action has effectively established a structural silence over military efforts and increased their scope in *all* areas including propaganda, in which it erodes visibility as well as responsibility to the troops.

Military solutions: academic expertise

The contracting out of the military propaganda apparatus increasingly, for reasons of credibility and of course subject knowledge, has brought in academics to assist in psychological warfare, among other activities. One proponent, Robert Thompson, criticised how the American military had traditionally been 'undiluted by civilian brains not bound by the rigid orthodoxy of the book' and welcomed the increased initiative this might bring (quoted in Nagl, 2005: 203). The former NSC Director for Strategic Communications and Information Jeffrey Jones also saw academics and think tanks as crucial to coordinating information strategy; he said regional centres of study at the National Defense University (NDU) and others 'institutionalize the self-help process through sharing the ideas and experiences of Western democracies and their free market economies' and 'new centers of this type should be proposed to meet theater needs' (2005: 110). Joel Harding, formerly Director of the IO Institute (2007–11), described his role at this professional organisation as:

> to bring government [...] the military [and] the industry together with academics and a lot of times the military or the government had a problem, they'd say, 'We have a huge need', a lot of the contractors are saying, 'We have all these products to help you with but we don't know how to get all the products in front of you to solve your problem.' Then the academics would help them walk through the technical procedures or the ethics or the legalities or whatever. And it's my job to bring them all together so we could solve all this. (Interview: 15th January 2013)

After the attacks on Washington and New York there began strong recruitment, and assistance in the counter-terror effort was often keenly given. Think tanks have played an intermediary role here. McBride at the Potomac Institute told how, 'when 9/11 happened we were getting calls from sociology profes-

d so forth saying, well "What do I do?", "how do I help?"' (Interview: ˍˍˍ ,ˍˍe 2009). As the father of PR Edward Bernays once said, 'If you can influence the leaders, either with or without their conscious cooperation, you automatically influence the group which they sway' (2004: 73). In 2009 McBride told me about a meeting he arranged 'a few years ago' to encourage this, between key figures from Social Science Discipline Associations including 'the American Anthropological Association … Executive Director; had Lee Herring, who's the Executive Director of the American Sociological Association' and he even got himself 'deputised by the American Psychological Society to be in this meeting', enhancing his credibility (Interview: 5th June 2009). This was not a meeting of independent academics, but was led by former US Navy Captain, military contractor, Georgetown University Professor and the Director of the 'independent' think tank the Potomac Institute, Dennis McBride. McBride's language below ('we') clearly shows that his allegiances lie firmly with the US military:

> I basically said, look … the Pentagon's … number 1 mission, is to prevent war, by being so damn strong, so smart, that no one would dare, mission number 2 is that if we fail that one, to get it over with, OK? I said, your communities have a role to play in mission number 1 … The Pentagon is engineering, it doesn't understand other cultures … We're not good at that. *We* wanna be good at it and *we* don't know how, absent your help. And I went through this and they said, absolutely, you know what? We're changing our minds, we're gonna support this. (Interview: 5th June 2009; emphasis addeed)

He recalled that one sociologist said they would be 'very uncomfortable helping with targeting'; McBride smirked at this concern: 'I said, I have to be honest with you, the military services don't need sociologists to determine a target sequence'. He argued that,

> things've changed a little bit but there's still this attitude that … we get from academic social science in particular that comes across as they're above, they're better than soldiers and … they're not gonna participate in what we call here 'baby-killing'. (Interview: 5th June 2009)

It is crucial that there is a dialogue between industry and academia, but this must be a dialogue that allows for criticism and is not solely aimed at hiring academics to more efficiently 'enable' already-determined strategies.

Encroachment on civil society also happens covertly. Former CIA officer Le Gallo in 2005 advocated 'covert action' using American universities, or 'any institution', to set up and run educational programmes that would offer an alternative to religious schools and teach in a framework 'emphasising the personal freedoms and free enterprise'. This would be done covertly when 'US or Western sponsorship would negate the effectiveness of the program' and filter US propaganda through civil society (Le Gallo, 2005: 39). Concern has been raised over the effects of military-sponsored research on academic freedom and curriculum.

An industry has grown up on this and in 2005 Britain and the US signed the Combating Terrorism Research and Development Memorandum of Understanding, which the British government's UKUSTrade website claims resulted in 'millions of dollars of mutual trade and investment' in 'counterterrorism'.[25] In the UK Mackay and Tatham have been influential and similarly argued that the networking of 'civilian and military' is 'urgently required' (2009: 33). Former DTIO Graham Wright argued that,

> Academia can provide really deep understanding. I mean if you want someone to go and analyse the deep relationship between ... Taliban and Al Qaeda in Pakistan, why not commission a few universities to begin studying this in-depth and grow departments that really understand this?

He favoured the (highly partisan) American 'think tank culture' which he thought was lacking 'back home', citing the Near East and South Asia Center for Strategic Studies and NDU as examples; Wright had a sideline working with one while in Washington, a 'sort of virtual think tank', and was 'thinking about setting something up back home [UK]' (Interview: Wright, 1st June 2009). He worked on a private sector engagement policy for UK cyber security before joining RUSI and Northrop Grumman.

One perceived benefit was seen as ending the extremely poor communication and cultural understanding in Afghanistan and (particularly the early stages of) Iraq. For example, Col. Glenn Ayers stated that:

> One of the, one of the bad things was ... we actually put out a ... message that said, we wanted the Iraqi military to 'capitulate' ... the Iraqis didn't know what 'capitulation' meant! Nothing is worse and ... Psychological Operation Forces didn't develop that particular message ... it was something that went out that was ham-handed ... and wasn't very effective at the time. So then we had [to explain that] it really means surrender, OK? ... So, that's anecdotal ... of what happened. (Interview: 17th May 2013).

Researchers are attributed much public credibility. The effects of military-sponsored research threaten academic freedom, will influence curriculum development and could bring clashes between the different professional values and interests. Montgomery McFate was a key author of the Human Terrain programme; she learned about 'COIN – History, Methods, Theory' doing field research with the British in Northern Ireland and sees it as important that military organisations don't ignore 'the social conditions in which they must operate' (Email: McFate, 7th March 2013). Since 2007 the US Army Human Terrain System (HTS) has embedded civilian social scientists in the field of war to provide cultural awareness and aid information-gathering (see Finney, 2008). Their contributions assist in, among other things, psychological warfare. Hired through contractors like 'CareerStone', writer John Stanton cited an example of $1,200 a day being paid out to recruits who 'hardly understand the US military culture they are embedded in' and are being targeted by insurgents (Stanton, 2010). Academics themselves have resisted this trend. McFate tells how anthropological writings were used to engineer oppression, blackmail and psychological techniques in Abu Ghraib (2005: 37). She recognised that

> Of course, there is some merit in the view that anytime one does applied work, objectivity is compromised as a result of the particular research interests of the sponsor, the effect of compensation, the problem of 'clientism' and so forth. Of course, there is also the possibility à la Foucault & Gramsci that the politics of knowledge production and consumption contaminate all knowledge through powerful interests of controlling institutions.

She appeared to see it as something which could be subjectively monitored, however:

> My personal view is that individuals who do research must always be the front line in any evaluation of whether they personally believe their objectivity will be, might be, or has been compromised or threatened in any way by doing research for the military – or any other client for that matter. Some anthropologists cannot do research for a sponsor without feeling compromised, yet others can. It depends on their level of sensitivity, their politics, their will power, and their notions of the meaning of 'objectivity'. (Email: McFate, 7th March 2013)

A recent report stated that HTS places 'potentially conflicting demands' upon researchers torn 'between serving occupied, studied populations, and serving the needs of the military' which it felt could 'undermine basic ethical principles that govern research' (American Anthropological Association, 14th October 2009). The American Network of Concerned Anthropologists has therefore been encouraging the discipline to pledge against attempts that, they argue, 'militarize anthropology in a way that undermines the integrity of the discipline and returns anthropology to its sad roots as a tool of colonial occupation, oppression, and violence'.[26] Ralph Arundell explained the need for human terrain analysts and his frustration at how this is often perceived:

> nobody in business goes off and does something because they plucked it out of the air that morning. You know what I mean? They prepare the ground, they do research … And yet when we do that in the military and prepare our business space, everybody looks at us as though we're, you know, some sort of evil, scheming merchants of death but we're not. You don't commit young men and women to operations or vast amounts of resource without understanding, and increasingly in the modern battlespace, the business of understanding target audience, human terrain analysis. We have just developed more sophisticated tools and are utilising a broad range of scientific methods and people from the private sector, if that capability is not there in the public sector – people with

intellectual backgrounds that you can capitalise on to better understand what it is you're doing. (Interview: 18th April 2013)

Mackay and Tatham have recommended the HTS idea be adapted for trial by the British military (2009: 32). Helle Dale from the Heritage Foundation has been a strong voice in the push to introduce a new USIA-style centralised coordinating body or structure. She was a strong advocate of pushing a Strategic Communication Act through in 2008 that it was hoped would establish such a structure (Dale, 2009). As a former journalist she has frequently appeared in the media, including on CNN, MSNBC, FOX News, C-CPAN, PBS and BBC (SourceWatch, 2009). The problem here is that academics affiliated with the military – and think-tank 'experts' from the Rand Corporation or Heritage Foundation among many others, which often claim to be independent or 'bipartisan' – carry greater credibility from their academic or institutional status, and are then sourced by the media for comment on different conflicts and counter-terrorism policies.

UK proposals included bringing social scientists into counter-terrorism and intelligence; Combating Terrorism by Countering Radicalisation received criticism and failed to have the impact of similar US programmes (Marrades, 2006–7). But since this was withdrawn in 2006, the ESRC ('the UK's largest funder of [academic] research on economic and social issues') has channelled funding into studies of 'security threats' and 'new security challenges', incentivising research that contributes to security policy (Marrades, 2006–7) – doctoral work is producing militarised knowledge for the defence industries. David Miller and Tom Mills have charted the rise of the 'terrologist' in Britain; a community of security 'experts' with backgrounds in government or contracting who dominate the media. Having few academic credentials, 73 per cent of these 'experts' were found to reproduce 'orthodox' statements supportive of official rhetoric and focused on violence directed *at* states, rather than state-sponsored violence (2010). The study cited Paul Wilkerson from St Andrews Centre for the Study of Terrorism and Political Violence[27] whose counter-terrorism expertise it argues helped the government rationalise permanent anti-terror legislation. A trend toward close supportive relationships between academics and government or industry is being imported from the US. America has a strong tradition of think tanks producing politically skewed research with conclusions that reflect their political or commercial sympathies. Conflicts of interest result from increasing ties between academic institutions and the government or security industry.

Think tanks enabled some unlikely oddball characters to try and capitalise on American insecurities. One example is Dr Tawfik Hamid (psychologist and former Al Qaeda recruit who had met senior members) who was Chair in Islamic Radicalism at the Potomac Institute. Hamid claims he 'predicted the attack of September 11th itself, two years before and no one believed'. He is a self-professed specialist in 'psychological warfare' with 'a complete strategic plan to defeat radical Islam' and described several 'educational techniques' he developed for children which use behavioural and 'cognitive psychology' intended to target 'the root of the problem' (Interview: 26th June 2009).

Hamid spoke of engagement in high-profile advisory activities in psychological counter-terrorism. These began when he spoke,

> at the intelligence summit, and the Director of National Intelligence. Then people were impressed. I was invite to speak at the Pentagon. The White House. The CI- ... I give lectures to huge variety. I met with Presidents, I met with the President of Italy and recently with the former President of England

– by which I believe he meant Tony Blair, though he had not yet visited Britain (Interview: Hamid, 26th June 2009). In commenting on British domestic tensions following 9/11, Hamid revealed extreme beliefs:

> Just imagine if ... these people manage to have more control ... So the UK would be like Somalia. The woman would be in the houses and have to wear that [unclear] and the hijab, man can beat you ... stoning of woman can happen. So we are talking about here an inevitable confrontation. It's just a number issue. Muslims behave very well as long as they are a minority. Weak. [does a squeaky voice] 'Oh we are *peaceful*' ... but I don't care about the words. (Original emphasis.)

Hamid has also spoken to US Congress and (being staunchly pro-Israeli) was invited to Israel 'by [Ariel] Sharon personally to speak at the President's summit' (Interview: 26th June 2009).

Conclusion

As the counter-terror efforts progressed, 'boundaries' traditionally constructed within the propaganda apparatus through either propagandists' doctrine or law to justify these British and American activities were increasingly considered a hindrance in addressing global asymmetric adversaries. This prompted a drive toward more 'flexibility' and the weakening or navigation of 'unhelpful' conventions. These efforts to deal with the demands of a modern propaganda war led to a sometimes piecemeal effort, with an extension of propaganda efforts both within government and beyond. Rather than the increasing openness implied by the breakdown of centralised propaganda as the USIA was incorporated into the State Department, this trend further normalised propaganda processes and led to extensive 'military solutions'. Private sector and civil society outreach made efforts to ensure credible sources delivered the government message, creating a perception of independence.

The internet also posed challenges to already weak traditional audience 'protections' and the effectiveness of traditional targeting. With the shift to US military dominance of propaganda came an increased use of 'the secret message' and covert action. A deniable campaign abroad could be easily picked up from the internet and enter domestic media, blurring PSYOP with PA and creating problems for PAOs. A lack of openness and attribution could disarm an intended audience to external messages entering domestic and international media, through Twitter for example. Covert propaganda impairs the audience's ability to make an informed judgement of the credibility of the source of the information. The responses to the changing security environment ultimately allowed wider access to a full range of capabilities.

By 2003 this apparatus was sprawling and a government need had been identified for coordinating these efforts. The next chapter will show how efforts were made by both countries towards formalised strategic control over propaganda systems. These changes posed problems for coordination within each country's bureaucracy, which were mediated within the institutional cultures and informal systems. But as former UK DTIO Graham Wright observed, the sheer scale of US bureaucracy made it easier for British IO to be more 'joined-up' (Interview: 1st June 2009). America in particular was hampered in these efforts by 'turf wars' and insular agencies creating conditions where informal relationships would need to be relied upon.

Notes

1 As do other countries, though their approaches differ and could also provide some resistance to attempts at coordination. Paula Hanasz, an Australian working for ISAF at the time, said, 'Generally the NATO forces were so paranoid about "contamination" from PSYOPS that the media ops folks stayed well away from us ... Then I went to Uruzgan, also as an FMT [Forward Media Team] leader, and the situation was completely reversed. The Dutch were so keen for me to promote their reconstruction projects in the PSYOPS media' (Email: 30th April 2013). Interestingly this might indicate a change in the Dutch practices, as Taverner reported that during his period in the MoD, 'of course you went to NATO. I had huge problems with the Germans and the Dutch ... and, in those days, they're absolutely *set*; they're in the business of public information. They were there to give out information. They were not there to try and if you like to shape the message' (Interview: 23rd January 2013).
2 Bloody Sunday refers to the 1972 shooting in Derry, Northern Ireland, of twenty-six civil rights protesters and bystanders by British Army soldiers.
3 An update is shortly being released reflecting changes in terminology – I am told fundamentals will be the same.
4 According to Dorril, this 'came across in the early 70s when it was discovered [MI6] had so few psychological warfare operatives' (Interview: 20th July 2010).
5 Figures for DOD spending on PSYOP, Public Affairs etc, are fragmentary within the defence budget. Sometimes costs are subsumed within other budgets (e.g. personnel,

contracts), making an overall figure elusive, though several interviewees put the figure higher than the State Department's for propaganda.

6 Though strategic coordination is a clearly stated goal of both governments as the next chapter will discuss.

7 The Institute was extremely important in instigating ideas in the information war; McBride recalled that 'The first idea that I remember came up ... at a conference at Potomac and John Bosnell was the man ... that we could get gazillions of wind-up ... radios and parachute them in' (Interview: 5th June 2009).

8 Wilkerson said the Office of Strategic Influence was set up by Rumsfeld (23rd June 2009); Thorp denied this (24th August 2009).

9 The number of stars on an officer's uniform equates to his/her rank in the US military:
One-star - Brigadier General in the Army, Marine Corps and Air Force, and Rear Admiral (lower half) in the Navy.
Two-star - Major General in the Army, Marine Corps and Air Force, and Rear Admiral in the Navy.
Three-star - Lieutenant General in the Army, Marine Corps and Air Force, and Vice-Admiral in the Navy.
Four-star – General in the Army, Marine Corps and Air Force, and Admiral in the Navy.

10 Another contractor, Tawfik Hamid, though not involved in the Office of Strategic Influence, was described as a respected contributor to academic life at Potomac. Hamid advocates variously targeting the 'woman issue' and claimed, 'if you showed [Muslims] that prostitution increased in Iraq or in Afghanistan as a consequence of Bin Laden attack on September 11th ... have to link it to Bin Laden ... you have to create the link ... because they can take it and link it to the war ... because of this man, now Muslim woman are into prostitution. So big for them, they can hate Bin Laden for this.' Hamid explained that at 'the ideological level there are ways through education, reformation, brainwashing tactics can be dealt through the media for example ... to encourage critical thinking ... hijab phenomenon can be weakened through ... certain ... I just can't say how exactly but it can be weakened ... by certain techniques. Psychological techniques and using the media' (Interview: 26th June 2009).

11 Not all agreed; Joel Harding said in fact 'IO has now been unshackled from the old five "components" and may now integrate and use anything as a tool or a weapon. Anything' (Email: 9th July 2013).

12 It should also be pointed out that Thorp was key spokesman on the Jessica Lynch story, held up as an example of Iraq War misinformation. Initial reporting of the story was factual, but reporting changed, and Thorp was reported to have said Lynch 'waged quite a battle prior to her capture. We do have very strong indications that Jessica Lynch was not captured very easily,' an inaccurate account of events. The identity of the 'US officials' that were the original source of the fictional account is unclear. Thorp stated that he confirmed press reports on the basis of other erroneous press reports he had seen, not knowledge of facts, and denied any deliberate attempt to mislead (House of Representatives, 2008).

13 100 per cent non-attributable military IIA can be authorised by the Defense Secretary, though this is rare as 'there are other people who do that' kind of activity (Interview: Ayers, 17th May 2013). Products can also be attributed to a 'willing participant', for example, the target nation's government, or another organisation. Ayers gave the example of a PSYOP Marvel comicbook they did 'in the mid-90s' that was not attributed to the US government (Interview: 17th May 2013).

14 This echoes Hamid's position not to emphasise arguments about US policy being 'just',

but rather to find ways to attribute poor social conditions of local concern (in this case prostitution) to support of the Taliban (see footnote 10, Interview: 26th June 2009).

15 After these events Lincoln Group reinvented itself as Fulcra, then was bought out and is now known as Strategic Social.

16 According to Singer, 'all of the translators and up to half of the interrogators involved' in abuse at Abu Ghraib were working for CACI International or another firm, Titan, and the 'U.S. Army found that contractors were involved in 36 percent of the proven incidents and identified 6 employees as individually culpable'. No contracted individuals were indicted, prosecuted or punished despite prosecutions of military personnel (March/April 2005).

17 Stelloh spoke of these origins in detail, and identified two key figures significant to PhaseOne's history as 'Peter Zeoellner and Dr John Dollard'. During 1941, in Lincolnshire, they worked for the 'Political Warfare Executive' which was headed by Sefton Delmer. Stelloh argued that 'the group had three objectives: develop demoralising propaganda targeting Nazi troops; measuring the effectiveness of the propaganda' and 'using some interesting tools, forecasting the course of the war'. Stelloh claimed that the original work and content analysis, 'was incredibly effective, considered a top secret capability on par with the Enigma machine and so people just didn't talk about it. They were accurate, anecdotally what I've heard is, they forecast within a 36-hour window when Germany would march into Poland' (Interview: 23rd June 2009).

18 He said 'I had the privilege of being with [Peggy Noonan] when I worked for George H.W. Bush' (Interview: Fitzpatrick, 30th June 2009).

19 'SMART' power meant the US working in partnership with practitioners and policy advisors like Richard Armitage to theoretically unite defence with economic and communicative forms of power. It sought to ensure 'American influence' through an 'integrated grand strategy' to 'match our strategies and structures at home to the challenges that face us abroad' utilising 'civilian instruments' (Armitage and Nye, 2008: 3). SMART power and Strategic Communication both sought to integrate influence into wider policy planning, to ensure its development was even more closely tied to the state's stability and foreign policy objectives.

20 According to the *Washington Post*, the consortium included Dr Craig Fox, a Los Angeles psychologist, as well as 'Susan T. Fiske of Princeton University; Samuel L. Popkin of the University of California, San Diego; Robert Cialdini, a professor emeritus at Arizona State University; Richard H. Thaler, a professor of behavioral science and economics at the University of Chicago's business school; and Michael Morris, a psychologist at Columbia' (Carey, 12th November 2012).

21 See also Chapter 5 where this theme will be developed further.

22 This will be developed further in Chapter 5.

23 The word 'clandestine' is used where actions themselves are secret/hidden; 'covert' specifies that the *sponsor* of the action is secret/deniable – a covert action may not be clandestine.

24 Rumsfeld denied this publicly at the Army Commander's Conference in February 2003 (Hersh, 2004).

25 See www.ukustrade.com/.

26 See Network of Concerned Anthropologists: http://sites.google.com/site/concernedan-thropologists/faq.

27 CSTPV have links to RAND Corporation in the US, a hugely influential think tank with strong ties to both government and the defence industry.

3

Formal propaganda (mis-)coordination

Introduction

The changes to propaganda in both the UK and US described above and the huge investment in expanding the propaganda apparatus prompted demands for strategic coordination. But as this chapter will show, we did not witness the coordinated, systematic response of a well-oiled propaganda machine. Improved coordination of capabilities such as PSYOP and Public Affairs, or between different government departments, was seen as a requirement of modern propaganda in a changing media environment. As Jowett and O'Donnell have argued 'successful propaganda campaigns tend to originate from a strong, centralized, and decision-making authority that produces a consistent message throughout its structure' (1992: 216). Coordination of every sphere is furthermore seen as a crucial element of counter-insurgency campaigns. John Nagl argues that 'the strategic vision ... to put the military component of a counterinsurgency campaign in proper perspective vis-a-vis the economic and political actions necessary to defeat the insurgents' is crucial to success in this form of warfare (2005: 195).

This chapter will show how the desired depth of coordination of propaganda proved challenging to impose on existing formal structures, particularly in the US. US bureaucracy is a loose sprawling mass compared to the British system, which is by contrast small, close-knit and relatively more disciplined. The chapter will show how insular agencies with strong institutional cultures impaired formal inter-agency cooperation and made strategic direction difficult. British and American military and political cultures differ markedly, with different cultures within sub-groups. Nagl argues that 'The varying strategic and organizational cultures of different organizations play a critical role in the organizations' abilities to adapt their structure and functions to the demands placed on them' (2005: 6). The chapter covers the two countries' domestic political contexts and integrates these accounts to develop a thematic argument highlighting changes in the apparatus and formal structure of propaganda policy-making. Cultural factors will be argued to contribute to institutional conditions that both maintain cohesive, functioning bureaucratic units and build insularity and competitiveness between government departments. The section will draw on insights gained from studies into organisational culture, recognising that such work has largely focused on *managing* cultures for the benefit of the institution, a problematic stance for sociology, which underestimates its contradictions and political role (Parker, 2000). The chapter highlights systemic problems and planning responses, which will in subsequent chapters be shown to have shaped the countries' relationship and the inter-country planning structures that coordinated joint propaganda efforts.

US strategic propaganda coordination and 'stovepipes'

According to Matt Armstrong there had long been a lack of focus on strategic coordination: 'The White House since the 90s had completely ended its interest in public diplomacy ... basically since the wall came down' and USIA was still active (Interview: 6th March 2013). Many attempts were made – through formal hierarchical relationships, coordination meetings and organising structures – to exert consistency of messages and coordination. American planners anticipated back in 1999 that structural coordination would be required if messages were not to conflict. Under a secret presidential directive, President Clinton ordered a formal International Public Information Core Group be established, in which the State Department was to be lead. It was chaired by its Under-Secretary and drew top officials from Departments of Defense, State, Justice, Commerce and the Treasury, along with the CIA and FBI. The International Public Information Group's role was crucially 'to synchronize the informational objectives, themes and messages that will be projected overseas ... to prevent and mitigate crises and to influence foreign audiences in ways favorable to the achievement of U.S. foreign policy objectives'. Their control over 'international military information' was intended to 'influence the emotions, motives, objective reasoning and ultimately the behavior of foreign governments, organizations, groups and individuals.' This would be done 'to enhance U.S. security, bolster America's economic prosperity and to promote democracy abroad' (International Public Information, 1999).

While their activities were marked only for foreign audiences, the International Public Information Group charter stated that Public Affairs should be 'coordinated, integrated, deconflicted and synchronized' with PSYOP to avoid contradictory messages – it was thus a precursor to efforts detailed above to weaken this partitioning of propaganda (International Public Information, 1999). While 'Public Information' functions continued to be incorporated across government, according to Pugmire, President Bush let this order lapse (2002).

Clinton's directive did not of course predict the events of 9/11, and, with further evolutions of the structure, this issue of strategic level inadequacies has returned time and again. Bradley Graham, Rumsfeld's biographer, spoke of

> an effort ... by Rumsfeld and Feith to draft an interagency strategic plan for the War on Terrorism and they kept groping all the way through 2002, 3, 4, 5 and 6 to try to get a document or ... blueprint for ... the larger war and the Pentagon took the lead in that, largely because they didn't see anyone else doing it. And there are several briefings with Bush where Bush seemed to sort-of 'buy into' the Pentagon pitch and order a National Security Directive to be drafted and then the process would bog down again. I think one finally did get signed and drafted in 2005–6 [of which] a major pillar [was] strategic communications. (Interview: 24th July 2009).

After Charlotte Beers's resignation, a report to the House on Public Diplomacy again linked Arab and Muslim resentment to American policies, calling for a new US 'Strategic Direction' (Djerejian, 2003). Similarly, the Government Accountability Office stated that, post-9/11, '[Department of] State acknowledged the lack of, and the need for, a comprehensive strategy that integrates all of its diverse public diplomacy activities' (Government Accountability Office, 2003). The Strategic Direction report stressed the need for a new White House office charged with wide-reaching strategic-level coordination of Public Diplomacy across government. The State Department would remain lead in this, but they too would follow the centralised 'unified strategic direction' (Djerejian, 2003: 14). Astutely, however, US government contractor (now retired) Sean Fitzpatrick identified a lack of strategic control and ownership. When asked if it was 'uncoordinated – the way they're going about this?', he replied that the problem was that 'There *isn't* a "they"' (Interview: 30th June 2009; original emphasis).

Rear Adm. Thorp, former Public Affairs chief, explained how coordination across the military propaganda boundaries must necessitate a re-think of the strategic level:

> in the twenty-first century what we really need is a reaffirmation of who has the lead for the communication element because as big as we are in the US, and I think it really [also] applies to the UK ... there has to be someone who is singularly responsible and accountable for public communication. And you can't have two different entities [PSYOP and Public Affairs] doing that. (Interview: 24th August 2009)

Strategic Communication was tasked to the NSC and White House where, as NSC Director for Strategic Communications and Information, Col. Jeffrey B. Jones filled the early strategic propaganda role, having previously run the PSYOP Group in Fort Bragg (Gerth, 2005). Jones has argued that while the activities of other government agencies were 'distinct' from defence, 'some of the means are the same'; for him 'synergy [of message] is impossible without coordination' (2005: 109). Later Jones headed the secret Counter Terrorism Information Strategy Policy Coordinating Committee; members included representatives from the State Department, Pentagon and intelligence agencies, and contractors including Rendon and Lincoln working with a sub-group. It was meant to coordinate efforts: 'everything from public diplomacy, which includes education, aid and exchange programs, to covert information operations' (Gerth, 2005). In a slightly evolved set-up since March 2005 the most senior propaganda position was the Deputy National Security Advisor (NSA) for Global Communications.

The Director role is subordinate to the Deputy NSA. Kevin McCarty performed this role between 2008 and 2010 as Director of Global Outreach and, with Deputy NSA Mark Pfeifle, oversaw and coordinated the information war. Ben Rhodes[1] is, at time of writing, incumbent Deputy NSA. Former Director of the Information Operations Institute, Joel Harding, saw this role as flawed:

the Assistant National Security Advisor for Strategic Communications ... Ben Rhodes ... has only been a speech writer and he's supposed to coordinate all this information ... I guess strategy ... for the White House. Well his job is as a political consultant so he doesn't do this. And then there's supposed to be an ... interagency process committee ... coordinating strategic communications across the government and it's supposed to meet every two weeks ... with all the Directors for Strategic Communication for the government. (Interview: 15th January 2013)

Matt Armstrong agreed that this post had never provided effective leadership:

the White House ... national security staff is *tiny*, uh, they're not [working at the] *operational* [level] – and because they're tiny, they're firefighters ... so they really can't be centre of the universe. (Interview: 6th March 2013; original emphasis).

Harding referring to Benghazi[2] as an example; the NSC 'is supposed to coordinate the United States on an ongoing basis but the problem is it's way too understaffed to coordinate such a large problem'. He said that 'there's also no national information strategy, and there's no ... continuity, there's no central planning effort' (Interview: 15th January 2013). Armstrong saw the post as little more than a figurehead for the US global outreach, observing that 'the title is a little inflated' and that often 'they're trying to justify what they're doing and why' (Interview: 6th March 2013). This also applies to many of the documents produced as 'doctrine' which claim to unify cross-government efforts.

Particularly for America, where the structural changes seen as necessary for coordinating the propaganda apparatus suffered after the USIA's dissolution, what is effectively a dispersal of propaganda functions into the bureaucracy of the State Department, then expansion of military capacities to pick up the 'slack', was never going to be easily coordinated.[3] Persistent challenges of interagency communication produced levels of discord between programmes and allowed conflicting messages. Efforts to coordinate across government created tensions in the large bureaucratic system with its traditional rivalries. Coordination of American formal structures has been historically lacking, exacerbated by the insular and protectionist ethos of agencies of the Federal Government, often called 'stovepipes'.[4] Wilkerson described propaganda responsibilities as increasingly divided between 'multiple prongs', each of which often produces work which is unknown to the others, and which create effects which 'are surprises to those who started them' (Interview: 23rd June 2009). The solution to the latter problem has been envisioned in an 'effects-based' approach (beginning from the desired outcome then working out how to achieve it) as detailed above. This section will focus on formal coordination and those 'multiple prongs' of the main propaganda players not working together.

The Pentagon resisted coordination with other agencies. As former National Security Council Director Franklin Miller observes, 'you shouldn't get the impression that these kinds of battles are unique to Iraq. I watched it for twenty-five years [through] the Soviet nuclear threat'; he observed how the Department of State always took the soft position, whereas Airforce took the hard line, and the CIA fell somewhere between (Interview: 3rd August 2009). Defense Department culture is seen as distinct from and conflictual with the CIA and State Department.

At the strategic level there was a feeling that the information war 'almost fell in the too-hard category' – Miller (who was responsible for interagency defence coordination at the NSC) said, 'I did have an extremely competent person on my staff [Col. Jeffrey Jones] who was dealing with that and I left them alone' to concentrate on traditional security concerns (Interview: 3rd August 2009). A similar tension also existed in the Department of Defense between the desire to control information, and the wish to delegate away an impossible task. This was observed at the operational level by Miller in 2003–4 when Sanchez commanded forces in Iraq (explored further in Chapter 6) but can also be seen in the bureaucracy. Part of the coordination problem was clearly due to leadership and personality factors, which contributed to both tensions, and ad-libbed solutions in all agencies of Federal Government.

Some actors managing the war took a monopolistic approach to coordination. According to Wilkerson, Rumsfeld regarded the sprawling DOD apparatus 'like a businessman running a company, that he could get his arms around most of the essential people and resources and he could manage them, if not lead them, he could manage them' (Interview: 23rd June 2009). Though leadership styles vary, the military's organisational culture encourages personal qualities. Pierce claims US Army organisational culture emphasises:

- An overarching desire for stability and control.
- Formal rules and policies.
- Coordination and efficiency.
- Goal and results oriented.
- Hard-driving competitiveness. (Lovelace in Pierce, September 2010: iv)

There was a need for coordination in the Pentagon, across the interagency, and finally in theatre. The US State Department has some strategic responsibility for US military propaganda so their coordination with the DOD is crucial to consistency in the propaganda war. Important strategic State Department roles were played by Deputy Secretary of State Richard Armitage (until 2005) and Chief of Staff Lawrence Wilkerson (August 2002–2005), both interviewed here. The State Department's remit goes far deeper than Public Diplomacy, and its relationship with the DOD is often unclear and confused, even sharing some strategic PSYOP planning. Frank Thorp said diplomats also needed to be coordinated: 'sometimes when you have Psychological Operations folks … coordinating with diplomats about what is going to be said publicly, and the Public Affairs folks aren't in the room, you're destined for disaster'; likewise if Public Affairs coordinate without involvement of PSYOP (Interview: 24th August 2009). The Pentagon is responsible for 'establishing national objectives, developing policies, and approving strategic plans for PSYOP' (Joint Chiefs of Staff, 1996: vi).

The Pentagon delegated much of the information campaign to the Combatant Commanders between whom US military responsibility around the globe is divided. Central Command, who are responsible for the Middle East, North Africa and Central Asia (including Afganistan and Iraq), established three Coalition Information Centres (CICs) in London, Washington and Islamabad that became crucial to the infrastructure of the coalition media campaign in Afghanistan. They were predominantly operated by Anglo-American personnel (Macintyre, 2002). CICs were designed for counter-propaganda and to maintain consistency of message, with a sharing of ideas, material and personnel as well as constant communication. But CICs did not coordinate well with the embassies, who answered to the Foreign Office and State Department, according to Graham Wright: 'CENTCOM can have a plan but that does not lock the diplomats in. So the diplomats can go and say things to congress and they can talk on the radio and completely screw around what they're trying to get done' (Interview: 1st June 2009).

One former British Flight Lieutenant argued that in Iraq, Central Command 'became almost a separate branch of the US military, reporting to the Secretary for Defense and bypassing the normal chiefs-of-staff route' (Email: Anonymous, 2010). As Rumsfeld's new Special Operations Military Information Support Teams grew in prominence, they left ambassadors unaware of in-country military activities and 'overwhelmed' some embassies with a 'growing presence of military personnel and insistent requests from Combatant Commanders' that turned embassies into command posts. Apparently 'in several cases, embassy staff saw their role as limited to a review of choices already made by "the military side of the house"' (Committee on Foreign Relations, 2006). Having delegated propaganda out to the CICs, Britain's Graham Wright found a subsequent refusal to engage with others on matters of the propaganda war at the Pentagon. Even *within* the DOD, across its forces, a lack of horizontal integration in the apparatus left the US campaign not being delivered consistently. McBride said,

> the administration lost an opportunity to prepare a ... thorough Strategic Communication plan, and ... instead ... relied on CENTCOM because that was the model that had been set up in Desert Storm. (Interview: 5th June 2009)

To compound this, the Americans had to get approval all the way up the cumbersome command chain. British PSYOP personnel argued that this contrasted with the British military who devolve decision-making to allow more flexibility and autonomy in the field of combat (Interviews: 15th Army PSYOP Group, 22nd November 2005). Adm. Fallon, who commanded CENTCOM from January 2007, said, 'I had ... challenges in communication with my own bosses sometimes who merely looked through a certain lens and made assumptions that were usually wrong' (Interview: 21st July 2009). This is particularly problematic when we consider US bureaucracy and military as having quite different cultures. A former British Flight Lieutenant described the Battle for Fallujah in 2004 as offering 'insight into the US mindset (soldiers vs politicians)'. He recalled that,

> These two operations were kicked off by a Bloody Sunday type incident where a number of protesters were shot by over-reacting US troops. This led to the infamous kidnap and killing of the security contractors. What is significant is that the US Marine Corps commanders[5] 'on the ground' emphatically did not want to 'take' Fallujah; instead they wanted to mount intelligence-led raids (as in Somalia), to kill and capture insurgents. But they were overruled at the political level and the costly and destructive battles followed ... almost the same casualties (military and civilian) as the Battle of Hue in the Vietnam War. (Email: Anonymous, 2010)

Miller said coordination between commanders and the strategic level eventually improved: 'We'd get on a video conference once a day, once a week, as time went on ... it changes where we do the surge' (Interview: 3rd August 2009). 'The surge' refers to a period in 2007–8 when the US government moved an additional five Brigades into Iraq and accompanied this with a 'controversial counter-insurgency strategy and an additional emphasis on diplomacy' – there was also a communications element, discussed below (McCarty and Pfeifle,

2011). Strategic planning was seen as improved at least for a time. Prior to 'the surge', direction was left 'to Rumsfeld and the commanders' and 'less interaction between, those commanders ... and President/Vice-President' (Interview: Miller, 3rd August 2009). The Defense Department's resistance to coordination had also compounded its traditional rivalry with the CIA, which shares responsibility for propaganda.

'Stovepipes': the Pentagon v the CIA

This section will discuss the 'turf war' over Rumsfeld's desire to ring-fence CIA capabilities for the Defense Department and concern over the coordination of CIA efforts with the DOD. The CIA and the Pentagon have a long-standing, conflictual relationship which began to feed on changing events. While exact numbers are classified, CIA resources in the propaganda war are certainly far smaller than those of the Pentagon[6] and State Department and Pentagon insularity and expansion contributed to an excessively protectionist CIA. It is unsurprising that Rumsfeld's encroachment into 'covert action' – CIA territory – was resisted by this historically closed organisation. Drogin described how 'the Pentagon did not have a ready-to-go plan to kick out the Taliban so the CIA went in ... got the credit for it really'; he argued that this aggravated Rumsfeld and contributed to the 'dramatically increased use of Special Operations forces from the Pentagon' (Interview: 22nd August 2009).

According to the former NSC Director Franklin Miller, 'CIA was a junior partner to DOD in what was going on out there, doesn't mean they were not influential'; he asserted that they may have been 'guiding things' (Interview: 3rd August 2009). The intelligence agency propaganda role seems also to have been evolving. Assistant Secretary of Defense for Public Affairs at the Pentagon (2009–12), Doug Wilson, stated that:

> in the time I've been in government, with stretches of service over forty years, there's a greater involvement now of intelligence Public Affairs Officers in discussions involving national communications strategy. Public Affairs Office Representatives of the NSC, the State Department, the Pentagon, and the intelligence agencies all on the same line talking together. (Interview: 14th May 2013)

The CIA has had people on the NSC staff tasked with coordinating an external communication strategy (Email: Harding, 20th May 2013a).

Former Deputy Secretary of State Richard Armitage also confirmed that the CIA's role was strategic level in the information war, aimed at perception management nationwide of the target country, and in contrast to the 'DOD [which] is generally tactical in nature', focused on a particular military campaign (Interview: 21st July 2009). Former Chief of Staff to the Secretary of State, Lawrence Wilkerson, stated that

> I know the CIA was running ... what we call black programs, secret propaganda programs aimed at you know in some cases ... on the far extreme destabilising a particular political leader or even a government and on the lesser extreme maybe just making a couple of local leaders that they had suspicions were Taliban-affiliated or Al Qaeda-affiliated seem less than they were or maybe more than they were, among the populous around them, in order to try and discredit them. (Interview: 23rd June 2009)

There has also been a move toward more overt communications in the US intelligence agencies. Doug Wilson observed that 'They've always had an understanding of the covert [message]. I think their Public Affairs personnel have a greater presence in the development of the overt messaging than there has been.' He said, 'I think the Public Affairs Officers of the intelligence agencies participate in overall Public Affairs messaging to a greater extent than they have in the past' (Interview: 14th May 2013).

Former Department of State Chief of Staff Wilkerson, who spent thirty-one years in the Pentagon, observed at times a 'bureaucratic hatred, and real visceral personal hatred' which was mediated by leadership and personality (Interview: 23rd June 2009). As Plame Wilson recalled, 'on working level sometimes ... the relationship is very good but obviously there are cultural differences and they have different missions' (Interview: 11th August 2009). Different chains of command structurally sustained cultural differences, which then form the basis of interagency relationships. This is typified by how the CIA sees the Defense Intelligence Agency – as military – and the CIA perception was dismissive of the military. As Bob Drogin put it, 'sort of shoot-first, salute, you know... go by the rules'. Drogin described how 'the CIA ... think they are the hot-shots and they're trained ... civilians'. The Defense Intelligence Agency were perceived as 'basically people who couldn't get into the CIA; which isn't really the case. So that they really look down their noses at them' (Interview: Drogin, 22nd August 2009).

Pincus suggests that Rumsfeld's covert operations inflamed the CIA rift when 'Pentagon operatives allegedly ... visited countries without prior CIA knowledge, although the local CIA Station Chief was supposed to have been told' (4th July 2005). If the military pursue covert missions independent from the CIA, this potentially compromises coordination of covert missions, which could end up operating at cross purposes. Wilkerson provided an example of this occurring which illustrates the CIA's own poor coordination with other agencies. He described how there was 'extraordinary inconsistency', saying:

> we have this problem with the CIA running a black program, let's say, out of Islamabad ... and the Station Chief ... the CIA's representative in-country, in Pakistan, not telling the ambassador, in whose embassy he works, what he's doing ... the CIA will say, that's because what we're doing is all lies, or semi-lies and we don't want the ambassador to be a liar ... What should happen is when the ambas-

sador is asked questions about what we have disseminated he should say well as far as I know that's incorrect or ... I don't know or something like that ... out of sheer honesty ... But that doesn't make for good, coordinated policy within a country [laughs]. And yet, I know that was happening.

The embassy risked making policy on false information and unwittingly became conduits for lies.

> So you have this huge um ... continuum of black stuff that they're putting out and the ambassador's there tryin' to figure out what's true and what's not true ... and he doesn't even know his own people are putting it out! And when I say putting it out ... when they concentrate resources I mean, they'll buy newspaper editors, they'll buy newspapers, they'll put ... stories in newspapers and so forth ... it's pretty powerful! (Interview: Wilkerson, 23rd June 2009)

As the CIA didn't inform the other agency about its programmes, messages became conflicted.

The Pentagon was also failing to keep the CIA in the loop. Miller concluded that 'That's the way this government functioned back then.' He described

> something called the synchronisation conference where once a week the senior people from the CIA and senior people in central command came together to talk about how the war ... was gonna begin ... and what would CIA's assets do ... when the military force would actually get engaged ... Rumsfeld found out that this ... was going on and pulled the plug on it. Said to [Tommy] Franks – you will not meet with [George] Tenet or his people. Until I approve it. (Interview: Miller, 3rd August 2009)

As Wilkerson's example infers, blame for mis-coordination cannot solely be placed at Rumsfeld's feet – apparently he and Tenet 'got on quite well' (Interview: Graham, 24th July 2009). When Porter Goss took over from Tenet as CIA Director in 2004 this increased tension in the agency and led to key staff resignations; Goss became resistant to any encroachment on CIA functions from John Negroponte in his new role of Director of National Intelligence (Thomas, 2009: 452). The role has been weaker than intended, with key agencies staying under the Pentagon, and a CIA that reasserts its dominance whenever issues over its responsibilities are raised (Interview: Anonymous, 1st June 2009). But in 2005 Goss and Rumsfeld made a written agreement designed to '"deconflict" the operations' and 'co-ordinate them as closely as possible' (Negroponte in Pincus, 2005). But new Pentagon guidelines in 2005 stated that the DOD 'reserves the right to bypass the [CIA's] Langley headquarters, consulting CIA officers in the field instead. The Pentagon will deem a mission "coordinated" after giving 72 hours' notice to the CIA' (Gellman, 2005). Rumsfeld vehemently opposed the subordination of intelligence under a new National Director of Intelligence (Kibbe, 2004). His creation of an Under-Secretary of Defense for

Intelligence was widely viewed as a plan to deflate these efforts. According to one Defense Department Official, the CIA was believed to be encouraging the negative media attention against Rumsfeld to support its own interests against the establishment of a Director of National Intelligence. A CIA negative campaign aimed to turn Congress and the national media against Rumsfeld and create the impression that he was trying to 'take over intelligence' and centralise power within the Pentagon (Interview: Anonymous, 1st June 2009). This is a powerful example of how a pragmatic CIA may have used populist tactics in a self-serving way to influence domestic media and power structures, and destabilised the interagency effort (Interview: Anonymous, 1st June 2009).

But even early on, the CIA looked to throw blame anywhere to protect itself. As American journalist Bob Drogin recalled,

> After 9–11, one of the things that came up was that ... two of the hijackers were out on the West Coast Al Hazmi and Al Midar and I get a call from ... the seventh floor in the CIA, the directors floor, telling me how absolutely outrageous it was that these hijackers had been in the country and the FBI hadn't caught them. Hadn't done anything about them. And, basically, I was being fed information about how the FBI had screwed up.

Drogin described how 'it came out that ... the CIA had not told the FBI that the guys were in the country until a day before the attack ... They'd sat on that information for months.' This reveals the importance of bureaucratic interests and domestic tensions in determining how propaganda often functioned. As Drogin argued, 'the enemy in the real world ... was Al Qaeda, but their enemy in terms of Washington, in terms of bureaucratic politics was to ... point the finger at the FBI' (Interview: 22nd August 2009).

The CIA felt threatened by the potential disclosure of questionable activities – something known in intelligence as 'flap potential' (Thomas, 2009: 24). This demonstrates a cultural attribute which Drogin described as 'a nature of secrecy ... used to ... conceal incompetence and ineptitude. Rather than simply to protect vital secrets' (Interview: 22nd August 2009). The CIA attempted to put propaganda in the service of limited agency interests when it felt its unique functions beginning to be usurped. It demonstrates how this is sometimes relative to *institutional* interests, not just national strategic goals. In intelligence an informer might sometimes be exposed (becoming a 'discard') to protect another, more important, asset – the culture and operation of intelligence is highly pragmatic (Thomas, 2009: 24). Function was not static within the organisation; it adapted to continually redefined needs. The CIA should not be seen as especially weakened; its role and identity are being renegotiated. Gordon Thomas argues that following 9/11 the CIA transformed 'from being primarily an intelligence-gathering organisation to a worldwide military police service' (2009: 412).

2005 onwards: 'Strategic Communication'

As this book is being written in 2013, there is still confusion about the concept of 'Strategic Communication'. It is often confused with the term 'strategic communications' which is applied to mean various types of persuasive communications and media used to support a particular strategy. As Steve Tatham has said, 'there remains an unresolved debate about what Strategic Communication actually is' and this applies to both the US and Britain (Email: 11th February 2013). In a recent example, Assistant to the Secretary of Defense for Public Affairs, George Little, sent out a memo stating that Strategic Communication was no more, saying he was no longer using the term.

As US former Assistant Secretary of Defense for Public Affairs Doug Wilson said, 'in the Pentagon all kinds of Strategic Communication terms and words were bandied about. "Strategic Communication" ended up becoming its own little academic world, and the words didn't mean much' (Interview: 10th May 2013). Paula Hanasz observed that 'There were ALWAYS new and better approaches, each with a sexier name or acronym than the last. As far as I could ascertain, nothing ever changed' (Email: 30th April 2013).

The goal was not just to coordinate military propaganda like PSYOP and Public Affairs, but to coordinate all government activities in the information sphere with *all* other government activity to create truly system-wide continuity. The discrepancy between the practice of US foreign policy and its propaganda efforts brought accusations of hypocrisy. America criticised Al Jazeera for airing dissenting views and footage of terrorists such as the Bin Laden tapes, whilst arguing for freedom of speech and a free and independent media. This was considered highly hypocritical among media outlets where Al Jazeera is accorded high respect for its journalistic standards, particularly in the Arab world and Britain, as many of its staff were BBC trained (Interview: Reeve, 20th April 2006). Phil Taylor recognised that it wasn't just messages that needed coordinating, as action communicates too (2002: 438).

According to former NSC Communications Director for Strategic Communications and Information Jeffrey Jones, in the US, leadership and strategic control of propaganda remained an unfulfilled task from Bush's first term; 'several attempts' to implement it had fallen short of a Presidential Directive (2005: 110–111): Jones argued that America still possessed 'no overarching ... information strategy at the national level' so any attempt to find a 'focussed and effective mechanism for coordinating dissemination to all prospective audiences around the world' was bound to fail (2005: 109). Jones, a key advocate of Strategic Communication, defined the term as: 'the effective integration of statecraft, Public Affairs, public diplomacy, and military information operations, reinforced by political, economic, and military actions' (2005: 114).

Key theorists of propaganda have observed how economic liberalisation can ensure the stability of certain basic assumptions within media coverage that are supportive of a capitalist state and destructive to democratic popular participation (Curran and Seaton, 1988; Chomsky, 1991: 59; Keane, 1991; McChesney, 2000). US media reform would be necessary to bring real change, but the prevailing system ensures elite power is preferenced (McChesney, 2000). And key government strategists interviewed here viewed US political, military and *economic* actions as needing to be better coordinated and further integrated with a broad framework of propaganda. Jones argued that an operational level, 'theater communications strategy' should be 'derived from' America's strategic level 'national communication strategy' by the commander but argued that often this didn't happen (2005: 110). Critical of the Pentagon's efforts, Jones sketched demands for a 'proactive' far-reaching information strategy for America where its Defense Department would coordinate information activities across government and beyond – not only PSYOP, intelligence, IO, USAID etc, but America's 'allied representatives' too (2005: 110).[7] At the same time came calls for the annual budget for PSYOP (stated at around $50m) to be raised further. Calling for coordination, Dr Christopher Lamb from the National Institute for Strategic Studies at National Defense University, and former Deputy Assistant Secretary of Defense for Resources and Plans, in a review of US PSYOP, argued, 'The British have a system for coordinating their information themes at the national level, and they are widely perceived to benefit as a result' (2005: 115). Jones underscored the need for a mechanism to coordinate interagency 'informational efforts' at the national level to 'shape the informational and intellectual environment long before hostilities'. He emphasised that it would be a pre-emptive, permanent entity, and even suggested it should be 'coequal' with the national political, economic and military strategies (Jones, 2005: 108). An important element of the Strategic Communication model is permanence, during peacetime as well as crisis (Jones, 2005: 110). Since Kosovo, peacetime PSYOP has been recognised as a key way to ensure the credibility of propaganda when used during a crisis. A 'crisis' campaign will be less noticeable to an audience that's used to similar 'peacetime' messages; this aids a campaign's 'invisibility'. This 'pre-propaganda' Ellul considers essential for successful propaganda (Ellul, 1973: 15).

Matt Armstrong agreed that before 2005 coordination was poor: 'Nobody [in the DOD] had any idea what was going on' (Interview: 6th March 2013). But Rumsfeld by 2006 was arguing that it was vital that the US make 'a strategic communications framework' central to its approach, with 'new institutions to engage people across the world' and 'develop the institutional capability to anticipate and act within the same news cycle' (Rumsfeld, 2006). Attempts to create this strategic focus coalesced into debate around a Strategic Communication approach similar to that described by Jones. Jones described the DOD as playing the central role in shaping information activities across government. He said that 'members of such an interagency structure would also work together to implement strategic information plans proposed by the affected geographic Combatant Commanders to both the Secretary of Defense and Chairman of the Joint Chiefs of Staff' (Jones, 2005: 110). But Rumsfeld predicted that

> Improving our efforts will likely mean embracing new institutions to engage people around the world ... We need to consider the possibility of new organizations and programs that can serve a similarly valuable role in the war on terror. (Rumsfeld, 2006)

Public information would essentially be defence-led. Yet commanders would even be expected to shape information activities beyond the interagency, encouraging allied partners and multinational organisations in 'development and implementation of such an information strategy' (Jones, 2005: 111). To ensure messages were complementary, theatre planning would need to be derived from a national strategy and would be 'proactive, influential and shaping (rather than reactive)' (Jones, 2005: 110).

As mentioned above, Rear Adm. Thorp said he was 'the creator of the doctrine for Strategic Communication for [America's] military' and defined it as 'ensuring that both actions and words communicated the same thing to create the desired effect'. This represented a 'very different' approach, he said, one that

> although it sounds very innocent ... it was a little controversial because ... what it was saying was you can't just say anything you want to try to achieve what you're trying to achieve – more importantly your words have to match your actions, your actions have to match your words, they both have to be focused on the desired effect and the idea of truth is more than just not telling a lie, it's ensuring that it is consistent with the actions and the policies of the commander. (Interview: Thorp, 24th August 2009)

The 'truth' presented has to be consistent with that communicated by other actions. This puts propaganda goals at the centre of policy-making and war planning through a need for coordination. It politically embodies the 'effects-based' approach to military planning. Thorp told how in 2008 'I was the Deputy Assistant Secretary of Defense for Joint Communications ... the first guy in the job'. He said that this 'really was Strategic Communication' but even with his Public Affairs-led version, 'we just didn't want to call it that ... because it was too controversial [*laughs*]'. Thorp said that 'In the United States it used to be thought that Psychological Operations' and Public Affairs 'should ... never talk to each other ... and we've evolved from that' – he saw 2005 as 'a turning point where we really recognised that we needed to coordinate it'. As he saw it, the post helped him become 'a leader in Strategic Communication'. Thorp argued that 'Psychological Operations folks ... are now succeeding in working in a more collaborative environment' alongside PA and other propaganda forms (Interview: 24th August 2009). It is not clear from interviews that anyone outside PA saw this as successful Strategic Communication, however. Thorp's vision of a 'homogenised' and 'coordinated' propaganda apparatus imagined Public Affairs leading the message, and others imagined a different future.

Col. Glenn Ayers stated that 'at the beginning, this whole strategic communications thing *was generated* by Public Affairs' (original emphasis). Thorp established the 'Strategic Communications Integration Group' (SCIG) in 2006[8], which Ayers said was 'Public Affairs, with another name on it' and 'did *nothing*' (Interview: 17th May 2013). He and others thought that PA dominance hampered attempts to coordinate and left PSYOP fighting Public Affairs restrictions. Some of Strategic Communication's advocates fought the influence of people like Thorp.

Later figures in the NSC role, Deputy NSA for Strategic Communication and Global Outreach, Mark Pfeifle (January 2007–January 2009), and Director of the same, Kevin McCarty, state that Strategic Communication is 'more than "strategic communications", or coordinated messages and campaigns. It is a way of managing the information environment to strategic advantage' (McCarty and Pfeifle, May 2011: 2). But this wasn't easy. In practice during 'the surge', this took the form of 'decentralised execution of a centralised plan' (McCarty and Pfeifle, 2011: 8), but this was not executed in a consistent way over time and changing events. Indeed not all positively appraised these efforts. Doug Wilson described a 'year-long exercise in futility on Strategic Communication' led by a non-communications specialist who had been seconded to the National Security Council during the first year of Obama's presidency (Interview: 10th May 2013). Rather than being set back by the change of administration, this approach was embraced and even gained ideological momentum into the Obama administration. The Pentagon also developed an official definition of Strategic Communication:

> Focused United States Government efforts to understand and engage key audiences to create, strengthen, or preserve conditions favorable for the advancement of United States Government interests, policies, and objectives through the use of coordinated programs, plans, themes, messages, and products synchronized with the actions of all instruments of national power. (DOD, 2010: 267)

The reality of how this Strategic Communication has been embedded in the US still seems inconsistent and at the time of writing its concepts seem not to be uniformly understood. Matt Armstrong argued that 'this concept of doctrine is non-existent, the definition of Strategic Communication is non-existent, or rather I should say *contentious*' (Interview: 6th March 2013; original emphasis).

Government employees still seem to regard the efforts as not going far enough. A senior State Department official suggested, for example, that there was still insufficient leadership for cross-government activities from the Obama White House (Email: 2013). Meanwhile Joel Harding argued that:

> In the future ... the Department of Defense is gonna understand that the information aspects of military operations are more important than the kinetic effects ... then Information Operations will be put down as a strategy and physical destruction will become a supporting action. That is when you're gonna see Information Operations become effective ... It's also probably blasphemous. But, and I don't expect that to happen for another ten, twenty years but it will happen, it has to. Which is gonna turn two hundred, five hundred years of warfare on its head. (Interview: 15th January 2013)

Some staff, like Little, saw Strategic Communication as encroachment on Public Affairs. Liberal use of the term may have been partly to blame for the confusion. According to Mark Pfeifle, '[The Department of] State wanted the authority, budget and staff – but was hurt by inherit inefficiencies. Some elements on the team didn't wish to be associated with nor fully appreciate the need to integrate gray and black areas to make the best decisions in a swift, coordinated way' (Email: 18th June 2013a). The State Department pushed against the coming together of the 'white' and the 'black', especially under its watch. So Republicans proposed new legislation to bring about change. The Smith-Thornberry amendment to the 2009 Defense Authorization Bill (H.R. 5658) sought to tighten leadership and strengthen interagency coordination. It called for a 'comprehensive interagency strategy for strategic communications', specifying the roles of the Departments of Defense and State, and introduced the idea of a new 'Center for Strategic Communication' (Blankley and Horn, 2008). The intention was to centralise everything (including 'information, educational and cultural activities') with a Strategic Communications Bill of 2008 (Dale, 2009). But Pfeifle said, 'it would have required decision making and funding moving from State/Defense to another, new agency' and bureaucracies often are reluctant for responsibilities to be shifted away (Email: Pfeifle, 18th June 2013b). Efforts stalled, but from them emerged the Center for Strategic Counterterrorism Communications, a 'truly interagency group with a specific mandate and a staff of about 35 people' within the State Department (Email: Dale, 2nd June 2013).

This Center was established by the efforts of Under-Secretary of State for Public Diplomacy and Public Affairs, James Glassman, and then Judith McHale in 2011, to target 'extremism' under the leadership of former ambassador to the UK, Richard LeBaron, with fifty experts from across government and a total budget of around $8m (DoS, 2011b). But its State Department role was not to coordinate the interagency effort; indeed Doug Wilson argued that it was 'In order to make Public Diplomacy and her office relevant again.' Wilson stated that

> Richard LeBaron, through no fault of his own, [was] coming in to head something that was considered by many to be entirely useless. It was meant to be something that in real-time would help provide communications to combat terrorism. It ended up being something where they would have guest speakers from academic institutions and they'd ask agency representatives to ask people to come and hear the speaker.

He stated that 'Strategic Communication no longer exists as a field at the Pentagon. They eliminated Strategic Communication.' However, he had a similar definition to George Little, seeing '"Strategic Communication" as its own communications entity' and criticising the imposition of this: 'We were putting money into developing a science that didn't exist' (Interview: Wilson, 10th May 2013). Doug Wilson explained that 'in the outside world – the world of companies like Hill and Knowlton and similar Public Affairs firms – Strategic Communication means developing communication strategy and using your different communications tools effectively so that your message is credible to each audience while your goals remain consistent' (Interview: 10th May 2013). Some conservatives would centralise control further (Dale, 2009).

Little's memo leaked and was shortly followed by a statement from Rosa Brooks who argued that, though it was confusing (and in the early Bush administration had been 'used to cover a multitude of sins'), it was still the best term available for what was an *ongoing* approach: 'reports of strategic communication's demise are greatly exaggerated' (Brooks, 2012). Joel Harding explained,

> Strategic Communication first of all is shared in the Assistant Secretary of Defense for Public Affairs *and* The Under-Secretary of Defense for Policy ... specifically Austin Branch's office. [Little's] memorandum that he put out was not coordinated. It was put out unilaterally by *his* office ... So it doesn't carry any credibility ... it's a waste of paper. [But] it exposes the *real* problem that we have now with Strategic Communication that there is no actual centre of gravity, as I like to say it, there's no belly-button for SC. (original emphasis.)

This, he said, was because:

> the White House puts out this national framework for Strategic Communication ... and names two officers within the Pentagon, to be in charge of Strategic Communication – which, by itself, you never put two officers in charge – but because Public Affairs says well we have to be involved in all communications, they put the Assistant Secretary of Defence for Public Affairs and the Under-Secretary of Defence for Policy in charge of Strategic Communication when it comes to the Pentagon.

Then there is the NSC communications structure, 'The other main belly-button for Strategic Communication' (Interview: Harding, 15th January 2013); three main points of government all trying to coordinate and be in charge of communication. Harding saw this as a problem particularly when there is a crisis, such as Benghazi, when he claimed that

> we have all this information that's flowing in, it's a fog of war ... the administration does not have a way to coordinate on a timely basis, in any crisis of this sort. The National Security Council does not – they have a crisis centre but they don't have oversight and they don't have control and there is no coordinating office within the United States government ... there is a formal coordination process that every two weeks doesn't ... do it. (Interview: 15th January 2013)

Despite the continuing efforts to engineer a 'whole of government' approach, in a recession budgets have been drawn toward America's powerful defence lobby. There is concern from industry that 'the "whole of government" strategy advocated in the National Security Strategy hasn't materialized'. With a troubled economy it has proved harder than anticipated to wrest control from the military and invest in a coordinating infrastructure for cross-government efforts. Figures for the State Department civilian surge in 2010 for Afghanistan were $6bn, which compares with $65bn just in emergency funding for the Pentagon, an amount which doesn't include 'war-related expenses that are already embedded in the baseline budget' (Erwin, 2010). Some continue to argue that the 'weakness of [American] civilian institutions of statecraft' is making 'the expansion of the DoD role a self-fulfilling prophecy' (Adams, 2010). This has bolstered traditional rivalries between the agencies of government and a defence-led system seems intractable. All sides asserted that counter-terrorism created a need for flexible, coordinated responses but the formal systems failed at the top to enable coordination further down. According to Kevin McCarty,

> you basically have to go back and restructure our government and change legislation to do that [coordinate] and I haven't really seen any national leadership that gives me hope that that's going to occur. (Interview: 13th March 2013)

There is some discussion of whether an organisation tasked with central coordination is needed. Harding said, 'we've been talking about it for ten years' (Interview: 15th January 2013). For some this might resemble the USIA, for others something looser, an interagency structure at strategic level. Glenn Ayers stated that 'you have to get a National Security Directive signed by the President stating that somewhere within the National Security Council, answerable to deputies, would be an office of Strategic Communication to coordinate the cross-government SC message or SC activities' to be successful (Interview: 17th May 2013). Joel Harding described how opinion often differs by agency: 'If you have a Department of State-centric background, things are fine and should remain just as they are ... If one has an IO, SC or USIA background, you will most likely think just the opposite.' Coming from an IO background, he argued that it was necessary: 'Take the current threesome of scandals in the US, at present. Benghazi, AP and IRS[9] ... the administration ALMOST did a good job dealing with three simultaneous scandals, but they did not get out in front of the scandal ... Additionally, the speed of technology appears to mandate a central "information coordination" service is needed' (Email: Harding, 20th May 2013b). And he spoke of current efforts he was involved in to strengthen ties and create a coordinating structure:

> Austin Branch [Then Senior Director for IO] asked that a very small IO planning group be put together to make recommendations for the future of IO. In its current state IO is going to vanish, the new definition is almost meaningless and some folks have taken that as an incentive to do bad things. (Email: 30th April 2013c)

> I've just been brought into [the] group, I'm doing up models now for how IO will look in 2020 and part of it involves the White House (if I get my way). (Email: 30th April 2013b)

UK strategic propaganda coordination

Britain too has had some bureaucratic difficulties in interagency propaganda coordination. Former British Ambassador Chris Meyer argued that 'there has been scant joined-up government between the soldier, the aid worker and the diplomat' (2008). According to Graham Wright this resulted in conflicting propaganda messages:

> other departments, like State Department and Foreign Office – they don't tend to plan. And so a diplomat will just be asked something when he's visiting somewhere ... and he'll shoot from the hip and say something. Now ... if you've gotta sort of cross-government plan that helps. (Interview: 1st June 2009)

Angus Taverner, former MoD Director of Media Operations and Plans, said 'We're just as bad' as the US and recalled how:

> experience of working in Whitehall leads me to feel that there's a ... very *strong* streak of independence between the ministries. So it's quite difficult to get a coordinated approach. It's not for want of trying either, there's lots of people who try very hard. (Interview: 23rd January 2013; original emphais)

Until 2003, Downing Street's Director of Communications and Strategy was Alastair Campbell, who 'used to hold a regular meeting where he had all the Directors of News round from all the various ministries' (Interview: Taverner, 23rd January 2013). He also oversaw the London Coalition Information Centre,[10] in the Foreign Office media suite, 'very actively' at times. It integrated structurally with links to policy-formers and 'from an early stage in the run-up to conflict, those involved with the CIC were regularly at [omitted] daily meetings on Iraq and were on the key distribution lists' (Foreign & Commonwealth Office, 2008).

In terms of intelligence agencies' coordination, while MI5 is under the Home Office and MI6 responds to the FCO, they both answer to Downing Street via the Joint Intelligence Committee (JIC) at the Cabinet Office. Before 9/11 Michael Pakenham, the former JIC Chairman, had already established a large committee to exert pressure on the media (Leppard, 21st March 2000; Nugent, 2008: 54). Similarly to the CIA, MI6's work is 'tied to operations' but is smaller scale and sometimes involves 'using the press as a central part of ... disruptive actions' (Interview: Dorril, 20th July 2010). Scott argues that a 'lack of clarity' about the term 'disruptive actions' reflects 'the determination of the British government to avoid disclosure of the activities involved' (2004: 325).[11] Black and grey propaganda operations being hidden from view in MI6 enables senior MoD Media Operations officials to confidently state at the MoD that they do not use the media for deception. One US contractor Sean Fitzpatrick (who worked for the UK in Northern Ireland) argued, based on his experience, that

> England has solved [strategic control of the information war] pretty well by having an MI5 and an MI6 ... I don't know how much the military gets involved in intellectual warfare ... but I would think that MI6 does most of it. (Interview: 30th June 2009)

In the run-up to Iraq Alastair Campbell collaborated closely with then-JIC Chairman John Scarlett (who later became MI6 Chief) on the so-called 'dodgy dossier'. He 'made it clear to Scarlett' that 10 Downing Street wanted the dossier 'to be worded to make as strong a case as possible in relation to the threat posed by Saddam Hussein's WMD' (Hutton, 2004: Ch. 12). Lord Hutton stated that this could have 'subconsciously influenced Mr Scarlett and the other members of the [JIC] to make the wording of the document somewhat stronger' (2004: Ch 2). The JIC gives a direct briefing to the Office of the Director General of the BBC on the right line to take on whether something is in the national and operational interest to broadcast. Angus Taverner 'was working very closely with people' who worked on the dossier. He said he thought they 'might have actually slightly overegged it ... in terms of the threat to the United Kingdom and that forty-five minutes piece ... but I think in fairness they believed it'. He went on to say,

> I suppose what I would say personally is that we used it as a ... um ... I was about to say a figleaf ... slightly too strong a word but I suppose we had used it as a justification for going ... It was a much deeper and more subtle thing that we wanted to go and do. (Interview: Taverner, 23rd January 2013)

Concerns over coordination emerged and the Foreign & Commonwealth Office (FCO) in 2002 said British Public Diplomacy, worth '£340 million of direct expenditure', was being conducted 'without any clear over-arching guidance on the core messages that we wish to put across to our target audiences' and lacked 'strategic direction' (Wilton, Griffin and Fotheringham, 2002: 3–4). The FCO also called for centralisation – under a Director of Communications – to ensure 'a closer alignment of our domestic and our overseas-targeted public diplomacy work' (Wilton, Griffin and Fotheringham, 2002: 5). This resulted in the establishment of the Public Diplomacy Strategy Board, which 'agreed and finalised' a ten-year Public Diplomacy Strategy in May 2003 (FCO, 2004: 35). The FCO had not before agreed such a strategy across government.

In his DTIO role, Graham Wright coordinated with those outside defence, including diplomats, and claimed 'it's not Information Operations but it's the same sort of thing ... it's about influence'. Wright pointed out that the Ministry of Defence generally does not do pre-emptive influence work, leaving this to the Foreign Office which, likewise, 'don't have the capabilities that [the MoD] do in terms of doing things on the ground in other places' (Interview: 1st June 2009) – the MoD and FCO had complementary functions if they could manage to work together. The MoD solution for the coordination issue led to a parallel MoD-originated 2003 cross-governmental strategy. They made links, particularly with the FCO and Department for International Development, to ensure that 'effects-based planning [would] complement wider strategic planning', and tying the tactical and operational into the strategic (MoD, 2003a). Taverner recalled how 'during Iraq we rather led the way in banging on the Foreign Office's door ... We actually *did* have very regular meetings between us, Foreign Office, DfID, Number 10. To make sure that we had our sort-of story coordinated' (Interview: 23rd January 2013; original emphasis). Senior bureaucracy at the MoD provided strategic shape and direction, and advice to ministers and the chain of command, particularly through the Defence Crisis Management Centre (Interview: Taverner, 18th July 2004). Within this a Current Commitment Team is assigned to a crisis, Afghanistan for example, and world events are monitored through media, diplomatic and intelligence sources (Interview: Taverner, 18th July 2004; MoD, 2004a). But Wright said they met with resistance from the diplomats who (like the State Department) held traditional 'boundary' concerns about working with IO and found 'trying to join all that up in Whitehall is actually quite difficult'. Within the Centre their answer was the Afghan Information Campaign Coordination Group, where a strategy was agreed between leads in each area who then implemented their particular area (Interview: Wright, 1st June 2009). This group met to achieve agreement on the broad themes and messages (Interview: Taverner, 18th July 2004). Taverner told how, for Afghanistan, it was 'in place from 2000/2001' and met under the chairmanship of the Director General at the MoD in Communication, and we normally met every, normally every week or sometimes every other week, to basically review a document on which we wrote down all the key messages that we were trying to get across, who was doing what, when we were gonna do them, how we were gonna do them, what media are we gonna use to get the message across, and so on. (Interview: 23rd January 2013)

This brought together key figures across government including Director General of Media and Communication Ian Lee; the Foreign Office, which represented the Cabinet Office; his two staff officers (Angus Taverner and Paul Brook); Director of Targeting and Information Operations (representing IO/PSYOP); and the Permanent Joint Headquarters (Interview: Taverner, 18th July 2004).

Direction from this *coordinating* meeting would then guide discussion at their lower level weekly Media Group meeting,[12] also attended by Permanent Joint Headquarters, to provide them with specific guidance.[13] When details were requested through Freedom of Information, it was claimed that the group did not exist prior to November 2008 (Read, 23rd September 2010). Yet this strategic level apparently operated above the Permanent Joint Headquarters of the Chief of Joint Operations and his 600 staff officers who command all UK overseas operations. The Chief of Defence Staff and his staff officers decide the shape and form of the mission, and rather than planning things in detail they assign resources to Joint Operations and give guidance on whether the military's approach to information should be passive, semi-active or active (Interview: Taverner, 18th July 2004).[14]

In 2001, procedures were laid into doctrine for the first time. Angus Taverner, during his time as Staff Officer for MoD Media Operations and Plans, was responsible for a more active engagement with the media during the Afghan conflict and planning for Iraq; he drew up MoD plans to embed journalists in the military. American Lt. Col. Tammy Miracle observed how media coverage became more positive with the strict measures and embedding imposed by both countries and coordinated during the Iraq conflict (2003: 41). Rear Adm. 'T' McCreary, former US Navy Chief of Information and Special Assistant to the Chairman of the Joint Chiefs of Staff, explained, 'what it gives you the opportunity to do is to ensure that disinformation on behalf of the enemy is not a viable option. You take away that element of his or her strategy' because the press bear witness to what happens on the battlefield (Interview: 15th October 2013).

The MoD also considered Media Operations in Iraq significantly improved, a positive attitude that reflects the fact that around 700 journalists were embedded with coalition forces, 153 of whom were war correspondents assigned to British units (2003b: 59). Kirsteen Rowlands was the MoD's Chief Press Officer (2004–6) and was in charge of approving the bids of who was going out. So ... I chaired a group, that still exists actually, that would look at the bids, get the feedback and the views from across government. (Interview: 17th April 2013)

Vickie Sheriff organised a daily itinerary of things to show the journalists, and as 'the Iraq border was officially sealed for everyone, even the media', they facilitated media access and

> looked after them 24/7, provided their fuel, their food, their protection and also put on press facilities for them. Even though journalists could leave our unit under their own steam there was a sense that this wasn't safe. Especially after the death of the ITN reporter Terry Lloyd, there was a real fear that the media themselves were targets [for the Iraqi regime]. (Interview: Sheriff, 18th April 2013)

The effect was 'a very ... artificial environment because [the media] were basically closeted with us and they couldn't really go anywhere without us' (Interview: Sheriff, 18th April 2013). Arundell also described a symbiotic relationship where changing safety concerns heightened dependence on MoD-facilitated access for journalists:

> they need us for access, we need them to tell our story. I would contend that certainly when we moved from Afghanistan in 2004 to the first Iraq elections in 2005[15] where I deployed my team to take people to Baghdad and beyond. British journalists weren't going to get there any other way. Other than paying *huge* sums of money to private security companies to get them there. (Interview: 18th April 2013; original emphasis).

Angus Taverner from MoD Media Operations had the role of operationally coordinating and instigating the ministry's media communications with those of the rest of government to achieve their own particular ends. He was responsible for

> getting agreement to the first British military doctrine for how we conduct Media Operations. [Prior to this] we had the Green Book ... and all that bit does is it sets out the basis on which the British military undertakes to work with the media on operations. But we had no doctrine for ... how we work with the media, if you like, in our 'battlespace'. (Interview: Taverner, 23rd January 2013)

His role therefore involved organisation at the cross-departmental and Ministry of Defence levels. On the Information Operations side, the lead role was Director of Targeting and Information Operations, at this time Mike Heath and then Ian Dugmore. Later this post was filled by Graham Wright from 2005 to 2008, helping ensure 'strategic direction' and coordination with other departments.

It was Wright's perception that even ministers needed to be reminded of the 'script of why we're there'. Wright argued that in the DTIO he tried to ensure, if there's a piece of paper that explains ... the core narrative, or the script of why we're there, that it's sent to all the departments. So if any minister is asked, they've all got access to the same thing. (Interview: 1st June 2009)

Taverner similarly noted how in Iraq there was conflict between political desire for the right domestic image, and the message the MoD felt was needed to go to war:

> You have your beautifully swept up information campaign, all carefully boxed up and ready for delivery ... but actually you had better be bothered to speak to the government of the day in the United Kingdom ... for example we wanted to make lots and lots of noise about going to Iraq to ... set the ground and unsettle Saddam, and we were not allowed to ... we were, we had to maintain a very sort of softly-softly approach ... We had Campbell, and ... things like the Secretary of State arriving in the desert to go and visit a laundry ... because we didn't want to be seen to be too 'warlike' ... I personally think ... behind that was a reluctance of the Blair government to appear ... it was almost as though we sort of went to war pretending we weren't. (Interview: 23rd January 2013)

Vickie Sheriff was in a Coalition Press Information Centre based in Kuwait City in the period of build-up before the Iraq invasion in 2003; she told how,

> before the conflict it was all about ... leaving space for diplomacy. So the sort of things we were doing on the ground were showing the media things like troops getting used to being in the desert, dogs in training, medical facilities ... but not show forces gearing up, teetering on a front line, weapons at the ready ... we tried to avoid aggressive images of tanks or guys with guns ... Right up to the last moment really. (Interview: 18th April 2013)

Alastair Campbell rang Angus Taverner before the invasion of Iraq and, according to Taverner, said, 'wondered if there's any possibility that the Ark Royal could go out at night? You know, so the media don't see!' (Interview: 23rd January 2013).

Mackay and Tatham argue that the lack of coordination results from 'each department having different aims, different cultures, applying alternative solutions' and additionally argued that the MoD itself was *internally* 'stovepiped' in propaganda between the Media Operations and PSYOP streams (2009: 11, 16). In Britain Kirke identifies four separate service cultures prompting particular behaviours, many cultures *within* the services, and regimental cultures (2010). Kirke observed how military groupings provided 'fertile ground for stereotyping' and rivalry; a sense that 'we (at whatever the relevant level) are better than you (at a comparable level)' (2010: 99). Rowland and Tatham point to a disparity between formal appearances, and what they see as a need for more cross-government formal coordination of influence:

For the UK, where doctrine appears to suggest that only the military conduct influence, it is important that the cumulative efforts of all government departments and NGOs are recognised as contributing to the influence effect. (2010: 6–7)

But in reality, practise often lagged behind the doctrine which claimed to coordinate influence cross-government. Britain's MoD is a department of state and senior military headquarters. It is the home not only of the Secretary of State and civil servants but also the Chief of Defence Staff and his staff officers. Originally these were intended to be quite widely separated, but increasingly civilian and military work extremely closely together since Media Operations were placed under the civilian Directorate General Media and Communications (Interview: Taverner, 18th July 2004).

Mackay and Tatham identify a disparity between MoD rhetoric about reducing 'kinetic over-reliance' and the lack of a real infrastructure (2009: 14). They argue that 'all Departments of State have an interest in influence and it might be seen as a tool for unifying cross government activity', one they see as 'far less intimidating' to the public than force (2009: 11). Integration is the often-stated goal, but one officer observed how '[not] every level up to the highest level Information Operations is part of the planning process' (Interview: Corcoran, 8th June 2006). Mackay and Tatham discuss the example of then-Brigadier Mackay taking British troops into Helmand in 2006; he felt operational success depended on 'influence-led deployment' (2009: 5). Mackay eventually got assistance from a visiting researcher at the Defence Academy and its small Advanced Research and Assessment Group (now closed) (Mackay and Tatham, 2009b: 14). But he had previously approached the Directorate of Targeting and Information Operations; they just offered 'generic strategic messaging' which was too inflexible for localised, tactical operations. According to Mackay, they viewed the assistance the Defence Academy gave as encroachment on their area/functions and put up 'ardent resistance' to it (Mackay and Tatham, 2009b: 14).

While problems in defence coordination continued, the MoD cross-governmental coordination strategy gained some support from the FCO. Lord Carter's 2005 FCO review acknowledged that already there was 'close contact at operational level' between the MoD and FCO Public Diplomacy efforts (2005: 35). But Lord Carter recommended that 'there could be more contact at *strategic* level between the FCO and MoD' [emphasis added], and that a future Public Diplomacy Strategy might consider ways the MoD and FCO could be mutually supportive and contribute to each other's efforts (2005: 35). In December 2005, despite 'recent improvements' and 'collaborative working', Public Diplomacy was reported by Lord Carter to still need 'central control' with a minister at the helm to 'focus the activity of its various partners in a systematic way' (2005: 4–

5). Essentially the top level coordination was still not being fully accomplished. But Graham Wright thought that 'everybody on the Information Operations side of things [in Washington] would recognise that we're more joined-up in the UK than they are'. This is mainly because 'we could walk out of the [US] Embassy and into the Cabinet Office and the FCO and back again in the space of fifteen minutes' (Interview: Wright, 1st June 2009).

Strategic Communication and the NSC

After the Hutton Inquiry,[16] censorship increased; there was a marked reluctance and increased caution in the MoD's interactions with the press. Angus Taverner told how

> I think Kelly/Hutton seriously damaged the MoD's appetite for being brave. I mean, we used to be quite good at trying to interact with journalists on a very background basis because we all felt it was important that journalists understood the background stories and so on, so we'd do a lot of background briefings, we'd give a lot of unattributed comments about things, an absolute blanket ban was on that after Kelly ... People talk about the BBC being much more nervous since Hutton, I think the same would go for the MoD. (Interview: 23rd January 2013)[17]

While Britain's issues with being 'joined-up' were less acute than those of the Americans, the Strategic Communication approach was also adopted as a goal. This is detailed in an influential paper by Steve Tatham (2008), who led British Media Operations in Iraq. Again it moves towards a 'whole-of-government effort' and has informed new counter-insurgency doctrine (2008: 1). Tatham reproduces a rhetorical American orchestra metaphor and diagram to explain Strategic Communication:

> The orchestra's conductor is the British government, the musical score is the Strategic Communication plan and the orchestra itself the various communities of practice &/or lines of operation. The music is the narrative. Depending on the effect you seek to achieve, different sections of the orchestra will be used at different times, or with different emphasis. The tempo of the music will also vary, depending on what effect the conductor desires. (2008: 3–4)

Past focus on Strategic Communication has evolved so these goals now are achieved by 'influence' operations. The fundamentals of Strategic Communication have been absorbed into current doctrine. But Steve Tatham spoke about future pressures and developments, saying:

> With less money we have to find cheaper and more effective means of achieving the desired effects. I would argue that the whole Influence piece is perfect for this and I have suggested that TAA [Target Audience Analysis] become a mainstay of Phase Zero [i.e. pre-conflict] Ops, indeed I have suggested that with proper

funding and support it could be part of UK's strategic deterrence. However, there is a problem. In times of fiscal stringency the three services can become quite parochial and end up arguing for ships, planes and tanks, particularly if there is no specific champion for the niche capabilities (and at the moment across UK defence there is not). (Email: 11th February 2013)

Departments also do not want to be seen to be dancing to the tune of another department. In the US, Joel Harding argued that 'The Department of State is only one Department and is not central enough to the White House to perform that mission [coordination] "near real time"' (Email: 20th May 2013). But in terms of coordination at the top, the British Coalition Government's establishment of a National Security Council (NSC) Communications Team finally established this layer of centralised coordination. Kirsteen Rowlands, Head of Afghanistan Communications in the NSC Communications Team, describes its role as to

> coordinate all the activity across Whitehall and theatre on communications … around Afghanistan … the overarching strategy, our objectives, the top line messaging and … the direction.

Now direction is strategic; Kirsteen Rowlands said of the NSC: 'obviously this is a policy-driven construct … it's PM-led' (Interview: 17th April 2013).

According to Rowlands, the establishment of this team has brought Strategic Communication considerations into the key stages of national security policy planning:

> we go to the key policy meetings, we contribute to it, we're involved in those discussions, so we see our role … as ensuring that communication issues are considered as part of policy formulation. (Interview: Rowlands, 17th April 2013)

No. 10's Press Office will deal with big breaking news around the Prime Minister, whereas the Cabinet Office is tasked with the longer-term and broader strategic picture, propaganda strategy that will feed into other departments' output and some communications from No. 10. There was felt to be more coordination occurring between No. 10, the Cabinet Office, the FCO and embassies than at the MoD. The MoD Press Office was 'almost like an incident room' fielding calls from media, theatre personnel and government. Rowlands was 'coordinating our … spokespeople in theatre who are dealing with … breaking incidents and reactive issues'. And with the media, 'to try and put across our view and explain what we did' (Interview: 17th April 2013).

The transition can be demonstrated through the example of the handover to Afghanistan and redeployment of British troops. Former MoD Press Officer Kirsteen Rowlands describes how

> Afghan confidence is our … top level priority at the moment … every time … one of our people make an announcement on draw-down, it has the potential to

be played as an abandonment story by the Afghan media. The messaging is therefore managed in theatre and at home through working relationships with Allies and Afghans. (Interview: 17th April 2013)

Now those responsible for the domestic message have accepted 'playback' of international messages in the UK, and vice versa, as inevitable and seek to avoid conflicting messages. The inclusion of the essential elements of key foreign messages that will be used for the theatre audience are being worked into the domestic Media and Press Office output. Rowlands said,

> We absolutely recognise that ... what we say to our domestic audience will be replayed to other audiences and ... we see one of our key jobs as banging home that message to all our people who are messaging on Afghanistan ... it's an easy one to forget when you're giving a message to domestic audiences, on for example, draw-down. That you need to balance that message ... recognising that it'll be picked up by Afghan audiences where the message is our long-term commitment. So we try to make sure we don't talk about draw-down without talking about our on-going commitment post-2014.

Rowlands, from her present NSC position, reaffirmed that

> There is no longer such a thing as a clearly defined domestic audience ... Anything that runs in our media gets picked up ... by the Afghan media. The growth of the Afghan media has been utterly explosive ...

The priority is consistency of message – prioritising the conflict outcome and overall defence objectives: 'We try to think more about the effect, rather than targeting to specific audiences' (Interview: Rowlands, 17th April 2013).

Rowlands described Libya as a particularly successful example of the NSC communications role. She said 'the [communications] response ... was very much led from the centre' by the National Security Communications Team, working with No. 10. There were 'daily meetings with the key ministers ... and ... a related daily comms meeting'. And, Rowlands said, 'the processes that were put in place to manage the crisis ... were very effective and would probably be replicated in any future model.' Also, 'there was very good linkage with the Americans, and I think at the comms level it was driven primarily between [No. 10 and the NSC Comms Team] ... and the people at the White House Communications Centre' (Interview: 17th April 2013).

Rather than explaining the UK's foreign and domestic priorities to different audiences, messages intended for the persuasion of a foreign or enemy audience are instead being incorporated into government output for the domestic media audience, which has now become integrated into the international realm.

In addition, direction on messaging for those involved in communicating NSC priority issues – including PSYOP – is coordinated through the NSC communications team. Rowlands described the example of

Afghanistan communications coordination: 'We have regular distribution of core narratives and weekly cross-Whitehall meetings ... with attendance from those who are involved in [PSYOP] as well as those involved in public media and stakeholder management.' Rowlands said that not only is '[PSYOP] direction, their messaging, what they're getting across ... influenced by top-level communication strategy objectives but they also have input in defining these objectives'. She explained that 'There is coordination between the NSC and [those who are doing the PSYOP side] and what we are ... setting as our core objectives' (Interview: Rowlands 17th April 2013).

The new doctrine 'Army 2020' in the UK is introducing the Security Assistance Group (SAG) to bring together PSYOP, Media Operations and all other supporting elements to be rapidly deployable influence units. Besides media and PSYOP they include the Military Stabilisation Support Group, the government's Stabilisation Unit and culture specialists. Army 2020, Tatham said,

> has the potential to be good for the niche capabilities that make up the whole StratComm piece. For example, 15 (UK) PsyOps Group was not only on the ORBAT [Order of Battle] of Army 2020 but it was also expanded in size by it. This is important, at times of austerity it is easy for non-mainstream capabilities to be over-looked. But, just having the capability on paper is not enough. It has to be manned and resourced.

Career motives and competition may be causing a reluctance to fill these positions:

> The various tranches of redundancy that are being implemented across the armed forces mean that various cap badges fear existential threats and are less receptive to putting their people into E2 appointments – i.e. niche capabilities where personnel from any cap badge can do the job. (Email: Tatham, 11th February 2013)

Conclusion

The extension of propaganda capabilities progressed in both the UK and US, with an underdeveloped strategic infrastructure. Meanwhile, as described in Chapter 2, operations have continued to be rolled forward. This raises the important question of how practice functioned. Practice in the UK has evolved conceptually with the goal of a 'Strategic Communication' approach. As we will see, its system was also historically better equipped to operate flexibly. But in America, across the interagency, Rumsfeld's attempts at formal control were being resisted and others' were advanced through struggles of influence or coercion. According to Nagl, for organisational change, 'The crucial first step [is] identifying a need to learn by recognizing that the institution is not accomplishing its objectives in the situation'; the problem for

America was its failure to 'achieve organizational consensus on required changes' (2005: 192, 221).

While Rumsfeld sought to impose *formal* transition, the form this transition took was quite often navigated *informally*. The trends noted in Chapter 2 were facilitated to some extent in both countries through initiative, using informal structures. According to Nagl, 'the key to organizational learning is getting the decision-making authority to allow such innovation, monitor its effectiveness, and then transmit new doctrine with strict requirements that it be followed throughout the organization' – but at the last two of these it laboured and stalled (2005: 195). The next chapter will argue that constrained formal mechanisms created conditions where aspects of the institutional cultures resulted in a more informal approach. This was characterised by a growth in initiative limited by institutional interests. The chapter argues that this enabled *individuals* to operate across the interagency and within the military, contributing to the gradual changes in propaganda systems.

Notes

1 Brother of CBS News president David Rhodes. Some have raised concern over the impact of their relationship on reporting (see for example: http://dailycaller.com/2013/05/11 /top-obama-officials-brother-is-president-of-cbs-news-may-drop-reporter-over-benghazi-coverage/)

2 'Benghazi' refers to an incident in which four Americans, including the Ambassador to Libya Chris Stevens, were killed in a raid on a diplomatic post in the city of Benghazi on 11th September 2012. There were notable inconsistencies between different US officials' statements and between their account of events and the accounts of witnesses.

3 The Advisory Commission on Public Diplomacy was responsible for making recommendations across the interagency, but had no actual powers and was not taken very seriously. When he became Director in 2011, Matt Armstrong (widely considered among interviewees to be an authority on Public Diplomacy) was frustrated that, 'Those that were aware of the Commission were generally aware of the non-action' (Interview: 6th March 2013). McCarty confirmed that influence resides with 'people who have a cheque book' (Interview: 13th March 2013). The Commission also faced opposition from the Under-Secretary of State for Public Diplomacy and Public Affairs, who resisted its oversight of their activities. Armstrong stepped up activities but was only in his role for a matter of months before the Commission lost its authorisation and closed.

4 The term 'stovepipes' is a metaphor frequently applied to describe bureaucratic organisations which communicate only within the organisation; the idea is that communications and processes are unable to permeate the 'walls' of the institution to coordinate with others so can only travel up and down within the established channel.

5 This refers to the critical comments made by Lt. Gen. James T. Conway, who was ordered to attack Fallujah by Lt. Gen. Ricardo Sanchez, the overall commander of US forces in Iraq at the time (see Chandrasekaran, 2004).

6 In stark terms, 'You've got a $50bn intelligence budget, $40bn is under Rumsfeld' (Interview: Wilkerson, 23rd June 2009).

7 He has suggested that multinational organisations could be encouraged to 'participate in developing and implementing' America's 'information strategy and to accept an increasing role' (Jones, 2005: 111).

8 This group brought together Director of the Joint Staff, Under-Secretary for Policy, Assistant Secretary for Public Affairs, and the Joint Staff's Strategic Communications Director to lead and coordinate communication on key issues.

9 'AP' refers to the Justice Department's secretly seizing two months' worth of records of telephone lines used by reporters and editors for the Associated Press in 2012 as part of an investigation into leaks (see McClam, 16th May 2013). 'IRS' refers to the revelation that the IRS was singling out Tea Party and liberal groups in examinations for tax-exempt status.

10 Later renamed 'Communication and Information Centre' (Foreign & Commonwealth Office, 2008).

11 The US does not use the term 'disruptive action'.

12 Chaired by the Director News Pam Tier (Interview: Taverner, 18th July 2004).

13 Minutes and correspondence relating to these meetings were not obtainable through Freedom of Information.

14 Passive is only answering questions when asked and acknowledging things if necessary, active is engaging every possible communication means, and semi-active is somewhere in-between (Interview: Taverner, 18th July 2004).

15 The elections included 'a very ambitious embed programme with over sixty journalists [from] print, radio and television' (Interview: Arundell, 18th April 2013).

16 The Hutton Inquiry was a 2003 judicial inquiry to investigate the circumstances surrounding the death of the MoD employee and former UN weapons inspector in Iraq David Kelly. He had been named as the source for BBC reports that Tony Blair's Labour government knowingly 'sexed up' what became known as the 'dodgy dossier': a report detailing claims about Iraq and weapons of mass destruction. Hutton's report cleared the government of wrongdoing and criticised the BBC, resulting in resignations in its leadership. The report has been heavily criticised in the media and its conclusions questioned (see for example Baker, 2007).

17 Former Flight Lieutenant Iain Paton provided me with a Senior Officers' Approvals Database which shows British ministerial approvals were required for contact with the media; he recalled being surprised 'at any level of ministerial scrutiny or approval for two-star officers and their speeches, as they are very senior with enormous responsibility and professional knowledge' (4th October 2010). There was also increased informality in communications, perhaps due to 'panic' about Freedom of Information (FOI) changes (Sumption quoted in Wheeler, 2010). Angus Taverner stated that 'we very rarely administered our meetings ... so FOI-wise there probably wasn't too much of a record, and what there might have been would probably be classified'. He mused that, 'How on earth people are going to do research ... about our era in even 20 years time, I have no idea, I mean the days of yore, people had diaries and written communications and everything else, we do everything now by email ... Most of what was done by way of planning and preparation and delivery of invasion of Iraq ... will be disappeared' (Interview: 23rd January 2013). Jonathan Sumption QC (who represented the British government in the Hutton Inquiry) reported that civil servants 'omitted significant information from internal documents, which in earlier times would have been included' and, 'in some departments it was quite common for politically sensitive matters to be omitted from

documentary records' (Sumption quoted in Wheeler, 2010). It seems civil servants therefore 'communicated ... informally instead, so that they would not be recorded in writing' (Sumption quoted in Wheeler, 2010). This censorship response is being used as an argument against extending Freedom of Information further. One Flight Lieutenant observed how, in Britain, 'there was almost certainly a culture change with more political considerations than in the past' (Email: Anonymous, 2010).

4

Domestic planners, initiative and propaganda

Introduction

This chapter will show how practical propaganda functions were maintained despite the failings of formal structures described above. British and US propaganda function continued of course, and inconsistent responses brought adaptation despite organisational problems. This chapter extends the analysis, begun in the last, of the domestic propaganda strategy of each country and develops a thematic argument, highlighting trends that were crucial to propaganda policy-making within the countries. It shows that, in spite of formal insularity, coordination *did* occur between proactive agents handling the propaganda war who were required somehow to fulfil their duties, though this coordination was very inconsistent. Strategic coordination laboured at the planning table but where the frustration of barriers prevented function, individuals sought solutions. Even in the US (where military 'initiative' has been said to be institutionally lacking), informal interactions and solutions were favoured to enable the navigation of systemic obstacles, and continue the pursuit of institutional goals. This chapter will show the importance of informal structures in coordinating defence planning in the information war and discuss the implications of this for accountability. Although diverse institutional cultures[1] comprise the two countries' governments, two characteristics will be highlighted in this chapter as especially relevant in the propaganda war across militaries and bureaucracies:

- Public Service
- Initiative

These will be shown to be in tension and to have varied subtly across government and military in each country. This chapter will argue that they were significant in framing how an evolving propaganda 'problem' was perceived and acted upon by planner. The chapter demonstrates, crucially, how government propaganda systems depend on continuing internal cultures and the activities of the individuals they comprise.

British and American 'public service' and propaganda

The notion of public service is rooted in established ideas of the state derived from classical social contract theory[2] and translated in contemporary society into the idea of a representative government in the service of citizens. In the contemporary system of representative democracy, public administration draws its legitimacy from the idea that decisions of elected policy-makers embody the wishes of citizens and they delegate responsibility for their enactment to administrators, clearly defining their roles through a hierarchy. This way

> complex missions could be separated into their individual components, each component could be assigned to individual administrators, and administrators would know what they were – and were not – charged with doing. The principle of authority would hold everyone in the system accountable. Policymakers delegated authority to the bureaucracy, and higher-level bureaucrats could use authority to control what their subordinates did. The application of these two principles – hierarchy and authority – would promote efficiency by allowing the creation of sophisticated bureaucracies full of highly skilled workers. It would promote accountability by specifying the relationship of each worker to policymakers. And it would do all of these things by carefully structuring the work within clear boundaries. (Kettl, 2002: 8)

Public servants, therefore, have varying views, as do the military, and they may not support the policy of the incumbent administration. For instance, Steve Tatham stated that 'When I was Spokesman in Iraq in 2003 I never bought into the lines and messages that I was being sent by the MoD and wider coalition to deploy; more importantly I could see that the intended audiences were not buying them either' (Email: 11th February 2013). Angus Taverner reflected on this, saying

> I suppose there is a sense where ... being a soldier is in some ways quite easy. You know, the government of the day says 'Right, we are going to go to Iraq and ... invade and ... overthrow Saddam Hussein and ... look for Weapons of Mass Destruction.' You know, the rationale for why we're going ... yes of course we're interested, but then we're not about to turn around and 'Well I don't think we're going, I don't agree with this'. (Interview: 23rd January 2013)

People are not automatons; they have conflicting views and, as the social theorist Raymond Williams stated, the public 'servant' is expected to subordinate 'his own interests' to 'a larger good' of society or national security (1958: 329). They therefore have a dedication to and belief in their role. Australian former Target Audience Analyst Paula Hanasz observed that, compared to other nationalities in ISAF, American and British PSYOP personnel in particular 'tended to have more of a dedication to their roles, had a broader appreciation of the strategic importance of PSYOP, and tended to see their country's engagement in Afghanistan as important' (Email: 30th April 2013). This belief in a 'larger good' ensures people with divergent political views can be relied upon to maintain a cohesive functioning institution. Angus Taverner was in MoD Media Operations and Plans when the notorious 'dodgy dossier' was compiled in justification for war:

> we used it as ... I was about to say a figleaf ... I suppose, slightly too strong a word but I suppose we had used it as a justification for going ... It was a much deeper and more subtle thing that we wanted to go and do, that was to do with the fact that Iraq was seen to be an extremely destabilising place in the middle of the Middle East ... certainly in America there were people who felt that if you could stabilise Iraq, encourage it to develop a democratic set of institutions then ... people would embrace that ... and it would grow. Quite an ideological belief and we can be rude about it, say it was very naive but a lot of people in America on the sort-of Neo-Conservative wing of American politics thought very deeply about ... And so, although we had to go to the United Nations to get a 1441 to sort of justify, *just!* ... going to do what we did. I think the justification was much wider than that. Now, did I believe all that? Yes, at the time I did; I bought into it completely. I believed my intelligence colleagues, they believed, they had lots of intelligence to send out. We can all be very wise ten years on ... But at the time, we didn't know a lot about what was going on inside Iraq ... I don't feel particularly proud of what we ... subsequently transpired ... but ... you, you trust the system I suppose. You *do* trust the system to get it right, and on the whole the system does get it more right than wrong. A lot of people in the intelligence community felt absolutely convinced that there was sufficient justification to go in. I looked at the intelligence briefing every morning, it seemed pretty compelling to me. 'I was only following orders, Guv' [ironic laughter]. (Interview: 23rd January 2013; original emphasis)

Williams spoke of the close relationship between the idea of 'service' and individualism, which he defines as 'an idea of society as a neutral area within which each individual is free to pursue his own development and his own advantage as a natural right' (1958: 328). While he examines the British cultural context, service is also fundamental to American bureaucratic and military service in a culture marked by its patriotism, and individualism is a defining value of American culture. Indeed Croft observes how representations of service and duty became a focus for remembrance and were one basis for delivering a 'shared' meaning for the 'War on Terror' response alongside an 'absence of blame within' (2006: 95, 101). But Rear Adm. 'T' McCreary did not see a conflict between debate of policy and the need to build 'support' for those executing the war; he said then-Chairman of the Joint Chiefs Richard Myers saw a 'lesson' from Vietnam, which was:

there's nothing wrong with bringing the horrors of war home. Because we should understand that this is the cost of war ... We need to be able to keep the support for the men and women who serve, even if people hate the policy. (Interview: 15th October 2013)

Valerie Plame Wilson often references strong values of 'public service' within her family preceding her CIA career and describes the traditional public service ethic:

I was at the working level and at the working level you don't think about policies, you're thinking about getting the best intelligence. Our mission is to get it to the senior policymakers who were going to make these decisions.

Plame Wilson demonstrates clearly how political beliefs and personal conscience can be subordinated to the role of servant:

you certainly don't serve overseas whether you are in an intelligence capacity or a military capacity or whatever, as a Republican. Or as a Democrat. You serve as an American. You are representing American interests and policy to the best ability. (Interview: 11th August 2009)

Likewise, McCreary described how Myers' job,

wasn't to explain policy, his job was to explain ... operationally why it was being done the way it was being done. So he was very good at really, publicly staying out of the policy debate. Some people accused him of being a 'yes man' but that wasn't the case internally and he accepted the fact that he would take that criticism because it wasn't his place to be engaged in policy ... When you realise that you have no role in policy *that* makes the ... decisions a lot easier and keeps your focus on the ball ... of what *you* have to do. (Interview: 15th October 2013; original emphasis)

In 'Politics as a Vocation' Weber argues that the honour of the civil servant is 'vested in his ability to execute conscientiously the order of superior authorities, exactly as if the order agreed with his own conviction'; it involves 'moral discipline and self-denial in the highest sense' (in Gerth and Mills, 2005: 95). But Williams points out that 'few men can give the best of themselves as servants; it is the reduction of man to a function' (1958: 330). Gramsci argued in his prison notebooks that 'patriotism' or 'nationalism' was the 'link by means of which the unity of leaders and led is effected' (Mouffe, 1979: 194). It is also crucial that this 'unity' with leadership is extended through to decision-makers in propaganda, and wider defence planners, to reinforce 'value' in their actions and frame their interpretation of situations and information to which they will be required to respond.

A revealing statement by Adm. Fallon demonstrates the assumption that American solutions are best – the dominative nature of American efforts in 'reconstruction' of Iraq. As CENTCOM Commander, his notion of 'service' is, of course, built on military cultural background, and he equates his institutional interests and assumptions with the interests of all. He states that:

> Back in late 2006, early 2007, I can't tell you the number of Iraqis who were helping us, working with us, at least with most of their hearts and minds, who would say, confronted with a difficult situation, 'Well just do it this way, that's how Saddam did it! It works, trust me, it works,' and revert back to the same thing.

From Fallon's point of view the Iraqis were 'helping us'; helping the US military to carry out US policy in Iraq, not rebuilding their own country. Of course the official message is that America was helping the Iraqis. While a return to Saddam's methods is clearly not desirable, Fallon is clearly confounded by the lack of comprehension by the Iraqis of the 'superior' American way of doing things. This gap between local ideas and American goals is used as a justification for propaganda, as a means to ensure the American way. The 'huge disconnects' driven between the perceptions of planners like Fallon (Interview: 21st July 2009) and the international or domestic audience are underpinned by an economic system which is sustained by material inequalities and individualism within wider US culture. As Croft points out, 'America's "response" to [the 9/11] attacks was not obvious, not natural, nor based on some objective standard of "common sense". Policy had to be built on' existing narratives, those of 'America's government, and importantly, American society as a whole' (2006: 2).

As Fallon argued, 'Money does not go to unstable places. Insecure places ... That's a really important message. That's a tough message to sell some illiterate bird farmer in ... one of these countries' (Interview: 21st July 2009). But from his perspective the solution is thus perceived as *justifying* this inequality through propaganda in order to influence opinion to support the externally imposed 'reconstruction' to bring 'stability'. This fails to consider the role Western foreign and economic policy plays in contributing to 'instability' in much of the developing world. And focusing the developing country's goals on economic liberalisation that will 'create wealth' in no way ensures that this wealth will be fairly distributed to the 'illiterate bird farmer'. 'Paternalistic' propaganda does not tangibly change the real world circumstances underpinning the situation, but seeks 'stability' through acceptance of Western solutions; it can thus only be dominative, and serve to *reinforce* such 'disconnects'.

In claiming propaganda as a necessity, propaganda practitioners (and theorists like Lasswell) make a claim often made by realists – a belief that they plan for the world 'as it is' rather than 'as we'd like it to be'. Governmental cultures are inherently conservative, as Nagl argues:

> Changes that conflict with the dominant group's ideas on preferred roles and missions – the essence of the organisation – will not be adopted. Leaders of the organisation, conditioned by the culture they have absorbed through years of

service in that organisation, will prevent changes in the core mission and goals. (2005: 216)

These cultures are self-perpetuating. One British Information Operations Captain (20 Armour Brigade in Iraq)[3] who found troops not 'clued-up' enough on how his role could help them, initiated a horizontal propaganda campaign and 'spent the first third of my operational tour educating the brigade that I worked for about what I could achieve for them.' He said,

> So I had a war, an information war to win … so I started by PSYOP-ing my own, conducting Psychological Operations on the Brigade, which is perfectly legitimate and within the doctrine. (Interview: Corcoran, 8th June 2006)

For both countries, horizontal propaganda[4] communicates the value of 'service' and contributes to a shared identity which is then reproduced informally; both militaries prioritise internal communication to support bureaucratic cohesion.[5] Doctrinal forms such as the presence of propaganda divisions and new doctrine favouring flexibility are also designed to shape the culture of the institution by communicating common goals, roles and values including the basis of legitimate practice. Doctrinal changes can be seen as embodying this intent, communicating to the interagency the value of 'working together'. Thus Armitage stated that for the US 'by using terms like SMART Power it's more *signalling* that we're gonna try and use everything in our power' and 'signalling to the bureaucracies that everyone has a role to play' (Interview: 21st July 2009). This implies that concepts like SMART power are designed to act as much as institutional propaganda, to ready the culture of this future bureaucracy, as they are to produce formal changes.

Nagl argues that US society historically 'felt a sense of ownership of its national army' (2005: 43). According to Herman and Chomsky, uncritical media organisations play an important role in 'manufacturing consent' (1988). Both patriotism and the military permeate cultural life in Washington DC, the highest honour being to 'serve' the country. In Nagl's words, American warfare is characterised by 'faith in the uniqueness and the moral mission of the United States' (2005: 43). British personnel interviewed seemed far more cynical about the idea of 'service' and the goals of their institution, something reflective of wider societal critique in that country. Many were very critical of the Iraq War. In foreign policy, however, a strong component of British 'public service' has been an underlying assumption that strengthening British value to the US, and British global political stature, are in the interests of the country.

Submission to institutional values, organisational accountability and orders does not, however, create a *resilient* system, adaptable to a changing environment. Initiative is also expected, desirable[6] and yet can be simultaneously dangerous to this system. This 'service' motive embodies an essential conservatism, which is in tension with individual initiative and keeps those initiatives in support of a self-contained belief-system (Williams, 1958: 329). It puts boundaries upon the range of initiative, which must fall within *institutionally defined* notions of what is in the public interest. Former Assistant Secretary of Defense for Public Affairs (April 2001–June 2003) Torie Clarke stated that after 9/11, 'the leaders of the time … Heads of State or … Defense Department, they all … appreciated that the information environment … required a very different approach and so they gave the guidance, they gave the incentives and they gave the support to people like *me*. They said OK, in this different environment, come up with a different strategy. Come up with different tactics' (Interview: 4th December 2013; original emphasis).

Differences in leadership and the importance placed on Strategic Communication or a particular region by those at the top also impacts on the range of what is possible for personnel lower down. According to Kirsteen Rowlands, 'there [are] individuals that drive the approach and clearly how high up an issue is on the political agenda of any … nation will directly impact on the assistance that you will get from people lower down the chain.' She explained that when senior ministers are involved, 'it has a very effective spill-down effect across Whitehall that makes things happen … If you look back over Afghanistan and Iraq, there are … individual ministers or Secretaries of State who will take a more … proactive view on these issues and drive it' (Interview: Rowlands, 17th April 2013). Of course, different ministers and politicians themselves will have approaches to the media which influence the way civil servants and special advisors will work.

Insular paternalistic cultures with a culture of 'service' confirm belief in institutional goals and encourage dismissal of and detachment from wider or conflicting arguments – even those of other government bodies. The cultures display a tendency to self-contained, self-justifying systems whose interests are seen as by definition in the 'public service'. A 'public service' motive is an aspect of public bodies which tends to discourage critical judgement in favour of internal cohesion (see the excellent analysis of Raymond Williams, 1958). In this way it supports the tendency to form the 'stovepipes' discussed above.

Institutional perceptions often embodied a set of assumptions based on superior insight into a 'real world' that those within that institution perceived, and which was misunderstood by naive outsiders and public (for Lippmann they were 'outsiders', 1954: 51–53). This provides a belief in the institution from which the legitimacy of propaganda and wider governmental or military action is derived. It can act as an enabler for ad hoc solutions that reach beyond circumscribed formal roles. Bureaucratic momentum and professional ambitions drove pressure to 'get the job done' and prioritised pragmatism and initiative by often well-intentioned individuals with a strong belief in what they were doing. First and foremost they had a job to do, Armitage stated:

I understand the shock to the nervous system of 3,000 of our citizens being killed ... by such a tremendous act of aggression, and we'd always been staying behind our two great oceans in the past. But for most soldiers, and most people who've been at war ... I tell you, for Powell and me it was a day in the office. Bad day, but it was another day at the office. (Interview: 21st July 2009)

Bureaucracy has a momentum in which people are swept up to enable continued function. Britain's Adrian Weale described how CPA Dhi Qar 'ran elections from September 2003 onwards ... and at times we were ordered to halt' by the Americans at CPA Baghdad, but 'The fact was that they'd taken on a momentum of their own and we couldn't stop doing them so we sort-of cracked on regardless' (Interview: 26th November 2010).

Bureaucratic momentum at times helped ensure dissent was not forthcoming. The legitimacy of 'public service' at times became permissibility for informal solutions. But personal and institutional priorities are separate from and could conflict with the declared service motive of the larger 'public good' and may have fuelled increased 'politicisation', competition and the suppression of dissent.

British initiative and propaganda

Initiative is defined by Occupational Psychologist Michael Frese as 'an active behaviour of employees, who show a high degree of proactivity (preparing for future problems and opportunities now), are self-starting' and persist in overcoming barriers (Frese et al., 1996; Frese, c.2009). The British military has historically been considered flexible and adaptable with regard to problem-solving, a past suited to counter-insurgency (including propaganda and political warfare). In contrast with the American approach, the British military has traditionally allowed the breaking of rules and considered boundaries flexible:

Doctrine is prepared in order that the Army should have some basis for training and equipping itself. You certainly don't fight based on your doctrine! If you actually do fight based on your doctrine you're letting yourself in for disaster. (British General Sir Frank Kitson, quoted in Nagl, 2005: 204)

Counter-insurgency expert John Nagl argues that a level of trust and autonomy can be found in British military culture that is absent from the US military; its military encourages 'junior officers' to 'seek out organizational performance gaps and alternative organizational paths of action' (2005: 191). He argues that 'It is a mark of British government's trust in the capability of her army that a single army general was given political *and* military authority' in Malaya (2005: 198). Dahrendorf observed that the confidence of 'members of socially homogenous elites' can make them *more* likely to take 'unorthodox' decisions (1988:

53) and Nagl links this to the British military (2005: 195). Angus Taverner observed that the British military, 'pride ourselves on ... British initiative and ... pushing and encouraging junior officers to use their initiative and that plays then at every level' (Interview: 23rd January 2013).

The British cynicism mentioned above may be related to self-reliance and autonomy. Charters states that in the British military, unlike the Americans, historically officers learned not to expect a flood of assistance from Britain – there was usually little to be spared – nor to look to some sacrosanct body of 'doctrine' for advice; there was none. Instead he must make do ... In short, he must adapt. (1989: 182)

As Britain has moved towards 'interoperability' with the US, its own doctrine has become increasingly written (Nagl, 2005).[7] But there was some cynicism about possible MoD responses to the Human Rights Act and UK membership of the International Criminal Court. One British officer expressed concern that 'legal mechanisms will be applied to the fullest level' where it is in the interests of the ministry to pursue infractions. The US, having avoided being a signatory to the International Criminal Court, has refused to allow US personnel 'to co-operate with inquests into so-called "friendly fire" incidents' involving British personnel.[8] While criminal prosecutions were rightly pursued in prisoner abuse cases, one officer observed that personnel expressed dismay at how the ministry then 'fought hard to limit its own exposure' when responsibility for service casualties was under question 'by successfully appealing the ruling that human rights obligations applied to British soldiers on the battlefield'.[9] In one example, the 'loss of an F-15 over ... Scotland ... the air traffic controller was court-martialled (although acquitted) despite concerns within the RAF air traffic control community that' responsibility lay elsewhere.[10] Recent reports[11] indicate that 'charges could be brought against British military interrogators who may have committed acts of "torture" that are not defined as "torture" by the United States, which is not a signatory to the International Criminal Court'. One former Flight Lieutenant argued that 'it is inconceivable that any interrogations ... would have been spontaneous or unauthorized by the chain of command, including the Ministry of Defence and United States' (Email: Anonymous, 2010). Therefore it seems likely that prosecutions would impact more widely on officer perceptions of the ministry if seen relative to American handling of personnel.

The relationship between notions of 'public service' and initiative is quite distinctive in Britain's military system; loyalties are to the battalion first (Interview: Weale, 26th November 2010). Wider concerns and a public service motive provided underlying legitimacy for this but loyalties were horizontally attributed because of a sense of being 'on your own' in carrying out the operation. This appears to be supplanted by faith in British military experience, shared difficulties and residual perceptions of military pre-eminence, all elements of its strong 'institutional memory'. The British imperial example shows how collective memory, institutional assumptions and propaganda become increasingly important systemically the further authority over propaganda is delegated. It adheres to the regimental system which provided a 'surrogate family' strong enough to sustain the morale of soldiers in far-flung stations when colonial administration largely involved 'a thin veneer of British officers' (Nagl, 2005: 37–38). Delegation, increase of trust and reduction of 'middle management' are argued by Nagl to be a crucial steps in ensuring American defence has the same flexibility to fight counter-insurgency operations.

To conclude that cynicism assumes British critical awareness or reflexivity would be complacent, though this belief was common among personnel. Propaganda is seen today as reducing casualties, and as democratically acceptable (see above). While problems were acknowledged, these were couched in terms of difficult circumstances, in which personnel lacked necessary support. Solutions were often seen in terms of improved training, integrated planning or target audience analysis. Officers prized their cynicism, and often distinguished their British worldliness from American self-belief and cultural subjectivity.

One function of the elaborate command process is not just to communicate orders, but to ensure people understand *why* they're doing something, and ensure that they feel that it's *right* (Interview: Taverner, 18th July 2004). It thus supports the sense of service. Adrian Weale claimed that 'that sort of established culture and tradition and so on means you have a short-cut to great cohesion within the unit, which contributes to welfare and tactical efficiency.' What this means is that members of an institution come to assist in maintaining the dominant ethos of their institution, and in pursuit of its ends initiative is enabled. Weale compared Britain's military to a 'feudal' system:

> individual commanders feel they own bits of the army. So if you become the Commanding Officer of an infantry battalion that is *your* battalion. And although of course, it's supposed to be working towards the greater good, it's also working towards *your* good. (Original emphasis.)

Everything is motivated by service, but this is linked to the battalion, its history and those who went before. This shapes the behaviour of personnel who 'want at some point to … command *their* battalion [and] don't therefore want to be too critical particularly of someone who they've worked with for a long time' (Interview: 26th November 2010; original emphasis).

The MoD's internal rivalries make it 'natural to want the maximum share of available resources' (Kirke, 2010: 99), something said to inhibit cohesiveness, cooperation and communication. British institutional priorities and its necessarily 'self-reliant' military culture may have hindered attempts at interagency cooperation. When the military were pressing to send troops to Helmand in 2006, concerns about being inadequately prepared were not emphasised upwards to ministers. This was blamed on a 'confused command and control structure' in Afghanistan by senior military and civil service figures (Haynes et al., 9th June 2010). But it shows autonomy. Battalions are tight-knit units and initiative is particularly strong in the institutional memory (Interview: Anonymous, 16th August 2010).

Nagl notes that British warfare was founded on sea power, and naturally favoured the 'principles of mobility and surprise' (2005: 36). He contends that throughout British colonial history its military evolved to see their function as 'the use of limited force' in the 'pacification' of potential British subjects, whereas it was the American belief that counter-insurgency was 'not the army's true business' (Nagl, 2005: 36, 46). Historically Britain's military was characterised by pragmatic expansions and contractions, forming ad hoc expeditionary forces to 'meet particular emergencies' (Barnett, 1970: xix). Postwar, its approach to warfare valued minimal manpower, a flexible, political warfare that recognised the constraints 'set by public opinion' (Nagl, 2005: 41). Flexibility is enhanced further still among non-conventional troops. British PSYOP in Afghanistan were supporting 'mostly [special forces] and specialised units' (Interviews: 15th Army PSYOP Group, 22nd November 2005). Unconventional forces 'are not soldiers who've served together all their lives' in one battalion; likewise British 'intelligence and PSYOP and so on groups, they're slightly more ad hoc than the ... established parts of the army' so tend to be less 'insular' and even more adaptable, though still driven by notions of service (Interview: Weale, 26th November 2010).

In Britain, people's attempts to work through informal channels and initiative appeared to respond to barriers they saw obstructing their fulfilment of functions. Mackay argued that commanders in Afghanistan were 'making it up as we [went] along' (Grey, 2009). Mackay and Tatham argued that the commander must 'place [influence] at the core of his thinking' but argued that during the Afghanistan and Iraq conflicts the MoD was not adequate 'philosophically, culturally and organisationally' to assist them in this (Mackay and Tatham, 2009b: 12). Mackay sought his own solution in Behavioural Economics. US behavioural economic approaches have helped structure planning of a new approach. Sunstein and Thaler's 'libertarian paternalism' (2003) was applied to Afghanistan's National Solidarity Programme in 2004. Their idea assumes people's preferences are often 'ill-formed' and can be changed by shaping the way choices are presented. This involves changing small conditions in the community that might affect choices – changing the 'Architecture of Choice' – to 'nudge' people toward 'beneficial action' (Mackay and Tatham, 2009b: 22). These 'nudges' were chosen to be locally specific and may not be explicitly linked to a narrow military objective. In an otherwise-disastrous Helmand campaign, Mackay's influence-led approach was held as a success (Farrell, 2010; Mackay and Tatham, 2009b).

But as recently as 2013 there were still reports of what was seen as a system still not embracing innovation. Lee Rowland and Jon Jenkins from the contractor I to I worked together on 'a major project' for the Defence Science Technology Laboratory (DSTL), with a sizeable budget to bring in 'four or five experts'. Rowland stated that 'unless there's something going on top secret that nobody knows about – I think it's the *best* work to date ... on measuring the effect of communications ... or influence'. But Rowland described their frustration, as 'We delivered what we think is *really* cutting edge ... I know the people at DSTL and I know that they are not doing anything at this level ... And yet they are not doing anything about it because of the way DSTL is organised' (original emphasis). He expanded on this further: 'We've heard recently that they're not going to move forward on any of it. ... Because it steps on the toes of other departments within DSTL who have a stake ... in doing [Measures of Effectiveness]' (Interview: Rowland, 5th July 2013).

Ian Tunnicliffe, former Iraq Desk Officer at the MoD, said that, having been in 'lots of different conflicts', he found during Iraq planning 'the super-sensitivity of it meant that politicians were reluctant to make decisions and there was constant ... absolute red-lining it in terms of when people were making decisions on things' which they had to deal with (Interview: 8th July 2013). Testimony to the Iraq Inquiry indicates that initiative was enhanced as a response to increased restrictions placed on planning. In one example, officers made arrangements themselves for organising US–UK data communications capability, leading them to establish informal planning structures (Paton, 2009). One key figure in MoD Media Operations and Plans was Angus Taverner, who talked about how interagency coordination in Iraq Media Operations was left to their own initiative and outreach: 'no one told us to do it. It was just that the worker bees like me, decided that it would be a good idea.' He said, 'You sort of make it up as you're going along' and described how it

> was down to the likes of [Paul Brook], lovely man called Captain Chris Palmer, Royal Navy, and me ... we were it! ... It was almost as though, we were sort of [an] area that the grown-ups didn't really understand and we'd to go away and sort it out. (Interview: 23rd January 2013)

He had Vickie Sheriff in theatre doing a similar thing to organise the tactical operation. She described how:

> my job particularly was to put on a menu of events for [the media], and that was *hugely* challenging, when there were very rarely comms ... you couldn't actually pick up a phone and say 'Hello, could we bring some journalists along?' so we had to be fairly intuitive and creative and work contacts at ... the divisional support headquarters, to find out what was going on and that would be helpful to sort of

demonstrate to the media, the public and wider regional audiences that we weren't going to just rush in and steal the oil. We were going in with journalists, and at the earliest opportunity demonstrating that we were a force for peace and not the ... hostile invader. (Interview: 18th April 2013; original emphasis)

The Press Information Centre that Sheriff was based in 'hosted *journalists*' (original emphasis) and she described how their efforts impacted reporting:

Because we were looking after them 24/7 [in a conflict zone] they couldn't [safely] go anywhere else and film anything else particularly ... there were very clear guidelines and they'd all signed up to the agreement so there wasn't much [if any] need to censor copy.

The Press Information Centre was offered little backing or resources from the MoD and Sheriff described the conditions they were presented with when she was part of the Field Press Information Centre supporting 1 Division during the invasion:

It was a unique organisation for that operation and we'll never do that again. In retrospect the concept didn't really work for the journalists and it didn't really work for us. The initial concept was a 'press office in the sand' for any journalist. But it turned out that would never be possible so we became an exclusive briefing unit for embedded broadcast journalists. And because we were created from paper for that operation, we were appallingly equipped ... we begged, borrowed and stole equipment, quite frankly, to make that unit happen. You know, on the plus side, it does show the ingenuity of people, you know when you are called upon to do something, you use your initiative and just get it done ... and we did. (Interview: 18th April 2013)

In response to this difficulty the Defence Media Operations Centre was set up to make available rapidly deployable teams and 'centralise the whole business of media training across defence'. Ralph Arundell said there was much autonomy for the team: 'Three million quid. Blank sheet of paper. Go and make it happen very enjoyable and exciting because it was working it out as you went along within a broad framework' (Interview: 18th April 2013). This was also confirmed by Angus Taverner who said with this Centre, Iraq/Afghanistan planning and developing wider doctrine often came down to

the initiative of pretty low-level creatures like me ... There was [no one above] saying, 'This is what I want you guys to go and achieve, now go away and do it.' It was very bottom-up.

Taverner said he needed to be proactive and push ideas forward:

And bizarrely I find myself sitting there thinking, I'm a Lt. Colonel, why am I sitting here having this bloody fight with all these Generals and Senior Civil Servants trying to push this idea through? They should be embracing it and telling me to get on with it. (Interview: 23rd January 2013)

Number 10's regular meetings under the Blair administration included the FCO, MoD Media Operations and Information Operations in the old War Office. Through these meetings Arundell and Taverner could 'understand the strategic level and what HMG was trying to communicate in conjunction with the Americans over Iraq'. Following these meetings Arundell would deliver 'the journalists to point of sale ... in Iraq and Afghanistan' (Interview: 18th April 2013).

In Iraq Adrian Weale described how the IO function had been assigned to the Italians whose capabilities were weak in this area. Getting little strategic coordination from the Americans in Baghdad, Weale's own proactive team 'did what we could' through speaking with local and international journalists, even though this was not in their remit; he said 'we ended up doing it all' (Interview: 26th November 2010). One PSYOP officer thought IO had insufficient prominence in formal British planning, and said he sought to achieve it 'by sheer force of personality', ensuring he was present at 'most planning meetings' in 2004. Initiatives can be shown crossing departments and penetrating Iraq civil society, privately contracting the local student body to assist the propaganda effort. Initially,

> guys were used by Information Operations at Division ... the [Measures of Effectiveness] gurus ... using them in soft effects to try and find out if opinion had changed ... They designed interview sheets that UK forces were initially using ... very early on, and by the time I got there you know, we're getting pretty much the same results all the time ... the results of these were going all the way to Downing Street ... someone eventually thought ... hold on, we've got a British guy with an interpreter asking an Iraqi what they think of the British ... maybe we should just get Iraqis to ask this question ... they formed, you know, a commercial ... with some direct, I think FCO funding ... not military funding ... it was through the military apparatus ... to train students to interview people ... the consensus rating was 70 per cent pro-UK military activity, it fell to 30–40 per cent overnight ... opinion hadn't changed, a guy wasn't asking a question with a rifle on his back. (Interview: Corcoran, 8th June 2006)

In Afghanistan too, some PSYOP output found distribution beyond the media, in a trusted and credible source: the English language version of PSYOP newspaper *Sada-e Azadi* got picked up and was used 'widely as a teaching prop' by local schools (Email: Gutcher, 1st June 2013). Former British *Sada-e Azadi* print editor Lianne Gutcher stated that 'I felt that people reading the paper for learning was a great way to get them to take on a message without seeming to ram it down their throats' (Email: 28th April 2013). She said also that 'it meant that at least people read and studied the newspaper – and hopefully picked up the message as a by-product' (Email: Gutcher, 1st June 2013).

US initiative and flexibility

Compared with the British system, the US military has been notoriously inflexible and resistant to individual initiative and adaptation, having failed to learn from the Vietnam experience (Nagl, 2005). According to Nagl, American history instilled a notion that 'politics ceases when war begins'; an overwhelming emphasis on hard power allowed no shades of grey (2005: 43). This can be seen in the debate that dominated much US defence planning after the 1990s over a new Revolution in Military Affairs (RMA). The ideas centred on technology such as 'smart missiles' and stealth and extended to Network Enabled Capacity: optimising links between allies, decision-makers, weapon systems and forces. A Congressional Report issued in 2004 stated that planners were shifting strategy to reflect an analysis that 'combat power can be enhanced by communications networks and technologies that control access to, and directly manipulate, information. As a result, information itself is now both a tool and a target of warfare' (Wilson, 2006). Andrew Marshall, of the US Defense Secretary's Office, defined it as 'a major change in the nature of warfare brought about by the innovative application of new technologies which, combined with dramatic changes in military doctrine and operational and organisational concepts, fundamentally alters the character and conduct of military operations' (quoted in McKitrick et al., 1995). Though it is sometimes used to discuss technologies, RMA is a theory about future warfare in which organisational change and strategy are key elements; it has been embraced in the US as a discourse of 'transformation'. It is argued that economic, political and social changes affecting the position of the nation-state in the international system are changing the ways its military must be organised and equipped (see RAND's Zanini and Edwards, for example, on counter-terrorism and 'netwar', 2001). Emerging out of the post-Cold War IT boom and the birth of the internet in the early 1990s (O'Hanlon, 2000: 7), RMA aims at utilising/responding to developments in information, communications and space technology, and has produced specific prescriptions for military and defence policy. Some, such as Michael O'Hanlon (2000), deny the emergence of RMA, and argue that these technological developments began long before the 1990s, yet RMA was influential in shaping US, and subsequently UK, defence policy.

With RMA, information warfare is seen as of increased importance, especially 'disrupting or defending the decision-making process' (Quille, 1998). Particularly significant advocates include John Arquilla who perceives an information age in its infancy in which America needs to gain an advantage (Arquilla and Borer, 2007: 1–2). With RMA, the focus came to be upon efficiency: 'minimal bloodshed and short battles' (O'Hanlon, 2000: 9). The clinical nature of their technological approach to war has come to epitomise for some an arrogant US 'detachment' in their foreign policy or propaganda to a misleading public image of 'bloodless war' (see Jenkins, 2007). Maj. Gen. Cordingley wrote of his command in the Gulf: 'The reporting of the very clinical nature of modern weapon systems and their effects on the bunkers and buildings in Baghdad led the public, especially the American public, to lose touch with the reality of war; a grim, ghastly and bloody affair' (1996). Gerard Quille of the International Security Information Service also warned against focus on technology over 'civil-military relations and other approaches to conflicts i.e. conflict resolution and third party initiatives' (1998). During the 'War on Terror' difficulties both in capturing Osama bin Laden and countering insurgency led some military experts to question RMA as a solution. Christopher 'Ryan' Henry, the Principal Under-Secretary of Defense for Policy, presented a briefing to Rumsfeld in 2004 emphasising the need for America to prepare to meet 'irregular challenges' (Ricks, 2004). His plans favoured troop strength over hi-tech weaponry, and generated opposition from the US defence industry, which risks losing out if there is a reduction in prized conventional weapons contracts (Ricks, 2004). Benbow argues that the new, modern approach to warfare offered by RMA is still largely suited to traditional inter-state warfare (such as Iraq 1991) and does not directly address new challenges (Benbow, 2006). Modern combat has increasingly been characterised by a need to respond to asymmetric attacks where, it is argued, high-technology solutions have limitations. Cohen has pointed out that a US preference for technological advances could always be surpassed by the innovation of an unconventional enemy (1996: 51).

Pierce's characteristics of the inflexible US Army contrast with the values officers considered *would* be desirable for the institution's culture, which include flexibility, participation, innovation and emphasis on professional growth (Lovelace in Pierce, 2010: iv). Out of the US Marine Corps, the '4th Generation Warfare' debate sought to address new, 'unconventional' adversaries with unconventional, asymmetrical and what were seen as 'innovative' responses. The RMA/4th Generation debate influenced the new 'effects-based' approaches the US and Britain developed after early failures of the 'War on Terror' (Benbow, 2006). One problem Matt Armstrong noted in the DOD is that they do '*want* to get an outside view' but sometimes the view they are offered 'naturally starts to become an echo chamber and the point of view that they want to hear' (Interview: 6th March 2013; original emphasis). By 2013 former Chief Pentagon Anthropologist Montgomery McFate observed that there *had* been a significant change towards recognising what she said was needed for counter-insurgency warfare:

> This represented quite a shift from the prior institutional orientation toward big wars, platforms, and technology. I think now, however, the pendulum has swung back and the US is again focused on peer competitor enemies, quite similar to the post-Vietnam environment. (Email: 7th March 2013)

Governmental cultures

As Bob Drogin asserted, the 'institutional systems and bureaucracies that are *always* feeding material upwards, not sideways' were the product of 'cultural differences that are hard to overemphasise' between government agencies (Interview: 22nd August 2009; original emphasis). Their comparative weight has an effect; as Ayers stated, the DOD 'have more people on the [USS] Abraham Lincoln, than they do in the entire State Department ... if you got together all of our military bands, our *bands* would be bigger the entire State Department' (Interview: 17th May 2013; original emphasis). Structural and historical factors have shaped State Department culture, as McCarty observes:

> The Secretary of State is the next person in line after the President and the Vice President in the Executive Branch. So they by nature are very defensive of their role as the senior cabinet member. They have very little ability to actually do anything because they don't have money or people ... but on the other hand they don't want to give up their image and role. So that kind of makes them obstructionary, by nature because they can do that. (Interview: 13th March 2013)

In 1999, most USIA functions were integrated into the State Department 'Office of the Under Secretary for Public Diplomacy and Public Affairs'.[14] The Defense Department remained the main player in US propaganda, but all agencies began to take greater responsibility for international public information. US former Assistant Secretary of Defense for Public Affairs Doug Wilson was in the USIA and led the fight against its consolidation into the State Department. Senators John Kerry and Joseph Lieberman led the Senate fight against consolidation. Wilson has since criticised what he sees as a devaluation of non-military Public Diplomacy activities in the post-USIA period. He argued that since the closure of the USIA, 'in my opinion Public Diplomacy in the United States has been severely weakened' (Interview: Wilson, 10th May 2013).[13] According to Matt Armstrong, since the first Under-Secretary was sworn in, in 1999, the post has been unencumbered 'over 31% of the time, but this was higher, over 37% during the Bush years'. There is a high turnover and the average tenure is 'barely over 500 days' with an 'average gap between departure and appointment of 248 days as of April 2013' (Email: 1st December 2013). There has also been a 'radical course change each time, so there isn't a lot of understanding of' what is needed (Interview: 29th April 2013).

Matt Armstrong, when it came to listening to outside advice in the information war, described the State Department as 'closed-minded, and ... essentially trained that way'. He said this was 'one reason ... they don't like the Advisory Commission – who needs an outside view? They believe they know best and outside views generally face resistance at best' (Interview: 6th March 2013). Doug Wilson argued that after the consolidation of Public Diplomacy, the State

Department has struggled to adapt to changing needs beyond traditional diplomacy. Wilson said, 'traditional diplomatic activities remain the template at State. Public Diplomacy activities and personnel are in a subordinate role. There has yet to be an effective meshing or synchronisation' (Interview: 10th May 2013). McCarty agreed that 'They're not *action* people, they're *process* people' (original emphasis). This is accompanied in shaping the culture by additional, structural, factors. It was a popular view that this 'doesn't make it a good environment for innovation and getting things done' and that 'the State Department reaction to anything, [was] "Let's have a meeting and talk about it"' (Interview: McCarty, 13th March 2013). It is true to say they can be more contemplative about foreign policy issues: the State Department is more 'outward looking' in the sense that it has a greater sensitivity to foreign interests and other cultures. Doug Wilson observed,

> the drones in Pakistan are one good example of the divergence of views and roles of Defense and State. The military and intelligence communities see the issue very much through the lens of counterterrorism and eliminating Al Qaeda. The State Department sees it primarily through the lens of damage being done to US–Pakistani relations. (Interview: 14th May 2013)

Matt Armstrong argued that the DOD in contrast was 'so very eager to get alternative points of view' that it *was* insular, but 'in a very different way'. This insularity, as noted above, is more in terms of control, information sharing and chain of command, along with a preference for technological solutions. Observations of the differences between agencies on the emerging approaches to dealing with the internet and social media were particularly interesting. Armstrong, for instance, observed how the State Department (home of Public Diplomacy) took a cautious approach with new technologies:

> State Department is attempting to muzzle everybody on social media ... whereas the Defense Department has gone essentially with [LTG William] Caldwell's four 'Es' – empower, educate, equip and encourage. And they know they can't keep everybody from tweeting and posting on Facebook so make sure they know the rules of the road. The State Department says 'no tweets unless you give us 48 hours'. (Interview: 6th March 2013)

Some interviewees argued that social media had gone too far, that the US government had been sidetracked by social media which is seen as a substitute for human engagement. Doug Wilson argued that 'the most effective current engagement, with many emerging leaders, particularly in places where there is or has been great public hostility to the United States, is being undertaken by NGOs and by media foreign correspondents' (Interview: 10th May 2013). Greater DOD openness may be because 'information' was often not felt to be a 'natural territory' of the military and the Pentagon saw itself as failing during the first five years of the war, but by around 2005–6 it 'actively, very actively sought outside advice' (Interview: Armstrong, 6th March 2013). This evidences some transformation within US defence. There were also rivalries in the US military that drove competition and expansion. Adm. 'T' McCreary said that with embedding,

> it was more inter-service rivalry quite frankly, that led to the numbers ... we had over 700 people embedded during the push up to Baghdad ... If the navy's gonna take 200 people out to sea, the *army* can't have 12! ... And all of a sudden you had a healthy size and ... what it allowed you to do was *really* tell *your* story across all domains. (Interview: 15th October 2013; original emphasis)

The UK's coordination problems were also partly lodged in differences of culture. According to one military source, 'there's a misunderstanding then that exists between both parties. I'm exaggerating for effect but, from the military it's of this bunch of twelve-year-olds with three-hundred-pound brains coming up with strategic vision papers, and from *their* side we're all shaven-headed maniacs who just want to kick doors in and kill people – neither view is of course true' (Interview: Anonymous MoD Source, 2013; original emphasis). Internal cultural perceptions of Media Operations personnel – nicknamed 'luvvies' (Interview: Anonymous, 16th August 2010) – are shaped by the fact that 'successful military careers ... are laid on hard power' (Mackay and Tatham, 2009b: 25). Angus Taverner observed how 'the military can understand Information Operations more readily than Media Operations – most people saw [the latter] as a very fluffy thing, sort of arty farty, yeah, luvvies. Handing out smarties to journalists' (Interview: 23rd January 2013).[14]

With its competitive individualism, American initiative in the 'War on Terror' has often been witnessed as increased 'politicisation', particularly where this resulted in influence and coercion. Nagl argues that 'the varying strategic and organisational cultures of different organisations play a critical role in the organisations' abilities to adapt their structure and function to the demands placed on them' (2005: 6). Through processes of resistance and change we can see how 'organisation' and its 'function' varied over time with function being often contingent upon an evolving relationship between individuals and their organisation (Scott, 2004: 332).[15] As practice changed, resistant institutional cultures did likewise. Where they could use informal power relationships, personnel took measures to navigate institutional barriers and fulfil functions for which they were responsible; solutions and priorities were developed within and pushed against the constraints of institutional culture and government structures.

Navigating formal systems

Evidence of a rise in initiative in US defence is surprising considering past work in this area. According to Nagl,

> Barry Posen argued that fundamental change in military organisations occurs as a result of the efforts of external civilian reformers, often with the assistance of individual military officers he called 'mavericks' – who were responding to a gap between doctrine and the emergent security threat (2005: 3).

Although whether military innovation can happen independently of civilian pressures is still in debate, some have suggested the importance of the relationship between them (Waddell, 1993). Avant argues that the civilian American leadership has more 'institutional incentives to act separately'; it traditionally 'found it harder to agree on policy goals and often chose more complex oversight mechanisms' that discourage innovation (1994: 130–131).

Given its history, it does not necessarily follow that America's military would respond to obstructions with initiative and attempt to negotiate systemic change. Where successful coordination *did* occur it appeared to be largely due to the initiative of individuals or using connections in informal planning in the military and wider bureaucracy. Torie Clarke talked about Secretary Rumsfeld's approach as encouraging innovation within the DOD itself:

> if someone is forward-leaning on the battlefield [and] makes mistakes, you want that person to learn from mistakes and move forward. He was willing to tolerate mistakes. Whether it was dealing with the media or building one of these programs. So ... 1) he gave the incentive, 2) he led by example, and 3) he was willing to let us try things even if there were not guarantees of success. (Interview: 4th December 2013)

Initiative and pragmatism by people trying to 'get things done' fed an increasing reliance on informal relationships. Plans proceeded in an ad hoc way across and between formal structures, and relations moved beyond the routine amicable relations necessary for maintaining ordinary function of a formal apparatus. While formal cooperative structures produced the *conditions* for informal ties, and informal relationships held together and drove them, the two could be mutually antagonistic. While the Pentagon was certainly insular during this period, at times informal dynamics broke through the autonomy of formal structures, utilising pressure and initiative to 'get things done'. Within the boundaries of circumstance, a clear tension emerged between existing practices, held in place by cultures and command chains, and the adaptation brought through the initiative and pragmatism of key individuals.

Tension, struggles and dissent

Particularly in the American case, the pragmatism and informality that kept the propaganda apparatus functioning was sometimes characterised by internal struggles and suppression of dissent. US efforts in initiative were emerging in a massive, unwieldy and increasingly politicised bureaucracy. The ideological neo-conservative elements of the US military were a powerful proactive minority in tension with other elements in the senior bureaucracy and military. Some embodied a more traditionally cautious, less activist, pragmatic tradition of American foreign policy; that of Henry Kissinger and George F. Kennan's Containment policies, which is rooted in the 'Structural Realism' or 'Neo-realism' of Waltz and his successors (Waltz, 1979).[16] In claiming 'You can't predict the future ... Once shooting starts a lot of bets are off ... human nature and the way things work out ... the path becomes very very unpredictable' Fallon articulated a widely held perception (Interview: 21st July 2009). Fallon himself identified the responsibility of the commander to 'set up some bounds', to try and 'keep it between here and here' (Interview: 21st July 2009). 'Bounds' are of course necessary in warfare, but can pull people along under poor planning as well.

To encourage cohesion and manage dissent in the bureaucracy, governments seek to exploit the pejoratively named 'herd instinct'; the tendency for people to 'go along with the group even when the group makes a decision contrary to privately held beliefs and values' (Jowett and O'Donnell, 1992: 224). Jowett and O'Donnell describe how rituals, sanctions, language, in-group references, clothing, activities and shared historical conditions contribute to the social practices and values that sustain institutional cultures and give value to its activities (1992: 217). Former State Department Chief of Staff Lawrence Wilkerson talked of gaining compliance of the bureaucracy – 'buy-in':

> You've gotta identify those portions [that may undermine you] and ... you gotta use them from the moment you begin arbitration over what you're gonna do, to the point at which you make a decision and you then oversee the execution of that decision, to however long it takes. You've got to have them. And you've got to be leading them not just managing them. You know, you've got to have them buy-in. And the only way you get them to buy-in is to make them at least *think* ... or even better make them a part of your decision-making ... feel like it's their decision they're implementing, or at least a part of it. (Interview: 23rd June 2009; original emphasis)

Chomsky has argued that for the educated 'political class' with 'some kind of role in decision-making' and who will 'play some role in the way economic and political and cultural life goes on ... consent is crucial'. He argues that 'that's one group that has to be deeply indoctrinated' (1992a).

In examining propaganda systems, the focus should be on a *process* – because within this process the practitioners' practices, cultures and ordering of their social structures and systems are as much a part of the *lived experience* of propaganda's effects as the effects that might result from its reception by the final audience. Means and ends are thus not separable measurable entities. The personnel involved as practitioners and planners in the propaganda hierarchy (many of whom distanced themselves from the politics and legitimacy of the wars) were crucial to its broader, more flexible and very political reconstitution. Practitioners of propaganda are not isolated from public definitions of right and wrong, nor are they entirely free from the influence of past formulations of 'just' propaganda and institutionalised assumptions.

Rumsfeld's Pentagon

During Iraq planning the American bureaucracy seized up. Rumsfeld reportedly shouted at people in meetings for taking notes, and restricted the circulation of information even to senior NSC figures like Franklin Miller and Condoleezza Rice. Miller was responsible for coordinating the interagency at the strategic level. His description starkly contrasts with Bradley Graham's account of Rumsfeld as taking 'the lead' in interagency coordination (Interview: 24th July 2009). Miller revealed how the cultures of the Pentagon and military were so insular that influencing them became impossible:

> Sec. Rumsfeld had made clear that he held the rest of the interagency in general contempt and that attitude was transferred to all his lieutenants … it was more difficult to get information and to get people to be interested in doing things that they hadn't thought of themselves.

He asserted 'that was not the case on the military side' (Interview: Miller, 3rd August 2009).

Most US strategic-level senior relationships were pragmatic, carrying out functions by whatever means necessary. Private interests also shaped some individuals' interplay with the structure. Rumsfeld rendered any attempt at strategic coordination impotent, according to Miller, who was one of those who chose to bypass him and rely on relationships:

> four-stars in the Pentagon … calling [about] things that they thought I needed to know, and [Condoleezza] Rice, [Stephen] Hadley and indeed the President needed to know, that would never have gotten out of the Pentagon on a front channel.

Dick Cheney and Donald Rumsfeld are often considered to have had an 'unholy dark power that … if Cheney knew something, Rumsfeld knew it' (Interview: Miller, 3rd August 2009). Wilkerson recalled this relationship: 'when you saw those two together, their body language, you didn't know which one was Vice-President and which one was Secretary of Defense' (Interview: Wilkerson, 23rd June 2009). Cheney's significance has been likened to a co-presidency (Warshaw, 2009), a dynamic that reflected how Rumsfeld used to be Cheney's boss. The relationship was long standing, as many political relationships were. However, Cheney and Miller were pragmatic, particularly where Rumsfeld was concerned:

> Cheney, through [his advisor, Scooter] Libby was getting once a day, twice a day copies of these Pentagon slides that I stole ... And any time, Cheney, who knew where they were coming from, could've said to Rumsfeld, 'Boy you better tighten up your computer networks, cause Miller and his people are all over you.' Not once, not him, not ever. (Interview: Miller, 3rd August 2009)

Job security became more tenuous, political and competitive in Rumsfeld's Pentagon; its transitional nature may actually have accelerated pragmatic solutions, risk-taking and private contracting. Kambrod implies (see Chapter 2) that 'young Majors and Lieutenant Colonels' are more driven by advancement than civilian staff, for whom 'job security' has a calming effect on their desire to take risks with new contracts and technologies (2007: 18). Initiative was enhanced by a more individualistic, competitive culture in the military and beyond; it became more politicised.[17] According to former CIA Operations Officer Valerie Plame Wilson, after 9/11 the traditional service motive was increasingly in tension with more individualist and political forces in the bureaucracy (Interview: 11th August 2009).

Miller argued that 'in the Department of Defense, when there's an election, probably 400 people change ... then you get it in each of the services ... and they're all at the top.' The culture, he said, is 'imported' through a large number of 'political appointees' (Interview: 3rd August 2009). A former Pentagon official claimed in a US military blog that

> The Pentagon is a rat's nest of military-industrial factions, factions inside factions, and ever shifting alliances – all competing with each other. The information game is easily played at all levels – which is one reason why this behavior is so intractable. (Spinney, 2010)

This was a practice encouraged by Condaleezza Rice, who Bob Woodward reports ordered 'if you can't do it through the front channels, call someone you know, and use the back channel' (2007). The former Pentagon official also stated:

> Colonels are always trying to manoeuvre generals into promoting their agendas. This is the way the real world operates, and the name of the game in this kind of staff work is always the same: remove all reasonable alternatives to your agenda to insure the decision goes your way. (Spinney, 2010)

Ultimately Miller had his people 'all over their internal networks' so that he 'had at least as much' information as needed. Cheney too was a pragmatist, and Miller worked this, such that Cheney was 'getting a lot less information from DOD' than via him (Interview: 3rd August 2009). Pragmatic initiative aimed at achieving particular goals was accompanied by cultural changes and tensions. Wilkerson described the pressure to 'get things done':

> You've still got people somewhere in there who are critical to the decision who are not gonna agree with the decision and who are going to be trying to undermine you or ignore you and their ignoring you is gonna hurt you ... So it's sometimes formidable ... even when you've got most of the bureaucracy you need to support, you may not have the kind of support you need in other elements of the government. (Interview: 23rd June 2009)

Intimidation, coercion and other informal pressures seem to have played a key role in the internal power dynamics that sustained American operations. Miller stated that he 'had no direct authority over' his 'virtual team' but claimed 'I could push them in certain directions and they would, by virtue of what it was, listen' (Interview: 3rd August 2009). Wilkerson also recalls how Vice President Dick Cheney

> went into the Republican caucuses, he went into the committee meetings, he went into the sub-committee meetings, and he strong-armed people ... more than any other Vice-President in our history. And the Congress was so feckless and so spineless they never kicked him out. (Interview: 23rd June 2009)

Similarly, when asked to comment on how dissenting voices were received, Armitage said,

> Oh it got through to Rumsfeld and then he'd fire people, remove them, and whatnot, and so I think to some extent senior leadership was cowed. In my personal view ... I can't prove it to you ... Mr Rumsfeld bullied Tommy Franks and others into having a very low number on the invasion force because he wanted to disenfranchise the so-called Powell Doctrine. (Interview: 21st July 2009)

Miller asserted that an unstable bureaucracy produces an environment unsympathetic to dissent:

> [when] you bring in people from the outside who have strong political views ... they only wanna hear about certain kinds of things and if ... you get in the way you're dead ... They sideline you. Reassign you a job fetching a glass of water and there's nothing you can do about it. There is no recourse, no court of appeal. (Interview: 3rd August 2009)

This most acutely affects the Pentagon, since unlike the CIA there are limited career professionals in the leadership positions of the DOD bureaucracy.

Informal relationships became increasingly important: beyond maintaining institutional integrity through shared culture, they enabled interaction between and within formal structures. Rumsfeld reportedly believed the reason he'd failed in Strategic Communication was 'he just couldn't get the bureaucracy to sort-of engage'; Rumsfeld found, 'he could rant and rave ... but the bureaucracy had a way of even confounding and resisting *him*' (Interview: Graham, 24th July 2009; original emphasis). Miller found in terms of planning and strategy the problems in the Pentagon impacted the propaganda campaign:

> there wasn't that much coming out of the political authorities, by which I mean President, Vice-President, Secretary Of State ... National Security Advisor, in terms of direction to the ground commanders. There was fretting, there was a feeling things aren't going right. The communications campaign was floundering, that we were taking casualties and not obviously responding in the right way. (Interview: 3rd August 2009)

Growing dissatisfaction raised a growing inclination for individuals in the military and wider bureaucracy to seek pragmatic solutions. A military initiative-drive introduced private sector solutions. Embedding was also emerging as a new idea in the DOD, as Rear Adm. 'T' McCreary said:

> It wasn't directed from above at all. We created it ourselves. As a matter of fact some people in the White House called the Secretary and said, 'Are you guys out of your mind?' (Interview: 15th October 2013)

Torie Clarke and McCreary both found that figures in the administration resisted embedding, but 'the winning argument' in that debate came because:

> We were getting our hats handed to us in Afghanistan [because] the Operational Commanders didn't understand the information environment. So we would launch a raid on a compound for example [and] what happens is if you wound somebody you cuff 'em, right? So that you can keep moving cause you don't have time to sit there and watch 'em ... so as you move forward you make sure the people behind you can't get up and kill you. And when you leave, just from a procedural standpoint, if you have the time to do it, you're supposed to unhook everybody and protect yourself on the way out. (Interview: McCreary, 15th October 2013)

However, with 'one or two people, even if they were killed you might put handcuffs on them because you didn't know. Or if somebody was wounded and they didn't get medical care right away before you pulled out they might've died and they still had the restraints on.' But he said,

> the bad guys would come in the next day, bring the press in because we didn't take press with us on these small raids ... and they'd say 'look, these guys are handcuff-

ing our people and executing them' so you say 'that's baloney, that's not what we're doing at all.

McCreary explained that 'In the heat of the battle, in the middle of the night, you don't take any risks' but 'when you see someone restrained that's dead you wonder why you had to restrain them right?' (Interview: McCreary, 15th October 2013).

McCreary said, 'So I was able to go in and say ... the good or the bad stories are gonna get out with pure transparency on the battlefield [but if we have embedded media it means the Iraqis couldn't] use that same disinformation that the Taliban did in the conflict ... Baghdad Bob's comments were immediately shown to be false by the fact that the press were writing' about what the forces did (Interview: McCreary, 15th October 2013). He and Torie Clarke said Rumsfeld himself was supportive of their fight to pass embedding.

Yet while 'there was a great deal of interaction between Rumsfeld and his commanders in the field', this communication was not always effective, and initiative was an intervening factor. Miller noted 'cases where Rumsfeld was clearly not cognoscente of what was going on' (Interview: 3rd August 2009). Commanders also differed in their approach to the communication environment. I asked McCreary if, where something had been said that was not true, there was pressure for a Public Affairs Officer to support it:

> I think that some commanders who don't understand the global communications environment, that that is the easiest course of action for them ... sometimes they do that ... I was in the unique position and I was never asked to lie or support a lie except one time, and that commander didn't last very long ... when I was fairly junior. If we raise our commanders properly to ... understand the international communication advice ... that wouldn't happen.

He stressed the importance of speaking out against 'bad ideas' (Interview: 15th October 2013).

High-level disagreements between PSYOP and Public Affairs had a ripple-down effect as systems were bypassed to push ideas forward. McCreary described how:

> The problems weren't when we had the meetings. When we had the meetings and we had planning ... those seemed to work very well. The problem was when people tried to run up programmes on their own side and get it to the boss and *not* do the coordination. And then you'd hear about it ... you had no choice but to go to the commander ... Don't wanna put all the weight on [PSYOPS'] shoulders, sometimes us in Public Affairs would do that *too*. Sometimes it was unintentional because you're in with the commander every day ... he asks you what to say about something ... and all of a sudden you're [finding you contradicted someone else] and, by the way, it's the *truth* and what [they're] trying to propose, it's not so much, or not as transparent. The problem was when it went up your own chain

and it wasn't shared with the other side, it was primarily done because you knew the other side would disagree with it. And so you probably shouldn't have taken it up to begin with! (Interview: 15th October 2013; original emphasis)

It is a commander's responsibility to resolve these disputes, 'but you don't want to go [to the commander] too often because then it'll show that ... you're unable to function together. So some people just avoided it ... But I know of at least three times where I had to kill something that came up through the IO side, with Gen. Myers' (Interview: McCreary, 15th October 2013). The British Army's Adrian Weale, who worked for the CPA in Southern Iraq, described how when communications came from the Americans in Baghdad, 'it was often difficult to work out what was the official order, and what was just somebody's bright idea'. Weale argued that 'what there wasn't was a clear chain of command. From Baghdad to us, or Baghdad to Basra and then on to us' (Interview: 26th November 2010).[18]

With sensitive cases there was military recognition, though, that it wasn't prudent to push people too far if they resisted an action. For example Wilkerson stated that, thankfully, when under pressure to use oppressive methods and torture, many of America's military personnel refused. Interestingly, their leaders did not force them to obey, but according to Wilkerson their lenience was motivated by pragmatism, not compassion. Leaders 'knew, from past experience, that when that happens, then you get whistleblowers, you get people who write to their congressman ... take pictures and so forth' (Wilkerson, 2009). It was overlooked because of the pragmatism of their leaders, who, fearing public opinion, sought to secure the silence necessary to allow others to continue as normal. Documents appearing on Wikileaks showing claims of torture were 'sent up the chain of command marked "no further investigation"' by the US military on the ground (BBC News, 2010b). Two documents that implicated British officers were also covered up in Britain (Cusick, 2010). Rumsfeld's lack of control over what appears to be a defensive army institutional culture was echoed by his biographer:

on *key* issues like Abu Ghraib, it was very much in his interest and in the Pentagon's interest to investigate the hell outta that as quickly as possible, take action ... jail 'em or fire 'em. (Original emphasis.)

Rumsfeld assigned the army to oversee the investigation, which

Took months ... years! ... it drove Rumsfeld nuts! To the extent, he really didn't wanna give the army any more important tasks if he could avoid it.

Later, when Rumsfeld wanted someone to build 'a plan ... to do reconstruction and stabilisation more efficiently', the army was the 'natural place in the Pentagon' to be 'executive agent', but 'Rumsfeld did not want to give oversight to the army, he wanted to give it to the policy branch ... because he just felt so burned by the army on Abu Ghraib' (Interview: Graham, 24th July 2009).

Assistant Secretary of Defense for Public Affairs at the Pentagon (2009–12) Doug Wilson found himself dealing with the legacy – what he called the 'Rummifications'. Wilson said that he 'came in with a very strong set of feelings that the civilian tools of Public Diplomacy engagement and communication had atrophied'. He observed that 'over the last ten years the military had, by default, assumed a number of these civilian communication and Public Diplomacy engagement roles'. In other words, it was

> Captains and Colonels and Majors … men and women in uniform [who found] it was not enough to know how to fire a gun or throw a grenade, you had to know how to deal with a shura and village elders.

Wilson said, 'the papers and articles that were written by some of these young military, reflected the *real* Public Diplomacy at that time' and argued their activities were prompted 'pretty much because they had no choice. This was what they had to do to be effective on the battlefield' (Interview: 10th May 2013; original emphasis). He identified several constraints or problems he argued were driving these captains, colonels and majors to act where they saw a need for 'engagement': 'an atrophied Public Diplomacy apparatus, embassies and consulates that were fortresses because of security requirements [and] a financially under-resourced system' for non-military engagement (Interview: Wilson, 10th May 2013).

'Rummifications' and resistance in Public Affairs

Within the Pentagon itself, initiative and the use of informal networks played out within an emerging struggle between PA personnel and those from an IO background. The Office of Strategic Influence (OSI) demonstrates the emergence of this as a problem. According to *US News and World Report*, its director was to be Simon 'Pete' Worden, who was given $100 million of Pentagon emergency funds. The chief weapon was to be a hi-tech radio and internet operation to open up information channels in the Middle East and, according to Worden, 'The target was the kids' (Worden, in US News, 2005).[19] Former Deputy Assistant Secretary of Defense for Public Affairs Frank Thorp said that Torie Clarke

> vehemently objected to [the OSI]. You know … there's one voice of the [Department of Defense] and that is the Assistant Secretary of Public Affairs. And her point was, 'Thank you very much, I'm very capable of coordinating that message across Government of the United States' as well as with her counterpart in the UK.

Thorp argued that the OSI was created as a tactic to exclude PA from taking a lead. He said: 'there were people in the policy division of the Department of Defense, who objected to the free flow of communication that was coming out' (Interview: 24th August 2009). IO experts were critical, holding PA responsible for its demise: Joel Harding said,

> It has been a historical problem with Public Affairs with ... with anyone else who does Information Operations or information activities of any sort. And one of the most publicly well-known events was back in ... 2001 the Office of Strategic Influence ... and everything that they did was legal ... and really with the best of intentions. But the people from Public Affairs leaked this story to the press that it was inventing stories, it was lying, it was doing all kinds of ... illegal things. And it was shut down ... And nobody's lost a taste for that, that was over ten years and people still remember what Public Affairs has done. (Interview: 15th January 2013)

Rear Adm. McCreary confirmed that

> A reporter for a national news outlet had run into Gen Worden (then running OSI) overseas and he talked openly about the office and its overall mission. So OSI gave the first insight to the reporters themselves. That started them digging. They had come across a brief where one of the slides would have been particularly damning, if printed, because it basically said they could lie to the press. Not necessarily in those words but it ... gave the impression that being misleading was OK.

McCreary observed, 'I don't think they [the news outlet] printed it though' (Interview: 15th October 2013).

Some internal politicking may have been involved in PA's resistance of what they perceived as a threat to their institutional role. Former Commanding Officer of the 9th Psychological Operations Battalion Col. Glenn Ayers argued that:

> As long as Public Affairs can control all information, they're happy. They would like nothing better, than every single ... programme or product that is made from Psychological Operations or IO forces, to go through Public Affairs for their stamp of approval. And they will kill everything, because they are totally reactive, they ... don't have a proactive bone in their body. (Interview: 17th May 2013)

Rear Adm. McCreary stated it was about 'ethics', however:

> You can talk about us throwing up roadblocks to the PSYOPS folks, or you can talk about us ensuring policies went into effect that would protect the truth, trust, transparency and credibility [of the organisation] ... I didn't look at it as a roadblock to them, I looked at it as *protect these goals and I'll never have an issue with what you do.* (Interview: 15th October 2013; original emphasis)

Wilkerson argued that, in an attempt to improve its ineffective but plentiful propaganda soup, during this period America resorted to '*the secret message, and we have this forlorn hope ... that it will never get out*' (Interview: 23rd June 2009; emphasis added).

Apparently Jeffrey Jones's attempts at strategic coordination of the interagency information war were thrown at this early point by media attention over the OSI. It caused the White House to become 'skittish' and the panel suffered when 'some agencies dropped out' and 'panel members soon were distracted' dealing with Iraq (Gerth, 2005).

Doug Wilson argued that one of the outcomes of the Rumsfeld Pentagon years, the 'Rummifications' for Public Affairs, was that Public Affairs was 'reactive' even into the beginning of the Obama administration. He said:

> Rumsfeld was seen as a saint by the press in the immediate aftermath of 9/11. There was 180-degree press turn as you got more and more into Iraq. That showed in the infrastructure of the Pentagon's Public Affairs office. The need to support the Iraq War dominated. (Wilson, Interview: 10th May 2013)

Seymour Hersh quotes a Pentagon official's claim that Public Affairs 'always want to delay the release of bad news – in the hope that something good will break' (2004: 285). When, on 28th March 2003, the army's senior ground commander Lt. Gen. Wallace told reporters that war plans were insufficient, both Rumsfeld and Gen. Myers's media approach (run by Thorp) was to defend them vigorously.

The Pentagon put retired military generals on US networks as analysts providing a more credible voice to deliver their message domestically, particularly as criticism of Rumsfeld intensified. Dorrance Smith explained that 2005–6 was a particularly defensive period: 'are you going to simply sit there and take incoming fire when you are the sitting Secretary of Defense or are you going to use the tools ... that you have, either through the secretary's office or through people will do it – honestly, transparently and openly – we're gonna do that'. They weren't doing the same thing in 2007 because 'we didn't change, the dynamic changed, there was a new secretary' to whom the media weren't hostile (Interview: 10th September 2013). Torie Clarke also said, 'Department of Defense has done that for years and years' and as a strategy it's 'fine ... but if someone from the business community in his environment stands up and says this is why I agree with this ... I may not agree with that ... that has far more impact' (Interview: 4th December 2013).

Doug Wilson observed that Public Affairs was gradually marginalised, and until 2008 or even later, 'most of the war-related communication that was done out of the Pentagon was done out of Information Operations' (Interview: 10th May 2013). This may have hindered their battle over propaganda rules, ethics and 'targeting', which are hard to separate from the institutional interests and struggles for influence. Informal and formal pressures challenged the extent to which the 'service' motive was a *limiting* factor in actions and saw it becoming increasingly visible as a tool subject to political and organisational imperatives.

According to Mark Pfeifle, it wasn't just Public Affairs in the Pentagon which wanted to be disassociated from black PSYOP; the State Department 'didn't want to be associated with nor understand the gray and black areas to make the best decisions in a swift, coordinated way' (Email: 18th June 2013a). Former CENTCOM Commander (2007–8) Adm. Fallon expressed frustration over how pragmatic military efforts to tackle the problem had been met publicly:

> it's this black and this white, it's this idiotic media obsession with it's either right or wrong. It's war, it's peace. It's fight, or love ... The world's much more complex. (Interview: 21st July 2009)

Not all embraced coordination across propaganda forms and it required a culture change. While *structurally* change was laboured, the *culture* change was beginning in how the information war was handled. Thorp sought a solution to the problem of coordination. During interview he said, 'The Public Affairs folks have also recognised the value of what Psychological Operations do, and recognised the value of coordinating with them' (Interview: 24th August 2009). He sought to enable a more collaborative working environment for PSYOP and PA teams but wanted PA to have primacy.

This was not good enough for IO operatives and the next struggle was over the emerging efforts to establish a policy for dealing with the internet and digital media technologies by coordinating activities. Col. Glenn Ayers said that when he was the Psychological Operations Division Chief on the Joint Staff (2006–8):

> we got the Deputy Secretary of Defense to sign two specific documents; one was a Trans-Regional Web Initiative [now Regional Web Initiative Program] ... and the other was the Interactive Internet Activities policy ... and we pushed those through.

He also was instrumental in changing the authorities for PSYOP to permit delegation to and approval by lower level officers. This meant that

> if you had a PSYOP-trained NCO on your staff, or an officer ... you could do tactical level Psychological Operations products, without getting higher approval, as a full colonel. Which never happened before ... prior to that [approval] was all the way at a two-star or three-star level. What I said is if you're gonna put out a, a leaflet or a handbill, in Arabic that says, 'Don't crap in the water and drink it', you don't need a two-star general to sign off on that! OK?' (Interview: 17th May 2013)

His mocking remark suggests that PSYOP will only be used for seemingly trivial 'public information' purposes. While many are of this kind, messages can also of course be focused on a variety of specific security objectives and may or may not be attributable or truthful.

Ayers, along with other interviewees, identified specific individuals whom they saw as responsible for preventing progress in both areas and obstructing approval of the policies:

There was more than reluctance [to coordinate Psychological Operations with Public Affairs], there was actual stonewalling, and physical, bureaucratic ju-jitsu to make sure that Psychological Operations authorities were *not* done. Frank Thorp and 'T' McCreary are both retired admirals from the *navy* ... The closest thing the navy had to IO is Public Affairs. OK? So that's the [direction] from which they come from, both 'T' and Frank. (Interview: Ayers, 17th May 2013; original emphasis)

But McCreary said that the army is

operationally focused and really doesn't put the premium on Public Affairs ... I think that's because many of them grew up with PSYOPS and they just don't understand the communication environment as well as they should.

He saw this as 'fairly cultural' and went on to say that 'Public Affairs is always the most junior and the smallest group of people in the ... room. Even smaller than Information Operations ... The only thing that brings them to the table is their relationship with the Commander', but that position is unlikely to be threatened (Interview: 15th October 2013). And Ayers said he found opposition generally at the higher level in the Pentagon:

any place in our government ... particularly in our command groups within the military, the Public Affairs Officer is a Special Staff Officer that answers directly to the Commander, which means they had direct entrée and intimate ... intercourse with each one of those primary people. *They're not gonna give that up.* You see what I mean? They're not gonna be *subordinated* to an IO officer or anything like that. (Original emphasis)

By contrast, in-theatre PA officers would fall in: – 'if you get outside of the Pentagon, IO, PA and Psychological Operations all coordinate very well at the combat theatre' (Interview: Ayers, 17th May 2013). McCreary explained that

The PSYOPPER normally works for the three-star, the PAO normally works for the Commander. But the PAO has to be integrated with – or have the respect of – the three-star because they do the bulk of the planning. And if they keep Public Affairs out at the beginning of the planning and only listen to PSYOPS, then it creates division. (Interview: 15th October 2013)

Ayers said he formed a plan to remove PA in the Pentagon from the planning process because

At the beginning of the conflict, we ... actually had to get ... all of our products that we were dropping over Afghanistan, approved by the ASD of Public Affairs [Dorrance Smith during 2006–9] and by the Under-Secretary to the Defense for Policy and Special Operations. We had people looking at our leaflets in DC ... this was back in 2001 and saying, 'This word is spelled wrong, or you have a comma in the wrong place' – it's because we had to send it to them in English!

He said this was one reason he got the PSYOP approval delegated to generals in the field when he was Joint Staff J-39 Deputy Director Global Operations:

we also got approval for the Psychological Operations Products ... *out* of the Pentagon, so I could get 'em away from Frank Thorp. And I could get him away from Policy.

This was a deliberate strategy to cut chain-of-command oversight and give greater autonomy in theatre:

> We were being second guessed ... and 'what if ...' and all this other kind of stuff by people who had no clue sitting in DC. So I took it upon myself when I came in on Joint Staff, *that* approval was gonna get out of ... the Pentagon. (Interview: Ayers, 17th May 2013; original emphasis).

Dorrance Smith recalled some of these discussions from his time in office and explained why it was important that 'front office' approval was gained:

> I pretty much was an advocate of Public Affairs being open and transparent in everything it did ... I think that my position was consistent with the people who went before me like Torie Clarke and Larry De Rita who were ... I think it's the role of [ASD Public Affairs] to *be* open and transparent and you can't have your foot in all of the various ... there's certain areas where, as Public Affairs, you really shouldn't be involved in the planning, the execution, the process ... I can't really remember a ... big conflict between what I was doing in Public Affairs and what some military operation was involved in. There were times where there would be these policy discussions and ... the PSYOPS people or the people who were in Special Ops would try to inculcate in doctrine or in policy that they could basically operate, you know, alone by themselves and without any transparency and of course Public Affairs would object to the extent that, that's where you get in trouble is where you do these 'off the shelf' operations that no one knows about and hasn't had anybody in the front office sanction and approve it and then when the press find out about it the first ... they don't go to the PSYOPS people for a comment, they come to *my* office for a comment. I think a general example, there were times in policy discussions where a General would try to argue a certain point of view to the Secretary in order to try and make it doctrine or make it policy and I would ... as Head of Public Affairs we would 'non-concur'. (Interview: 10th September 2013; original emphasis)

Smith said 'I never felt that Secretary Rumsfeld ever put the Office of Public Affairs or me personally in a position that would've compromised our ability to do our jobs' and 'whether or not he satisfied the itches of the PSYOPS community' he wasn't sure (Interview: 10th September 2013). Messages can re-enter the country through the domestic media and, as Smith noted, the press came to his office for comment and Public Affairs 'non-concurred' because they were concerned with managing this problem. This was because it excluded them from influencing the other messaging, which then might re-enter the domestic arena and PAOs would need to respond to media questioning.

Dorrance Smith also said coordination that goes beyond 'sanction' or a check and approval by Public Affairs was potentially problematic:

be careful what you wish for because you then become complicit in whatever it is ... and so how do you then have deniability? Or how do you then have credibility? When it then goes awry or becomes public and then you have to then go out and defend it ... internally that might be brilliant ... in terms of long-term relationship, I'm not sure that it's all that wise ... Public Affairs is not PSYOPS and once you go down ... you have to be very careful about when people were ... convincing you that it's in *your* best interests for them to deceive people for whatever reason and use the media as part of their deception, I just have no comfort in that. (Interview: 10th September 2013; original emphasis.)

This was happening, however; McCreary presented two examples, one of which he saw as coordination done badly, from Iraq:

Fallujah – and I sent a note blasting folks for this – the PAO had to stand up – was *forced* to by the Information Ops folks and by the commander – to say that we've crossed the line and we're starting efforts to retake Fallujah. That was not the truth. The truth was we were doing a *fake* to try and get the bad guys to move so we could see 'em ... If they had done it the way the *PAOs* would normally do it, it would probably have been more effective. The media were in the area, all the firing would have got their attention, and they would have said, 'Ah, you've started to retake Fallujah'. The right answer for the PAO ... was, 'We don't discuss current operations, we will move on Fallujah when we're ready' but the media would've said, 'There's gunfire, they *have* to be moving.' Whatever the case would've been, it would've been a much more effective answer. Because the way the PAO said it, what happened back in Washington, both from the political and the military side, everybody had to tell the reporters back there 'No that's not true'. (Original emphasis.)

This had to be done because there were press in Fallujah to witness the truth. In McCreary's second example he saw Strategic Communication as working well during Desert Storm (1990–91):

it was a plan to fake but the Public Affairs Officers were read into it and it *worked* [We were] gonna conduct an amphibious landing ... we did an exercise, we invited press to the exercise and said, 'This is one of the capabilities' [and the press asked] 'Where are you going to conduct the landing?' [then the PAO replied] 'We don't discuss potential future operations' ... but *everybody* was convinced we were going to do an amphibious landing. And as a result we kept many of the Iraqis on the *coast* ... But no one ever told the press ... we were going to conduct an amphibious landing ... no deception necessary ... in utilising the press. (Interview: 15th October 2013; original emphasis)

The utilisation of the press is indirect and done by control of information, without utilising lies. McCreary argued that actions communicate far more effective propaganda.

Ayers described how they put pressure on Thorp with internet policies:

Remember I told you about TRWI [Trans-Regional Web Initiative] and IIA [Interactive Internet Activities] and the authority for O-6s [colonels]? He *specifically sat on those packets* and would not either approve them or disapprove them, for *months.* Until, until I, and my, my boss ... I had to get ... my one-star air force boss to go in and sit down with Frank Thorp, *in his office*, and read through the *entire* message about TRWI ... And he kept on saying things like, [whiney voice] 'I don't understand this' ... my IO force boss, said ... this great thing. He looked across the table at him ... one-star to one-star and said, 'You did go to university right? What about this message is not apparent to you, that you don't understand Frank?' (Original emphasis)

Ayers used his influential networks to press changes through and navigate resistance from those who were concerned at the PSYOP content leaking back into domestic/international media. Public Affairs needed to approve it:

Well, er, here's how I got it through. I always punched above my weight as a full colonel in the Pentagon, so I got my three-star boss, I got the Director of the Joint Staff, who was another three-star ... I got a couple of SESs ... Senior Executive of Services within USDI [Under Secretary for Intelligence] within policy, to ... help me push this through ... Because ... my first assignment at the Pentagon was, I was the Military Assistant for Secretary Rumsfeld and for Secretary Wolfowitz. So I went for a year to the war college and I came back in, and I still knew all the networks at the Pentagon. I was friendly with quite a few high people, so ... I used my powers do that. Those three things that I pushed through ... it was the IIA,TRWI and the O-6 thing and every single one of those I had to *use* the Pentagon ju-jitsu and get around Public Affairs. Public Affairs was the *key* impediment to everything we tried to do, because once again going back to what I said ... they look upon all information as in the realm of Public Affairs information ... but Psychological Operations uses the same information. But we only may choose to use ... 80 per cent of it ... to *modify* the behaviour of a target audience. Public Affairs thinks everything needs to be totally open, everything needs to be spoken about, everything needs to be ... attributed. Not the case. (Interview: 17th May 2013; original emphasis)

Since Deputy Assistant Secretary of Defense (Joint Communication) Frank Thorp retired in 2009, there has been less opposition with PSYOP in coordinating Public Affairs with the other tools. As Matt Armstrong put it, 'what was starting the revolution in there [was that] you had Rosa Brooks over in policy, and Doug Wilson in PA, and Austin Branch at IO. You had three very competent, respected people who got along very well ... and you did not have Frank Thorp in there anymore' (Interview: 6th March 2013). Doug Wilson came in to the Pentagon as Assistant Secretary of Defense for Public Affairs in 2009 and had a very different approach to coordination. He described this change: 'I never thought Information Operations was a bad word. I wanted to diffuse the tensions between the Public Affairs and the Information Operations shops. My approach has always been that communications is a broad spectrum, from the overt to the covert, and it's a matter of using the tools in tandem.' He observed that some in the PA branch 'thought that if you dealt with the dark side of communications, you were getting your hands sullied. I think that's the result of spending too much time carving up the field into stovepipes … I brought with me a desire to be a holistic communications team. And not feeling that Austin Branch was, you know, from planet Mars' (Interview: 10th May 2013). This impacted his approach when he was the 'point person on Wikileaks in the Pentagon'. He explained how his coordination was international, cross-governmental and of course, between PA and IO:

> It was international in scope because [the emails] ranged from things that could be embarrassing to people, to things that could be life-threatening. It involved several different agencies – the military, intelligence, diplomatic – cooperation among the communicators was superb really. It was something that was done in real time. You had issues of free press versus issues of national security. And I was quite proud of how our government handled it. We met with the *New York Times*, we were able to go through. We couldn't prevent the publication but we were able to work with them in terms of identifying things that truly would put lives at risk. There was tremendous cooperation between the military and intelligence communities, great cooperation between the United States and foreign governments … communicating in advance things that could be embarrassing, and things that could be a national security risk. And when it came to … between me and [Senior Advisor, then Director of Information Operations] Austin Branch, I mean he certainly was aware of and part of the discussions about how we were going to be handling it. (Interview: Wilson, 14th May 2013)

It was suggested that it was 2009 before Public Affairs were able to 'get around the planning table' again:

> During my tenure, some under Gates, but particularly under [Leon] Panetta, Public Affairs started to regain its seat at the table as the place that developed and coordinated communication strategy for the Pentagon. (Interview: Wilson, 10th May 2013)

From this time, he argued, communications became

> an integral *part* of policy – a *part* of policy-making. And I believe that particularly under Panetta that that became *reality*. I was able to do what any person dreams of, if you want to be an effective communicator: to say at the very beginning of the development of policy, 'Here are the kinds of things that you need to take into account because this is how people are going to hear them and react to them'. (Interview: Wilson, 10th May 2013; original emphasis)

Doug Wilson said,

> Reconciling that coordination of information activities is important and in fact that happened on the battlefield. In Afghanistan you had … [Director of Communications, ISAF] Adm Greg Smith, who headed Public Affairs under Gen. Petraeus and who coordinated all of the communications elements at ISAF. It wasn't that Public Affairs then *ran* everything else. There would be one communications coordinator, everybody would be in the room on a daily basis, the communications goals would be outlined and updated and each element would take what was in their field and implement their part of it. And that's how it should go. (Interview: Wilson, 14th May 2013; original emphasis)

Doug Wilson said the way it worked 'in Washington, in government, it was not the same thing as on the battlefield'. He recalled, 'there were times when it was discussed [with Austin Branch and Rosa Brooks] and I was asked 'Shouldn't we move everything into my shop [Public Affairs]?' and I said, 'No', I wasn't interested, and it wasn't a matter of building an empire … it was a matter of everybody doing the job they were supposed to do' (Interview: Wilson, 14th May 2013).

Small struggles continued. According to Hastings, Gen. Caldwell in Afghanistan gave wide-reaching orders to Lt. Col. Holmes – the officer in command of his Information Operations unit – to target 'NATO populations' and pushed for generals to have PSYOP-trained personal spokesmen (instead of PAOs). Caldwell wanted Holmes to target PSYOP at visiting US policy-makers, think tank analysts and foreign dignitaries seeking to sway decisions and funding in favour of projects under his command, but Holmes refused on the grounds that PSYOP should not target Americans (Hastings, 23rd February 2011). He originally received an official reprimand for his refusal to follow orders. Again this occurred through a General's attempts to navigate structures to ensure outcomes he believed necessary in the propaganda war. In many cases, particularly in the American system, institutional and informal means of coercion appear to have been put in service of individuals' intent to ensure the continuation and success of their occupational goals, securing both cultural and functional changes. Distrust of the perceived informality of higher-level decisions led others at the lower levels to come up with their *own* informal, ad hoc solutions, implying a continuing system (Interview: Weale, 26th November 2010).

This confirmed a contemporary line for acceptability. Caldwell's orders to use PSYOP on US Senators overtly crossed this line and challenged newly defined aspects of authority and legitimacy. The *intent* to target within propaganda boundaries was not present, raising conflict for Holmes, and prompting him to speak out. But after they had established new-found limits of function, *PSYOP-trained* staff were permitted to target a 'PR campaign' against both US and worldwide audiences, though not presumably the US Senate. Attempts to redefine the culture and assuage any question of legitimacy were cloaked in a change of language; Holmes describes how the Information Operations Unit was renamed an 'Information Engagement Cell' in response (in Hastings, 23rd February 2011).

The Iraq War: 'cherry-picking' intelligence

Initiative is an important element of the culture of operations in all intelligence agencies. Former CIA Station Chief Stelloh told how it was through a 'back-channel' that his then Deputy Director of Operations, Jim Pavitt, told the Domestic Chiefs to 'redouble' and immediately begin 'scrubbing the ... private sector for tools' to use in the propaganda war (Interview: 23rd June 2009). Former CIA Division Chief Tyler Drumheller claims there is pressure in Federal Government and an ethic that discourages questioning and dissent (Drumheller, 2008). Miller described President Bush's 'tendency to be somewhat impulsive' but that 'had someone thrown themselves in front of that train and said – Mr President, we need 48 hours to sort this out' he would have trusted that. Yet Miller recalled a sense that culturally it couldn't happen:

> the way Hadley and Rice were, I mean, when I went to Hadley after that meeting ended [the last before they went to war in Iraq] and said – oh my God! [Hadley] said 'Decision's been made. It's done.' (Interview: 3rd August 2009)

A culture of non-questioning in US government agencies emerged within a 'public service' mindset; personnel were expected to follow decisions.

Official doctrine and formal organisation moved too slowly for individuals responding to a changing situation: people tackled problems in an ad hoc manner and relationships were crucial, with everything arranged informally. Miller organised a 'virtual team' for example:

> various different people in the NSC would gather in my office twice a week to kinda talk about what else they were doing, humanitarian stuff and people who were doing the intel stuff ... the guys who did WMDs just didn't come. (Interview: 3rd August 2009)

This extract from Miller's interview shows how formal structures and informal structures worked increasingly in tandem.

> In the ... interagency system, NSC staff is not empowered to make a decision that binds a cabinet government. So ... you bring people together and you try to convince them that it's the right thing to do. Or coerce them that it's the right thing to do. Or to *embarrass* them that it's the right thing to do! ... And if things aren't happening then you would generally, in prior administrations, forward the issue for decision to the Deputies' Committee which could ... make a ruling. And

if that failed then it would go to the Principals, the Secretaries of Department, and if necessary the President. In the Bush 43[20] administration that was much more difficult because Rumsfeld did not recognise the Deputies as a decision-making body ... a really tough issue that needed to be decided ... had to go all the way up to the Secretary of State, Secretary of Defense ... And even ... if the President signs something ... Pentagon staff wouldn't necessarily follow it ... Rumsfeld said ... if I haven't heard it personally from the President it's not important ... So it was much more challenging to get things done ... you had to be more wiley and just try and convince and coerce, jolly people along, etc. (Interview: 3rd August 2009; original emphasis)

This also demonstrates how people responded to rigid systems in informal ways which could lead them to use pressure and coercion as tactics. Dissent was dealt with in the name of public service. Through pragmatism and initiative actors met their institutional goals, with 'bright ideas' navigating obstacles to bring them about. Bureaucratic momentum and the mindset of the 'public servant' accorded a means of suppression to enact such ideas. Personnel had their own agendas, and 'bright ideas' that could conflict with senior officials' own planning, which meant that 'every day they're gonna undermine it' according to Wilkerson. He said 'you discount that [Public Service mentality] at your peril'. In some cases where cooperation was lacking, 'we know best' was sometimes replaced by 'I know best'. Wilkerson explained that competing pragmatic interests left out the 'big picture' of gaining agreement of staff, in favour of coercion. Cheney 'understood that George Bush could be that way if you rubbed him right, and Cheney knew how to rub him. And George Bush could be that way: "I'm right ... that's the end of the discussion. Period"' (Interview: 23rd June 2009).

The 'service' motive primarily binds public servants' commitment to the organisation's and politicians' goals, to its other members and decisions. In fact, the intelligence organisations in *both* countries tried to warn against an invasion. The US events are well documented, and emerged quickly via journalists like Seymour Hersh. Similar pressures were applied in UK intelligence, politicising it and preventing reliable intelligence from emerging. In the UK, however, the pressures are less well documented even today (see Davies, 2012 on both countries). Many of the justifications for the Iraq War were built on analysis of the evidence of German intelligence's 'Curveball' informant. It was the European Division of the Clandestine Service, operated by Drumheller, who began investigating 'Curveball' in late 2002 and voicing concern. When Colin Powell visited the CIA with concerns prior to speaking to the UN, he was assured it was a '100% completely reliable source' and wasn't told about a 'furious heated debate' between the Directorate of Intelligence and Directorate of Operations concerning the evidence. The Clandestine Service was not present, though the Deputy Director of Central Intelligence, John McLaughlin, was; Drumheller had warned McLaughlin 'just the Wednesday before' that 'we thought this case might be a fabricator' (Drumheller, 2008). By autumn 2002, CIA analysts had already built the case for war on the basis of this information. Pressure may have been heightened by Dick Cheney and Scooter Libby's visiting CIA analysts (Interview: Wilkerson, 23rd June 2009), though Miller, who worked closely with Cheney, argued he was simply trying to deepen his under-standing (Interview: 3rd August 2009). Ultimately an individualistic and pragmatic desire to 'please the principals' in government contributed to a momentum in which 'people were caught up', and it became hard to back-pedal (Drumheller, 2008).

Bureaucracy operates in an atmosphere of inevitability where a sense of inertia can be generated among personnel caught in its momentum, a sense of a larger system of which people are a small part. Drogin points out that 'The Curveball case is a fascinating case because ... it's not a single bad guy, it's about a system that, at every possible stage you have people going along, saying "Well shit I don't know if this is right but he must know, or she must know" so you know they're gonna pass it on' (Interview: 22nd August 2009). He stated in this case that:

> the [chemical weapon] analysts ... were very sceptical about the intelligence until they began seeing these ... classified reports from the bio-weapon people. And the bio-weapons people were relying internally on the Curveball reports. So the chemical weapons people simply changed their analysis. They didn't wanna be left behind. (Interview: 22nd August 2009)

The momentum of occupational pressures helped this to culminate in Powell's notorious 2003 speech. Plame Wilson said:

> For me personally, it wasn't until Colin Powell's speech before the United Nations in late February 2003 that I realised the extent to which the administration was twisting and turning intelligence. Because what he was talking about in his speech had no bearing on reality ... until that point ... I had been just working so hard making sure that my intelligence operations were secure, they were efficient, effective ... There was just so much coming over ... Chalabi's shovelling leaves at us[21] ... and you've gotta go through *all* of them ... it takes time to validate an asset and to corroborate their information. Time. We ran out of time. (Interview: 11th August 2009; original emphasis)

This led to the CIA responding to pressure by 'cherry-picking' intelligence that supported the popular ideas about Iraq and drove messages in the prop-aganda war (Drumheller, 2008).[22] Ultimately, the CIA worked bureaucratically to give the 'principals' the justifications they had asked for to support the war; the problem lay in the inflexible, unapproachable form of the strategic level coordination, which left a gulf between the image and the reality on the ground. Drumheller mentions 'another source' which was 'ignored' and now acknowledges that 'maybe I should've gone to Powell directly, that's what he said'; however, he argues that 'it's still a disciplined organisation and it's hard to go around that' (Drumheller, 2008). Ultimately the internal pressures ensured that dissenting views did not escape the Agency. However, Drogin also recalled how

> The DO guys – Tyler Drumheller, Margaret Henoch ... were making a stink about this, taking it all the way up to John McLaughlin, then the number two guy at CIA, until they were essentially ordered to stop by their [unclear] at the Clandestine Service who said this isn't our case.

He claimed 'the head of the Clandestine Service ... Jim Pavitt' told him 'at the time it wouldn't have mattered. ... he said I could've tap-danced nude on top of the White House and it wasn't going to stop the war' – an irresponsible attitude, according to Drogin, that was not uncommon (Interview: 22nd August 2009). As Miller states: 'After the fact, a lot of people came up and [said] "See, I told you they never had it" but these people were not obviously in evidence during the run-up to war' (Interview: 3rd August 2009). The repression of dissent eventually culminated in the name of Valerie Plame Wilson, a CIA operative, being leaked to discredit her husband Joe's claim that Iraq had not obtained WMD from Niger. She recalled how 'right before my husband's op-ed piece came out' a number of anonymous 'analysts' had been in the press 'talking about the pressure that they had felt in the run-up to the war'. Plame Wilson told how

> both Joe and I feel strongly that [her exposure] was in fact a very clear signal. Those that would speak out, that – look what we can *do* to you. We'll not only take you down we'll take your family. (Interview: 11th August 2009; original emphasis)

Drumheller asserted that the CIA 'is still a bureaucracy and people are still looking for ways to get ahead' (Drumheller, 2008). According to an anonymous source, and confirmed by Miller (Interview: 3rd August 2009), the world of the analysts works similarly to academia; progression is based upon publishing, and your work being read. So a reversal, as Drumheller recollects, was 'not something that was gonna be done in this White House ... the atmosphere was not conducive to that' (Drumheller, 2008).

The Iraq War: strategy for the 'surge'

Director for Global Outreach Kevin McCarty felt there were constraints on what could be done even at the White House level; that when he came to his position he was 'naive' in thinking 'I'm at the White House ... I can make things happen' but, even faced with a large bureaucracy, it *was* a hub where contacts made planning and coordination possible, with a creative approach. He said:

The hub at the White House gave us a lot more ability to *apply* innovation ... we could go to [Ambassador] Crocker, we could go to [Gen.] Petraeus, we could ... invite people to do things. If I'd been in the Department of Defense in some division somewhere I would never have been able to do anything like that. Where you sit has a lot to do with how big you go with your innovation. (Interview: McCarty, 13th March 2013; original emphasis)

In the White House, McCarty found he needed to *prioritise*:

to make change you can only pick two or three things that you really want to change because you have to put a lot of your own personal time and effort into making sure that change happens.

He said 'we started devising how we could make strategies like the surge strategy work. But not [wielding] a big bureaucracy ... Bureaucratic changes don't happen so how do you make things happen without them?' (Interview: McCarty, 13th March 2013). As Pfeifle put it, 'we were attempting to drive the train because nobody else was at the wheel'. He told how for each conflict,

several times a week ... we would have the people from across the interagency on a secure video-conference from State Department, Defense Department, IMNF [Iraqi Multi-National Force] ... the Embassy ... the leadership in US Central Command, Tampa, USAID officials both in Washington and on the ground.

For Afghanistan, they would include the same kinds of officials, plus 'the embassy officials in Pakistan' (Interview: Pfeifle, 12th July 2013).

According to McCarty and Pfeifle, their NSA at the time, Stephen Hadley, sought to 'institutionalize rapid response' to Al Qaeda, particularly in Iraq, and ensure 'a long-range planning component that amplified [US] messages' (McCarty and Pfeifle 2011: 9). Under his direction Pfeifle (then Deputy NSA for Strategic Communications and Global Outreach) and McCarty (Director for Global Outreach, working for him) designed and executed small-scale high-impact campaigns to accompany 'the surge' and turn around perceptions both in the national media and in theatre. According to McCarty,

There's ways to make things happen but you don't need big organisations and you don't need BBCs and VOAs. It's a whole different environment and we actually did some interesting things before I left the White House that worked really, really well and it didn't gain much public attention. The secret to the success was, we were smart and innovative about how we did it, not by going big in budget or programme.

After the surge, they felt that 'public opinion in the US was a very much Iraq was our new Vietnam ... it was a morass and nobody was going to win, it was falling apart, nothing good was happening'. But the White House saw the surge as a success:

> All the things we were looking for – improvements in governance, security, education, agriculture, business, finance – all the things that were part of that strategy, we were getting back that this stuff was working. (Interview: McCarty, 13th March 2013)

They set out to change this public perception and match it with what they perceived as the reality.

One of the problems was credibility; that 'nobody would believe anything Bush said at that time'. They needed to find credible voices to deliver the information, disseminate the supportive media coverage that was already available more widely, and do that using voices that were already trusted and drawing the audience. McCarty describes the approach:

> we got about four or five people together and we just started collating all of the . . . articles that were being written, all of the things that . . . we knew was really happening but weren't written by us . . . official reports, other people that were there, local media, whatever . . . and we put that out to a large distribution list of thought leaders . . . just sent this stuff out every day to them. And say look, here's what's going on, but don't believe us, read this stuff, go talk to *these* people . . . And then we offered trips to these people, said you know, don't even believe this . . . go look for yourself. We'll pay your way over and you can go look at anything you want to. So what this did is it began generating a whole new stream of information into the environment about what was really going on that was coming from other people, not us. (Interview: 13th March 2013; original emphasis)

It's important to note that this was not just aimed at supporters but also at critics: 'a total of 2000 domestic and international reporters, bi-partisan congressional staff members, think tank experts, columnists, radio and television producers, bloggers, and government officials in the US, Iraq and Afghanistan' (McCarty and Pfeifle, 2011: 10). A key element of the approach was changing the position of what were called 'responsible sceptics'. McCarty described these as 'the opposition party . . . but . . . known for being thoughtful people. And they weren't just pure partisan, they're strong with their side, but they were very thoughtful people' (Interview: 13th March 2013). The key with 'sceptics', after demonstrating credibility of the government information, was enabling unprecedented access and encouraging interest and take-up of information. McCarty describes how what Hadley dubbed the 'Fusion Cell'

> started setting them up and bringing them in. Saying, 'Why don't you interview anyone you want to, we'll sit you down, we'll talk, we'll tell you what we're doing, you guys can write what you want about it but come on in and talk to us.' Well we just brought them in and laid everything open to them and then most of them wanted to go see for themselves and they started writing about what was really happening. (Interview: 13th March 2013)

'Sceptics' included Michael O'Hanlon and Kenneth Pollack, who returned and wrote that the administration's critics 'seem unaware of the significant changes taking place' in theatre (O'Hanlon and Pollack, 2007). The 'Fusion Cell' used the 'viral' nature of modern media to spread the word; those journalists and 'thought leaders' were cited by others 'then they would send things out and then people would reference them and write their things and that would make the information grow' (Interview: McCarty, 13th March 2013). Their stated aim was to saturate as many channels as possible with a 'consistent flood of information that was factual … with credible, direct links to verify its credibility' (McCarty and Pfeifle, 2011: 11). McCarty and Pfeifle state that

> in any given week dozens – if not hundreds – of outside influencers and experts would receive information first-hand in the White House Situation Room, participate in conference calls with Iraq War fighters and diplomats, travel to Iraq or Afghanistan to learn on the ground or respond with questions about email fact sheets or other documents that moved the message to a large audience. (2011: 11)

As a result, 'armed with first hand insights' from visiting the country and the information that had been provided, 'we found that the sceptics moderated, or in some cases, changed viewpoints' (McCarty and Pfeifle, 2011: 8). Mark Pfeifle also told of a 'congressional staff delegation trip to Iraq and Afghanistan in 2008' that they organised (Interview: 12th July 2013). He named two delegates who he said 'gained more perspective' on the surge:

> Mr. Jim Manley, Communication Director to U.S. Majority Leader Harry Reid – Democrat from Nevada … had said publically that the 'war was lost' in Iraq. Jim told us he was very skeptical of our operations in Iraq before he left on the trip. He came back with a renewed understanding of the complexity of the situation – he didn't support our efforts completely, but he said that the future public statements from his boss would be more nuanced and would likely add the new perspective that he saw firsthand. (Email: Pfeifle, 13th July 2013)

The second, he said, was Congressman Brian Baird, a Washington State Democrat who Pfeifle said was highly critical before he left but then after, on MSNBC, said 'I think we are seeing signs of progress', linking this turnaround to his trip (Baird, 2007). O'Hanlon commented on his experience:

> These kinds of trips can be outstanding but the quality can vary greatly from one to another, depending largely on the honesty of who you meet with, and also on the degree of knowledge and informed skepticism that the group of scholars is armed with. (Email: 18th July 2013)

Pfeifle and McCarty also realised they needed to address media handling of the insurgency in theatre during the surge. With 'the backing of the seniors' they planned a high-level strategy, coordinated with 'Ambassador Crocker in Iraq and … General Petraeus' (Interview: McCarty, 13th March 2013). The then-

White House Chief of Staff Josh Bolton emailed Pfeifle, stating it was part of
"THE top priority of your humble Chief of Staff" and that he would lend any
and all help in breaking through the bureaucracy to put a team together at
lightning speed', and within two weeks they had seven experienced detailees
from across the interagency dedicating long hours to the task. Secure Video
Tele-Conferences began three times a week with 'the White House and the
National Security Council, US government strategic communication leaders in
Iraq, US Central Command, Department of State and Department of Defense'
(McCarty and Pfeifle, 2011: 10). They circulated a document with key messages
and supportive evidence 'coordinated all war on terror, Iraq and Afghanistan
public events, media interviews, significant dates and events' (McCarty and
Pfeifle, 2011: 10). The operation was also coordinated with the PA teams in Iraq.

The strategy they implemented started from the premise that 'a terrorist
fights a media war. He creates an event to draw attention to something and get a
message across' – the message being 'despite all these big armoured guys
protecting themselves, they can't protect *you*' (original emphasis). They
developed a strategy to

> take that away from them ... so what we did was we sped our media cycle up,
> instead of an attack happening ... the terrorists putting out their propaganda
> message, then us reacting to it. When you're reacting you've lost. We set up our
> meeting and as soon as there's an attack we put the story out first.

Key to this was getting the media there early, so the attack could be framed to
emphasise that 'These guys killed a bunch of women and children again in this
area that was unprotected.' This wasn't difficult as 'there were always people
around when these things happened ... But the priority was to do the security.
Not the media. We just ... told them the media is more important, make sure
that happens.' This first element of the strategy helped them to change the
public perception of the surge's impact. Secondly, they highlighted the crimes of
the insurgents – 'We showed their torture-camps. We showed their torture-
manuals. We showed their mapped burial grounds' (Interview: McCarty, 13th
March 2013) – and increased their credibility by pointing to 'independently
verifiable facts' that supported their position (McCarty and Pfeifle, 2011: 8).
Finally, they supported the strategy by ensuring that coalition announcements
had 'an Iraqi face on it, rather than Ambassador so-and-so saying what we're
gonna do, we have an Iraqi', and

> only highlighting the positive stuff that we were doing ... building this, making
> that ... we didn't want people just thinking we were dropping bombs ... we didn't
> ignore that, but we weren't out there to *highlight* it. What we did is we changed the
> way we told the story ... The story was now about all the positive things. (Original
> emphasis)

The key was coordination: McCarty said Crocker and Petraeus 'were a great team and they took to this like ducks to water'; the NSC coordinators had 'regular conferences with them about this. We were in constant touch with their people and they were very, very good' (Interview: 13th March 2013).

McCarty is not alone in believing that image must be prioritised. It is a common belief among those who strongly subscribe to the 'Strategic Communication' approach that emerged at this time. Joel Harding argued that

> until the trigger-pullers and the jet-fighters and all those people that live at the Department of Defense, when they realise that perception has to be managed first ... then we can think about the bombs and the bullets. (Interview: 15th January 2013)

A propaganda campaign that hinged on ensuring that the media image was prioritised over the security situation might have been controversial among Iraqis and might not be appreciated in the local community. It also could create a dislocation between their lived experiences and the media image of the conflict, as they see the US military as more concerned with image than safety.

Gen. Petraeus brought big changes, placing greater priority on the information sphere and the role of culture in warfare. The Defense Department was more receptive to these ideas but individuals who wanted to enact change still found they needed strong networks to achieve these goals. Montgomery McFate described the efforts to bring about the Human Terrain System:

> HTS like most other stuff that happens in DOD involved a lot of personal networks. Steve [Fondacaro] had a large network based on his classmates from West Point, and his 30 years in uniform. I had a large network from just living and working in DC. Just to give one example, a personal friend of mine was a senior staffer at Undersecretary of Defense for Intelligence, and when HTS was looking for DOD executive oversight we asked her, and she brought it to her boss, and her boss brought it to his boss. That's how HTS ended up in USDI instead of USD (Policy). It was more of an accident than a plan.

She described how they did this:

> My approach is always to align my interests with those of others, so when we encountered resistance, I was always looking to find out ways that everyone could benefit. Steve's approach was a lot more direct! (Email: McFate, 7th March 2013)

Meanwhile, in both Iraq and Afghanistan, reality for the local people still diverged greatly from the 'message', to the frustration of some working in PSYOP and PA. Paula Hanasz, who worked in a Target Audience Analysis (TAA) team, criticised how during 2008–10:

> what I saw in Kabul was that nothing much changed. There were still soldiers who had to walk from compound to compound in full battle rattle[23] while I wrote strategic advice saying our media should propagate the notion that ISAF is there

to make Kabul safe. How is Kabul safe if even the ISAF soldiers have to walk around in body armour? That sort of inconsistency between our media efforts and the behaviour of soldiers sends the most powerful message of all – we are all full of shit. (Email: 30th April 2013)

And propaganda will not necessarily be believed – as Armstrong put it: 'The Baghdad bomber ... was spewing out propaganda... so what?! Was it effective? No!' (Interview: 29th April 2013).

Also, during the surge, the 'Fusion Cell' sought to saturate opinion leaders with a 'consistent flood' of evidence of their successes by taking them on trips to see these things themselves. It is important to note that how 'successful' the US surge strategy was, and the relative importance of the US role in quelling violence in the country, have been questioned by planners. For example, while Sen. John McCain called the surge the 'fundamental factor', the Secretary for Defense Chuck Hagel criticised both the surge and decision to go to war (Szoldra, 2012). This is because 'indicators' on which the US government based claims of surge strategy 'success' had complex causality, even by their commanders' own accounts. For instance, Army Lt. Col. Daniel Davis interviewed commanders, and stated in his report that

> the surge of troops in 2007 was *instrumental* at best and according to one senior ground commander who led much of our fight in the Anbar province, '75% to 80% of the credit' for the surge's success lies elsewhere. (Davis, 2012; original emphasis.)

NSC work gained the approval of other interviewees also. Doug Wilson, the former Assistant Secretary of Defense for Public Affairs, said, 'In my view the Obama National Security Team on Communications was the best I have seen in forty years in government and most effective' (Interview: 10th May 2013). It was the locus of coordination and strategic control, and Wilson stated that

> In this administration, I think it's been the case in recent administrations, the National Security Staff has really become kind of the hub; they've really become an effective coordinating mechanism. The various communication elements report into them and work with them. (Interview: 14th May 2013)

After Pfeifle, the Deputy NSA for Strategic Communications position was filled by Denis McDonough (January 2009–September 2009 when he became Chief of Staff) and then Ben Rhodes (previously Obama's chief speechwriter then Deputy NSA September 2009–present). Doug Wilson 'maintained very close communications' with Rhodes and McDonough, and 'the people who were overseeing communications at the White House and the National Security Council'. He found that those relationships also reinforced his credibility in the Pentagon (Interview: Wilson, 10th May 2013).

Afghan reconstruction: in-theatre impacts

The ability to wield initiative in both countries' political and military systems was subject to variation in circumstances, personalities and institutional differences. Former ISAF Afghanistan PSYOP Senior Print Editor Lianne Gutcher observed how, at the tactical level, 'I think for many people the barriers were insurmountable and they gave up trying' (Email: 28th April 2013). But both there and in Iraq, or back in Washington, the ability to draw on informal contacts or apply innovation seemed limited – or enabled – by differing circumstance. Military on the ground in Iraq found differences in coordination very much depended on the divisional commander; for instance, the CPA in Nasiriya

> were in a building in the middle of the town so we continuously interacted … whereas for example in Maysan our equivalent group were constantly living under mortar fire in the civic house. And in Basra [the Americans] were all locked behind the palace walls. (Interview: Weale, 26th November 2010)

In Afghanistan, late in the 'reconstruction', whether or not US tactical PSYOP units benefitted from TAA depended on their own outreach and the pressures of war. From 2008–10 Australian Paula Hanasz worked in Afghanistan as a Target Audience Analyst for the Combined Joint Psychological Operations Task Force (CJPOTF). She observed that in US-only tactical PSYOP units,

> a lot of this depended on the initiative of those US PSYOPS unit chiefs. Some were very keen to get as much information and support as they could from us at HQ level, while others had no interest at all.

Initiative and ad hoc solutions were reported to be driven by the fast pace of change and pressures on the ground and those with longevity could wield more influence there, leaving the military at a disadvantage. Hanasz stated that 'The organisation was so fast-changing there was barely enough time to figure out who was supposed to be in charge of what, let alone time to develop a process.' Her civilian colleagues were mainly British and American and were closely networked, but with military colleagues it was harder because of high turnover:

> By the end of my time there, I even stopped bothering to learn some of their names because I knew they would leave so soon.

Again it was down to their place in the system; in Kabul, civilians like Hanasz and her British and American colleagues had 'full freedom of movement and extensive networks in Afghan organisations, ministries, as well as the international community' (Email: 30th April 2013). She said,

> The TAA team was pretty autonomous of the rest of CJPOTF, and so we mostly got things done without having to ask for permission first … As civilians, we had

on average spent a lot more time at ISAF HQ than any of our military colleagues, and therefore always knew the 'right' person to ask things such as information or how to get our strategic communications advice passed up to senior level.

Regarding the military chiefs she said,

> In the end we (in TAA, and other civilians in CJPOTF) knew that we would remain and they would leave sooner or later … So we didn't stress too much – we also knew we could insist on our own ideas and guidance because we had the longer experience, and were generally more trusted because of it by the Chief of CJPOTF. So in that sense it wasn't too difficult to get things done.

Female personnel were also used as a tool to get greater influence:

> My boss would regularly send me, the only female on the team, to meetings with senior military officers he knew would be more receptive to a young, attractive, civilian woman than to some scruffy bloke … I would often be sent to meetings specifically because [I was] a woman. It was true that senior male officers would give more face time to a female civilian, even if they were doing it subconsciously and didn't mean to be creepy. (Email: 30th April 2013)

Hanasz in ISAF recalled how when military chiefs (of any nationality) imposed their new initiatives, this often had disruptive impacts. She said many of the military chiefs, including Americans,

> would have ambitions of shaking things up, 'fixing' everything, creating some grand campaign that would win Afghan hearts and minds once and for all. Of course in the accomplishment of that, whatever had been established previously would have to be scrapped. So every four to six months we'd have a brand new campaign plan, brand new ideas that the military, with their short term deployments, thought were novel, but that we civilians with two, three, four and even five years experience in-country knew to have been tried before. (Email: 30th April 2013)

'Cultural understanding' at *Sada-e Azadi*

In Afghanistan, Stanley McChrystal's COIN strategy was heralded as placing a greater emphasis on 'cultural understanding' and the information campaign. But some accounts indicate that those actually imposing these latest initiatives sometimes focused on demonstrating effort that was pleasing to the bosses, attempts to 'look busy' in their job, rather than attempting to understand the local population or focus on long-term goals. Lianne Gutcher was Senior Print Editor for *Sada-e Azadi* (2007–11) and reported that changes placed TAA in a lead position. But she argued that in actuality they prioritised their desire to keep seniors happy:

> When I started the team of journalists and the team of analysts were considered to have the same authority over copy. Then a new PSYOPS Commander took over

and made the [Target Audience] Analysts senior to the writers. This meant that whatever the analysts wanted included or changed had to be done ... I often felt the analysts were more concerned with writing something that would appeal to their military bosses than the actual target audience.

At the same time, Gutcher was strongly critical of the TAA, considering it far from being tuned in to local cultural sensitivities and concerns. She said they

mainly formed their opinions and views by participating in focus groups rather [than] by going out and interacting with Afghans in a regular manner ... I often felt that the analysts were rather lacking in subtlety and tended to think of Afghans as quite stupid. (Email: Gutcher, 28th April 2013)

She recalled how 'we were often [told] by TAA to spike stories or change the tone' (Email: 28th April 2013). In one example Gutcher describes how:

The American boss of TAA was really into ratcheting up the aggressive tone of the newspaper. So when mentioning for example, a Taliban attack, he would want to really drill home to readers what 'bastard scum' (this is the expression I seemed to recall him using) the Taliban were. (Email: 1st June 2013)

Paula Hanasz was of the opinion that between 2008 and 2010 some of the more ineffective activities had been 'mostly used by us and other western or ISAF personnel to illustrate the PSYOPS work being done', for example the work of the Combined Joint Psychological Operations Task Force 'newspaper and radio network' Sada-e Azadi website, which looked good back home but 'had a very low readership among the target audience' in Afghanistan (Email: Hanasz, 30th April 2013). English-language versions of publications were also produced for this reason: 'the magazine was the only tangible thing the CJPOTF commanders had to hand out to their own military bosses ... if it lacked English their bosses would not be able to easily assess their work' (Email: Gutcher, 1st June 2013).

There was a sense of the precarious nature of the budget share relative to kinetic resource, and the need to prove effectiveness was a common concern among interviewees. This helped drive the development of Target Audience Analysis and Measures of Effect forward. As Ralph Arundell noted, there is a belief that 'influence activity, can achieve disproportionate effect to what it's going to cost you' but 'how do you turn that into a provable fact so that you can then turn to the budget men and say, you spent this and I delivered this' and ensure long-term investment (Interview: 18th April 2013). Influence budget depends on, often short-term, measures of effectiveness. Arundell said its effectiveness, though, depends on the post-conflict continuation of the campaign:

we should be retaining our strategic communications activity effort long after we've finished having troops on the ground to help maintain that perception. You don't suddenly chuck a bit of Strat Comm in there and ooh look, everything's changed. It happens over time and it's then got to be sustained. (Interview: 18th April 2013)

Arundell thought that 'increasingly we're going to shift' to 'messaging an audience directly', but this needs to be credible. A younger audience's chief information source is 'stuff that's relayed by their mates through social networking sites – Twitter' and 'if I say I'm Col. Ralph Arundell from the British Army they'll go "I'm not listening to that"' but if 'done in the right way' it might go viral. This gives an advantage as 'Nobody looks at a viral video on YouTube ... and goes who planted that?' But it needs to be from a known source (Interview: 18th April 2013).

A 'democratic propaganda service'?

The notion of a democratic propaganda has a modern history; expertise developed throughout the twentieth century into what Phil Taylor argued was a more credible 'democratic' tradition (2003: 322). Yet as propaganda sits in conflict with democratic values embodied in the culture, any changes to its operation are reconciled in some way with the notion of service to a 'common good'. Propaganda boundaries have contributed to a sense of legitimacy for the propagandist. They descend from a traditional institutional culture to provide a cognitive separation between democratic values of openness and debate, and belief in the necessity of the propaganda function. This belief is also tied to the 'public service' motive; propaganda often operates paternalistically. According to Williams, public service ensures the necessary divide between public servants and a public viewed *passively* (1958); it appears to endow the former with the sense of authority, the 'insider' superior knowledge necessary to justify paternalistic propaganda. On the basic underlying assumptions of 'service', a broad consensus appeared across liberals and conservatives interviewed, and between institutions.

During interview Adm. Fallon described succinctly an attitude that formed an underlying perception articulated in other interviews:

> the business of messaging to influence people to make decisions; critically important and in my book, influencing people to do the things that I'd like them to do, assuming that they're in our own best interests for mankind, is the way we ought to be going. (Interview: 21st July 2009)

This frequently used justification[24] for individual actors' roles in the continuation of paternalistic propaganda is built on values not dissimilar to Lasswell's conception of public opinion (1934). It demonstrates a fear of 'majoritarian democracy' which is perceived as dangerous 'mob-rule' (Williams, 1958: 298). The public is there to support decisions that have already been made. Similarly, in terms of morale, it was perceived as more crucial that British troops feel their loved ones support their actions, than to believe they are just themselves

(Interview: Taverner, 18th July 2004). Yet British research points to a public not prone to 'panic' (Oates, 2007; Sheppard et al., 2006).[25] Raymond Williams notes that systems of mass communication are paternalistic, based on 'an arrogant preoccupation with transmission' by 'agents' who assume the position that 'the common answers have been found and need only to be applied' by those in power (1958: 314). Here we can see contemporary equivalents in British and US propaganda.

In interview former CENTCOM Commander Fallon expressed the importance of 'debate' in Britain and America, echoing commonly expressed values of democracy:

> Pretty much everybody in this country, in your country, will [agree] yes we gotta have a strong economy, yes we gotta be vibrant and growing ... but the fundamentals of how you get there ... huge debates about ... but at least there's debate here. Many other countries around the world there's no debate at all. And one guy calls the shots.

Clearly this idea contradicts Fallon's earlier statement – the accepted 'reality' of his institutional position – that 'influencing people to do the things that I'd like them to do ... is the way we ought to be going', justified by reference to the service motive. Fallon proceeded to lament the difficulties of knowing what could be trusted in the internet age, before returning to say 'you've gotta start figuring out how you're gonna get in the people's heads to get them to do what you want them to do' (Interview: 21st July 2009). Similarly, Franklin Miller asserted that 'first and foremost the US government cannot, does not and should not propagandise its own people', a clearly contradictory position alongside his frustration at Public Affairs' concern about the message becoming corrupted and lines that could not be crossed (Interview: 3rd August 2009).

Regardless of whether he may feel 'influencing people' to be in the interests of mankind, Fallon's ideas were clearly compartmentalised. According to Garratt, most people 'get into such a routine with their work' that within a particular context they 'view all problems in a similar way' (1994: 42–43). Switching between contexts occurred with ease of habit and did not arouse observable conflict between Fallon's values. It seemed important for Fallon to believe both in the importance of propaganda and in the importance of the existence of free debate, as represented in his comments above. It allowed him to define public interest in terms of the goals of the institution, and public service as what action served those goals. This potentially allows for much flexibility of action and initiative in 'service'. As Ellul evocatively argued, propaganda 'is comparable to radium and what happens to radiologists is well-known' (1973: 242–243).

E.P. Thompson was dedicated to building into his theoretical analysis the experiences of the people who constitute the social structure and their experience of it; in so doing, his detailed empirical attention revealed evidence of active engagement with their position. He argued that these tendencies to see people as passive passengers on the boat of capitalist history 'obscure the agency of working people' (Thompson, 1991: 12). Fallon and others occupy key positions within a dynamic class process of relationships engaged in wider society and it is important to highlight how institutional cultures and decision-making are mediated within an active process, often by well-intentioned people. McCreary recognised that a tension existed between practitioners' institutional desire for a positive public image and the public need for a rich debate:

> To me, the worst thing that coulda happened during media embed is … a TV reporter being hit with biological weapons, with his last breath making a live report with his cameraman on the air bleeding from everywhere and turning colours and gasping his last breath and showing soldiers … doing the same thing. … The fact is, this is the horrors of war and we would probably have a better handle on whether you enter a conflict or not if our entire nation, or any citizen of any democracy understood the true cost of war. (Interview: 15th October 2013)

In many ways, an outlet to air dissent in controlled circumstances was seen by some as a useful way of operating and securing conformity, loyalty and belief in 'service'. Wilkerson argued that,

> If the leader understands what the dissent is about and accepts some of the dissent or all of the dissent and changes and does so publicly and with an explanation for why in the … group, let's say it's a meeting of the principals or a meeting of the National Security Council, formal meeting, it can be very salutary, it can be very helpful. And you can count on that person who dissented to be your strongest disciple thereafter … If on the other hand you don't listen to him, you build a Chief of Staff as George W. Bush did, Andy Card, or you build an apparatus in your Vice-President's office … so you never hear the dissent or through your own arrogance you refuse the dissent, or even as JFK did several times, you listen to it, you ponder it, you bring a person back, you listen to it again and you ponder it some more … and then you still refuse then at least you've attenuated some of the person's ability now or desire to block you, because he … or she feels like she's got her hour, and the President still didn't buy it. (Interview: 23rd June 2009)

In a democratic state, separate identity need not be obliterated by 'total identification with the organisation' the way Bauman argues it is in a totalitarian state (1988: 488). The ideals of pluralism and 'freedom' become a crucial factor in securing observance. All public servants implement policies which may not be of their choosing, but motivations are not simply deference to authority. Personnel are free to disagree personally with actions and policies of their department, and do. Belief is negotiated. Dissent reconciles a concern that freedom and plurality are embodied in the society and its government and gives legitimacy.[26] The 'inclusive' principle of the US government as embodying a plurality of views means dissent is dealt with, without a personal responsibility to act. Dissent is for the election box.[27]

The service motive clearly creates a gulf of understanding between those putting out government messages and those on the receiving end. When I asked about how PSYOP messages were increasingly filtering through to American audiences, Adm. Fallon expressed frustration. The reasonableness of military understandings (of external audiences needing different propaganda and the resulting inevitability of cross-over) seemed irrelevant to the reactions of the public it was meant to be in the 'service' of, who should, it seems, be more discerning:

> people they see something, hear something and they assume, this message was intended for them. And they take affront, they're offended. That wasn't aimed at you at all! (Interview: Fallon, 21st July 2009)

But there is an inherent institutional motive in even the most 'safety'-oriented campaigns, as the British Army's Adrian Weale explained:

> material about unexploded ordnance that they were circulating ... apart from the ... public health and safety message, is also good for getting people on-side and making them think that you're looking after their interests. (Interview: 26th November 2010)

Williams argues that 'those who are ruled by the idea of service are genuinely dismayed when the workers do not fully respond' (1958: 330); or in Fallon's case, when the people do not appreciate that the public servant's activities are 'in our own best interests for mankind' (Interview: 21st July 2009). But the interests are different; Williams argues that, if the audience 'cannot feel that this *is* their community' being served, then 'education in their responsibilities to' that community will fail (1958: 330). The gulf between the public servant and public 'served' was never more visible than during the UK anti-war protests. They embodied people's rejection of the notion that the actions taken were intended to serve their 'community' and the government response was furthering top-down persuasion. Furthermore, in theatre, the perceived failures of persuasion to impose any change in attitudes in support of strategic goals in Afghanistan and Iraq have led to the emergence of behavioural techniques, which focus on changing behaviour regardless of attitudes.

Williams argues that any respect we accord to people submitting to admirable public service motivations should not prevent us recognising the inherent error in a system which operates to sustain wider social division (1958: 329). In justifying a paternalistic propaganda approach, the values of civilians and social science were sometimes ridiculed or resented for being unrealistic and too liberal if their views departed from an institutionalised 'common sense' world-view. Propaganda was 'misunderstood'. As noted above, McBride observed this attitude that ... we get from academic social science in particular ... comes across as they're above, they're better than soldiers and ... they're not gonna participate in what we call here 'baby-killing'. (Interview: 5th June 2009)

When America and Britain's propaganda apparatus makes claims about 'truth' it is crucial that we remember that this 'truth' is negotiated within ideological boundaries influenced by the institutions and wider society.

But as a clear 'insider' McBride dismissed the notion that anyone outside the institutions of government can make sound value judgements, since those on the military's 'list' are officially ethical:

> McBride: My fellow military *understand* the role of, at least, military interrogation and enhanced techniques and so on ... not letting someone sleep for days at a time ... and so forth. So it becomes ...
> Briant: So they're better at judging these?
> McBride: I don't know about better but ... as I said before, the fastidiousness of the five-sided building is ... rather than, 'Oh, this feels like it's torture' ... Well, we don't do that, we have a list of things. This is the list allowed, and this is not allowed. And it's over with. And they're obeying those laws ... That doctrine.
> Briant: A kind of scientific approach to it?
> McBride: Yes. Whereas civilian reaction has been all about being judgemental as opposed to critical. (Interview: 5th June 2009; original emphasis)

An unquestioning faith in the 'fastidiousness of the five-sided building' and a commitment to totally submit to the authority of an institution's rules over personal responsibility and critical judgement demonstrate a belief that the Pentagon is above morality as defined by those to whom it is accountable. Again, McBride, this time discussing public distrust of the military:

> A lot of that is all about so-called torture ... this is I think the most overblown thing I think I have experienced. People need to do their *research* and find out that enhanced interrogation techniques, as they are being called, are done as any coercion, or any interrogation is done, with the presence of the Inspector General. The IG's job is to catch people misbehaving and turn them in and get promoted. OK, IG is very motivated to catch someone disobeying the law. And I have to tell you just in terms of doctrine and law that no nation can stand next to the United States in terms of its torture rules and regulations. Do you honestly think in Somalia when one faction grabs another they don't torture the hell out of 'em? I mean I'm not justifying it, I'm just saying ... We've got a process of self-inspection that is, is er, so motivated and everything is on video ... at Guantanamo[28] and so the [laughs] I've talked to people a lot who do that and ... the [chuckles] waterboarding ... I'm sure you know what it is ... and noone's ever drowned, there's never been any tissue damage but I guess it could scare the hell out of them ... but I'm told that the mode number of dunks is one ... 'mmm, OK, whaddya wanna know!' (original emphasis)

This flies in the face of massive international, independent evidence, and international legal judgements condemning torture practices. Of course, as a former military public servant, McBride was confident that 'it's not my job to evaluate that sort of thing', but in his view it did mean that 'it's important the Strategic Communication thing here is very big' (Interview: 5th June 2009).

It would be naive to think that such judgements would not affect the presentation of the 'facts' within even a white propaganda campaign under his authority. According to Jackson, within the confines of their 'rhetorically constructed reality, or discourse, the "war on terrorism" appears as a rational and reasonable response; more importantly, to many people it feels like the right thing to do' (2005: 2). Despite earlier claiming to be 'fiercely objective', McBride's views, expressed in good faith, betray his blind belief in the infallibility of the American system, and military bias (Interview: 5th June 2009). It is clear that for McBride these claims are 'fact' and 'truth' – it is others who have not 'done their research'. As McBride's statement shows, the problem with propaganda is not simply about lies. Systemic position and the value judgements connected with it shape the 'fact' and 'truth' honestly perceived, and likewise could shape propaganda from policy-making to pamphlet.

For example, in 2005 Public Affairs Guidance discussed the horrific case of four soldiers from 101st Airborne Division who, after drinking, went to the house of a local family in Iraq, and 'allegedly raped a young woman . . . and set her on fire. They are also thought to have murdered her family. To include a 5-year-old child' (US Army, 2005b). But these facts were marked 'not for release'. The charges could be given, in a very detached format – '1 specification of rape' – without human details. There are no words of sympathy. Themes for statements were solely focused on defence of the institution: 1) innocent until proved guilty; 2) the Division does not condone crimes by service members; 3) soldiers must adhere to core values; 4) 'The overwhelming majority of 101st Airborne Division soldiers have performed exceptionally well throughout the last year, and continue to perform well every day.' Beneath this last, points to stress included the language 'we are taking the proper measures', 'tremendous sacrifices our soldiers are making', 'proud of the job our troops are doing' and:

> These incidents cast a negative light on our operations, *but it's important to remember that 20,000 young Americans are making the right choices* day in and day out in the toughest conditions. (US Army, 2005b: emphasis added)

It hardly seems appropriate in the circumstance to be celebrating the fact that most are choosing *not* to rape and murder.

Values obviously differ between individuals, and not all military personnel or contractors would agree with McBride's defence of torture. Yet American interviews did reveal great personal belief in the US systems of government. This strength of belief in institutional frames of understanding as 'common sense' was particularly heightened within a context of paranoia over the vulnerability of the American and British infrastructure to 'enemies within'. Wilkerson described how,

> you always need an enemy, you need an 'other' ... in both our countries, we've always had the majority with a very distinct impression of the 'other' and it was easy to manipulate ... propagandise and so forth. (Interview: 23rd June 2009)

Social prejudice is an easy pragmatic tool manipulated divisively against groups targeted as the present leadership's 'enemies within'.

Nagl also identifies a historic 'general mistrust of theory' characteristic to *British* warfighting, which was born out of the colonial experience, where there was rarely procedure relevant to an arising situation and emphasis was on finding a 'real world' solution, or 'hitting hard' (2005: 36–37). In Britain some accounts also observed in this a 'we know best' attitude – a PSYOP officer reported the paternalism of how intervention was perceived as officers slipped into 'colonial mode', helping these 'poor blighted states', something that was reflected in propaganda (Interview: Anonymous, 16th August 2010). Likewise founder member of the British Armed Forces Federation Adrian Weale argued that British officers were 'arrogant' in their dealings with the Americans (Interview: 26th November 2010).

A direct result of the service motive is therefore the acceptance that the public don't know what's best for them and a tendency to understand a situation through the institutional frame. As inflexible formal structures constrained individuals' actions, institutional perceptions often embodied a 'real world' seen as misunderstood by both outsiders and public. Individuals had a great deal of belief in the importance of what they were doing. Weale described a perennial sense that they are 'on the right path towards truth and justice and everyone else is wrong' (Interview: 26th November 2010). This starkly contrasts with the idea that democratically elected policy-makers divide responsibility in a bureaucracy 'carefully structuring the work within clear boundaries' according to strict principles of authority and hierarchy to ensure efficiency and accountability (Kettl, 2002: 8).

There was pressure from above in the UK too; Mark Etherington, who helped write Britain's cross-governmental plan for Helmand, argued that 'there was a real sense of the clock ticking, that "the Minister is jolly keen to get into Helmand – don't bring me bad news, bring me good news"' (in Haynes et al., 2010). Perceived alternatives are determined by the practice and shared ideology of the institution to leave just two polarised extremes: force or top-down manipulation with propaganda. Alternative models would require systemic overhaul that is impossible to comprehend within the institutional boundaries of thought. We can see few alternatives in Fallon's account:

there are ways to do it otherwise ... you can do the Saddam Hussein method; put a boot on people's throat and shoot 'em in the head if they don't do exactly as you tell them ... gun-barrel diplomacy. That's still a way to do it. We can *force* people to do stuff. In Baghdad we had to do that for a while. 2007. But, is that how you ... is that really the best way to do it? Answer's probably not.' (Interview: 21st July 2010; original emphasis)

Alternative approaches to communication were not conceptualised as a possibility. And indeed a less dominative approach would require significant changes in policy.

Notes

1 Wilson defines organisational culture as a 'persistent, patterned way of thinking about the central tasks of [an organisation] and human relationships within an organisation' (1989: 91).
2 Especially Hobbes (1651), Locke (1690) and Rousseau (1762).
3 Between September 2003 and April 2004.
4 Horizontal propaganda is defined and discussed in Chapter 1.
5 The 'Pentagon Channel' and AmericaSupportsYou.mil are just two American examples. 63 per cent of staff surveyed by the Ministry of Defence said they read its internal magazine 'Focus', and its 'The Sandy Times' newspaper targets troops in Iraq (MoD, 2004a).
6 Though the extent to which it is encouraged/tolerated differs according to culture (see below for British and US historical differences).
7 Conversely, this weakens one of the qualities it prides itself on, 'flexibility'.
8 See also BBC News (2007).
9 See BBC News (2010).
10 See Pprune (2010).
11 See Cobain (2010).
12 Headed between 2001 and 2005 by Secretary of State Colin Powell (succeeded by Condoleezza Rice).
13 One key problem has been the turnover in the position of Under-Secretary of State for Public Diplomacy; Matt Armstrong said 'Since this ... position was established in 1999, when USIA was abolished, a confirmed Under Secretary has been on the job only 70% of the time. If Tara [Sonenshine] departs July 1, 2013, she will have been in office 452 days. The average tenure of the six preceding U/S's ... is 512 days. Since 1999, the average gap between the resignation of an U/S for Public Diplomacy (and Public Affairs) and the swearing in of a successor has been 248 days' (Email: 29th April 2013).
14 Similarly, Intelligence Corps officers are referred to as 'green slime' due to their green berets; Taverner noted they tend 'to be slightly thought of as a slightly odd organisation. Nobody really knows what it does ... It's called the green slime by the rest of the army ... They're the blokes who stand up at the beginning of the morning brief and tell us all about the enemy and then they sit down again' (Interview: 23rd January 2013).
15 As Chapters 5–6 will discuss, this also applies to the Anglo-American relationship, which changed over time. Informal relationships helped Britain's personnel to sustain a prominent role.

16 Realism begins from a Hobbesian starting point, seeing 'human nature' as leading to an international system characterised by power-hungry states (see Morgenthau, 2006). Neo-realism later abandoned this essentialism. Its adherents often begin from a 'structural' analysis; they too view actors in the international system as essentially self-interested; see Waltz (1979) for example.

17 Politicisation is perceived also as a growing problem in Britain, as Blair imported American-style Public Relations approaches, buying in 'spin' professionals like Campbell and 'political advisors'; yet this faced resistance, unlike the long-established individualism and private sector approach of the US (Jones, 2001c).

18 A direction came from Baghdad in this way for a 'Clean-up Nasirya' campaign, 'a sort of a crude info op'; CPA staff 'had about 5 days' notice ... to set up a recruitment process and buy overalls for these guys to work [and] be identifiable as working for the CPA and this would be great'. Apparently, when it was announced 'about 20,000 people turned up' leading to a riot (Interview: Weale, 26th November 2010).

19 Worden compiled a database of '210 million publicly available Facebook profiles' for research and social profiling (http://petewarden.typepad.com/searchbrowser/2010/02/how-to-split-up-the-us.html).

20 US officials often refer to an administration by the number of presidents – Bush was the 43rd.

21 Ahmed Chalabi, an Iraqi politician with the Iraqi National Congress, provided false information about Saddam Hussein possessing WMDs and having ties to Al Qaeda, on which US intelligence agencies based their justification of the Iraq invasion.

22 This has also been argued to have occurred in Britain, with Alastair Campbell (see Chapter 6).

23 This began to change in mid-2009 when officers were finally able to walk between bases in Kabul without flak jacket and helmet.

24 Often the motivation compelling individuals to use their initiative in propaganda planning beyond the formal structures was either the admirable concern with 'understanding' and communication with the theatre audience or concern with ensuring the message was sufficiently culturally appropriate to be 'received', and very often involved a confusion of the two.

25 In interview Mike Berry of the Glasgow Media Group commented that 'Research carried out in June 2005 showed that insurgent attacks in Iraq did not necessarily lead members of the public to support withdrawal of British troops. For some people insurgent attacks actually had the opposite effect of strengthening their conviction that troops should remain until stability was achieved'. Apparently 'The relationship here was complex and it is not possible to say that reports of atrocities carried out by insurgents would necessarily erode support for the occupation forces' (Interview: 30th May 2006).

26 This notion is related to Ellul's argument that democracy is ideologically linked to 'truth' and 'progress' and must be seen to triumph (1973: 232–235).

27 Rousseau once claimed that 'the people of England think they are free. They are gravely mistaken. They are only free during the election of Members of Parliament' (1968: 141).

28 McBride disclosed that 'Dan Gallant – yet another Potomac person who was working for Rumsfeld' came up with the idea for Guantanamo Bay (Interview: 5th June 2009).

5

Anglo-American relations in the counter-terrorism propaganda war

Introduction

This chapter will begin by tracing developing patterns of divergence and convergence in the perceived interests dominant in each country's leadership. The international system which permitted the emergence of a predominantly Anglo-American 'war on terror' was a security environment in transition. Former adversaries now competed in the marketplace of capitalism, with China a rising economic competitor to the US. The period was also characterised by the emerging international position of non-state actors; both as factors causing perceptions of insecurity (i.e. international terrorism) and as mediating forces (e.g. international institutions). The nature of the 'threat' was perceived as changing to one that slipped across national boundaries and rendered states devoid of solutions. As governments contemplated tackling an uneasy 'multi-polarity', the idea of 'collective security' became frequent in Western rhetoric. Yet the threat and promise of America's 'unipolar' hegemony still dominated international perceptions.

Material factors such as these shape every state's interpretation of 'threats' and 'needs', but besides economic, political and military security concerns, as stated in Chapter 1, social and cultural factors also play a role. The principles and ideological standpoints dominant in a society's leadership, and the nature of its bureaucracy and armed forces, are also determiners of such 'needs', assessments and responses. This chapter will present a very broad introductory overview that in no way seeks to encompass the significant political differences within each country's leadership. Instead it will underscore certain underlying assumptions and dominant arguments which drove the course of planning. It will show how, post-9/11, the Anglo-American relationship was perceived by many in each leadership as having utility. The chapter will argue that Britain's defence strategy was pragmatically steered towards complementing US capabilities (see also Miller 2004a) and spinning its 'expertise' in counter-insurgency warfare, for example, to engineer inroads for relative influence. The chapter will show how in some instances US restrictions and the perceived 'obstacles' mentioned above could be navigated through Anglo-American relationships.

Anglo-American relations and 9/11

The processes of media globalisation and the growth of trans-national issues blurred traditional borders, drawing international politics beyond mere state-to-state relations. By 2001 the question had been raised of whether the US was suffering imperial overstretch. Its rates of defence spending were seen as unsustainable, leading some to advocate cuts to America's readiness to fight: from 2.5 wars to 1.5 wars (Denoon, 2001). While escalating costs left America's economy increasingly strained, its ideological objectives and security concerns continued to sculpt interventionism into the heart of American policy. From isolationism, America has had a historic tension between its need to prioritise the domestic political context and, since the Cold War, to ensure its international dominance. A heightened sense of insecurity at the shifting security environment brought an American foreign and defence policy structured around the core objective of creating a global security environment dominated by the American values of 'freedom, democracy and free enterprise' (Office of the President of the United States, 2002). Only states which allied their political and economic system with the principles at the core of these US political interests could be tolerated. The systematic pursuit of these goals is confirmed by the military's 'Joint Vision': that 'America' might be 'persuasive in peace, decisive in war, pre-eminent in any form of conflict', increasingly, of course, in the information realm (Defense Technical Information Centre, 2000). Propaganda operations were intended 'to advance U.S. interests and security and to provide the moral basis for U.S. leadership in the world' (US Department of State, 2004). Consequently we have seen an increase in the use of economic policy, multilateral resolutions, high technology, propaganda and diplomacy over military means (as being less costly financially and politically), as America has been forced to broaden its approach, and in turn engage with its allies. Gradually America's military has moved from a position where it was 'too heavily relying on hard power' to a post-Iraq realisation 'that we had a lot more tools', even if it has sometimes struggled to coordinate them (Interview: Armitage, 21st July 2009). But as Nagl points out, 'The demands of conventional and unconventional warfare differ so greatly' that an 'organisational culture that makes it effective in achieving one is counter-productive in accomplishing the other'; therefore 'organisations should focus on achieving one critical mission' (2005: 219). Differing capabilities appear to favour an assistive, complementary relationship between the British and US defence arrangements.

American assessments of its external security environment have historically been in promoting a Europe that can protect its *own* interests (Nye, 2002a). Larger political frameworks such as the EU have played an increasing role in its vision of a stable Europe. European support for US ideological/strategic goals has not always been forthcoming and as Douglas Hurd observed during the Gulf War, Britain's relative independence from Europe enabled it to 'give a lead to Europe' which was 'an enormous help to United States policy' (Hennessy and Anstey, 1990: 27–28). As former White House advisor Robert Blackwill has noted, the US would rather deal with one coordinated body (a united Europe) than individual governments (Hennessy and Anstey, 1990: 28). The American vision for Britain to be a gatekeeper to this Europe has often conflicted with *British* political priorities: to swing the US's interests from its Pacific to its Atlantic shore.

Of course, the Anglo-American relationship has seen many changes in administration, and occasions where differing British and US interests led to diverging security needs and policies. Notably, despite reluctant US support for the Falklands War, Britain did not reciprocate in supporting the invasion of Grenada (Hennessy and Anstey, 1990). No international arrangement, even one this close, is ever viewed as irreversible and concrete by the states concerned. Leaderships change, as do geo-political, social, political, environmental and military conditions. Where cooperation occurs, ultimately states back collective agreements with unilateral defence strategies. While cultures change more slowly, and states seek to maintain the image internally and externally that they are peaceful and committed to any agreement, if the leadership perceive it as no longer suiting their needs they will pursue other means to achieve their security goals, as America did in Iraq. The quest to gain power and influence that drives much of each country's foreign policy is thus coupled with attempts to neutralise or nurture other interests and actors.

Under Blair, the reformist ideology of 'New Labour' blamed the British Labour Party's former image and ideology for perceived domestic and international failures. With Germany the lead economy in Europe, Britain as a state has balanced its interests carefully in order to maximise its respective power and influence in the world. Since alienating Europe could prove extremely damaging economically and strategically, Blair maintained relationships pragmatically. And although Labour had *traditionally* embraced Anglo-American relations, New Labour challenged what *they* saw as a move away from the US (Morgan, 2002: 182). There were more ideological differences with Bush than with Clinton, who had shared Blair's vision of a 'third way', something that caused Chris Meyer, the British Ambassador in Washington, 'massive anxiety' at first (Meyer, 2009). But Blair's transformation led to an acceptance of Thatcherite economic principles, embracing business and the role of the market, which brought Britain closer to the US in ideological terms – so much so that the claim of dominant American neo-liberal theorists that an open international economy would promote stability (Nye, 2002a) was accepted as a strong element of coalition strategy for post-conflict 'reconstruction'. Ultimately, one of the most fundamental UK defence policy aims in 2003 was 'maintenance of the transatlantic relationship', and Europe's strategic importance was defined in relation to global threats to British and 'wider Western interests' (MoD, 2003a: 4; MoD, 2003b: 5). The Prime Minister did not encounter the indecisiveness in foreign policy that frustrated him with Clinton (Sharp, 2003: 60) and shared Bush's tendency to see situations in a simplistic, ideological way. As Roy Jenkins put it, they saw 'matters in stark terms of good and evil ... and with a consequent belief that if evil is cast down good will inevitably follow' (Jenkins, 2002, quoted in Sharp, 2003: 63). Even setting aside ideological factors, Britain's ongoing commitment to the alliance was so central to its foreign policy that solid support was a certainty.

On top of this, 9/11 brought mutual insecurity; as such a close American ally, Blair's government now saw Britain as a possible target for Islamic extremists. Beyond its physical threat, 'terrorism' demonstrates the conditional nature of the sovereign state to its citizens, weakens its power and interrogates perceptions of its unquestioned permanence. Britain's large Muslim population meant policy decisions would have unique implications for domestic stability. This was true also of the subsequent invasion of Iraq. And with ties to Pakistan, the Middle East, ongoing involvement in Iraq, Iran and even Afghanistan itself, Britain had historic interests in the region. According to one Iraq expert's belief, in Basra 'there is a perception that the British, before the invasion, back in the 50s and 60s contributed toward the local infrastructure, and the running of local oil companies. So ... the British have a good reputation' (Interview: Anonymous 2010).[1]

Defence Secretary Geoff Hoon considered Iran of greater British concern than Iraq, but with a twenty-first-century reduced-capability Britain unable to respond to all perceived security interests, the leadership saw diplomatic links (particularly American ties) as of crucial importance (MoD, 2003a: 10, 11, 19). As late as 2006 it was predicted that 'The US will remain the most influential global actor'; this increasingly unsound prediction shaped and legitimised planning throughout (Foreign & Commonwealth Office, 2006). Like the American leadership, Tony Blair perceived the emergence of an international perception of Britain that ran counter to his government's foreign policy goals. British propaganda capabilities, like wider defence resource, are dwarfed by American capabilities and Blair sought Britain's response to its concrete and informational insecurities in Anglo-American emphasis. If a state risks more by going it alone, even if this means maximising gains, then committing trust to a cooperative agreement can often be seen as the most advantageous and economical way to provide for its security (see Glaser, 1994–5). While the leaders' bond was not immediate, Bush and Blair were brought closer by the events of 9/11, the

American people finding Blair a reassuring ally. Elite perceptions sought propaganda and wider security solutions in a closer cooperation, both to limit potential harm to their own national priorities and ensure their concerns fed into coalition outcomes. As Prime Minister, Gordon Brown furthermore continued to support the war and US commitments made during Blair's administration.

Pimlott has observed how during the 1960s Britain had little choice but to embrace the Anglo-American relationship, and its comparative strength when its leadership considered Iraq gave it more power (2002: 191). It seems likely that shared fears and ideological visions, combined with domestic political and economic concerns for 'stability', and desire for influence in the region, drove Blair's foreign policies more than any dutiful obedience of America. This is supported by Woodward's observation that Bush called Blair on 9th March and offered an opt-out; an

> extraordinary opportunity to essentially remove the UK from a combat role in Iraq and the Prime Minister said: 'Absolutely not. I have made the commitment and I am with you to the end.' (2004: 338)

Some pointed to this as another sign that Britain was non-essential. Yet beforehand it seems Condoleezza Rice told Bush that Blair might lose his government over the deep domestic discontent with the Iraq War, so Woodward suggests Bush was offering appreciation for loyalty and commitment (2004: 338). Loss of Britain would have damaged American credibility and the 'opt-out' would have been a way to 'cut American losses' were Blair to fall. It pre-empted a disaster in perception management and optimised operational (and competing domestic) objectives. According to Blair's Iraq Inquiry testimony, in early 2002 when the decision to go to war was made, Bush apparently described his fear to him that 'if we weren't prepared to act in a really strong way, then we ran the risk of sending a disastrous signal out to the world' (Blair, 2010). Blair confirmed how this meant 'Our own strategy was going to have to evolve in the light of that' commitment to America (Blair, 2010). As Iraq was 'essentially a British and American operation', rather than 'a NATO operation', Anglo-American link-up and coordination were deeper during this conflict (Interview: Arundell, 18th April 2013). Blair's policies sought to provide capabilities that would complement US defence systems and responsive solutions for American problems. Some might suggest the UK leadership was therefore operating in the 'service' of America, but this would be reductive. It was a facilitator with a stake in the outcomes.

Providing complementary capabilities

Despite claims of a desire to juggle relationships with both Europe and the US, the decisiveness of British policy shows this to be a hollow image, with America solidly at the forefront of Blair's foreign policy. Following 9/11 British support was immediate, and in Iraq, Britain's official foreign policy position remained unwaveringly loyal to the US. An FCO report declared that:

> The USA has achieved unequalled power. It is an indispensable partner for our security and it shares our values. A close relationship with Washington that serves and protects UK interests will remain a vital asset for this country. (Foreign & Commonwealth Office, 2004: 147)

Despite overtures as a pro-Europe leader, Blair snubbed European allies, particularly on the issue of Iraq. In 2007 David Miliband still maintained America was 'the single most important bilateral relationship' (Miliband, 2007). A significant military contribution was perceived by the leadership to be the way to secure influence with America, but British resource was quite limited. This section will argue that in terms of fire-power and net resource, much of the British contribution brought negligible comparative weight. But politically and in its flexible planning responses and propaganda it was valuable to America and the propaganda war. British military value depended on:

- Providing unique capabilities;
- Complementary provision;
- Closing potential capability gaps with its ally.

British policy emphasised 'interoperability', converging doctrine and providing unique capabilities in an attempt to secure 'fit' and relative value to America, all factors which shaped the propaganda war.

Both countries' leaderships sought to maximise overall resource in meeting coalition objectives and thus sought to ensure each country's capabilities were utilised to best effect. This resulted in a security strategy where Britain was increasingly focused on ensuring it could provide unique capabilities to complement its key ally's abilities, rather than providing comparative forces. The maintenance of a division of labour was intended to meet the leaderships' 'shared' goals in the conflicts. Britain strove to 'provide those capabilities that deliver the greatest impact when operating alongside the US' (MoD, 2003a: 8). While this is generally concerned with formal kinetic military systems, similar trends can be observed in the information realm. One example where 'unique' capabilities were offered to the alliance was propaganda, including processes in which one partner is able to offer a capability which the other lacks or would find problematic to obtain themselves. The power of information and communication can arguably allow a militarily inferior country such as Britain to punch above its weight (Keohane and Nye, 1998). While America also assisted Britain, this was a deeply established British defence strategy. One writer has stated that about 40 per cent of CIA activities to prevent terrorist attacks on America are focused in Britain (Shipman, 2009).

Of course, trans-national structures such as NATO play a powerful role in cementing the kinds of commitments we are looking at here, as well as bringing policies and interests closer together. Kirsteen Rowlands describes the current position:

> the construct if you like is the NATO framework is the top level ... which influences our NSC Communications Strategy, which provides the umbrella from which other departments can then create their own communications plans, but taking their objectives and initiative directly from the top. (Interview: 17th April 2013)

Britain's positions relative to America and relative to NATO are inter-dependent and are operated likewise. Accordingly, British forces were the 'Allied Rapid Reaction Corps lead for NATO when the ISAF operation was ramped up in 2005'. British privileged American access in Iraq still went beyond that of other NATO members (Email: Anonymous, 2010). This has relevance too in the information realm. Interoperability and the homogenisation of doctrine have been assisted through NATO and increasing multilateral force participation. Some see a key US role in 'encouraging' multinational organisations like NATO in the development and implementation of American propaganda strategy (Jones, 2005: 111).

There was a homogenisation of doctrine between the two countries. To have utility it was considered necessary for British expertise to complement American expertise and for British forces to be interoperable in command and control as well as operationally (MoD, 2003a). Doctrine emphasised interconnectivity as crucial to coordinating their counter-terrorism wars so that the countries could work together with fluidity (MoD, 2003a; MoD, 2003b). Interconnectivity rests in large part on forces ensuring interoperability – the ability to 'fit' together and function in a complementary way. UK policy underscored a move towards adapting British capabilities into an American-centric system (see MoD, 2003a). US arms exports to Britain in 2001 were an incredible $1,247M (SIPRI, 15th July 2013).

The MoD now considered it crucial to ensure 'doctrine is coherent and relevant to US-led operations' (MoD, 2003b: 36). The discussion of a 'Revolution in Military Affairs' (RMA) might be said to have triggered a homogenisation of doctrine as it brought a redefined image of the future of defence as exploitation of information advantage. RMA built on conventional forms of military action, and going into Iraq it influenced MoD doctrine and investment in networking the military with allies (MoD, 2003a). '4th Generation Warfare' was seen as providing an 'agility' that also became the cornerstone of the MoD's new doctrine (MoD, 2003a; MoD, 2003b). The RMA/4th Generation debate influenced the new 'effects-based' approaches that the US and Britain started to develop out of the early failures of the 'War on Terror'.

Likewise, there were attempts to develop complementary systems such as Britain's Defence Media Operations Centre, where personnel were trained, which was established by Taverner and drew on an American model:

> I got quite friendly with ... my opposite numbers who ran a thing called DINFOS ... the Defense Information School, it's where they train *all* their Public Affairs people ... it came out – we did a lot of interaction with the Americans just to see what their school looked like, how it worked and what lessons we could draw from it. (Interview: 23rd January 2013)

Torie Clarke said this type of exchange happened a lot between the two countries (Interview: 4th December 2013). Moves toward complementary 'systems' and strategy such as RMA, 4th Generation warfare and a striving towards interoperability in general have functioned to secure American preference, formed the basis of a working relationship and demonstrated commitment.

Working against US systems: NOFORN for the British

As established above, the American bureaucracy was insular and structurally resistant to cross-government coordination, let alone Anglo-American collaboration. This was not uniform though, and a growth of informal networks led to variation. Informal information 'priority channels' formed between the countries where organs of government were most receptive. Some senior bureaucratic coordination efforts were strongly focused on maintaining consistency and allowed inlets through which informal coordination between the countries took shape. This enabled the adjustment of statements to facilitate the partnership and propaganda, mediating perceptions both of the alliance internationally and of each ally by the other. The Anglo-American links were nurtured to enable British in-roads into American planning, and, for sections of the American government and military, were crucial channels enabling them to navigate obstructions in the American system. Britain acted as a necessary enabler alongside a US system that struggled against insular agencies. Facilitating operations in turn enhanced perceptions of British relative 'value' to America, but in a huge government this occurred only among those who saw the immediate benefits.

Despite their efforts to enable 'interconnectivity' and closeness with the US, the insularity of the Pentagon and other American agencies impinged on formal Anglo-American cooperation. John Sattler, former Director of Strategic Plans and Policy for the Joint Chiefs of Staff and Commander of US Troops in Iraq, argued that allies were not treated as 'members of the team' (in Erwin, 2009).

Franklin Miller argued that a lack of outreach by the Pentagon to British counterparts was exacerbated by a huge purge of staff from the Pentagon after each election and

> the people coming in don't necessarily know the people they're dealing with ... Two weeks wouldn't go by without me talking to one of my British counterparts about something. But unless that's in your bloodstream you don't know that. (Interview: 3rd August 2009)

Miller observed that Obama's Defense Department was better but 'their experience is not with allies, it's with US Force Structure Issues' having come in after the coalition assault. Despite these issues, an America where elements were becoming more receptive to informal ways of operating was a crucial inlet for British planners. Miller observed that the Ministry of Defence had a more constant culture, a crucial factor in securing relationships, and that Britain would be forced to do the outreach 'until the relationship was an equal one' (Interview: 3rd August 2009). Formal systems were a constant problem which worsened as turf wars affected the US defence structure and ensured British inroads had to be negotiated informally.

Classification

With Rumsfeld's Pentagon impeding coordination within the US it is unsurprising that they were also obstructive with allies. British personnel reported that additional security clearance was required on top of that normally demanded when working with Americans. Former Flight Lieutenant Iain Paton described at the Iraq Inquiry the level of security in Iraq planning as greater than during 'Operation VERITAS [Afghanistan] and ... other military tasks during my career', a level 'rarely employed or encountered except for extremely sensitive matters such as intelligence, cryptography or strategic nuclear defense' (11th March 2010). One commentator has stated that

> allies are being asked to participate in coalitions that exist only on paper. In the real world of military operations — where the United States is the dominant force ... allies play on the sidelines, if at all. (Erwin, 2009)

In guidance sent to CENTCOM around the beginning of August 2002, for distribution to propaganda planners, senior Pentagon officials had plans for an ultimatum to Baghdad. But the document, described as 'an update of work done months ago', warned that 'we should aim to delay Saddam's recognition of the *imminence* of his downfall for as long as possible' (DOD, 2002). It is likely that this thinking limited US defence openness both with the public and allies during the run-up to war and restrictions became institutionalised by Pentagon insularity and momentum. US bureaucrats, if pushed for time and unsure of the security status, stamped documents with 'NOFORN' (no foreign) by default, restricting distribution according to one US official (Interview: Anonymous, 1st June 2009). Joel Harding described how,

> the declassification process is sometimes overseen by some intelligence prude [who] gets a wild hair up his backside, but that's getting less frequent. When I first began doing intelligence work I threw all kinds of declassification exceptions on everything I wrote, citing all kinds of really flakey reasons (none good). (Email: 3rd May 2013b)

In 2013–14, Edward Snowden, a US intelligence operative, leaked thousands of classified documents to the media. He revealed massive domestic and global surveillance by the NSA, GCHQ and other 'Five Eyes' governments (Australia, Canada, New Zealand), along with the cooperation of companies such as Google and Verizon. It also emerged that the NSA was funding GCHQ's activities (see Hopkins and Borger, 2013). For Torie Clarke it was not the activities themselves that were the problem, but over-zealous classification by intelligence personnel who then neglected the really important secrets:

> It's terrible it happened, not necessarily for all of the reasons that most people say ... But one of the reasons it happened was ... we and other governments classify way too much information ... that information that really *should* be protected doesn't get the care and attention it needs and ... we give way too many people access to classified information so it has the effect of 'cheapening the brand' if you will, and ... there aren't serious enough consequences for those who do leak classified information. (Interview: 4th December 2013)

Franklin Miller's recollections of the Pentagon were that 'just after the first phase of combat ended' in Iraq a bureaucratic trend towards over-classification and 'US only communications and US only intelligence began to reappear', becoming obstructive to the alliance (Interview: 3rd August 2009). The MoD's Angus Taverner observed from his experience that 'The famous share of intelligence is ... it's not very good' (Interview: 23rd January 2013). Miller said he tried to overcome these problems: 'we took steps to get an interagency agreement, which the President signed that knocked all those barriers down only to have bureaucrats in the Pentagon refuse to carry out the order' (Interview: 3rd August 2009).

One purpose of the sharing of information is what Jeffrey Jones called an 'enduring requirement' to 'assess ground truth and the resonance of [US] messages' (2005: 111). Intelligence is different from Target Audience Analysis (TAA), as it does not use

> qualitative and quantitative research methods to determine the motivations for specific group behaviours in advance. It is very good at telling you that a group of men have laid IEDs on a road, for example, but not why they decided upon that course of action in the first place. (Email: Tatham, 11th February 2013)[2]

But intel *can* be used to assist with profiling by the Information Operations staff within the MoD who have security clearance (Interview: Taverner, 23rd January 2013). This access of course depends where they sit in government.

Taverner explained that with, 'SIS, CIA, DIA, NSA, GCHQ ... It is extremely difficult then to declassify that lot to a level where you can push it forward and that makes our lives difficult' even within the country. There were no informal solutions either, as 'firewalls even between the various agencies are really quite firm'. This has implications, as

> the profiling you may have done is such that you don't want to then push that down to – out to a much wider audience. Because the sources from which you've drawn that profile are vulnerable ... this is where this trust thing comes in ... trust is placed in the attending staff to get it right. So it's not for me to sort of sit there and say 'How did you find that out?' Which is perhaps me being w– perhaps a weakness in me ... being a soldier. (Interview: Taverner, 23rd January 2013)

The US Human Terrain System (HTS) which was established under Petraeus in 2007, was intended to 'augment [traditional TAA] with better understanding of local views, concerns and preferences' (Email: McFate, 7th March 2013). But its insights weren't available to all; one Australian analyst complained that HTS findings

> were on a classified system I didn't have access to. Even the Americans I worked with couldn't always get into the information. Ultimately we gave up trying because it was too difficult.

During 2008–10 access was still seen as a problem for allies; one former Australian ISAF Target Audience Analyst talked about working in multinational groups and the difficulties of

> all the different classification systems, and computer networks and databases that some of us could and some of us could not access. The rules kept changing and it was always difficult to keep up. But in the end it didn't matter – the 'intelligence' was never nearly as useful as the information we'd get from our Afghan colleagues ... Invariably, if a bomb went off in the city they would know before the military intelligence guys where it was, who it was targeting, etc. Of course as soon as the intell folks got hold of the information, parts of it would become classified and we could no longer discuss this with the Afghans. (Email: Hanasz, 30th April 2013)

The Americans may not always have even been aware of the extent of British discontent. Having had a strategic level vantage-point and involvement in 'pre-war meetings', Franklin Miller said,

> I don't know that every piece of advice the UK offered was followed. But ... I was close enough to my British colleagues that I believe I would've gotten blow-back from people saying 'Why do you keep ignoring us?' or after the fact, you know, 'Well ... if you guys had listened to us in the first place it would've been better.'

Nobody ever said that to me and so I would crawl out on that limb and assert that
in large measure ... the British voice was heard. (Interview: 3rd August 2009)

Former Deputy Secretary of State Richard Armitage observed that the British
'had access everywhere, Secretary of State, Secretary of Defense, National
Security Advisors. They knew fully what was going on' (Interview: 21st July
2009). Miller thought that cooperation 'probably happens more at the State
Department'. He said that he 'was never aware of a significant outreach by the
Defense Department civilians to the leadership in UK' (Interview: Miller, 3rd
August 2009). As Armitage recalled, State Department dialogue was 'always very
in-depth and ... when they came in to us they got the Queen's jewels. As we felt
they were engaged in this endeavour and they deserved it.' He recalled that

> even before the decision that we made ... I'm pretty proud of being part of it ... to
> give the British and Australians much more access up to about 99 per cent of our
> intelligence ... they were probably about 92–93 per cent before.... There were very
> few secrets, that's the one thing about the, quote, 'Special Relationship' that is true.
> (Interview: Armitage, 21st July 2009)

Anglo-American planning was still difficult. Interviews with Miller and others
indicated that insular systems began to be resisted and navigated by individuals,
realising occupational demands as best they could through informal channels.
When questioned about whether a lack of dialogue with the Pentagon made the
British relationship more difficult, Miller responded 'Definitely not. I think that
the informal contacts facilitated that' (3rd August 2009). Significantly, there
appears to have been British primacy in facilitating these channels with receptive
Americans, performing an essential function for the US executive.

Managing cultures

The continuation of the 'special relationship' (as supporting the working
alliance itself) operates as an easy focal point with ready discourse. Supported
through wider culture and propaganda, this functions conceptually as part of
(especially British) *national* institutional cultures and the 'community' of close
Anglo-American elite relationships. It feeds into the domestic institutional
cultures, contributes to perceptions of 'mutual interest' and provides a
framework for pursuing relations.

Kier argues that 'the organizational culture is the intervening variable
between civilian decisions and military doctrine' (1995: 66). Mutual cooperation is thus essential for an alliance to be strongly woven into the institutional
culture of each country and its discourse. Just as the media can be seen as
'contested space' (Eldridge, 1995: 25), so too can the discourse of the bureaucracy and military. Elaborating a concept derived from Foucault, Stuart Hall

argues that discourses are 'ways of talking, thinking, or representing a particular subject' and 'this knowledge influences social practices, and so has real consequences and effects' (1996: 205). Discourses 'are part of the way power circulates and is contested', effectively 'organizing and regulating relations of power' (Hall, 1996: 205). So, while material interests remained very real, within government history, ideology, horizontal propaganda and converging doctrine also framed goals within an image of unity, bridging differences and solidifying mutual perceptions of Anglo-American commitment. An underlying acceptance of common interest was reinforced on both sides. By former Deputy Secretary of State Richard Armitage's account, 'We shared a general value and a general enemy. So that's a pretty good basis to start. We'd consult constantly about how we'd determine the outcome' (Interview: 21st July 2009).

Cultural construction of British 'expertise'

The British viewed enduring positive American assessments of British 'unique' capabilities and 'expertise' as key to sustaining their connections. Indeed, Sir John Reith argued in his Iraq Testimony that his experience from the Gulf War added crucial credibility with the Americans including CENTCOM Commander Tommy Franks, saying they 'very much work on ... do they trust somebody, is he of the right calibre for him to work with' (Reith, 2010). The continuation of perceptions of British historical 'expertise' particularly in counter-insurgency (discussed in Chapter 4) helped sustain connections, keeping British prominence in US planning and thinking, where kinetically their utility was questionable. Indeed, Chris Meyer described in his Iraq Testimony how as Ambassador in Washington

> wherever you went – you didn't have to do anything, just walk through a door – people would rise to their feet and give you a sort of storming round of applause. So you had to – you know, you had to be careful not to be swept away by this stuff. (26th November 2009)

But within US culture, Col. Ralph Arundell learned 'very quickly ... that British self-deprecation and understatement doesn't work and if you don't stand there going "Do you know what, I'm bloody marvellous, I'm bloody brilliant" – they look at you as though you're completely stupid' (Interview: 18th April 2013).

Former NSC Director for Strategic Communications and Information, Jeffrey Jones, said to build 'enduring bridges of understanding' America needed an integrated strategy, to include '*reassurance* for friends' and '*persuasion* of friends, allies, adversaries and neutrals' (2005: 111). Britain was demonstrably the weaker partner and US attentions were widely drawn, so for the British leadership showing 'value' was the natural bedrock of building coordination that might influence US objectives. Propaganda and diplomacy communicate the image of its intentions that each state wishes to transmit to its partner and globally; to redress any perceptions that do not complement its security arrangements. They provide a reassuring counterbalance, with which each country is able to act according to its own foreign policy goals, whilst also sere-nading those of its partner.

A sense of agreement over histories, 'shared' interests and the cultivation of perceptions of each country and the alliance itself helped adhere the informal relationships which became important to coordination. Given the power differ-ential, ensuring influence over perceived 'shared' interests is a function of the relationship which was of great significance to Britain's leadership, both in terms of 'selling' this notion to its *own* public and military, and in terms of ensuring continued *American* value through the maintenance of the relation-ships. Notions of British 'expertise' were emphasised during the 'War on Terror' as a means to unify Britain's domestic military, and also played on American sentiment for tradition. Conceptually British 'expertise' within the wider notion of a 'special relationship' was a means for Britain's leadership to demonstrate the value Britain offered. Through building connections of value to American partners it could negotiate and shape 'shared' interests that conformed to contemporary British leadership interests.

Underpinning the notion of British 'expertise' are past colonial experiences (that of Major-General David Lloyd Owen OBE, the late British Commander and Military Assistant to the High Commissioner in Malaya, for example: 'my generation and above have spent so much of their career doing colonial policing that we'd better bloody well be good at it' (quoted in Nagl, 2005: 205)). Some argue that residual pride, confidence and expectation stem from British geography and 'freedom from foreign conquest' which built a historic 'confi-dence in victory' into military culture (Woodward, 1947: 530–547). David French (2011) points out that British 'expertise' in COIN and 'hearts and minds' is a highly romanticised construction and de-emphasises the coercion, bloodshed and fear that were integral to its historical colonial 'expertise'. To US planners like the State Department's Richard Armitage Britain's relationship in the region, and its having historically 'had a bad experience in Iraq', meant it was still seen, militarily and bureaucratically, as having valuable insight. He said he found 'some of [Britain's] Iraq-watchers to be extraordinary' (Interview: 21st July 2009). Similarly, Franklin Miller argued that

> in some places ... [British] regional and country expertise is much better than ours and I think that's true even today ... And in part because you've got relations with Iran, so you have Diplomats who've been on the ground in Iran, whereas we have not since 1979. So I think in many areas your talents and capabilities are deeper than ours yes ... And I've done what I can to try to get people, even ... at your Embassy here, with these kind of backgrounds to be more well known to their American colleagues. (Interview: 3rd August 2009)

This was common throughout the diplomatic and bureaucratic realm, and militarily Britain's experience in Ireland was often referenced as an example of greatly respected counter-insurgency skills.

Contractors offered a more stable concept of experience than British forces due to their ability to specialise, but with varying results. For example, the central $293m contract in Iraq was controversially granted to Aegis, a UK company established by former British Col. Tim Spicer whose troops in Ireland were implicated in a human rights violation. Aegis was to act as a coordinating interface between the US military and its other contractors.

Former Pentagon anthropologist Montgomery McFate had studied British counter-insurgency in Northern Ireland and sought to bring this to the US, stating that 'deep cultural knowledge is inherent to the British approach' (McFate, 2005). Some British personnel believe that the more experience the Americans get, the fewer the capability gaps, and the less vital British 'expertise' becomes (Interview: 15th Army PSYOP Group, 22nd November 2005). Also, Heginbotham observes that traditionally 'reliance on a combination of single-arm regimental standards and on ad-hoc guidelines issued by theatre commanders permitted continued innovation' for the British military, but this meant 'little accumulation of knowledge' (1996: 1–2). British military personnel change post frequently compared to America's career officers; British PSYOP personnel are largely reservists but from related civilian positions. They have 'a strong sense of institutional memory' that serves to sustain this sense of British 'experience' but very little training to accompany the British military 'initiative' and confidence (Interview: Anonymous, 16th August 2010).

Language reflects wider domestic military relations, and functions to solidify perceptions, bonds and status in relation to the partner. Cultural stereotypes underpin relationships (both within the same institutional culture and between each country's personnel), and can preserve consistency in understandings, hierarchy and assumptions in a fast-changing, unsettling world. The Anglo-American military culture generated often paternalistic 'cynicism and amusement' about 'the "spams" and the "septics" (from Septic Tank = Yank)' from the British side (Email: Anonymous, 2010). References to the affinity between the cultures was frequently apparent in interview and interviewees seemed to use these as a way to build a relationship and rapport. While I did not refer to the history of the 'special relationship' in my questions, the predominantly white, American elite interviewees were keen to reference history and personal or societal 'roots'. The language of the relationship slipped easily from tongues. This is an elite discourse in which the two countries' dealings are often still shackled. Franklin Miller referred to the 'grand relationship' (Interview: 3rd August 2009) and former Deputy Secretary of State Armitage mused that there were 'No more Yalta moments ... No more Yalta moments for the Brits' (Interview: 21st July 2009).[3] Similarly, when interview discussions probed

Anglo-American cooperation in intelligence agency propaganda, and responses became vague, it proved an easy non-confrontational way to dispel difficult questions. Having diverted the subject from intelligence agency propaganda collaboration, Miller continued through the ease of historical cliché:

> But, broadly put ... the symbiotic relationship between the American and British intelligence communities is terribly, terribly important. We each bring something to that game, which is unique, even if it's only perspectives, and so it's an area which has been fundamental to the special relationship. (Interview: 3rd August 2009)

While American society offers great rewards for the powerful, there remains an unsatisfied desire for history and ceremonial tradition. Its pragmatic ally seeks to exploit this void and provide symbolic fulfilment.[4] Armitage explained:

> Well I'm very, very proud ... and perhaps the biggest surprise in my professional life was receiving a knighthood. And the reason I was so surprised, I think it happened ... And I've determined my own mind ... it was all about communication. It was a great appreciation that both Powell and I went out of our way to ensure that our key ally in this endeavour never got surprised. And that is not the reason listed in the KCMG, but I am quite sure that happened. As ... we never got caught out.

A possible implication was that Armitage's knighthood may have been conferred on an unwritten understanding that it represented British gratitude for American efforts in coordination of information release so that Britain 'never got surprised' (Interview: 21st July 2009).

As Gorman and MacLean have noted, propaganda's effectiveness to a great extent 'depends on its success in tapping into people's existing beliefs and direct experience' (2003: 118). The notion of British experience, realised through 'collective memory', thus also provides a horizontal propaganda function which could be built upon. As Shy points out, in military organisational culture beyond power and interest 'a remembered past has always more or less constricted both action in the present and thinking about the future' (1971: 210). Maintaining preference for British expertise was one way in which Britain would be able to maintain the connections it needed to enhance its position vis-a-vis America. Nagl argues that 'understanding how [past] is remembered by those who direct an organisation's present and future, is essential to understanding how that organisation will adapt to changes in its environment' (2005: 216). 'Unique' capabilities and cultures and British 'experience' functioned domestically as a source of pride, but also functioned within the relationship, playing on the predilections toward history and tradition of an often ex-military American leadership.

The social theorist Raymond Williams argues that the 'residual' or received cultures of the past are 'always easier to understand'; that culture can often default back to meanings and values which were created in actual societies and actual situations in the past, and which still seem to have significance because they represent areas of human experience, aspiration and achievement which the dominant culture neglects, undervalues, opposes, represses, or even cannot recognise. (1989: 123–124)

British history and tradition were reported to be a source of great respect for US personnel and Britain's PSYOP officers said this meant in real terms that people listened to them and clear dialogue was enabled between the US and UK at all levels (Interview: 15th Army PSYOP Group, 22nd November 2005).

American perceptions of free thinking, wider experience and flexibility of British personnel translated into greater powers, with British PSYOP personnel routinely being given a higher rank than normal when posted to work with US troops. British assistance in the 'planning component' was said to be given 'considerable weight'. With PSYOP 'on the ground' there was considerable Anglo-American 'co-operation with liaison officers in both national' headquarters (Interviews: 15th Army PSYOP Group, 22nd November 2005). American respect served to boost British personnel's view of the American troops and confirm their sense of pride. A British Flight Lieutenant perceived Americans he encountered as 'very courteous and usually well educated, certainly at the [Non-Commissioned Officer – NCO] and officer level. Highly professional as well ... their word is their bond.' US personnel were generally highly regarded by British personnel, reportedly far from the 'gung-ho' stereotype; the Flight Lieutenant joked that this was more at a political level (Email: Anonymous, 2010). Correspondingly the British military's institutional memory is argued to be very conservative (Interview: Anonymous, 16th August 2010), based on a strategic culture still influenced by the 'legacy of great power status' and a 'political culture that values evolutionary change, continuity and tradition' (Macmillan, 1995: 34–36). This has shaped its engagement both with American allies and within the theatre of war.

Class remains a persistent issue within the British military, and one former PSYOP officer described how certain reservists were 'excused certain types of duties and have certain types of privileges' despite only an 'absolute minimum' of military skills. My interviewee argued that 'basically the difference between the two is your accent, and the school you went to. There's still an awful lot of that' (Interview: Anonymous, 16th August 2010). This ingrained sense of class made lunch in the Officers' Mess at the PSYOP base in Chicksands feel like high tea at an Oxford college. A former PSYOP officer painted a vivid caricature of 'British experience' impacting approaches in the field, as something apart from actual 'practical experience', more a

collective memory, self identity and understanding within the British armed forces that they are good at colonial warfare, that they are good at turning out in

Nyasaland, talking to the chiefs, getting the natives in line, lining people up with a picture of Queen Victoria, and giving them all a Martini-Henry rifle. (Interview: Anonymous, 16th August 2010)

Human rights lawyer Phil Shiner has contended that this fed into British abuse of Iraqis which could not be dismissed as 'one-offs', but was 'colonial savagery' reflective of a wider systemic problem (Cusick, 24th October 2010). The CPA's Deputy Governor of Dhi Qar province Adrian Weale argued that in reality

There was a problem certainly among the British ... a lot of British officers had read Lawrence of Arabia and ... they had a rather romantic idea about ... the social structures within modern Iraqi society which didn't quite fit in.

Thus Weale argued that 'Iraqi society had changed a lot under Saddam Hussein' and now

many Iraqis that I spoke to felt that this was ... an anachronistic process that we were encouraging ... that they'd been happy to get rid of the tribal influence over the years and the British Army ... were trying to engage [tribal leaders] and giving them a sort of power and status which they hadn't had. (Interview: 26th November 2010)

This contrasted with perceptions of American personnel; a PSYOP officer said there was a general American attitude of 'Why can't these bloody Iraqis be more like us!', which translated into a PSYOP policy on the ground of 'Liberating means turning into Americans.' He observed that 'at the *officer* level, it was that failure to' recognise that

other countries *exist* ... are not just *behind* on a path to reaching the American ideal, they are actually different and I think the British had a much greater sense of that but the British went into colonial mode. It's all about 'how you treat the natives'. So the Americans were all brash and ... the British approach was basically to treat them a bit like ... poor blighted states. (Interview: Anonymous, 16th August 2010)

The PSYOP officer observed that both approaches embodied the notion of superiority; for the British, that 'we're better and we're different, and we *acknowledge* the difference, whereas the American approach is we're better and there is no difference and you're going to be like *us*' (Interview: Anonymous, 16th August 2010). However, attitudes toward Americans were seen to embody a certain arrogance that emerged from a British institutional culture which emphasised its own 'expertise' (Interview: Weale, 26th November 2010). This was presented in interviews as a sense of paternalism; that we might not like what 'they' (the Americans) are doing, but it would be a lot worse if 'we' weren't there. Both allies and enemies alike have an evolving relationship relative to the British 'institutional memory'.

Limits of British counter-insurgency 'expertise'

As war progressed in Iraq it became glaringly obvious that British unique capabilities and thus 'expertise' could not be defined by its conventional kinetic activities. US adaptation began to crystallise in 2007 with the rise of Gen. David Petraeus, a fan of the British Special Forces flexible approach, who collaborated with 'Military Initiative' expert John Nagl on America's new counter-insurgency doctrine. It was Petraeus's surge-and-soft-power that brought in 'Human Terrain Systems' and the 'whole government' approach to warfare (Schaub, 2008). Increasingly American troops were brought in to support Helmand in Afghanistan, as British regular troops were seen as *kinetically* 'not up to the task'. An embassy cable from 2008 suggests that the counter-insurgency was achieving 'progress' but the Afghans agreed that American troops were necessary to secure Helmand (US Embassy, Kabul, 2008). Although, as Robert Fox observes 'much of the new Petraeus thinking comes from British experience' in counter-insurgency, its regular forces had slowly been devalued in American eyes (24th April 2008). In 2008 the *Daily Mail* quoted a Whitehall anecdote: when prompted to justify what makes Britain's military unique, a serving Chief of Staff reportedly said, 'We're the only nation in the world that doesn't make military ceremonial ridiculous – and we have the SAS' (Hastings, 22nd April 2008).

British counter-insurgency in Ireland is even referenced as an example in the US Army guide (DOD, 2007: 3–18). But Corcoran warned that while 'intelligent influencing activity' was 'much lauded' as 'an area of historical strength', officers 'shouldn't take it too much for granted' (Interview: 8th June 2006). Regarding British experience of insurgency and fighting terrorism in Ireland, Armitage noted that

> Originally, around 2003, British were sayin' look, we had the Northern Ireland experience, this is why we don't walk around in hard hats and helmets, we walk around with our berets. Well, you can guess what happened ... pretty soon they start to get picked off ... and Muqtada Al-Sadr started acting up. And the next thing you know we're not only wearing full body armour and helmets, but they're hunkered down in the airfield! Which caused us to say ... what about the Northern Ireland experience? It didn't work. So what're you gonna do now?

In a restrained evaluation of the British approach he concluded, 'I don't think it was wildly more successful than ours' (Interview: Armitage, 21st July 2009). In interview, British personnel indicated how they prided themselves on a soft approach, soft berets, talking to the Mullahs etc, and boasted of the success of this approach relative to US heavy-handedness (Interviews: 15th Army PSYOP Group, 22nd November 2005; Interview: Taverner, 18th July 2004). To this Armitage responded, 'Great, and at the end of the day – what happened? How's Basra now? It's controlled by gangs' (Interview: Armitage, 21st July 2009). This contrasts with the impression created by the Anglo-American propaganda campaign which accompanied the step-down. In reality personnel 'assumed that it was going to be much like our experience in Northern Ireland' (Interview: Weale, 26th November 2010).

Britain's Adrian Weale confirmed it as a wider issue; while

> British Special Forces have a very high reputation with the Americans ... with conventional forces [an American perception developed] in the first year or so of the campaign that the British were very arrogant and patronising ... There was all this bollocks about ... British troops are patrolling in soft hats in Basra so they didn't seem threatening and the Americans quite rightly pointed out that the Brits were able to patrol in soft hats because nobody was attacking them at the time. [When they did] there was all helmets on and body armour and shoot back. I think the Americans *deeply* resented all that crap. Because a lot of British officers were encouraging it and the British media ops people in Basra were ... using this as our *unique selling point*. (Original emphasis.)

A rift developed 'to the extent that ... a lot of Americans were secretly rather pleased when we *did* wind up getting our arses kicked in Basra' (Interview: Weale, 26th November 2010). One former British Flight Lieutenant even described a more extreme account of the 'attitude of "US first and sod everyone else"' among troops, something more prevalent among American personnel than other nations, which he argued contributed to incidents of fratricide (Email: Anonymous, 2010). Recent leaks imply that British forces were attacked by US forces so often that it was seen as an occupational hazard and in one 2005 friendly fire incident British 'convoys continued on their journey without stopping' (Meek, 2010). Weale argued that with the British 'there's a great deal of reluctance to admit how badly it all went wrong'. This reluctance to recognise that British 'expertise' had not been wholly helpful related back to culture and 'normal careerism and so on within the military', 'where a mythology continues because' 'if you start getting too critical about it all then you're not going any further' (Interview: Weale, 26th November 2010).

Despite this, a combination of horizontal propaganda, complementary systems and doctrine helped demonstrate commitment and solidified the informal relationships on which Anglo-American cooperation and assistance depended. Shared indulgence in cultural history allowed Britain to sustain the dominant image of its historic 'expertise' with its ally despite US closed systems and personnel turnover. While hollow in some ways, they functioned to maintain a workable dialogue and the joint planning necessary for accommodating inevitable differences in interests and structural discontinuity. Hopkins (1998) has observed how open to foreign influence, and particularly British influence, the American system has traditionally been. 'Expertise' had limitations in-theatre and ultimately weakened the faith of American officials. Weale agreed that 'they do tend to listen to our suggestions, though I think less so now than ten years ago' at the start of the conflicts. As America has become more experienced Weale thought this 'introduced a degree of uncertainty and unhappiness about British self image and what they're *doing* it for' (Interview: 26th November 2010). Cynicism directed at the MOD appears to have been enhanced by the recent conflicts, particularly in relation to the inquiries into 'friendly fire' incidents and prosecutions mentioned in the last chapter. This may mean that today the maintenance of this 'collective memory' is more significant to the robustness of Britain's internal military culture, and in how it relates to its American partner, as 'real' expertise dwindles. But particularly in the early years of Afghanistan and Iraq, it helped in creating the in-roads that British personnel used for coordination, planning and organisation – channels they used to address what they saw as US failures.

Complementing capabilities in propaganda: whose line is it anyway?

Going into conflict, Blair's support was decisive. But his government brought its own challenges and respective 'needs' to the table. Distinct strategic priorities shape each state's respective 'propaganda needs', harbouring a potential for conflicts of interest in the information realm. Continuity of the alliance's message was crucial; national conflicts of interest would inevitably affect messages in the propaganda war, creating a constant tension between the domestic and international context, and between the partners. As former US Navy Chief of Media Frank Thorp observed, 'different countries out of an alliance have different priorities' (Interview: 24th August 2009). Their political and military elites claim unique insight into the country's 'needs'. These national priorities are *constructed* within, and serve to *limit*, the existing belief systems and cultures discussed in Chapter 4.

The implications of the Anglo-American imbalance are enormous in propaganda. To ensure complementary messaging between allies, an overriding strategic message must be agreed; not only cross-government, but *across governments*. It seems likely that such a strategic message would be driven by the dominant country. NATO was previously restricted from strategic level PSYOP, which were considered a national responsibility (Collins, 2002). Especially post-Iraq, multinational security forces are essential to build the appearance of legitimate power in overt warfare and Strategic Communication attempts have developed under Obama. Thus, both within NATO and within an Anglo-American relationship embodying great power differentials, it is important to consider how 'strategic messages' will be defined and delivered internationally when debating propaganda.

Concerns arose over the potential interference of national priorities and cultures in these converging elite goals in the conflict. For example, each country's domestic political structures, tensions and indeed its different media culture created demands that necessitated a different geographical focus for the propaganda war. Personnel worked hard to mediate this. Air Cmdre Graham Wright was Chief of Defence Staff's Liaison Officer to the Chairman of the Joint Chiefs of Staff when I met him in 2009. He observed how America's culture 'of the media, is not as critical and probing as ours tends to be. So over [there], it's ... more driven by what needs to be done in operational theatres.' Conversely in Britain, Wright argued,

> what worries ministers ... is how the media portrays them back home. They don't care about what's happening in theatre, I mean they should do 'cause they should care about winning, but the thing that actually influences them most is how they're being portrayed in the media. (Interview: 1st June 2009)

For instance, for Britain with its multicultural population, a war which was directed at 'radical' Islam had to be handled delicately and the domestic population were a priority. Correspondingly, media image became of greater concern to the bureaucracy, since if the government feels it has the full weight of public support behind what it's doing then departments are more likely get the resources and go-ahead they need (Interview: Taverner, 18th July 2004). While Blair was sceptical of the neo-conservative elements influencing Bush there was some continuity in the Christian ideals which helped drive their world views; yet Blair was highly cautious of the alliance being perceived as a crusade against Islam, as was Bush, once off US soil. The concerns of the British political elite split between the global influence it gained whilst warming itself on American afterburners, and a growing awareness that it was riding on a rapidly dissipating vapour trail of public opinion. Diverging interests had to be mediated within its US relations.

An ongoing discourse which proposed the 'mutual' importance of, often particular, interests was crucial in communicating through each bureaucracy understandings of 'what line to take' in the propaganda war. Strategic dialogue and coordination was a priority for the states to ensure that underlying national interests and bureaucratic differences didn't cause conflicting messages. The following sections will detail mechanisms that were hoped to avoid political discontinuity and embarrassments in the relationship before moving into a discussion of how in reality persistent barriers to progress were often encountered.

Strategic level

Messages formulated independently and filtered in isolation through different leaderships' national objectives would be inconsistent in the information realm.

Graham Wright observed that 'the logical extension of ... joining up Whitehall is, we're in a coalition ... how do we join that up and meanwhile back here [Washington] you've got people doing the same sort of thing?' As he said, 'it would be helpful if we were both saying the same thing', and for the overall message to be consistent, 'where it needs to be joined up is at the strategic level' (Interview: 1st June 2009). Formal mechanisms of Anglo-American relations began organising around this function, solidified by a desire to promote domestic and what were presented as 'mutual' Western interests in the face of a new common enemy. Between the British and American executives information exchange was regular and cooperative. Richard Armitage recalled the close leadership tie feeding into wider bureaucratic relations: 'we had understanding that our President got along with Mr Blair ... so that always helps the bureaucracy' (Interview: 21st July 2009).

Despite Britain's smaller resource, following the 9/11 attacks Blair demonstrated from the outset a clear desire to be a leader in the information realm. This was also crucial to his own leadership's interests. He was the first world leader to give a coherent public response to the terrorist threat: within an hour and twenty minutes of the attacks he articulated a need for democracies to stand up to the threat and 'fight it together', at a time when Bush had only stated a need to find those responsible (Blair, 2001; Bush, 2001). Blair also called Al Jazeera to No. 10 for an interview days before the US did.

Jeremy Greenstock (the UK's Special Representative in Iraq, September 2003–March 2004) observed that Blair and Bush consulted more often than any of their predecessors throughout history (Foreign & Commonwealth Office, 2004: 37). According to former NSC Director Franklin Miller, in Iraq coordination was maintained through 'video conferences starting in the summer 03' between Bush and Blair, initially every four weeks then 'regular two-week meetings or three-week meetings'. Miller said this coordination 'at the macro level' extended 'between 10 Downing Street, David Manning, Condi Rice, Jack Straw, Secretary of State or me, and Blair and the President'. So while Blair and Bush were the faces of strategic-level relations, their meetings were complemented by other major points of intersection between 'less senior' officials (Interview: Miller, 3rd August 2009).

Given the close relationship George Tenet had with President Bush and his senior advisor Karl Rove, it seems likely the CIA's strategic role was important in coordinating the campaign at this level. Having once said, 'Everything is mano-a-mano, everything', Tenet believed in forging personal relationships both at home and with heads of intelligence abroad (Woodward, 2004: 67). It is no accident that SIS's leadership is peppered with Anglo-American ties. According to Risen, the 'American and British intelligence services are so close that under normal circumstances, they hold an annual summit to discuss a wide range of issues' (Risen, 2006: 113). The SIS chief at the time was Richard Dearlove, a neo-

Conservative who had been head of SIS Washington DC Station in the 1990s and built strong ties in the US, where officials regarded British Intelligence highly. Woodward writes that in early February 2002 Tenet had retorted to his Iraq Operations Chief, 'How come all the good reporting I get is from SIS?' (Tenet in Woodward, 2004: 107). One CIA official reported to Risen that 'the MI6 station chief in Washington was in CIA headquarters all the time, with just about complete access to everything, and I am sure he was talking to a lot of people' (Risen, 2006: 114–115).

The level of intelligence agency involvement in strategic planning and coordination is clear from the Downing Street Memo sent to David Manning on 23rd July 2002 containing minutes of a meeting about Dearlove's discussions with Tenet regarding the decision to go to war in Iraq (Rycroft, 2002). Risen reports that it was written three days after 'candid' discussions at a 'CIA-MI6 summit meeting held at CIA headquarters' that was called 'at the urgent request of the British' who had put great pressure on the Americans to meet (2006: 113). According to Risen, 'Tenet had an especially good personal relationship with Dearlove' and spent most of that day talking, including one and a half hours spent 'mano-a-mano' (2006: 114). Dearlove had observed that military action was seen as 'inevitable' and would be 'justified by the conjunction of terrorism and WMD'; his report to Downing Street hinted at the nascent propaganda campaign, that 'the intelligence and facts were being fixed around the policy' (Rycroft, 2002). On probing propaganda coordination at the strategic level, Franklin Miller said,

> I don't think ... that CIA and SIS were operating completely independently in Iraq. I think that there was some sort of overall game plan ... And it *was* coordinated to some degree or another ... while parts of it may have been uncoordinated there were parts that were coordinated.

The agreed 'game plan' was then coordinated 'with the military, and with the embassies' (Interview: Miller, 3rd August 2009).

From an early stage in Afghanistan, Britain's executive engaged the propaganda apparatus and its formal and informal Anglo-American channels in building international and domestic support. The Downing Street Director of Communications and Strategy until 2003, Alastair Campbell, was crucial in communicating British leadership concerns, putting them forward as of mutual concern to the Americans. Taverner attributes the idea of Coalition Information Centres (CICs) to Campbell who after Kosovo was aware of different time-zones creating dysfunctional operations between NATO headquarters in Brussels, the MoD in London, and Washington (Interview: 18th July 2004). The CICs were born out of his visit to Washington in early October 2001, to meet with Under-Secretary of State for Public Diplomacy and Public Affairs, Karen Hughes, and Director of the Office of Media Affairs, Tucker Eskew (Macintyre,

2002). Campbell emphasised British importance and responsibility in handling the news, before Washington had even risen, on stories that had become established hours before at Taliban press conferences in Pakistan. The Americans gave Campbell's idea an enthusiastic reception (Interview: Taverner, 18th July 2004). Through his former employee Alan Percival who helped to set up the Islamabad Centre, Campbell had significant influence in the coordination of the whole operation (Dillon, 2001),[5] and Britain was the 'first nation to send military representatives and campaign planners' to the CIC on 18th September 2001 (Coalition Information Centre [n.d., 2003?]). The White House based its Office of Global Communications on this design (Meade, 2005) and it was 'linked directly' to the CIC 'mainly through daily conference calls and e-mail' (Foreign & Commonwealth Office, 2008: 1). CICs effectively fed into Britain's Information Campaign Coordination Group (ICCG), through NCOs and the Cabinet Office into the MoD (Interview: Taverner, 18th July 2004).

A further instrumental role was played by coordination and planning between Campbell and his American counterparts, Karen Hughes and Tucker Eskew. Vickie Sheriff, a recent Head of News at No. 10, described day-to-day relations under the present (2013) UK coalition government, a close cooperation which would have been greatly heightened during the Iraq and Afghanistan conflicts:

> We cooperate really well ... and have a really good relationship with the White House at the press office level too. If for example there's been communication between the Prime Minister and the President we do have a desire to at least inform people of what the sort of subjects [were] that were discussed ... we would agree between us what would be briefed out from that conversation and of course our briefings would mirror, so what's being briefed to the journalists in the White House briefings would be the same as that which Downing Street would brief the UK press. What you don't want is 'Well they said that, and they said *that*'. Lots of good cooperation. Or certainly when things happen we keep each other informed. (Interview: 18th April 2013)

During Campbell's 2001 trip he was shown a copy of Bush's speech to Congress before it was delivered. Likewise, an article in the *Independent* reported that 'Eskew was shown the Prime Minister's statement to the Commons after the Taliban lines had finally been breached; after consulting Washington he succeeded in having a few of the more triumphalist lines toned down, and Blair referred to the Taliban "collapse" rather than to an allied "victory".' This is indicative of an informal 'consideration' where messages can be included which assist the partner, and which perform an important role both in solidifying the sense of alliance and in ensuring consistent (credible) propaganda. Importantly, from early November, Tucker Eskew was quietly based at the FCO in London for five months, and began meeting daily with Alastair Campbell to plan the coalition's media strategy (Macintyre, 2002). Campbell headed a team there charged with monitoring the Islamic media and daily London briefings began to engage more with Muslim journalists (Dillon, 2001). Campbell discussed the appearance of Blair on the 'Larry King Live' show (6th November) with the White House, and this gesture was reciprocated by Colin Powell when he spoke to the London Information Centre before his BBC interview (Macintyre, 2002). Campbell was concerned to ensure consistent adherence to certain 'key messages' which centred on 'mutual' goals, though censorship remained a key policy (Dillon, 2001). Early publicity was considered to have failed in some areas, for instance in publicising the level of support gained internationally, so four aims emerged for the strategy:

1) To emphasise generally that September 11 lies behind the current bombing campaign.
2) To publicise that the breadth of support for the campaign is greater than usually credited.
3) To challenge arguments that the strategy is not working.
4) To publicise negative arguments relating to Bin Laden and the evidence against him within the Islamic world. (Watson and Webster, 2001)

Initially a hostile stance was taken towards the Muslim media. Culture Secretary Tessa Jowell cautioned British media against using Al Jazeera footage in their broadcasts on 29th October, for example, and announced that the ITC had been monitoring it for signs of incitement of racial hatred (Jowell, 2001). Eskew was reproachful of the press in Britain, especially in response to Guantanamo Bay critics, yet considered the Information Centre to have been highly successful in managing an exercise to 'impede great lies and propel great truths', including 'rebutting' Taliban stories about civilian casualties (Macintyre, 2002).[6] In correspondence with Richard Sambrook (former BBC Director of News) at the time, BBC correspondent Nicholas Jones noted a change in Campbell's strategy, 'a charm offensive with the foreign media' (Jones, 2001b). Likewise in the US, Bush toned down his rhetoric to emphasise that 'we have much more in common than people might think' (Watson and Webster, 2001). The approach changed from the demoralising agitation propaganda of an 'enemy' to integration propaganda from a long-lost 'friend'. The assistive propaganda relationship was also underscored. According to Dillon, Campbell wished to ensure central figures involved in the conflict timed key speeches and trips so as not to detract from each other's publicity, thus maximising the overall profile of the coalition side of the campaign (2001). To facilitate this there was a 'swapping of ideas, material and possibly staff between Downing Street and The White House in what officials describe as a "constant co-operation and co-ordination at every level" between the two governments since September 11' (Watson and Webster, 2001).

Campbell's message was imposed with a heavy hand; one particular article, written for the Prime Minister for Remembrance Sunday and reproduced by the *Mail on Sunday*, was taken over suddenly and 'Campbellised' – rewritten with its message strictly controlled. Nicholas Jones said they 'hijacked Remembrance Sunday' and pushed wearing poppies 'as a way of showing support for British forces at risk in Afghanistan' (Jones, 2001a). He stated that his contact 'said this was a typical example of Campbell' who 'used Remembrance Sunday as a way of promoting the need ... for solidarity' (Interview: Jones, 14th March 2006). The government press office released a statement that 'This year there will be added poignancy as we remember not only those who died in the service of their country in the First and Second World Wars, but also those who lost their lives on 11 September in tragic circumstances as a result of terrorism' (10 Downing Street, 2001).

On his departure from London, Eskew underlined how formative his experience had been, stating that it had increased his appreciation of the need to address Arab and Muslim media, many of whom were London based (Macintyre, 2002).[7] The leaderships began to emphasise the Muslim death-toll from 9/11 and that this was not a war on Islam, but within two years Arab sentiment around the world had become decidedly hostile to US foreign policy (Tatham, 2006). As the Iraq invasion became likely, a key element of the 'coalition-building' process was gaining access to the region. Britain therefore increasingly focused Public Diplomacy in 'emerging trouble spots', and courted unlikely friends that might prove Britain's value in coalition-building to the US (MoD, 2003b: 34).

MoD, Pentagon and military coordination

The key site for strategists to then 'deconflict' was the MoD Afghan ICCG, a group which managed Britain's cross-government message. According to Graham Wright, former Director of Targeting and Information Operations, after 9/11 their focus for Britain's strategic message was finding an answer to 'Why are we in Afghanistan?' An observer might expect this to be simple for the MoD to answer. Yet their aims extended beyond merely answering this question, to ensuring that the answer chosen would bolster the wartime goals of Britain's leadership, 'shared' coalition goals, and respond to each level of the campaign. Wright stated that if they found a line to take, 'the question was, had the Americans got to the same point?' He found that though 'often they did', continuity between these answers had to be ensured (Interview: 1st June 2009). In interview, US PSYOP Division Chief on the Joint Staff (2006–8) Glenn Ayers said, 'We would always coordinate with [Graham Wright] on what the Brits were doing ... he was always interested in how we were trying to do IIA and that kind of thing' (Interview: 17th May 2013). But there were limits, Wright said:

'we end up with some good ideas ... which we plug in with [the Americans, and] their machine is just so cumbersome that we can't actually influence' (Interview: 1st June 2009).

Angus Taverner stated that when he was at the MoD (until 2004) coordination wasn't easy:

> [The US] didn't have military people sitting alongside their civilian press people so it's quite difficult in a way to actually get a handle on who was doing what. So we just got on with what we were doing and they got on with what they were doing but of course, it does mess tunes up. (Interview: 23rd January 2013)

FCO/MoD cooperation[8] did aid coordination with the US through the ICCG, a group that talked with the Pentagon, CENTCOM and other governments (Interview: Taverner, 18th July 2004). Some MoD officials saw their Anglo-American coordination as inadequate in the early stages of the Afghan conflict though; Taverner observed that

> Our relationship with the Americans sort-of developed, but only slowly ... There was a bit of communication between our bosses. There was obviously No. 10 to White House communication ... We talked to each other about embedding ... I talked to the Press Attaché in Washington quite a lot ... He'd tell me what the Americans were doing ... think it was probably a massive area of weakness was that [the military] had very little interaction with our American counterparts. I mean, surprisingly little actually.

He added, 'I was still far too busy trying to build relationships with the Foreign Office and No. 10!' (Interview: Taverner, 23rd January 2013).

Isolated efforts sprouted up to do what was possible, bringing a lack of continuity; permanent structures of government gave birth to ad hoc groups or meetings. Taverner described how close informal relationships with the FCO enabled coordination and told how his team needed to problem-solve and develop strategies and initiatives to progress the information campaign (Interview: 23rd January 2013). The MoD, for example, stepped in to meet needs for the Afghan elections in 2004. While Foreign Office communications were felt to be 'under-resourced', this raised 'an opportunity' for both British Embassy Kabul and those piloting the new Defence Media Communications Centre. For Ralph Arundell, 'it meant I could demonstrate an initial operating capability for the team I was setting up and do it earlier than was anticipated'. They set up facilities for print and broadcast media and 'an embed programme dedicated for Islamic journalists', while reporting back 'in the MoD but also to the FCO and No. 10' (Interview: Arundell, 18th April 2013).

Through collaboration at CENTCOM, British IO expertise influenced doctrine that helped shape the US attempt to impose a 'Strategic Communication' approach. Special Assistant for Public Affairs Frank Thorp was 'in charge of policy for the coordination of Psychological Operations and Public Affairs, from the Public Affairs standpoint'. Thorp asserted that during his five months in Qatar as Special Assistant on Public Affairs for the Joint Chiefs of Staff:

> When it came to the British, I never saw one set of Psychological Operations talking points and another set of Public Affairs talking points. I always saw … It was always coordinated. It oughta be.

He observed during his five months working alongside them that British PSYOP and Media Operations 'weren't totally different cultures' – their relationship 'was more coordinated and more together, and more homogenised' in goals and messages. When I pointed out that British officials often stress the separation he responded that 'it's separated, but it's homogenised' in its goals and messages. This was something Thorp considered 'very healthy' and borrowed from when he 'briefed the Joint Chief of Staff on how [Public Affairs and PSYOP] should be combined and coordinated' in the US military (Interview: 24th August 2009).

Special forces, covert and clandestine activities

An assistive necessity for British policy meant that strategic-level dialogue did not always produce tangible victories for Britain's particular national interests, which were at times subordinated in 'service' to wider 'mutual' interests, American-influenced goals. For instance a tangible rift existed concerning potential targets in Afghanistan following the 9/11 attacks. According to Risen's CIA source the British 'were screaming' for these targets to be bombed since most of the heroin in Britain originated there (2006: 154). The State Department argued for armed forces to tackle opium production. The Pentagon and White House refused (2006: 154–155). But this was not allowed to disrupt the image of the alliance. Following the American refusal to bomb drug-related Afghan targets, Britain took on much of the initial anti-narcotics campaign (including propaganda initiatives) despite limited military and intelligence resource to do so (Risen, 2006: 154–155). In Afghanistan, some diplomatic 'reconstruction' programmes, set up by Britain and seen as successful, were then reportedly co-opted by American control. An official stated:

> they wait until some project is, you know, being seen to work … and then they pour in, and this is on the information side, they pour in with promises of millions of dollars for the Afghan government and lots of consultants and they want to take it over. They want to control information programmes. (Interview: UK Diplomatic Official based in Afghanistan, 2006)

While dominant national interests could still cause dispute, the perception of a stable Anglo-American campaign remained a priority. Thus in terms of perceptions, at times the UK approach prioritised strategic outcomes over the leadership's particular perception of 'national' interests. The maintenance of an effective alliance, and the uncomplicated perception of this, necessarily relies upon effective dialogue and coordination of message, even where interests diverged.

Rumsfeld's Special Forces-centred approach required the intervention of UK forces in one early failure. The US dramatically misjudged the level of resistance at Mullah Omar's residence near Kandahar on 20th October 2001, and twelve Delta Force members were injured. Gen. Myers reported in a Pentagon briefing the ease with which Special Operations Forces were able to operate with only 'light' resistance in this 'successful' mission, a stance the military supported with selective television footage (Hersh, 2004: 122). Neither Myers nor Rumsfeld subsequently acknowledged the near-failure but the following day it was reported that America had requested Britain's entire SAS regiment to deploy (Hersh, 2004).

Britain's SAS was seen by many as a model for US capabilities, but in Iraq, former military intelligence officer Adrian Weale criticised how SIS and Special Forces had been pulled in to support a very American strategy. American concerns became central to Britain's strategic planning: this meant that 'the agencies which had the funding and the capability to start dealing with the insurgency were focused on something else entirely'. This represented a difference of approach to counter-insurgency, and Weale further described how 'In Nasiriya we were talking to Muqtada Al-Sadr's number two, who was a moderately reasonable Shia cleric ... He was certainly open to reason and would pass messages back to Muqtada.' It was an important 'channel of communication. But the Americans wanted to ... sweep him out of the way and deal with' Saddam as this would demonstrate the public image of American strength. Weale said he 'personally discussed this with Graham Lamb, the General who's in Command in Basra, who came to see us' and 'the Brits opposed it generally' because 'Muqtada was the real problem. Saddam was just hiding low.' Weale described how especially in the first year after the Iraq War the strategic intelligence set-up meant that 'SIS and Special Forces were focussed almost *entirely*' on the Americans' 'pack of cards' to the detriment of counter-insurgency operations. Propaganda concerns were criticised for likewise reflecting this focus on high-profile cases:

> the effort that was being expended on information campaigns on tracking down Saddam ... would've been ... better focused on more relevant things like potential insurgents, what Muqtada Al-Sadr was doing. (Interview: Weale, 26th November 2010)

Britain is seen as providing particular and complementary skills in covert Information Operations. Col. Arundell confirmed this: 'the Americans like to think we're very good at this sort of activity. Because we have a long historical background with it' (Interview: 18th April 2013). An anonymous MoD source observed that the US tends only to do 'delayed attribution. There's a big differ-ence between delayed attribution and completely non-attributable – it requires a whole different level of sophistication [in practical terms/planning]. They do produce some fabulous material but again, it's not dark. It's all very sort of positive – it's mum and dad, apple pie and it's disguised as not coming from the Americans. Delve far enough into the website you'll find this is a product of US CENTCOM or whatever. It's not half as dark as they might like you to think it is.' (Interview: 2013). Attribution can have a significant impact on credibility for the audience.

British expertise was also sought as the intelligence agencies of the two countries worked together, and attempts were made to draw on any propaganda capabilities that might complement each other's objectives. Historically, Britain has provided the CIA and US Special Forces with certain expertise in propa-ganda, enabling the strategic messages to filter into the public domain. According to US journalist and author of *Curveball*, Bob Drogin,

> The CIA was designed ... built on the model of British Intelligence ... the early days they worked hand-in-glove, and still to a certain extent do. (Interview: 22nd August 2009)

MI6's budget limits its use of contractors, but it developed a 'classic technique' known as 'surfacing'. An expert on British intelligence, Stephen Dorril, said he thought the Americans had 'been taught it by MI6'. The technique has the potential advantage of circumnavigating domestic audience targeting rules by distancing the propagandist from the propaganda, again reducing accountabil-ity and giving the message some wider credibility. An SIS agent would

> plant a story in a third country, you tell the journalist who's your contact that there's an interesting story in Poland. He gets the story ... he comes back to you [the agent] and you say yeah it's true, they can build a ... nuclear weapon in six months. Then he puts the story in the press that intelligence sources confirm that.

This 'double-sourcing' adds credibility to the story, yet 'the person who usually backs it up is also the person who planted the story in the first place'. In 2010 Dorril said, 'they started the same process with Iran about two years ago ... people on the *Telegraph*, they were running a lot', and he observed how in the run-up to the Gulf War then again for the war in Iraq the CIA were engaged in these activities. He said 'it happens quite a lot' but 'some of it wasn't *by* them. It's pretty clear that some of it was done by surrogates ... Chalabi ... he did a lot' and 'nobody's quite sorted out his relationship to MI6 or CIA' (Interview: Dorril, 20th July 2010). Clandestine activity's inherent deniability allows governments to negotiate with other governments, insurgents or terrorist groups outside public scrutiny.

Legal restrictions are massaged and this reaches beyond propaganda, as McBride stated, referring to rendition:

> here again, when we're trying to be too *good*, if we pick up a foreign agent and he's suspected of conspiracy for terrorism or has committed a terrorist act there are many mechanisms which, it's *claimed,* that US forces can use which is – well we picked him up ... in, say, India, and we could turn him over to the Indians for interrogation, they don't have the restrictions we do, and guess what, they get their answers! And ... we have to be very careful that it doesn't look like we're goin' – you know, here's this bad guy, give us your answer once you get done torturing him.[9] Because we're against torture. Exactly, like we can blow you up with a hundred shots to the head but we can't make you feel uncomfortable. If we capture you. (Interview: 5th June 2009)

Two CIA rendition flights used the UK's territory of Diego Garcia to refuel despite British opposition to the practice and divergence of the US/UK position on torture. To this, Foreign Secretary David Milliband said, 'The breach is not the defining element of our relationship with the United States' (quoted in Robbins, 21st February 2008).

The CIA's use of 'surrogates' for propaganda (and, of course contractors) functions for deniability or credibility of message, and it is possible that the CIA relationship with SIS operates in a similar way. For example, Seymour Hersh reported an SIS I/Ops programme during the Clinton years. It was 'known to a few senior officials in Washington', one of whom commented that 'We were getting ready for action in Iraq, and we wanted the Brits to prepare.' Hersh reports that in 'a series of clandestine meetings with MI6', the CIA provided very unreliable 'inactionable intelligence' – documents that MI6/SIS then fed to the press. The intelligence officer is quoted as saying, 'It was intelligence that was crap, and that we couldn't move on, but the Brits wanted to plant stories in England and around the world' (Hersh, 2003).

Former Executive Vice President and Vice Chair of the Board of McCann-Erickson World Group Sean Fitzpatrick, as a CIA/DOD contractor, also worked for the British in Northern Ireland. He said, 'I think your country has [counter-terrorism] better handled'. MI5, he said, is not bound by the constraints that the FBI is, as a law-enforcement agency, and doesn't have to prove a *criminal* act:

> And if you screw up they'll lock you up. Well you know, you're in much more dangerous territory [as a government]. But ... nothing sharpens the mind like the prospect of hanging in the morning. (Interview: Fitzpatrick, 30th June 2009)

Drogin related the same argument to propaganda:

> it's certainly my understanding that in the UK, MI6 has fewer of those kinds of restrictions about operating in-country ... the British Intelligence services do in fact have British correspondents working for major ... organisations ... operating on their behalf. (Interview: 22nd August 2009)

Potomac Institute for Policy Studies Director Dennis McBride also commented that 'the British are very clever, and ... don't have the restrictions we do'. On domestic/foreign propaganda restrictions he said, 'the British were less concerned with that kind of problem ... no matter where the perpetrator is in the world the same intelligence gathering machine can be put to use' (Interview: 5th June 2009). All this supports recent (2013) evidence from Edward Snowden that shows that in Britain's Government Communications Headquarters (GCHQ) surveillance, British oversight is more flexible than that of the US, and that the US seeks to exploit the differential: the weakness of British laws was considered to be a 'selling point' with the Americans (Hopkins and Borger, 2013). Different 'capabilities' in the intelligence community or military could clearly prove the Anglo-American relationship advantageous in wartime.

It is known that GCHQ works collaboratively with the National Security Agency (NSA) on ECHELON (mentioned earlier), PRISM and TEMPORA, among other surveillance programmes. PRISM and TEMPORA are massive domestic and international surveillance programmes revealed by Snowden that have raised questions about privacy and ethics, and which indicate that the speed of technological adaptation in intelligence has left policy and oversight behind (Hopkins and Ackerman, 2013).[10] Documents reveal huge British dependence on the US, which is driving a dominant fear that 'US perceptions of the ... partnership diminish, leading to loss of access, and/or reduction in investment ... to the UK' (Hopkins and Borger, 2013).

Any apparent imbalance of power is significant when we consider how just as each country can utilise surrogates to deliver their message, the scope of each country's intelligence and defence activities is complementary. The two countries have worked together increasingly as 'threats' were seen as requiring global 'solutions', and attempts were made to draw on any propaganda capabilities that might complement each other's objectives. Besides weak restrictions, some interviews indicated that Britain is seen as providing particular or complementary skill in covert IO (as Armstrong notes below). Dorril argued that the British '*do* it... but probably not as necessarily as much as they had to' due to greater American scope of action (Interview: 20th July 2010).

Wingfield stated that US restrictions should not be seen as 'prohibitions' anyway, but more as different 'domestic approval chains'. He also stated that the UK's slightly weaker restrictions were of 'little operational significance' (Email: 1st May 2013). The 'restrictiveness' that interviewees observed may relate more to US formal hierarchical approval structures and oversight being cumbersome and bureaucratic. Indeed, Miller didn't see CIA oversight as *restrictive*, saying that during wartime 'I don't know that we've had that many [CIA] operations ... actually ... denied' (Interview: 3rd August 2009). In fact, in contrast to the beliefs of many interviewees about the CIA's ability to target Americans, in 1996 a Council for Foreign Relations independent task force recommended taking a 'fresh look ... at limits on the use of non-official "covers" for hiding and protecting those involved in clandestine activities' including journalists. John Deutch, then Director of Central Intelligence, responded that there was 'no need to change U.S. policy as [former Senior NSC Director Richard] Haass had advocated, since the CIA already had the power to use U.S. reporters as spies' (Houghton, 1996).

The two militaries may have slightly different capabilities that can complement each other. Wright explained that,

> if we wanted to do something in the Maghreb, because our military say, 'Look we're worried about [Al Qaeda from Mesopotamia]'. Our policy people in the MoD would say ... We're not doing military operations there.

This would mean Britain relying on embassies, something restrictive, as the FCO 'don't have the capabilities that [the MoD] do in terms of doing things on the ground in other places'. In contrast, America could act where a military response was deemed necessary due to its wider reach; in this case 'doing influence activity, in its broadest sense, in Africa to prevent operations ever happening' (Interview: Wright, 1st June 2009).

Some evidence suggested each country helps the other to navigate its boundaries and enables it to do different things. As Matt Armstrong notes, different countries including Britain also have different areas of specialism in '"The black arts" ... what I mean is covert Information Operations. Their PSYOP and MISO type of stuff' and this means 'there are things ... we look for from our allies and they look for from us' (Interview: 6th March 2013). The remarks of MoD Assistant Head Defence Media and Communications Operations Plans (and former Assistant Head Targeting and Information Operations) Ralph Arundell were noted above on the existence of US constraints to 'non-attributable' campaigns and 'activity that could potentially play back against the US audience'. Importantly, these US restrictions are those which McCarty and others, in Chapter 3, designated outdated, and which Ayers and other IO operatives were pushing to change. During interview I asked Arundell whether this meant Britain was of high value to the US in this kind of activity. He replied, 'Yes, of course it is.' He then clarified this:

> And that's not because we can be used as a pawn to do America's bidding. *We* could come up with a bright idea and say, 'Right, we want to do X.' The Americans might go '*That's fabulous*, you crack on and do that. We'll ensure we deconflict with that.' (Interview: Arundell, 18th April 2013; original emphasis)

From this account, for the UK to be of high value in this area would require it to be proactively connected with the US in order to be able to anticipate, provide complementary operations and de-conflict, connections that do seem to be firmly in place.

Responding to this question of where US restrictions have made British assistance valuable, a Senior State Department official also confirmed that this applies to a specific area, when 'there are restrictions on its *ability* to have *covert* information, unattributed information, intentionally come into the United States' (Email: 2013). Former NSC Director Franklin Miller nervously said, 'If it's influencing our own people, which is I know, forbidden by law . . . then you wouldn't really want your ally to be doing for you what you're not allowed to do yourself' (Interview: 3rd August 2009). But Joel Harding, former US Special Forces and Director of the IO Institute, confirmed:

> Both the US and the UK can take advantage of one another's laws to skirt around restrictions, legal and otherwise. If the UK could not do something with a UK citizen, for instance, the US can assist. I'm especially thinking of extremists. That could be a repugnant situation, however, as we honestly think of you guys as family. At least I do, as do most veterans.
>
> But as a former intelligence officer I've used that relationship a few times . . . especially when I was working in Special Operations. 'nuff said. (Email: 3rd May 2013a)

Since, with Arundell's account in Chapter 2, the extent of British military information activities is not revealed to all personnel, it is possible such activities are unknown to them for deniability. According to Mark Pfeifle this depth of coordination is more about individuals' initiative than an overall policy; he said, 'I would *hope* that there were that much coordination and insight, I would *think*, to a point, but not from a global or overall level' (Interview: 12th July 2013).

Somewhat ironically, on the Snowden revelations, Harding commented on his blog that while he supports 'what NSA do, what they have done and what they are going to do', he continued, 'As much as I detest [Snowden's] actions . . . I must credit him with giving transparency where none existed previously.' He states, 'Snowden has exponentially increased awareness of what the US government is doing not only against other governments of the world, but possibly illegal operations against US citizens' (Harding, 2013).

The legalities and checks regarding US covert PSYOP re-entering the country have been presented in full above with analysis from Thomas Wingfield, an expert in this area. Allies delivering IO would of course follow their own country's doctrine and oversight. But inter-country coordination seeks to ensure a common purpose is maintained and allows the partner to consider the content and evaluate 'risk'. Matt Armstrong stated that, in the case of covert information coming back into the US, 'What somebody will *say* to that, might be to watch, what we would call the Washington Post-test . . . "Am I comfortable with seeing this on the front page of the Washington Post?" – That's not *law* . . . That is probably the bigger *driver. . .*' as far as whether objections might be raised or a plan approved (Interview: 29th April 2013; original emphasis).

According to US 2007 rules, a commander can avoid attribution of online content by attributing activities to a 'partner nation' if both that country and the US Chief of Mission agrees (Deputy Secretary of Defense, 2007). This surrogate to which a US PSYOP campaign is attributed is usually the targeted country (Iraq for example) or an organisation. With such countries dependent for their security on the US and its allies, their governments have little choice but to comply in the use of propaganda by an external power. This weakens the authority of the government and any notion that its message represents its people, as well as showing the hypocrisy of claims to be setting up a 'free and independent media'.

As mentioned above, as part of an overall war effort, coalitions account for differing skill-sets and capabilities of their members in producing a division of labour that will allow members to perform an assistive, complementary role, and optimise their overall resource in meeting operational objectives. To this effect, operationally the Americans 'only need us in areas where they're not well covered' (Interview: Dorril, 20th July 2010). While the two states' power within the coalition is certainly imbalanced, engagement at this level is inevitably going to be restricted by both sides. Close ties are drawn upon pragmatically, according to need. Therefore, American ties did not stop John Scarlett (2009) distancing MI6 from the CIA publicly when evidence of US torture became public, stressing that 'we are our own service' and 'working to our own laws'. This act was crucial to public perceptions and would probably have been discussed at length with American intelligence. Gordon Thomas argues that Scarlett ate regularly with the CIA London Station Chief with whom he shared similar views (2009: 24). And when the unpopular Porter Goss was replaced by Michael Hayden in 2006, the CIA Director cultivated a close relationship with Scarlett (Thomas, 2009: 452). The CIA's use of covers in US domestic media is clearly a carefully protected ability known to few, and would probably be cautiously exercised, whereas activities performed by British intelligence would probably be subject to no US scrutiny, and indeed little domestically.

Certainly, Dorril also said, MI6 and the CIA do try to complement each other's abilities (Interview: 20th July 2010); MI6's role is unclear largely because of its secrecy. According to Thorp the tactical, focused nature of the intelligence agencies' activities in the propaganda war (as opposed to their strategic-level aims) mean that 'the *coordination* there is much more at the tactical level' (Interview: 24th August 2009). Significantly, the intelligence operatives' activities rely on networks of informal contacts and resourcefulness. Their autonomous approach can create a tension at the tactical level with overall Anglo-American cooperation,[11] at the same time as crucially building wide-reaching connections.

In one example, Adrian Weale, whose wide contacts as a former intelligence officer helped greatly in his position as CPA Deputy Governor of Dhi Qar Province, recalled how

> an American intelligence guy was appointed to CPA South to be intelligence link-man with CPA Baghdad and CIA ... from NCIS ... the Americans perceived that the guys who ... I'd been talking to were British assets ... they didn't have access to ... he basically came up to Nasiriya ... and he wanted to take over all my sources ... somebody'd obviously put him up to do this ... and there was lots of sort-of offers of we can do this for you and we can do that for you ... didn't quite offer me money, but it seemed that way.

The officer made unsuccessful appeals to Weale's notion of public service to gain acquiescence; 'couching it in terms of "It's all for the good of the CPA"' (Interview: 26th November 2010). Yet this breached Weale's understanding of what was appropriate to expect from British cooperation. The expectation exemplifies in an extreme example how boundaries of 'shared' interests and, correspondingly, British 'value', were subject to negotiation between the Anglo-American institutional cultures by individuals in pursuit of optimising their own occupational outcomes in the service of their state. Scott makes the argument that intelligence officers 'may be more than just a conduit' for denia-bility of governmental actions, that 'their own initiative may be an important element' and he emphasises the 'role of the individual' (2004: 336). Furthermore McBride's statement above regarding rendition and the sanctity of the 'five-sided building' also highlights how easily a notion of what is acceptable can be extended conceptually by the individual through interaction with distinctive organisational interests and cultures that rationalise and incrementally legit-imise restricted or unethical acts.

Notes

1 The British government's stance was also influenced by 90 per cent of Britain's burgeon-ing domestic heroin having come from Afghanistan's glut opium crop of 1999 (Travis, 2001).
2 Rowland and Tatham argue that Afghanistan has become 'the most polled population on earth' (2010: 2).
3 Armitage refers to the Yalta Conference between Roosevelt, Churchill and Stalin in 1945. As Anthony Eden recalled, 'The President shared a widespread American suspicion of the British Empire as it had once been and, despite his knowledge of world affairs, he was always anxious to make it plain to Stalin that the United States was not "ganging up" with Britain against Russia. The outcome of this was some confusion in Anglo-American relations which profited the Soviets' (1965: 593).
4 Miller also received a knighthood in 2006 for 'services to UK–US relations', as did CENTCOM Commander Tommy Franks the year before (House of Commons, 2006).
5 MP Pat McFadden, a No. 10 Special Advisor, based in a team run by Coalition Spokesman (former USIA Foreign Service Officer) Kenton Keith in the Islamabad

Coalition Information Centre. The staff was hugely varied: analysts, experts, civil servants, speech writers and political advisors from No. 10, the Ministry of Defence, the Treasury, the Lord Chancellor's Department, US State Department officials, Republican White House political appointees, and US and British forces personnel (Interview: McFadden, 20th April 2006). Keith took a lead role in organising all their activities to counter negative stories in the media and give journalists' briefings, issue statements, anticipate negative coverage and generally manage Media Operations.

6 These activities were viewed as crucial to Anglo-American relations and staff at the Islamabad CIC were keen on a more proactive role in media management. McFadden got frustrated at being unable to provide information until it was confirmed as this left an information vacuum and discontent among the press. He thought that the team was established too slowly and fed his concerns back to No. 10 in time for Iraq (Interview: McFadden, 20th April 2006).

7 It is worth noting that focus groups have shown the British public were far less sympathetic to the coalition message; for example, see Oates, Kaid and Berry (2009).

8 Described in Chapter 4 above.

9 McBride's response to public opinion and accepted ethics is to emphasise the importance of separating the image of these acts from the mechanisms themselves in terms of operational activity, so that each becomes a separate task necessary for battlefield success.

10 This data is shared between US and British governments. The NSA's PRISM programme uses the Foreign Intelligence Surveillance Act Amendment of 2008 to demand mass internet and communications data from companies such as Google, Microsoft and Apple (Hopkins and Ackerman, 2013). TEMPORA is a GCHQ-run surveillance programme which, through fibre-optic intercepts, accesses telecommunications and internet-users' data including massing Facebook posts, internet browsing history and calls (McAskill, 2013).

11 And vis-à-vis parallel organisations.

6

Iraq War case study

Introduction

The UK media subjected the Iraq invasion to more scrutiny than their counterparts in the US, but this was constrained by strong and increasingly coordinated strategic efforts to 'manage' public opinion regarding the war (see, for example, Tumber and Palmer, 2004; Miller 2004b). In 2014, over a decade after the invasion of Iraq, the idea of the release of the Chilcott Inquiry report in the UK seems a futuristic fantasy. Nichols and McChesney were right to talk in the US of 'tragedy and farce' (2005): they give an extensive account of a 'hawkish' media complicit in selling the war to the US public, a failure of journalism that meant 'The government said "jump." And the media responded "how high?"' (2005: 67). As this book goes to press, the 'war on terror' conflicts driven by this propaganda, in producing a power vacuum within the region and fuelling resentment over imperialist arrogance, have had a long-term destabilising impact and allowed the rise of ISIS.

In light of the worsening situation, it is timely to revisit the role of the British and US governments' propaganda in Iraq during the early planning and 'reconstruction' periods. Many argued that this propaganda might reduce casualties and the need for force by changing attitudes and behaviours; counter-insurgency warfare is often said to hinge on winning the consent of the local population (as detailed in Chapter 1). This chapter will explore further the themes developed in the last two chapters and consider Anglo-American planning during the Iraq War in more detail, particularly post-invasion.

Post-invasion planning

During the Iraq War some British personnel made a strong effort to use informal channels as in-roads to 'fix' what were seen as American propaganda and coordination 'failures'. As America's Iraq information war was delegated to CENTCOM in Qatar, British personnel found engagement from Pentagon staff dried up along with their engagement in the propaganda campaign (Interview:

Wright, 1st June 2009). They met the barriers to coordination within America's government and military by working around them where possible, with inconsistent outcomes. Initiative appears to have been enhanced in some cases in *response* to the barriers to formal coordination in broader Iraq planning.[1] And the MoD's London-centred bureaucratic links with receptive Americans (discussed previously) and the embassies became crucial once the Coalition Information Centres were disbanded in 2003.

British relationships were influential for Frank Thorp when he was Deputy Assistant Secretary of Defense for Public Affairs (2005–7) in planning his effort at forming strategic communications doctrine, and coordinating operations and messaging. Thorp had worked alongside the senior British officer running the information campaign in Qatar, saying 'he was tremendous and he ran a great operation'. In planning of messaging, according to Thorp,

> it goes right down to the unit commanders on the ground, you know the coalition forces commander in Iraq or forces commander in Afghanistan ... they have tried to put together an organisation where there is better coordination and better oversight so that everybody is working together.

He came to prefer his British colleagues' style of media management; asserting that

> I think there was actually a freer flow of communication with the Brits ... And [British media] were more focused on context rather than individual sound bites ... the openness was tremendous.

Thorp saw his role as 'definitely trying to encourage' US troops to take a similar approach to UK PSYOP/Media Operations, and among the forces he asserted that 'there was not resistance where *I* was. There was very little tension between what I was doing and the Brits were doing' (Interview: 24th August 2009).[2]

As we saw in Chapter 4, there were divisions within the military between Rumsfeld's supporters and critics, and the military began to bypass Rumsfeld in planning. Often this still depended on 'Rumsfeld not vetoing it' as he did in the 2004 Fallujah example mentioned in Chapter 3. By summer 2004, Rumsfeld's authority was being seriously undermined by the navigation of informal channels within and without the American system, as in Franklin Miller's account:

> where [Gen.] Casey[3] says 'I'm gonna bring Iraqi units to patrol with US units' and Rumsfeld said, 'No – No – that's not happening yet, I haven't approved it.' Well it was happening ... right then and there, I knew it was happening. I'd seen it. (Interview: 3rd August 2009)

The British government contributed to processes which effectively undermined the Pentagon, as traditionally flexible institutional cultures and the pace of war brought ad hoc responses. Adrian Weale, the Former Chief of Staff and Deputy Governor and Coordinator of Dhi Qar Province (Southern Iraq), observed that 'it was a long time since we'd invaded a country and tried to rule it and I think everyone was feeling their way' (Interview: 26th November 2010).

In Iraq we can see channels of military operational control taking over early in Basra, and planning had begun moving beyond the bureaucracy and beyond Rumsfeld. Miller recalled effective links with 'people like' Rumsfeld's CENTCOM Commander Tommy 'Franks and others ... clearly interacting with counterparts in the UK', hence 'the US marines who went into Basra went in under British command' (Interview: 3rd August 2009). After the invasion, from 21st April 2003 Coalition Provisional Authorities (CPA) were set up to govern. Ian Tunnicliffe, in the Office of Strategic Communication (StratComm) at Baghdad, said 'nominally underneath us we had all the PSYOPS capability ... In reality, we never did. Because they were military and they did what they wanted' (Interview: 8th July 2013). From his strategic position Miller recalled that

> from ... May '03 for far too long, it was no coordinated effort. If you were the Division commander in Tekrit you did it one way ... if you're the Division Commander in Baghdad you did it another way.

He stated that Commander Lt. Gen. Sanchez 'tended to treat the multinational division South as if it ... was the British zone of Berlin', seeing events as 'the UK's responsibility not his, as opposed to taking a holistic approach to Iraq.' As a result 'each of Sanchez's Division Commanders was essentially on his own. There was not a coordinated message coming out of Baghdad' (Interview: Miller, 3rd August 2009). Adrian Weale confirmed that coordination differed according to commander (Interview: 26th November 2010).

American and British forces were of course operating in different areas in Iraq but there was some initial coordination. In Basra at first the British and American PSYOP teams 'all lived together and worked together as one unit', and a British team visited the American area in Baghdad (Interview: Anonymous, 16th August 2010). British officers working with the Americans in a joint PSYOP unit engaged in Basra early on described US products as embodying an aggressive and imperialist attitude (see Chapter 5), and as often poorly researched (Interview: Anonymous, 16th August 2010; Interview: 15th Army PSYOP Group, 22nd November 2005). As Basra-based Americans recognised that mass-produced American leaflets were inappropriate they adopted British methods, assisting their tactical level in-theatre production of PSYOP products (Interview: Anonymous, 16th August 2010).

After July 2003, the joint unit split and forces went to different bases, which mean that cooperation broke down. After the split, one PSYOP officer claimed,

Figure 6.1 Personnel inside the palace at CPA Baghdad.

Figure 6.2 Ian Tunnicliffe inside the palace at CPA Baghdad.

as far as I could see they didn't actually do much from that point on ... our organisations became more separate and we would still go and meet with them from time to time ... But it wasn't very effective coordination ... we'd say 'We've done this' and they'd go 'We've done that' and 'That's nice'.

The Americans reverted back to importing products designed in the US. British PSYOP 'were based at the Divisional Headquarters ... at Basra Airport. The Americans were based in Saddam's Palace in Basra' (Interview: Anonymous, 16th August 2010). One Iraq expert said that the decision of the US Chief Administrator in Iraq, Paul 'Jerry' Bremer, to use the Presidential Palace in Baghdad led to a perception that 'America had simply replaced the dictatorship by installing itself in its old palaces and putting a wall around preventing Iraqis from gaining access' (Interview: Anonymous, 2010). There was evidence of building British resentment too:

> they were in the palace, they had a swimming pool and they were eating lobster ... all they could get to us was chicken nuggets and yellow jelly. (Interview: Pennett, 15th February 2011)

Bremer responded directly to Rumsfeld and, according to Tunnicliffe, 'had ridiculous power that I will probably never – I think he had $19 billion budget to roll out in a few months' (Interview: 8th July 2013). According to Dorrance Smith who was Senior Media Advisor to CPA Baghdad for Ambassador Paul Bremer from September 2003,

> I saw my role as ... a problem-solver ... and I had pretty much carte blanche in terms of resources and support to do whatever was necessary in order to fix it ... I pretty much was unencumbered in terms of having support from the White House.

He stated that neither the Pentagon nor the State Department were actually driving the CPA effort:

> the Defense Department ... was not actively involved in the strategic communications side of it. And, even though Bremer was Ambassador – he had to write up and do cables back to the State Department, I never found that the State Department was taking over strategic communications either.

But Dorrance Smith said,

> There were different departments that were operating ... that were not coordinated. My sense was that the CPA which was being funded by the Defense Department was *really* being run by the National Security Council ... It was pretty much, in terms of my chain of command working through the CPA and the NSC and the White House.

The entire NSC and White House 'were impatient and we couldn't do it fast enough, which helps an operation like that because whoever gets in your way, you can find a way to get beyond them' (Interview: Smith, 10th September 2013).

There were separate streams of activity not coordinated into the Bremer/Smith-led CPA activities and sometimes running against them: 'I pretty much figured out within a few weeks of being there that they didn't have the capabilities and the personnel to accomplish what we needed to do so we did this with the White House and [President Bush's Deputy Communications Director] Scott Sforza and a group of people that we set up' (Interview: Smith, 10th September 2013).

CPA Baghdad was insular, according to Adrian Weale, based in the south, a 'self-licking lollypop':

> For all the thousands of people who were working [there] we heard virtually nothing from them. We got the odd email … or phone call telling us to do something. But they were never based on any kind of analysis of the local situation and they were utterly unrealistic. (Interview: 26th November 2010)

The CPA was 'hugely American' and according to then-DTIO Iraq Desk Officer at the MoD, Ian Tunnicliffe, in August came

> the defining moment … the bombing of the UN compound. And it was at that point that … one could call it a collective shudder of panic … Brits decided to gather a whole bunch of people with relevant expertise and throw them into the CPA in an attempt to positively influence on what the Americans were doing.

This included John Sawers, mentioned below. But Smith said the British 'were working as part of Strategic Communications, which wasn't operating in terms of what the White House, the CPA and *we* were trying to do' (Interview: 10th September 2013). Ian Tunnicliffe flew in to become Director Plans at the CPA's StratComms and found acute operational and tactical coordination problems there. These, he believed, were often political, arguing that some personnel used the operation to further their ideological quest or career goals:

> Quite a few people who were actually in the [Office of Strategic Communication] were there because they were actually Republican idealists … serving their time doing something on a positive note which would then go back into the Republican system in the US … so it was considered a good tick. And there were a number of people who were there for ideological reasons … they were supportive of Bush. … Often … the real emphasis was on the American audience, not on any other audience … If you're gonna really piss off an audience, which one do you do? Well inevitably … it was the Iraqi one. (Interview: Tunnicliffe, 8th July 2013)

MoD planning was key, Tunnicliffe said: 'I was on the Iraq Communications Group, the ICG, and heading that was Alastair Campbell … either my boss or myself would go to No. 10 meetings … [Campbell] was a *brilliant* operator …

Figure 6.3 Slide from presentation by Ian Tunnicliffe, Baghdad, 2003.

but he was operating one week ahead and we had been trying to do plans that would cover months and the political sensitivity' (Interview: 8th July 2013). With a divided CPA Baghdad, and little internal or external communication, some British personnel began to utilise informal relationships with American officers to get things done. In one example, Weale described how a British official, Charles McFadden in CPA Basra, was overwhelmed due to the poor coordination. Weale navigated the problems he encountered informally: 'we found ... a US Air Force contracting officer who could also approve these projects if they were you-know, handled in the right way ... and so we just short-cut and went to them' (Interview: 26th November 2010).

It was among these struggles that in October 2003 the new broadcaster, Iraqi Media Network (IMN), which became Al Iraqiya, was being set up by the CPA and US contractor SAIC (Science Applications International Corporation).

When he first arrived at StratComms, Tunnicliffe said, 'I had ridiculous resources compared to the UK' but he said of five million PSYOP leaflets produced, only about 3 per cent would get to the target audience – satellite TV had taken off. Iraq was watching Al Jazeera, so for election preparations he decided to push out adverts through Bell Pottinger. Tunnicliffe said, 'I went direct to Bremer [who] liked the idea, and ... he said "Yeah, sure do it" ... So we arranged the $6m contract in about a week.' Tunnicliffe saw it as successful,

Figure 6.4 Slide contrasting US/Arab media images.

Figure 6.5 Slide contrasting US/Arab media images.

because 'A lot of people *did* want to vote, so we didn't actually have to *persuade* them. We had to tell them about it' (Interview: 8th July 2013). Dorrance Smith (later in 2006 the Assistant Secretary of Defense for Public Affairs) fought him on it; when Fallujah happened, Tunnicliffe left for a few days: 'Dorrance stopped the adverts from going out and I came back and started them again.' Smith was opposed to putting anything out on Al Jazeera, according to Tunnicliffe. Dorrance Smith explained his position:

> I don't recall having an opinion about the Bell Pottinger ads being on AJ. And I categorically deny having anything to do with stopping the ads on Al Jazeera. My job was to oversee the Iraqi Media Network IMN – which was fully funded by the USG – including Al Iraqiya over which I had oversight. We believed strongly that Al Iraqiya could only be credible if it was operated by Iraqis and that Iraqis maintained editorial control. We [thought that] to insert ads or [Public Service Announcements] paid for by the CPA would pervert that process, and undermine the credibility we were trying to establish. With Bremer's backing, we didn't put the ads on Al Iraqiya, and it was the right call.

For him, the problem was that

> there was no communication apparatus set up from [the military] side and from the civilian side, be it the state department, the CPA, or Public Affairs at the Pentagon, there was pretty much no strategy other than trying to buy ads ... to influence the Iraqis ... and they brought in that British group ... Bell Pottinger ... threw a whole ton of money at them to make ads ... Well there were a couple of problems, the ads ... were made in Kuwait using Kuwaitis not Iraqis. I got into something of a battle, because they wanted to air them on Al Iraqiya, and it sort of reeked of US propaganda, buying print ads on the Iraqi Media Network which we owned ... even Ambassador Bremer was confused as to what they were trying to communicate and so we didn't put them on the air, which they were very resentful of.

Smith said, 'I was very sensitive about [it appearing to be "Bremer TV"] and letting the Iraqis run their own network' (Interview: 10th September 2013).

In one such example, when told by CPA Baghdad to halt the election preparations (probably by Smith) the former Chief of Staff for the Coalition Provisional Authority, Deputy Governor of Dhi Qar Province (July–December 2003) Adrian Weale in Nasiriya said they 'cracked on regardless' (Interview: 26th November 2010). The situation in the CPA weakened coordination with the British areas, however; one IO Officer who arrived in Basra in September 2003 said that specific coordination of messages didn't occur at the level of production:

> So the strategic messages *were* reaching the area that I was responsible for. But it's ironic that even though I was [a] public well for the messages, I wasn't aware of what the [American] products were [without] that ability to monitor them. (Interview: Corcoran, 8th June 2006)

Tensions between British and American bureaucracies and the disarray at CPA Baghdad culminated in 2004's Fallujah debacle (see Chapter 4 and above). At this time, a British diplomat, Hilary Synnott, was in charge of the CPA but reported to both Tony Blair in London and Paul Bremer in Baghdad (Foreign & Commonwealth Office, April 2004). Synnott and Lamb, during the Iraq Inquiry, both described the lack of coordination in the CPA (Iraq Inquiry, 2010) and Hersh blames Bremer for mid-ranking Baathists rising 'to control the insurgency' (2004: 281). Some personnel used informal contacts where information was not forthcoming. Weale recalled using his informal intelligence connections to help him deal with the lack of coordination out of Baghdad:

> my background is in military intelligence, so I had good connections with our intelligence set-up in Basra and [would] generally go down there once a week and just get myself briefed up on what was going on ... The CPA eventually got some security and intelligence people ... so I would talk with them [and] the Iraqi Police ... various Iraqi political parties [with] informers and ears on the ground [even] Muqtada Al-Sadr's people [the Islamic Supreme Council of Iraq]. (Interview: 26th November 2010)

Crisis-managing US defence: strategic networks

A need for British personnel to maintain communication channels with the receptive State Department, whilst not alienating an insular Defense Department, may have contributed to some variability in coordination with both. Whereas Blair was close to the State Department,[4] this would position him in opposition to Rumsfeld. Just before the invasion Rumsfeld commented that Britain's role was 'unclear' (BBC News, 2004). His biographer said those who knew him would say 'don't mind Rumsfeld', he was 'undiplomatic' and 'didn't treat the allies any differently than he treated Congress, or the Joint Chiefs, or the Press' (Interview: Graham, 24th July 2009). Despite the Anglo-American power imbalance Torie Clarke said,

> My sense is it was much more *equal partners* [with the UK] across the board, across the planning, in the strategy, the execution of the military in the classic sense and also in the information space in which I operated. I didn't see it as *them* complementing *us* or vice versa so much as working together. (Interview: 4th December 2013)

In the Pentagon, Clarke remembered the coordination and relationships with the UK as particularly strong for her, in a 'consistent' way. She cited an example:

> early on in the Iraq War when some journalists ... were trapped in a hotel or something like that. And they were not embedded journalists, they were ... unilaterals and they got themselves in a bad spot and their organisation contacted us and said 'We need help' and it was Brits who went in and helped them out ... it

was very easy for me to pick up the phone to whoever my counterpart was at the time and say this is what's going on and he spoke to the right people in the British Headquarters and they got it done. (Interview: 4th December 2013)

Blair made some efforts to strengthen more liberal elements in the US administration, like Colin Powell, and modify public outcomes, which was crucial to his leadership's *domestic* interests to nurture international perceptions of legitimacy. Some would argue Blair was attempting to complement perceived American weakness at the political level. In fact Armitage argued that British efforts hadn't gone far enough; when it came to Iraq War planning, the State Department struggled to get their support vis-à-vis the Defense Department, even though 'some in the [British] defence establishment thought that the ... operational plan was not as it should be'. Armitage said that

The Foreign Office was a little worried we hadn't done complete planning, same thing that Powell and I worried about. But we ... failed to get sufficient attention by our President and we couldn't get Mr Blair to raise it with the President. (Interview: 21st July 2009)

However, Franklin Miller said one concern that was raised was the US government's information campaign; it was 'a point the Prime Minister raised repeatedly with the President during the summer and fall of 2003' – perhaps trying to fire-fight public opinion in the wake of a poorly planned invasion. Miller observed that Bush had confidence both in Blair and in British capabilities, stating that

at one point the President, who was frustrated by the US government's inability to get the message out, said that 'If I haven't fixed it [the propaganda campaign] by Christmas Tony [Blair], I'm gonna give it to you' ... but he never did fix it and the responsibility never was given to the UK. So in that sense there was discussion. (Interview: 3rd August 2009)

This may have come too late – Dorrance Smith, who was then in his post at CPA Baghdad, said,

I remember in 2004, at some point Tony Blair got involved, cause the Brits were very frustrated with the way things were going and he sent ... someone who had been in charge of Sky News or I think it was a friend of his to come to Iraq do a survey of why things weren't ... working. I showed them what we were doing ... And they went away quite satisfied ... but it was April, May and we were about to depart anyway. There wasn't a whole lot they could've done about it. (Interview: 10th September 2013)

While Armitage concluded that British influence during the period overall amounted to 'not much' (Interview: 21st July 2009), in the White House, Miller perceived British strategic influence as crucial:

I don't think the President would've gone back to the UN in the fall of 02 ... if not for Tony Blair. Absolutely. The President was inclined to say, 'Damn the torpedoes, full speed ahead'. And I think the Prime Minister convinced him to do that and gave Powell an opportunity to jump on the bandwagon. But I think the Prime Minister absolutely was significant in driving Bush back to the UN. (Interview: 3rd August 2009)

Blair's administration ultimately played a role in addressing US concern. They allayed American fears of UN scrutiny as a threat. The NSA's Frank Koza requested a 'surge' in intelligence-gathering at the UN Headquarters in New York, to gain 'insights' into country reactions to the ongoing debate and voting intentions (2003). The scope was huge, highlighting priority countries but, Koza said, 'minus US and GBR of course'. Koza stated he was drawing in 'the full gamut of information that could give US policymakers the edge in obtaining results favourable to US goals or *to head off surprises*' including communications with both Security Council members and non-members (Koza, 2003; emphasis added). For Blair's administration, political support hinged on domestic public perceptions of the war and strategic objectives were seen as dependent on the Anglo-American alliance. Any strategic gains in relative influence that might have been made by Blair vis-à-vis America may have been constrained by the domestic political cost, however, as any influence was not immediately apparent to the public.

Rumsfeld may have been 'unclear' about Britain's role, but with formal planning structures failing under his command of the Pentagon, Britain's utility was palpable to the White House. Miller denied that a lack of dialogue made the British relationship with the Pentagon more difficult since the informal links were still open; it meant he 'was able to do a great deal' through informal relations (Interview: 3rd August 2009). Lawrence Wilkerson laughed that 'you use the informal processes to make the decision and you use the formal processes to announce it' (Interview: 23rd June 2009). In planning and policy-making, interactions were often free-form and informal. Richard Armitage described how discussion enabled them to coordinate the message at the strategic level:

So they'd be talking ... all the time. Yeah, here's what we're gonna say here, here's what gonna say there, or if there was a question ... we saw you said X yesterday, is this indicating change of policy? That kinda ... *slight modulation ... we all have different ... audiences. We're not contradicting ... I don't think we ever contradicted each other. And that's the way you do that*. (Interview: 21st July 2009; emphasis added)

They were agreeing plans without being rigidly prescriptive. In the bureaucracy, Wilkerson observed how 'the informal relationships are very often far more important than the formal relationships' (Interview: 23rd June 2009).

A British joint planner based at CENTCOM, Sir John Reith, described how, as an information vacuum emerged in Washington, MoD official channels also dried up. But his initiative enabled him to become 'the conduit' back to the MOD through Permanent Joint Headquarters for 'a flow of information as to what the Americans were doing'. This was facilitated by a 'close relationship' with Commander Tommy Franks, who 'jokingly used to call me his deputy commander'. Reith stated his role had to be 'dynamic' and he compared it to playing on an ever-changing sports field (Reith, 2010). Problems within the Pentagon were feeding US military frustration and, accordingly, the importance of British dialogue at the political level to daily war-planning in Washington.

This appears to be significant to how Iraq operations progressed. Miller said that he was in regular contact with 'friends of at least a decade, sometimes many decades' in the senior MoD bureaucracy and British military (Interview: 3rd August 2009). For Wilkerson, small differences in working practices made 'all the difference in the world' (Interview: 23rd June 2009). At the strategic level, the State Department's Richard Armitage described his 'relaxed, sometimes ribald relationship' with the Foreign Office. Personal, long-standing relationships seem to have contributed fluid ties between what might otherwise be a rather frustrated formal structure with two potentially discordant bureaucracies with idiosyncratic internal dynamics. Strategic level relations were reported to have been smooth and Armitage couldn't 'remember a major difference' occurring before he left in 2005. He believed rapport 'was a little less, 2006–7–8' and thought this change in dynamics was due to different 'personalities. Dr Rice … and … people changed. [Britain] changed Foreign Ministers … it certainly wasn't a conscious policy choice' (Interview: Armitage, 21st July 2009). Miller described his own 'very close relations with the senior staff in the main building [MoD]' and recalled being in 'almost daily touch, at least comparing information and talking about what's happening and what wasn't' (Interview: 3rd August 2009).

In fact, the Pentagon was so highly controlled that information links with the White House and State Department were effectively shut down, but the breakdown of coordination made this informal information exchange *essential* to daily functioning. Former NSA Director for Strategic Communication Col. Jeffrey Jones considered the embassies to be crucial to 'reinforce perceptions of American engagement and outreach' in a properly coordinated communications strategy (2005: 114). Indeed Armitage remembered much dialogue with the UK who 'were right with us at CENTCOM headquarters', and 'Chris Meyer and David Manning – the two ambassadors the time I was there, now Nigel [Sheinwald] – I nearly every day was on the phone or in person with them' (Interview: 21st July 2009). Miller recalled that the crucial relationship was 'David Manning, or later Nigel Sheinwald to [Condoleezza] Rice', meeting one-to-one (Interview: 3rd August 2009). Though Manning declined to comment, his importance was echoed by Armitage along with 'Ambassador Meyer' both of whom 'were damn good. Energetic'. He said that

> All of us in the bureaucracy had pretty long-standing relations with Manning when he was in 10 Downing, and ... Chris Meyer ... In cases some thirty years of relationship. So, for a bunch of reasons beyond ... I mean the *personal* reasons, beyond the special relationship. I don't have any complaints. (Interview: Armitage, 21st July 2009)

The embassies and proactive British Ambassadors performed an enhanced role in the coordination of information under these pressured circumstances:

> There was nothing that I knew ... which I did not share promptly with my friends at the embassy ... absolutely nothing that I had that didn't get passed on immediately, and I believe the same is true from them. (Interview: Miller, 3rd August 2009)

The flexible nature of informal relationships helped facilitate an important assistive and complementary role for British officials. As Miller recalled, even before Paul Bremer got to Baghdad in May 2003, 'the White House was getting no reporting from any source on what was happening on the ground' (Interview: 3rd August 2009). Sir John Sawers, Britain's Special Representative to Iraq (MI6 chief from 2009–2014), arrived around the same time as Bremer and found the CPA in 'serious disorder' (2009). There 'was very limited information flow from Baghdad back to London' at this time, and his aim was to 'initiate a flow of reports back to Whitehall' about the problems in Baghdad. For some time after, he was the White House's only source of information:

> John Sawers ... sending reports to the Foreign Office ... the Embassy here would share those reports with me and Rich Armitage. And then I would obviously send them up the line.[5]

This meant that for the President and White House,

> situational awareness of what was going on in Baghdad for the first four or five weeks after Saddam fell [April] came from Her Majesty's Government. And again, this is all, you know, this is through informal channels and communication. You won't find this in a front channel. (Interview: Miller, 3rd August 2009)

Informal Anglo-American relations effectively acted as a prosthetic channel, bypassing formal systems at the Pentagon to facilitate strategic-level awareness and planning necessary for success in the propaganda war and beyond. According to Miller, with formal systems 'You've got lined up diagrams and boxes but at the end of the day it's how the people interact one with another that makes the difference' (Interview: 3rd August 2009). After he arrived in

September to tackle the situation in CPA Baghdad, Dorrance Smith reported that 'there was a very healthy relationship between the CPA and the White House' and very regular communication (Interview: 10th September 2013).

But interviews revealed that even after this, Bremer's side of Baghdad's CPA was being navigated through British personnel's informal relations at the top of the bureaucracy. Armitage recounted tactical-level difficulties 'primarily in Baghdad' with 'Jeremy Greenstock[6] and [Paul] Jerry Bremer' who 'didn't get along at all' (Interview: 21st July 2009). This was crucial to political-level understandings of the position on the ground, and there may have been resistance from the Defense Department to this British prosthetic communication channel to the top. Though their staffs worked closely, Greenstock stated that Bremer (who was in 'the office next door') would not take advice or keep him briefed (15th December 2009). Greenstock was a preferred Iraq contact, which may have helped secure the UK political position with the State Department, a pragmatic necessity for navigating US in-roads, but it seems likely that it inflamed British enmity with Bremer and the Defense Department. But Richard Armitage in the State Department also stressed the value of these British relationships compared to US contacts under the DOD:

Figure 6.6 The 'Green Room' – Office of Strategic Communication, CPA Baghdad.

whenever I went … I went eight times to Baghdad, I always walked right under Bremer's office and right over to Jeremy [Greenstock]'s office to get *his* appreciation … So I benefited much from [the British]. (Interview: 21st July 2009)

Crisis-managing CPA Baghdad: Iraqi Media Network

CPA Baghdad's effort in the propaganda war was seen as highly problematic. Tunnicliffe explained that 'Saddam … used propaganda incredibly effectively and frightened everyone into putting it back on the list.' In an initial attempt at censorship, the CPA

destroyed millions of pounds worth of TV stations and aerials … And in the meantime of course we didn't have any communications and in that first year satellite TV really *absolutely* took off … Al Jazeera and Al Arabiya, which were … broadly hostile to what was going on. (Interview: 8th July 2013)

Having put him in the position of Minister of Culture, British reservist and media contractor, Miles Pennett said Janet Rogan of Basra CPA Senior Staff[7] 'directed' him to 'have a look at the media side'. One of the largest US intelligence contractors, SAIC, had been contracted to rebrand the Iraqi Media Network (IMN) and roll out a network more widely. Despite Dorrance Smith's statement above about the station he initially ran appearing a truly Iraqi station, this former British PSYOP station, Pennett said, 'was seen as Bremer TV'. Pennett began as 'liaison' for these projects; SAIC were to supply equipment. Pennett said he went to 'find out why nothing was happening' with SAIC. Various contractors had been identified as not following through. The CPA Communications Director at the time, Lt. Col. Iain Picard, informed the press of the situation and made international headlines (see Shadid, 2003 and Halpern, 2003). He said, 'The U.S. contractors have their own agenda and that is Washington's agenda' (Halpern, 2003). Pennett said, 'he got removed the next day. No MBE for him' (Interview: Pennett, 15th February 2011).

Pennett reported that 'SAIC were obviously trying to get their own transmitters out' and inaction continued 'from June 2003 to December and eventually … on my leave, I had to go to the Foreign Office [London] and we said "Well how much is it gonna cost to put some sort of comms into the South?"' So, Pennett said,

we brought around a cheap option [about £300K], the Foreign Office turned around said 'We'll pay for it.' [So they went ahead.] That was our self-help really as a British point of view … I sat down with John and said, 'We're gonna do this from a British point of view. I can get Foreign Office sponsors here.' The problem was they were buying all … the latest digital … the Iraqis didn't want that they wanted all 1980s big hand-held cameras that you can't break that they know how to edit.

SAIC were eventually 'binned' around the time Pennett left the British military in December 2003, and Harris Corporation were brought in. Pennett helped Harris 'put a proper studio' together and issue a 'shopping list' which took 'another ten or eleven months to go to America to their division and back' (Interview: 15th February 2011). This left a vacuum. This was mainly, Ayers said, because Mike Furlong (Pentagon, Joint Psychological Operations Support Element) had 'gathered up just about every radio transmitter and print press or whatever' for security reasons but they were then in 'a big holding yard and we couldn't get it ... the reason they *needed* it was because all the other stuff had already been *gathered up!*' (Interview: 17th May 2013).

Pennett argued that crucially for their propaganda effort:

> The basic camera equipment we'd ordered from the FCO came out fairly quickly ... that 12 months would've been a gapfill of no broadcasting had that FCO kit not come in ... It actually kept the South on-air for that extra year and a half until our stuff with Harris came in. (Interview: 15th February 2011)

Harris approached him to 'run Southern Iraq' as 'programme manager' and he stayed managing the network until April 2005. Apparently lines of communication in the UK were strong. Pennett reported that Tony Rowlands, Head Information Operations, Iraq Directorate, UK Foreign & Commonwealth Office, 'was brilliant, because I think they were sensing the frustration on the home turf and the problem was, in a way, we could have just gone straight to the PM's office'. Pennett put many of the problems down to the rigidity of the American system:

> America had the umbrella over everything and I think this was a problem from square one in Iraq ... there was obviously no policy that you *can't* go do your own thing but [the FCO] eventually turned around and said well we're going to have to do our own thing. Because if we're not *seen* to be doing anything, it's getting labelled, 'Well the British aren't doing anything either' ... 'Well hang on a minute, no, we're actually ...' and we can't actually turn around and say 'Well we've got to do what America says', and we'd *hate* to say that! And so for £350,000 or whatever it was we got to not say that and took care of the South. (Interview: 15th February 2011)

SAIC became so significant during the Iraq conflict that *Vanity Fair* referred to it as a 'shadow government' (Bartlett and Steele, 2007). At the same time this of course enabled British personnel in CPA South to continue propaganda function without being abrasive in their relationship with the Americans. In a US report, Lamb noted that

> JFCOM [Joint Forces Command] and CENTCOM reports also noted that the JPOTF [Joint Psychological Operations Task Force] has limited capability to produce TV programming. No live broadcasting in Arabic ... By comparison, the

United Kingdom provided world news programming within 2 weeks of request submission through its liaison office. The British Broadcasting Company and Sky News produced a 1-hour program in Arabic, costing the United Kingdom $15,000 per day. (2005: 116)

Pennett himself differed with IO personnel in his approach to running the station, however, as he didn't want it to appear as a propaganda entity. Pennett did what he called a 'land grab' and strove to remove Al Iraqiya network's army connections with the help of money 'they took from Saddam', which meant they could say 'the Iraqi people' were funding it. When I enquired about the strategic guidance Pennett was getting from British PSYOP, he responded that 'I completely ignored them' (Interview: 15th February 2011). Indeed, British IO Officer Corcoran reported that he 'didn't appreciate his work', that 'the guy didn't do anything' (Interview: 8th June 2006). Pennett therefore apparently said 'I'll help you put out what you want to put out but ... at the end of the day I was there to set up an Iraqi network.' This was largely about credibility of the message, as he argued: 'PSYOP, you know, if it's good, you don't actually know you're being PSYOPed ... it can be done' (Interview: 15th February 2011).

Indeed, as a contractor, Pennett was able to take a lot of delegated responsibility for decision-making; 'When my country director came in, he ... would let me make ... at times ... big decisions.' In one example, Pennett claimed he 'wasn't allowed to do' advertising at the newspapers he was running; 'Bremer wouldn't allow it' as 'they wanted this BBC-type format' but had been using US money so had no claim to independence. Pennett said he was able to navigate this; 'I got my *regional* people advertising'. This meant that although 'when we handed over in April, the Finance Minister refused to let the pay go out' and 'the people didn't get paid for three months' this did not affect them – 'I got emails saying, you know, good job you were advertising in the South otherwise you would have to shut down.' Pennett essentially ensured the propaganda by working with those he trusted and navigating US policies he found unhelpful. Pennett was working closely with CPA Baghdad's Gary Thatcher who had been brought in as CPA Communications Director for the whole of Iraq by this point and provided a much-needed American point of influence with CPA Baghdad. He was 'very approachable' and always available to 'hear what could be changed, what could be shaped'. It was apparently 'a case of him being much more worker/user-friendly with [Strategic Command]. That link didn't seem to happen before' (Interview: 15th February 2011).

British Contractor for SCL Nigel Oakes was very critical of how contracting had been operated in the US, particularly out of Joint Military Information Support Command (for example to Bell Pottinger, Leonie and Lincoln Group). He said, 'whatever you said in your proposal ... the more dishonest you were, the higher chance you had of winning the contract', which disadvantaged a quality bid. He said, 'anybody can do it for a couple o' hundred grand if you're not gonna do it properly. [There were] a number of [contractors] who were found to be making the data up' (Interview: 24th October 2013). He went to the US Congress with a proposal: 'we said, look, you can resolve all this with ... an assessment framework' to ensure effectiveness of the output. He worked with NSC Director Jeffrey Jones who 'was absolutely key to getting this assessment thing in' although, as he 'was also tied to Booz Allen ... there was slight commercial conflict of interest ... hoping to get Booz Allen to do the assessments rather than anybody else' (Interview: 24th October 2013). It went through in 2007–8.

This helped Oakes gain recognition more widely, in the 'Counter-terrorism Communications Centre [which] very much realised ... what we [were] trying to do and ... were big supporters [as well as] Doc Cabayan ... the Chief Scientific Advisor to the Pentagon, he's very powerful'. Oakes saw a positive future for 'influence' in the US, with 'Austin Branch, who's just left the office of Secretary of Defence' and was 'moving in the right direction and his new shop in NCTC ... is gonna be thinking again more in this area [behaviour change]' (Interview: 24th October 2013).

Coordinating the 'surge' propaganda

As British forces were pulled out of Basra in 2007, Tony Blair declared that the operation had been 'successful' (Blair, quoted in Tempest, 2007). Despite US concerns about British handling of the campaign, it was taken for granted that the perception would be managed together to maximise gains. Coordination would achieve the optimal information outcome for both leaderships by balancing announcements and producing an agreed, consistent message.

Graham Wright, DTIO at the time, described how, 'when the surge in Iraq was announced, America was to announce [it] at about the same time as the UK was going to start drawing down in Basra'. They determined that this would create the perception of incompetence or disconnect. People would ask since they're 'here as a coalition, why are the Americans putting more in and the Brits are taking stuff out?' The answer they decided they needed to convey was 'Basra is fixed and we've gotta go home ... Baghdad's not fixed and it needs to be fixed and it needs more people.' The concern was that the British voice would not be the most credible; the perception would be 'they're bound to say that aren't they?' – it would seem like an excuse for pulling out. So for Britain it was

> really helpful ... for an American to say ... the Brits are going home because they fixed Basra and actually we want to get to that position ourselves and we're not there yet so we've had to bring some more people in. (Interview: Wright, 1st June 2009)

The feeling was that the perception of the UK position 'would be much stronger if it was an American saying it about us' and so 'sometimes joining up is about trying to do that'. In this case, the coordinated US announcement was planned and a speech by Blair delayed until after it, but Foreign Minister Margaret Beckett 'happened to be in-country' and 'said something earlier than the announcement was due'. This created a perception-management situation where

> our General, who [was] in Baghdad working with the Americans, spent the next three days rushing around ... saying 'Look, this is not what's happening, this is the deal and it wasn't quite as she portrayed.' (Interview: Wright, 1st June 2009)

The public opinion contexts of Britain and America's differing national propaganda channels functioned as differing 'capabilities' which they used to complement each other. The coordination of the announcements above[8] clearly shows a willingness on the part of the Americans also to assist Britain to ensure the message conveyed did not contradict *British* domestic interests, indicating a propaganda relationship that could be mutually beneficial. It also emphasises how negotiation in how the countries handle information can make or break the perceptions within and of the alliance. Formal structures are highly dependent on informal relations, and the domestic understandings of each partner play an important intervening role.

Conclusion

It is somewhat debatable whether the oft-cited 'special relationship' has really been 'special', particularly at certain points since the decline of the British Empire (and compared to US relations with Israel or Saudi Arabia for instance). In practical outcomes the contemporary relationship could be said to be rather one-sided and there has been a marked change in perceptions of it. At times the material basis of the partnership has been doubted as having any worth beyond propaganda. However, there has undoubtedly been a sustained relationship that varied considerably in basis, strength, power balance and role in domestic and international politics over the course of post-war history. Crucially, this is because both countries valued cooperation (or avoiding contradiction) in the way the alliance is perceived by each partner and the rest of the world. A desire to maximise influence within the coalition for dominant interests of the British leadership made the British 'value' perceived by American eyes extremely important to the British leadership and drove a continued effort to forge positive perceptions. Despite Britain being demonstrably the junior partner with US attentions so widely drawn, the two states' institutional cultures allowed key channels of influence which they used to advance their institutional objectives in the Iraq War.

Notes

1 British Flight Lieutenant Iain Paton described how in London, Iraq planning was 'so restricted' that 'we had to make our own arrangements for data network planning with US coalition partners' which was 'organised at our own initiative independent of any direction from the chain of command' (Interview: 19th October 2009).

2 Thorp's efforts to shape the US 'Strategic Communication' were contested, however, as mentioned above, and increasingly US Public Affairs efforts were marginalised.

3 Iraq Commanding General, Multi-National Force, June 2004 to February 2007.

4 Wilkerson had 'a lot of respect and admiration for him' (23rd June 2009).

5 And, of course, these informal ties are likely to have been carried to Sawers's next post as political director of the FCO, then in SIS.

6 Greenstock ultimately criticised the invasion, calling it 'of questionable legitimacy' at the Chilcot Inquiry (15th December 2009).

7 Rogan, according to Tomlinson's evidence, has worked for MI6; Pennett described her as 'British top floor' (Interview: 15th February 2011).

8 This demonstrates the process using an unsuccessful attempt; successful coordination attempts would be unlikely to be revealed publicly as this would expose the enduring perception.

7

Countering terror, denying dissent

Given the dramatic period of adaptation that followed 9/11, it's important to reflect on the changes in propaganda and deconstruct the role played by the Anglo-American relationship, with a view to bringing wider discussion in academia, policy and wider society. This book has examined the extent and manner in which Anglo-American relations shaped the direction of propaganda strategy, within the wider 'counter-terrorism' adaptation of both countries. It showed how the domestic structures of each country's bureaucracy, its wider propaganda apparatus and cultural idiosyncrasies were crucial to its adjustment to what was seen as a new security context. This influenced the nature and extent of the coordination between the two states. An underlying imbalance was drawn into this analysis – US superiority in 'hard power', economy, and pretty much everything else, compared with much-lauded British 'expertise' in counter-insurgency. This balance was crucial to perceived and actual roles in the conflicts as well as organisational forms. The approach taken here moved beyond crude structures to consider practitioners as agents in international relations, and the author rejects the examination of foreign policy in isolation from the institutional cultures within which change is negotiated. The latter approach fails to problematise planners' assumptions about foreign policy or examine the struggles within systems and attempts to exclude some from decision-making. Nor does it account for the ways in which dominance is established within the social structures that underpin the international system, through human action and culture as well as material factors. Only by considering international politics this way can we understand the relationship between global policy changes, publics, planners and propaganda; a relationship that is fundamentally shaping our world. During the resolute examination of the research evidence presented here, a series of central implications arose which have been unpacked fully through this book. The evidence demonstrates important changes affecting propaganda, and also details how Britain came to play a significant role in the Anglo-American propaganda effort, particularly during the Iraq War. The present chapter will situate the research findings within a wider discussion of legitimacy. In so doing it will emphasise the need for debate and comment on the shape of change in propaganda, and the future of British Atlanticism.

Changing practice, stifling debate

As we saw above, practitioners in UK and US government institutions often argue that propaganda is a tool of foreign policy and 'limited' war which is used (by their government) to serve the public interest. Arguments like these imagine a democratic tradition in propaganda, focusing on the desired 'end' of public interest – of protecting and 'serving' the public, preventing conflict and countering enemy lies. It is a *paternalistic* argument for propaganda, which puts it in the realms of bureaucratic and military 'service' for the common good.

Here it is important to discuss what 'ends' are served in the public's name. The declared goals being served by the 'hearts and minds' campaign were nominally to end 'terrorism' and ensure domestic and global security. Domestically within the US, around 3,000 people were killed on 9/11, but the number of terrorist attacks has fallen and stayed low since 2001, and the danger posed to Americans by terrorism has decreased despite continued discussion of ongoing 'threat'. The introduction discussed how this 'War on Terror', whilst being geographically unlimited, was also theoretically unlimited in its duration; its ultimate goal (to end 'terrorism') being an essentially unachievable end.

As for 'ensuring domestic and global security', Western powers continue to export arms to developing countries responsible for human rights abuses, the US being the largest supplier, followed by Russia, France, Germany and the UK (Perkins and Neumayer, 2010: 3). The 'War on Terror' conflicts had a long-term destabilising impact: Iraqi casualties are estimated at 1,455,590 (Just Foreign Policy, 2013).[1] Refugees fleeing the conflicts placed a strain on neighbouring states: for example, in 2007 there were 2.1 million Afghan refugees in Pakistan (UNHCR, 2009).[2] Globally, 'terrorism' and attacks attributed to Al Qaeda are reported to have proliferated in this period (START, 2011). In June 2013, as Britain and America approached 2014 withdrawal, a UN report showed that Afghan civilian casualties had increased by 23 per cent, comparing the first six months of 2012 and 2013 (UNAMA, 2013). Voice of America acknowledged that 3,000 civilians were killed and wounded in the first five months of 2013 (Behn, 2013).

Where once propaganda audience targeting added an additional layer of legitimacy to propaganda's image, since 9/11 this has eroded. Propaganda has historically been justified in relation to state-centric assumptions of relative security, which assume easy demarcation of national audience targets. Richard Shiffrin, former Deputy DOD General Counsel for Intelligence and Compartmented Activities has argued in defence of the US domestic ban:

> When the government tries to sway the American public ... it imperils the
> essential relationship between the governed and the governing ... while a particu-
> lar undertaking may be intended to be benign, even ameliorative, what is to
> prevent a partisan effort or a malign one in the future? (2006: 3)[3]

These issues have not been resolved, but as the operational reasons that made
clearly defined audiences possible have disappeared, the new operational imperative was the 'consistency' of the propaganda message, and coordination was
prioritised to ensure effectiveness. Werner Levi once argued that 'the nation-
state system compels statesmen to place national interests above morality, so
that in most cases moral norms serve rather than determine interests' (1965:
226) and of course, the 'national interests' are institutionally defined.

Changing structures and doctrine, the stated use of international relationships to evade restrictions, the use of profit-driven contractors in setting
propaganda messages, as well as the expressed concerns of some practitioners
about changes taking place all indicate that curbs on propaganda must be re-
examined. The adjustment of the propaganda systems occurred largely
internally, undebated and isolated from outside pressures. It was a particularly
difficult transition for the US whose rules are more codified. The infighting on
this subject between streams in the military is partly a power-play between
personnel who tend to forward their own department and position. The
streams also have slightly differing cultural qualities, which change their understanding of what is 'legitimate' propaganda. It would be wrong to say genuine
concern was not present in some interviews regarding the extent of persuasion.
This research found the propaganda 'War on Terror' involved a cultural
struggle, not just with the in-theatre audience, the international community or
the British and American publics, but also played out within and between
cultures in the two states' administrations. Indeed the circumstances in the
propaganda war were ripe for a culture change; to rework and internalise
adjusted definitions of legitimacy to support the extension of an alternative
approach. This opposition failed to gain momentum and ignite public debates
outside of practitioners' communities and left-wing blogs. Where concern *was*
vocal among Public Affairs and the State Department it was systematically
smothered, marginalising Public Affairs for several years. In the world of
surveillance, these same processes of government adaptation to the changing
information environment (again driven by a priority on effectiveness over
ethics) have recently emerged. Government openness to social science is only
insofar as it is seen to be contributing to or supportive of policy and government actions. Only transparency and openness to critical social science and
journalistic enquiry can ensure planning and policy changes are genuinely in
the public interest. The aggressive attempts to censor recent whistleblowers are
very concerning, particularly the campaign of intimidation against the

Guardian, in which equipment was seized and Alan Rusbridger, editor of the *Guardian,* had his patriotism challenged by Chair of the Home Affairs Select Committee, Keith Vaz (see Greenwald et al., 2013; Hopkins and Taylor, 2013).

Of course, to be effective, propaganda must be hidden from awareness. But at the very least, the rules *governing* propaganda use should, in a democratic society, be transparent and subject to enquiry. Whether or not the population in a democracy chooses to support propaganda use and how it chooses to regulate this, it is imperative that those rules which govern it (when, how, if and where it is used) are debated. Yet if we take as evidence the views of many of the public servants interviewed here, still today public opinion is viewed as ignorant and unstable. Public opinion (whether it be domestic or foreign) must with this reasoning be conditioned to correspond to the objectives of a US or UK privileged elite with exclusive authority over knowledge and the decision-making behind its release. The extent of secrecy and self-governance in this area, particularly in the UK, also makes academic enquiry problematic, but, as this book demonstrates, not impossible. Documents, though widely available on Wikileaks and from other sources, are not always a reliable reflection of actual practice. In the US there was a greater willingness to contribute to research and it is important for independent researchers to be able to contribute to an informed debate in this area. Fresh perspectives based on strong evidence could inform attempts to reform systems and would encourage an informed electorate.

Debating contemporary propaganda

Regarding the existing rules, the American system offers huge scope for propaganda abroad but constitutional legal protections for its own public that Britain lacks. This at least makes it much more difficult, for instance, to *intentionally* target its own population with black propaganda. Shiffrin clarifies his defence of the domestic propaganda ban, saying 'the only activity under discussion here is one intended to influence a domestic audience and not one which may do so inadvertently' (2006: 3). It is *not* absolute and the US public should be aware that some manage to evade restrictions, for example by relying on the help of trusted allies. Yet US personnel did find these laws impeded their range of action. The UK's less codified system with greater secrecy and a reliance on doctrine (often seen as 'guidelines') by comparison appears to offer little public protection, and more potential scope for abuse in this area. Any review of the guidance in this area could re-examine this exception since a government might be expected (given the fluidity of the current information environment) to have a duty of care to ensure any of its foreign output is suitable for its domestic audience whether intended for that audience or not.

Externally imposed 'democracy-building' propaganda has if anything merely exposed a sustained lack of understanding of non-Western cultures, particularly in the US, and perpetuated a fear of terror attacks that does not match the reality for those countries. Former PSYOP Battalion Commander Col. Glenn Ayers mocked Public Affairs as ill-equipped for communicating with foreign audiences: 'if you don't understand I'm gonna talk to you *louder* in English' (Interview: 17th May 2013). He has a point. The separation of foreign and domestic has been counter-productive in many ways in how it divides us from and defines our relationship with the international community. Questions that prompt concern internationally regarding these conflicts are still hanging unanswered and unaddressed. For example, while the response to the 9/11 attacks by the US and UK was swift and decisive with respect to the Taliban in Afghanistan, fifteen of the nineteen hijackers were Saudis. Despite the conclusions of the 9/11 Commission that the Saudi Arabian government and leaders played no role, questions have been raised over this even within the US by former Senators Graham and Kerrey (Lichtblau, 2012). Charges of hypocrisy have understandably been lodged at British and US arms sales to this country, as mentioned above (and in debate over the 2013 Foreign Affairs Committee Report) and there is international concern over US sales to Israel ($30 billion from 2009–2018 or an annual average increase of 25 per cent) and its support for that country's actions in Palestine (Reubner, 2011).

Increasingly, defence strategy is embodying what Martin Shaw (2005) has called 'risk-transfer militarism' – reduction of risk to Western intervening forces through drone strikes, for example. Drones are seen as representing the unacceptable combination of arrogance, technological hubris and invulnerability. Foreign policy fall-out cannot be fixed by propaganda. Military practitioners make much of their 'cultural awareness' – the use of anthropology, polling, focus groups, psychological profiling and target audience analysis, not to mention internet surveillance. Many see this as 'listening' to the Iraqis or Afghans and improving 'communication'. But profiling to create a message that will drive attitude or behaviour change is not engaging with that audience; it is not listening, it merely seeks to more effectively dominate. Communication is something that is not to be found in any of the solutions offered by practitioners nor the examples discussed in this book.

Any debate over governance in this area will be hampered if publics do not think of themselves as within an international community, rejecting nationalistic ideas of 'foreign' and 'domestic' as categories determining whether to show concern. 'We' are no longer separate from 'them'. External propaganda comes back within our own media discourse, and may indeed be intended to, perhaps through the collusion of our government with another. It also means that what our government *does* say in our name has no credibility. Dominative foreign propaganda cannot create lasting peace and stability, indeed it shuns true intercultural understanding. By perpetuating dominative forms of communication governments do not 'communicate', they do not learn and they do not make foreign policies that promote international stability.

As discussed in Chapter 1, historically the propagandised image of the 'special relationship' and real-life cooperation hid a struggle for influence then, as today. Both Britain and America targeted propaganda within each other's borders, sometimes with agreement, sometimes not. Each government always sought the other to share a sympathetic world-view. The passivity of the recipient in these processes of 'mass-communication' and the transmission of messages by an elite excludes the possibility that the recipient's interests are represented. Propaganda is being justified more by ends not means, becoming increasingly paternalistic: Williams argued that this represents 'an arrogant preoccupation with transmission, which rests on the assumption that the common answers have been found and need only to be applied' (1958: 314). This book shows that the common answers have definitely not been found, and must continue to be debated.

In many ways Taylor was right in drawing our attention to the intentions and goals of the propagandist – the *interests* served; yet any ideal of 'democratic' propaganda for the public good seems hollow when we consider on what the wider public must base their judgement. Many of the 'lessons' the MoD identified in Iraq are kept in a database in Shrivenham, 'overclassified, to prevent criticism becoming public' (Mackay and Tatham, 2009b: 27). Since it is in this way that conflicts of interest remain unseen, the suffocation of differing agendas in propaganda, and in the decision-making process itself, is at least as significant as the nurture of a dominant message; more so. Lukes argues that power can be exercised over a person 'by influencing, shaping and determining his very wants' (2005: 27). Behavioural propaganda in particular often aims to produce 'consent' by engineering the situation whereby people will produce the 'right' behaviour without their rational awareness that they are being influenced.

The real question is not just the moral or immoral intentions of the propagandist, but whether we can really *know* the intentions and goals of those employing propaganda, if propaganda forms the knowledge-base through which we judge them and they can change the rules with little recourse to consent. Philo and Berry of the Glasgow University Media Group have shown how 'official' messages ultimately dominate media output, and come to influence 'whether the use of force is understood to be legitimate' by the media audience (2004: 257). The essential divide created by the relationship between the citizen and the state means a 'service' culture where it is desirable for practitioners to see beyond the 'weakness' of 'popular' concerns to a constructed realism in which pragmatic military decisions about war-planning's more immediate, operational 'ends' are made. Steven Lukes observes how non-decision-making is a crucial element of any effective analysis of power (2005: 22–23).

Around the time of the 'surge' in Iraq, thinking in the NSC prioritised the saturation of existing *credible* sources, away from establishing new government propaganda outlets – a push through hegemony to strengthen penetration of the US message and create apparent independent media 'consensus'. Prior to this, Torie Clarke also called on propagandists to 'flood the zone' (2006: 79). Matt Armstrong recognised that the problems with propaganda arise from *monopolising* information sources and drowning out or excluding competing voices or critics:

> The real lessons of propaganda, and we ... understood them in the 30s ... in '43, '44, '45 – we got it. The modern person says propaganda is bad information, and the assumption there is that you are going to believe that information ... Propaganda only works when you don't have the competing information! The lessons of Nazi propaganda was not that *government control the media*, it was that *it eliminated all the other voices*. (Interview: 29th April 2013)

Lukes rightly points out that it cannot be assumed that the 'absence of grievance equals consensus'. For him, 'the most effective and insidious use of power is to prevent ... conflict from arising in the first place' (2005: 28, 27). Behavioural influence aims to do this by providing short-cuts to the 'best' option without awareness that rational decision-making has been evaded. Conflicts of power and domination are to be found in what decisions have *not* been made or even appeared on the agenda. This does not necessarily mean they have been censored – saturation can have the same effect.

Within the dominant propaganda cultures of both countries, separation of propaganda powers in the state provided a basis for rational-legal authority. This supports an ideal of Western policy-making as moderate, rational and based on 'limited' war, despite a reality of extensive practice. While there might be 'hot wars' in Afghanistan and Iraq, the 'War on Terror' became an ongoing global conflict being fought through increasingly unconventional, ideological means. Beyond addressing terrorist acts, propaganda has far wider implications in that it aims to *prevent* conflict with the status quo from arising. The 'unlimited' nature of the 'War on Terror' ideological conflict blurs the boundaries between 'wartime' and 'peacetime' operations and renders problematic the traditional geographical limits that democratic states such as Britain and the US previously used to define their security.[4] Institutional assumptions seep into the paternalistic idea that propaganda must address the audience 'as they *really* are' (as a potential threat to stability) not as we'd 'like them to be' (in the ideal world of reasoned debate).

According to a recent classified document within a target country, PSYOP or MISO are now 'usually well coordinated with other US Government efforts', so attention has shifted to reinforcing regional coordination (GAO, 2013: 11). The US continues to make serious attempts to create a centralised controlling propaganda body and this recent classified document states 'improvement' in coordination. Meanwhile, Britain's propaganda apparatus has become increasingly coordinated and centralised under a new NSC and 'influence' activities are now seen as a prized new commodity to be traded abroad, something that could define the country internationally.

Unquestioning Atlanticism and Britain's role

The counter-insurgency response needed for fighting the US 'War on Terror' in a globalised media environment demonstrably posed a significant challenge to the US defence infrastructure. Britain's foreign and defence policy hung on the need to provide a function alongside America, complementing its capabilities. By supporting the US in its 'War on Terror' Britain's leadership was in a position where it was then committed to managing the consequences of the conflicts, 'reconstruction' and insurgencies. In particular it was committed to the 'crisis management' of US 'failures' within which it would be implicated through its unreserved support of the conflicts. Ironically, the two countries' failed efforts to coordinate their apparatus have been shown to be one factor which drew out adaptation in actual activities. Pressure was placed on staff who in turn worked their informal relationships and drove forward whatever solutions they could muster to make the propaganda more effective.

While both countries were seeking to redefine propaganda practice, for Britain this was already more flexible and less codified. Propaganda tactics were often judged relative to America, and seen as standing within a British 'democratic' tradition. British personnel saw a need to 'manage' the US approach through small informal renegotiations, avoiding conflict with Britain's powerful ally and seeking a consistent outcome that would meet objectives in the war. For British personnel, their actions in the 'War on Terror' were seen as a pragmatic necessity – based on the institutional assumption that the partnership is de facto essential. In enabling prosthetic routes of informal planning and communication, Britain was shown here to have made itself extremely useful to American strategic planners, and increased its perceived value with them. This is highly significant because when the problems of the insular American infrastructure *also* constrained the formal mechanisms of Anglo-American cooperation, this not only threatened *British* involvement; potentially it jeopardised both British value to America, and domestic *American* lines of communication. The networks that maintained these functions were supported, particularly where British resources were lacking, by the wide ideological emphasis on British 'expertise'.

America remains dominant in British foreign policy planning. When the qualitative relations between the two countries are considered during this period, the extent to which this was a negotiated, and yet unquestioned, British relationship emerges. The public paid a high price for continued government 'influence' with the US. This has come to be felt in the military also. According to Adrian Weale, who is a founding member of the British Armed Forces Federation, the period was marked by the emergence in the military of a 'degree of uncertainty and unhappiness about British self image and what they're *doing* it for' (Interview: 26th November 2010). Despite this, and increased public mistrust, this defence relationship does not show signs of being tangibly weakened by the public inquiry over Iraq. With public attentions overtaken by the economic crisis and a rhetorical emphasis on the coming 'draw-down' in Afghanistan, defence policies are shifting. Increasingly covert action (mentioned at length above) and drone warfare are being favoured. A recent MoD 'Development, Concepts and Doctrine Centre' report recommends minimising 'the numbers of Service Personnel committed to the battlespace' and advocates increased use of special forces as their losses have less impact on public opinion (MoD, 2012). Not only does this reduce public debate and accountability, but 'Unmanned Aerial Vehicles' lead to a great many civilian casualties and have potential destabilising effects both internally, regionally and in the future relations of the US and Britain within those regions and states.

Propaganda in both countries has been transformed since 9/11, largely through the initiative of key government personnel in both countries who drove adaptation using informal relationships, with US planning enabled during times of strain by British efforts. With fewer restrictions and improved coordination, these propaganda processes they helped ease in will play a central role in supporting current policies, by both the US and a UK Conservative-dominated coalition that surpasses Blair in its Atlanticism.[5]

Notes

1   Comparable independent counts are lacking for the Afghan war (Crawford, 2011).
2   There was also little acknowledgement of UK responsibility toward refugees fleeing these wars, and seeking asylum in Britain, with successive legislation seeking to curb what was often viewed as 'illegal immigration' (see Philo, Briant and Donald, 2013).
3   Armstrong criticises Shiffrin's analysis, because it recommended 'that in the absence of a clear instruction (i.e. law) from Congress, the Defense Department should consider the law as applicable to its activities' which is both 'equal to Defense making law' and an inaccurate interpretation of the intent of Congress (17th May 2012).
4   While the British military was already well suited to ideological and asymmetric warfare, this is of course still operating according to a state-centric definition of security.
5   As evidenced by its stance on Europe and attempts to create stronger links with US power. For example, as early as April 2008 the US Embassy in London's Deputy Chief of Mission, Richard LeBaron, relayed the contents of a conversation with William Hague back to the National Security Council. After confirming that a Conservative replacement for Gordon Brown was likely, the Americans were keen to press the question 'whether the relationship between the UK and the U.S. was "still special"' in Conservative eyes

(LeBaron, 2008). Hague reportedly 'said he, David Cameron and George Osborne were "children of Thatcher" and staunch Atlanticists' – importantly, he recognised that this contrasted with the British public but Hague felt that politicians 'sit at the top of the pyramid'. LeBaron recounted that Hague reassured him that whatever public opinion says, the relationship was 'essential', that 'we want a pro-American regime. We need it. The world needs it' (LeBaron, 2008). Indeed in a later cable, the US Embassy reported back favourably that 'the relationship will be especially close in the defense sphere under Tory leadership' (Susman, 2009).

References

Emails

Anonymous (2010), RAF Flight Lieutenant.

Armstrong, Matt (23rd April 2013), US Chairman of the US Broadcasting Board of Governors, former Executive Director of the Advisory Commission on Public Diplomacy (28th March 2011 – December 2011).

Armstrong, Matt (29th April 2013), as above.

Armstrong, Matt (30th April 2013), as above.

Armstrong, Matt (13th May 2013), as above.

Armstrong, Matt (16th June 2013a), as above.

Armstrong, Matt (16th June 2013b), as above.

Armstrong, Matt (17th June 2013), as above.

Bergman, Simon (Maj.) (8th August 2006), 15th Army PSYOP Group Training.

Carroll, Rory (16th August 2004). Journalist at the *Guardian*.

Dale, Helle (2nd June 2013), Senior Fellow for Public Diplomacy at The Heritage Foundation.

Gutcher, Lianne (28th April 2013), UK Senior Print Editor of *Sada-e Azadi, The Voice of Freedom* newspaper ISAF HQ (December 2007–February 2011).

Gutcher, Lianne (1st June 2013), as above.

Hanasz, Paula (30th April 2013), former Australian Target Audience Analyst and Psychological Operations, NATO International Security Assistance Force, Afghanistan.

Harding, Joel (30th April 2013a), US Former Special Forces, SAIC (2005–2007) and former Director of the IO Institute.

Harding, Joel (30th April 2013b), as above.

Harding, Joel (30th April 2013c), as above.

Harding, Joel (3rd May 2013a), as above.

Harding, Joel (3rd May 2013b), as above.

Harding, Joel (20th May 2013a), as above.

Harding, Joel (20th May 2013b), as above.

Harding, Joel (20th May 2013c), as above.

Harding, Joel (27th May 2013), as above.

Harding, Joel (24th June 2013), as above.

Harding, Joel (9th July 2013), as above.

McFate, Montgomery (7th March 2013), US Former DOD Senior Cultural Anthropologist, Minerva Chair at the Center for Naval Warfare Studies at the US Naval War College.

Naylor, Sean (23rd August 2004), Journalist at the *Army Times* (US).

Nelson, Erik (14th May 2013), former US Editor of *Sada-e Azadi RC-East – The Voice of Freedom* newspaper ISAF HQ, Afghanistan.

O'Hanlon, M. (18th July 2013), Brookings Director of Research: Foreign Policy.

Paton, Iain (4th October 2010), former RAF Flight Lieutenant.

Pfeifle, Mark (18th June 2013a), Deputy National Security Advisor for Strategic Communication and Global Outreach (2007–2009).

Pfeifle, Mark (18th June 2013b), as above.

Pfeifle, Mark (13th July 2013), as above.

Rowland, Lee (7th May 2013), Behavioural Scientist at the Behaviour Dynamics Institute, London.

Senior State Department Official (2013).

Shadian, Scott (21st July 2007), State Department: US Embassy Kabul's Counter-Narcotics Public Information Campaign Program Manager.

Tatham, Steve (11th February 2013), UK former Commanding Officer 15th Army PSYOP Group.

Treadwell, J. (6th May 2013), former Director of the Joint Psychological Operations Support Element and Commander of 4th Psychological Operations Group in Iraq (2003).

Wingfield, Thomas (1st May 2013), Professor of International Law George C. Marshall European Center for Security Studies and Civilian Rule of Law Advisor to Gen. Stanley A. McChrystal's Counterinsurgency Advisory and Assistance Team (October 2009–February 2010).

Wingfield, Thomas (10th May 2013), as above.

Wingfield, Thomas (21st May 2013), as above.

Wingfield, Thomas (22nd May 2013), as above.

Wingfield, Thomas (29th May 2013), as above.

Wingfield, Thomas (8th June 2013), as above.

Winters, Jim (31st July 2006), US Army Capabilities Integration Centre Staff.

Interviews

15th Army PSYOP Group (22nd November 2005), group interview with three Personnel: Chicksands, Bedfordshire.

Adams, Paul (22nd March 2006), BBC Chief Diplomatic Correspondent: BBC TV Centre, London.

Anonymous (15h July 2010), British intelligence contractor recently returned from Baghdad: telephone interview.

Anonymous (2006), former British intelligence officer.

Anonymous (1st June 2009), DOD Official: Washington, DC.

Anonymous (16th August 2010), Staff Officer at 15th Army PSYOP Group, deployed in

Iraq March to September 2003: Glasgow.

Anonymous (2013), UK official.

Anonymous (2013), MoD source.

Armitage, Richard (21st July 2009), former Deputy Secretary of State, Department of State: Armitage International, Washington, DC.

Armstrong, Matt (6th March 2013), US Chairman of the US Broadcasting Board of Governors, former Executive Director of the Advisory Commission on Public Diplomacy (28th March 2011–December 2011): telephone interview.

Armstrong, Matt (29th April 2013), as above.

Arundell, Ralph (18th April 2013), UK Assistant Head Defence Media and Communications Operations Plans and former Assistant Head Targeting and Information Operations, MoD: London.

Arundell, Ralph (20th February 2014), UK Assistant Head Defence Media and Communications Operations Plans and former Assistant Head Targeting and Information Operations, MoD: telephone interview.

Ayers, Carl Glenn, Col. (17th May 2013), Commanding Officer, 9th Psychological Operations Battalion (Airborne) (2001–2003), Psychological Operations Division Chief, Joint Staff (2006–2008), Assistant to Secretary Donald Rumsfeld and Deputy Secretary of Defense Paul Wolfowitz (2003–2005), Contractor SAIC (2008–2012): telephone interview.

Berry, M. (30 May 2006), Glasgow University Media Group researcher: Glasgow.

Bulmer, Elliot (16th August 2010), former Lieutenant at 15th Army PSYOP Group, deployed in Iraq March to September 2003: Glasgow.

Clark, James (18th July 2004), former *Sunday Times* correspondent: MoD, London.

Clarke, Torie (4th December 2013), former Assistant Secretary of Defense for Public Affairs: telephone interview.

Corcoran, Peter (8th June 2006), Information Operations Officer, Captain of 20 Armour Brigade in Iraq during Op Telic 3 (September 2003–April 2004): Ankara, Turkey.

Dorril, Stephen (20th July 2010), academic, investigative journalist and author of numerous key texts on MI6: telephone interview.

Dorril, Stephen (22nd November 2012), as above.

Drogin, Bob (22nd August 2009), *Los Angeles Times* Intelligence and National Security Correspondent and author of *Curveball: Spies, Lies, and the Con Man Who Caused a War:* telephone interview.

Fallon, William, Adm. (21st July 2009), former Commander of CENTCOM 2007–2008: Washington, DC.

Fekeiki, Omar (12th May 2009), Iraqi journalist, the *Washington Post*: Washington, DC.

Fitzpatrick, Sean K. (30th June 2009), former Chief Creative Officer McCann-Erickson, Creative Director National Center for Unconventional Thought at Potomac Institute for Policy Studies: Williamsburg, VA.

Geran Pilon, Juliana (31st May 2013), Faculty Chairman at the Institute of World Politics: telephone interview.

Graham, Bradley (24th July 2009), Donald Rumsfeld's biographer and *Washington Post* journalist: Washington, DC.

Hamid, Tawfik (26th June 2009), psychologist, Chair of the Study of Islamic Radicalism and former Al Qaeda recruit: Potomac Institute for Policy Studies, Washington, DC.

Harding, Joel (15th January 2013), US former Special Forces, SAIC (2005–2007) and former Director of the IO Institute: telephone interview.

Harding, Luke (29th July 2004), journalist at the *Guardian*: telephone interview.

Hastings, Richard (2nd June 2009), FBI Office of International Operations: Washington, DC.

Jenkins, Jon (28th October 2013), Director, I-to-I Research: telephone interview.

Jones, Nicholas (14th March 2006), author and former BBC Correspondent: London.

Marcus, Jonathan (13th March 2006), Correspondent for BBC World Service: London, BBC Bush House.

McBride, Dennis (5th June 2009), Director, Potomac Institute for Policy Studies and former Naval Captain: Washington, DC.

McCarty, Kevin (13th March 2013), US former National Security Council Director for Global Outreach: telephone interview.

McCreary, T. (Rear Adm.) (15th October 2013), former US Special Assistant to the Chairman of the Joint Chiefs of Staff, former US Navy Chief of Information, former Director of Strategic Communication for the National Counterterrorism Center: telephone interview.

McFadden, Pat (20th April 2006), MP for Wolverhampton North and Former Information Officer: London.

McNair, William (15th August 2006), Public Relations Executive: Edinburgh.

Meek, James (18th July 2004), Journalist at the *Guardian:* London.

Miller, Franklin C. (3rd August 2009), former Senior Director for Defense Policy and Arms Control on the National Security Council staff; US Strategic Command Advisory Group; Council on Foreign Relations: The Cohen Group, Washington, DC.

Oakes, Nigel (24th October 2013), CEO SCL Group, Chairman BDI, former Senior Producer for the Saatchi Group: telephone interview.

Pennett, Miles (15th February 2011), former British reservist and PSYOP/media contractor Al Iraqiya/Nahrain and former Programme Manager for Southern Iraq: telephone interview.

Pfeifle, Mark (12th July 2013), Deputy National Security Advisor for Strategic Communication and Global Outreach (2007–2009): telephone interview.

Plame Wilson, Valerie (11th August 2009), former CIA Undercover Operations Officer 1985–2003 and author of *Fair Game*: telephone interview.

Reeve, William (20th April 2006), former BBC Correspondent and Head of Counter Narcotics Information Programme Afghanistan: London.

Rowland, Lee (5th July 2013), Behavioural Scientist at the Behavioural Dynamics Institute, London: telephone interview.

Rowlands, Kirsteen (17th April 2013), UK Cabinet Office NSC Comms Team, Head of Afghanistan Communications: London, UK.

Sheriff, Vickie (18th April 2013), UK former Head of News at 10 Downing Street and former Territorial Army Media Operations: London, UK.

Smith, Dorrance (10th September 2013), former Assistant Secretary of Defense for Public Affairs and former Senior Media Advisor to Coalition Provisional Authority, Baghdad: telephone interview.

Stelloh, Ren (23rd June 2009) Chief Operating Officer/President PhaseOne Communications and former CIA Station Chief: Washington, DC.

Taverner, Angus (Lt.) (18th July 2004), Director Media Operations (Policy), Office of Director General of Media and Communication MoD: MoD, London.

Taverner, Angus (Col.) (23rd January 2013), former Director Media Operations (Policy), Office of Director General of Media and Communication MoD: Glasgow.

Thorp, Frank (Rear Adm.) (24th August 2009), former Special Assistant for Public Affairs, former First Deputy Assistant Secretary of Defense (Joint Communication) and former US Navy Chief of Information (retired): telephone interview.

Tunnicliffe, Ian (8th July 2013), former British Army Intelligence Corps, former Director Plans in the Office of Strategic Communications of the Coalition Provisional Authority MoD: telephone interview.

UK Diplomatic Official based in Afghanistan (August 2006): London.

van Buren, Peter (24th January 2013), former US State Department Foreign Service Officer, Lead 2 Provisional Reconstruction Teams in Iraq: telephone interview.

Weale, Adrian (26th November 2010), former Chief of Staff for the Coalition Provisional Authority, former Deputy Governor of Dhi Qar Province (July–December 2003) and founder member of British Armed Forces Federation: telephone interview.

Wilkerson, Lawrence (23rd June 2009), former Chief of Staff to Secretary of State Colin Powell, Department of State 2002–2005: Georgetown University, Washington, DC.

Wilson, Doug (10th May 2013), US former Assistant Secretary of Defense for Public Affairs: telephone interview.

Wilson, Doug (14th May 2013), as above.

Wood, Paul (22nd March 2006), BBC Defence Correspondent: BBC TV Centre, London.

Wright, Graham (Air Cdre) (1st June 2009), former UK Director of Targeting and Information Operations, MoD and British Liaison to Joint Chiefs at Department of Defense: British Embassy, Washington, DC.

Zinni, Anthony (Gen.) (2nd June 2009), former Commander of CENTCOM 1997–2000, Acting Director BAE Systems: Washington, DC.

Publications

10 Downing Street (2001), '10 Downing Street Lobby Briefing on Friday 9th November', in *10 Downing Street Online*, available from: www.pm.gov.uk/output/page2359.asp.

Adams, G. (2010), 'McChrystal-izing a Problem: The Militarization of American Statecraft', in *Budget Insight Blog*, 23rd June, Available from: http://budgetinsight .wordpress.com/2010/06/23/mcchrystal-izing-a-problem-the-militarization-of-american-statecraft/.

Adler, Selig (1957), *The Isolationist Impulse: Its Twentieth Century Reaction*, New York: The Free Press.

Aldrich, Richard (2002), *The Hidden Hand: Britain, America and Cold War Secret Intelligence*, London: John Murray.

Alexandrovna, L. (2007), 'CIA Running Black Propaganda Operation Against Iran, Syria and Lebanon, Officials Say', in *Raw Story*, 4th June, available from: www.rawstory.com/news/2007/CIA_running_black_propaganda_operation_against _0604.html.

American Anthropological Association (2009), 'AAA Commission on the Engagement of Anthropology with the US Security and Intelligence Communities: Final Report on The Army's Human Terrain System Proof of Concept Program', *Executive Board of the American Anthropological Association*, available from: www.aaanet.org/cmtes /commissions/CEAUSSIC/upload/CEAUSSIC_HTS_Final_Report.pdf.

Anonymous (2011), 'Forum Comments – MISO: Is it Soup Yet?', in *Small Wars Journal*, 24th June, available from: http://smallwarsjournal.com/blog/2010/06/miso-is-it -soup-yet/.

Aristotle (1984), *The Politics* (trans. Carnes Lord), Chicago: University of Chicago Press.

Armitage, Richard and Nye, Joseph (April 2008), 'Implementing Smart Power: Setting an Agenda for National Security Reform', in *Statement Before the Senate Foreign Relations Committee*, 24th April, available from: http://csis.org/testimony/imple-menting-smart-power-setting-agenda-national-security-reform.

Armstrong, Matt (2010), 'Rest in Peace, Jeff Jones', in *MountainRunner.us*, 11th February, available from: http://mountainrunner.us/2010/02/jeff_jones.html.

Armstrong, Matt (2012), 'Smith-Mundt Act', in *MountainRunner.us*, 5th June, available from: http://mountainrunner.us/smith-mundt/#.UX-VqyqF9e0.

Armstrong, Matt (2012), 'Smith-Mundt Modernization Act of 2012 Introduced in the House', in *MountainRunner.us*, 17th May, available from: http://mountainrunner.us /2012/05/smith-mundt-modernization-ac/#.UYP42iqF9e0.

Arquilla, John and Borer, Douglas A. (eds) (2007), *Information Strategy and Warfare: A Guide to Theory and Practice*, London: Routledge.

Avant, D. (1994), *Political Institutions and Military Change: Lessons from Peripheral Wars*, Ithaca: Cornell University Press.

Azubuike, Samuel (2005), 'The "Poodle Theory" and the Anglo-American "Special Rela-tionship"', in *International Studies*, Vol. 42, No. 2, pp. 123–139.

Baird, B. (2007), 'MSNBC 'Tucker' Interview with Rep. Brian Baird', in *Votesmart*, 21st August, available from: https://votesmart.org/public-statement/283817/msnbc-tucker-interview-with-rep-brian-baird-d-wa-interviewer-tucker-carlson#.UehLGo3 VCSo.

Baker, Norman (2007), *The Strange Death of David Kelly*, London: Methuen.

Bamford, James (2005), 'The Man Who Sold the War', in *Rolling Stone*, 17th November, available from: www.rollingstone.com/politics/story/8798997/the_man_who_sold _the_war.

Barnett, Corelli (1970), *Britain and Her Army 1509–1970: A Military, Political and Social Survey*, London: Penguin.

Bartlett, D. and Steele, J. (2007) 'Washington's $8 Billion Shadow', in *Vanity Fair*, March, available from: www.vanityfair.com/politics/features/2007/03/spyagency200703.

Bauman, Zygmunt (1988), 'Sociology after the Holocaust', in *The British Journal of Sociology*, Vol. 39, No. 4, pp. 469–497.

Baylis, John (1984), *Anglo-American Defence Relations, 1939–1984*, London: Macmillan.

BBC News (2004), 'Blair "Rejected Iraq War Offer"' *BBC News*, 20th April, available from: http://news.bbc.co.uk/1/hi/uk_politics/3641615.stm.

BBC News (2007), 'US Troops "Won't Attend Inquests"', in *BBC News*, 29th August available from: http://news.bbc.co.uk/1/hi/uk/6967982.stm.

BBC News (2010a), 'Judges Quash UK Troops Human Rights Ruling' in *BBC News*, 30th June, available from: www.bbc.co.uk/news/10450556.

BBC News, (2010b) 'Huge Wikileaks Release Shows US "Ignored Iraq Torture"', in *BBC News*, 23rd October, available from: www.bbc.co.uk/news/world-middle-east -11611319.

Beers, Charlotte (2003) in Stout, David 'Official Hired to Improve US Image Resigns', in *New York Times*, 3rd March, available from: www.nytimes.com/2003/03/03 /international/03CND-BEERS.html.

Behn, S. (2013), 'UN: Afghan Civilian Casualties Up Almost 25 Percent', in *Voice of America*, 1st June, available from: www.voanews.com/content/un-afghan-civilian-casualties-up-twenty-five-percent/1679527.html.

Benbow, T. (2006), 'The "Revolution in Military Affairs" and Asymmetric Warfare: Irre-sistable Force or Immoveable Object', Paper at 56th Political Studies Association Annual Conference 'Liberty, Security and the Challenge of Government', 4th April, University of Reading.

Bentham, J. (1843), '"Of Publicity", in an Essay on Political Tactics', in J. Bowring (ed.), *The Works of Jeremy Bentham*, Vol. 2, Edinburgh: Simpkin, Marshall & Co.

Berger, J. (2012), 'Covert Action', in *Joint Forces Quarterly*, Issue 67, 4th Quarter, pp. 32–39.

Bernays, Edward (2004), *Propaganda*, Brooklin: Ig Publishing.

Billingslea, Marshall (2003), 'Testimony to the House Armed Services Committee', in *Department of Defense Online*, April, available from: www.dod.mil/dodgc/olc /docs/test03–04–01Billingslea.doc.

Blair, Tony (2001), 'Tony Blair's Statement Broadcast 10.12EDT', in *BBC News*, 11th September, available from: http://news.bbc.co.uk/1/hi/in_depth/world/2001 /war_on_terror/tv_and_radio_reports/1619536.stm.

Blair, Tony (2010), 'A Six-hour Defence of his Fateful Decision', in *The Independent Online*, 30th January, 30th January, available from: www.independent.co.uk /news/uk/politics/a-sixhour-defence-of-his-fateful-decision-1883654.html

Blankley, Tony and Horn, Oliver (2008), 'Strategizing Strategic Communication', in The Heritage Foundation, 29th May, available from: www.heritage.org/Research/Reports /2008/05/Strategizing-Strategic-Communication

Bomford, A. (1999), 'Echelon Spy Network Revealed', in *BBC News*, available from: http://news.bbc.co.uk/1/hi/503224.stm.

Bower, Tom (1996), *The Perfect English Spy: Sir Dick White and the Secret War 1935–90*, London: Heinemann.

Broadcasting Board of Governors (2013), *Budget FY 2014*, available from: www.bbg.gov/wp-content/media/2013/09/FY-2014-CBJ.pdf.

Brook, Paul (Col.) (2004), 'Chapter 15', in House of Commons, *Select Committee on Defence Third Report*, 3rd March, available from: www.publications.parliament.uk /pa/cm200405/cmselect/cmdfence/63/6302.htm.

Brooks, R. (2012), 'Confessions of a Strategic Communicator', in *Foreign Policy*, 6th December, available from: www.foreignpolicy.com/articles/2012/12/06 /confessions_of_a_strategic_communicator?page=0,0&wp_login_redirect=0.

Bryant, D.C. (1953), 'Rhetoric: Its Function and Scope', *Quarterly Journal of Speech*, Vol. 39 (December), pp. 401–424.

Burnell, P. and Reeve, A. (1984), 'Persuasion as a Political Concept', in *British Journal of Political Science*, Vol. 14, No. 4, pp. 393–410.

Bush, George, W. (2001), 'President Bush's Statement Broadcast 9.30EDT' in *BBC News*, 11th September, available from: http://news.bbc.co.uk/1/hi/in_depth/world /2001/war_on_terror/tv_and_radio_reports/1619536.stm.

Byrnes, Jimmy (1945), *Foreign Relations of the United States, 1945–1950: Emergence of the Intelligence Establishment, Document 28*, 16th October, available from: http://history.state.gov/historicaldocuments/frus1945–50Intel/d28.

Carey, B. (2012), 'Academic "Dream Team" Helped Obama's Effort', in *New York Times*, 12th November, available from: www.nytimes.com/2012/11/13/health/dream-team -of-behavioral-scientists-advised-obama-campaign.html?_r=0&adxnnl=1&page-wanted=all&adxnnlx=1368720100-+07TOkJxUaZXrPB5cPf6Ig.

Carlile, Lord (2007), *The Definition of Terrorism*, London: Home Department. available from: www.official-documents.gov.uk/document/cm70/7052/7052.pdf.

Carter, Lord (2005), 'Lord Carter of Coles' Public Diplomacy Review', in *FCO Online*, available from: www.fco.gov.uk/resources/en/pdf/public-diplomacy-review.

Chandrasekaran, R. (2004), 'Key General Criticizes April Attack In Fallujah' in *The Washington Post*, 13th September, pp. A17.

Charters, David (1989), 'From Palestine to Northern Ireland: British Adaptation to Low Intensity Operations', in David Charters and Maurice Tugwell (eds), *Armies in Low-Intensity Conflict: A Comparative Analysis*, London: Brasseys.

Chermak, S. (2003), 'Marketing Fear: Representing Terrorism After September 11', in *Journal for Crime, Conflict and the Media*, Vol. 1, No. 1, pp. 5–22.

Chiefs of Staff (2004), *JSP 383: Manual of the Law of Armed Conflict*, available from: www.gov.uk/government/uploads/system/uploads/attachment_data/file/27874/ JSP3832004Edition.pdf.

Chomsky, N. (1991), *Necessary Illusions: Thought Control in Democratic Societies*, London: Pluto Press.

Chomsky, N. (1992a), *Excerpts from Manufacturing Consent: Noam Chomsky Interviewed by Various Interviewers*, available from: www.chomsky.info/interviews/1992—— 02.htm.

Chomsky, N. (1992b), 'On Propaganda', *Interview on WBAI*, available from: www.chomsky.info/interviews/199201—.htm.

Chomsky, N. (2002), *Media Control: The Spectacular Achievements of Propaganda*, New York: Seven Stories Press.

Clarke, Torie (2006), *Lipstick on a Pig*, New York: Free Press.

Coalition Information Centre (n.d., 2003?) p6, *Campaign Against Terrorism: A Coalition Update*, available from: www.law.kuleuven.be/iir/nl/onderwijs/terrorisme /ECOterrorcoalUpdate.pdf.

Cobain, Ian (2010) 'War Crimes Charges Aagainst Military Interrogators Would Put MoD on Trial', in *The Guardian*, 9th November, available from: www.guardian .co.uk/uk/2010/nov/09/war-crimes-charges-military-interrogators-iraq.

Cohen, E. (1996), 'A Revolution in Warfare', in *Foreign Affairs*, Vol. 75, No. 2, pp. 37–54.

Collins, S. (2002), 'NATO and Strategic PSYOP: Policy Pariah or Growth Industry', in *Journal of Information Warfare*, Vol. 1, No. 3, pp. 72–78, also available from: http://ics.leeds.ac.uk/papers/vp01.cfm?outfit=pmt&folder=64&paper=985.

Committee on Foreign Relations (2006), *Report to Congress: EMBASSIES AS COMMAND POSTS IN THE ANTI-TERROR CAMPAIGN*, available from:

www.fas.org/irp/congress/2006_rpt/embassies.html.

Conlin, Joseph (2008), *The American Past*, New York: Cengage Learning.

Cook, R. (2003), *The Point of Departure*, London: Simon & Schuster.

Cooper, K. (1944), 'Freedom of Information', in *Time Magazine*, 13th November.

Cordingley, Maj. Gen. Patrick (1996), 'In the Eye of the Storm', London: Hodder & Stoughton, quoted in Ministry of Defence (2001), *Joint Warfare Publication* 3–45 *Media Operations*, available from: http://ids.nic.in/UK Doctrine/UK (9).pdf.

Crawford, N. (2011), *Civilian Death and Injury in Afghanistan 2001–2011*, available from: http://costsofwar.org/sites/default/files/CrawfordAfghanistanCasualties.pdf.

Crewdson, John M. (1977), 'CIA: Secret Shaper Of Public Opinion: C.I.A. Established Many Links To Journalists in U.S. and Abroad', in *New York Times*, 27th December.

Croft, Stuart (2006), *Culture, Crisis, and America's War on Terror*, Cambridge: Cambridge University Press.

CRS Report for Congress (2004), 'Information Warfare and Cyberwar: Capabilities and Related Policy Issues' in *CRS Web*, 19th July, available from: http://digital.library.unt.edu/govdocs/crs//data/2004/upl-meta-crs-6058/meta-crs-6058.ocr.

Cull, N.J. (1994), *Selling War: The British Propaganda Campaign Against American 'Neutrality' in World War II*, Oxford: Oxford University Press.

Cull, Nicholas (2012), *The Decline and Fall of the United States Information Agency: American Public Diplomacy, 1989–2001*, New York: Palgrave Macmillan.

Curran, J. and Seaton, J. (1988), *Power without Responsibility: The Press and Broadcasting in Britain*, London: Routledge.

Cusick, James (2010), 'Wikileaks Fall-out Reaches UK' in *Sunday Herald*, 24th October, p6.

Dahrendorf, Ralf (1988), *The Modern Social Conflict: An Essay on the Politics of Liberty*, London: Weidenfeld and Nicholson.

Dale, Helle (2009), 'Improving the International Marketplace of Ideas' in The Heritage Foundation, 5th March, available from: www.heritage.org/Research/Commentary/2009/03/Improving-the-International-Marketplace-of-Ideas.

Datta, Monti (2014), *Anti-Americanism and the Rise of World Opinion*, Cambridge: Cambridge University Press.

Davies, P.H.J. (2012), *Intelligence and Government in Britain and the United States*, London: Praeger.

Davis, Daniel (2012), *Dereliction of Duty II: Senior Military Leaders' Loss of Integrity Wounds Afghan War Effort*, 27th January, Draft Report on Rolling Stone Website, available from: www1.rollingstone.com/extras/RS_REPORT.pdf.

Defense Management (2009), 'MoD Eyes "Big Rise in Outsourcing"', in *DefenseManagement.com*, 18th November, available from: www.defencemanagement.com/news_story.asp?id=11309.

Defense Technical Information Center (2000), *Joint Vision 2020*, Joint Chiefs of Staff, available from: www.fs.fed.us/fire/doctrine/genesis_and_evolution/source_materials/joint_vision_2020.pdf.

Denoon, D.P.H. (2001), 'Economics and National Security: The Dangers of Overcommitment', in Richard L. Kugler and Ellen L. Frost. *The Global Century: Globalization and National Security: Volume 1*, Washington, DC: National Defense University Press.

Department of Defense (2001), 'Directive 3600–1', in *Cryptome*, October, available from: 3600.1http://cryptome.org/dodd3600–1.htm.

Department of Defense (2002), 'Memorandum for the Commander of US Central Command' in *National Security Archive (Online)*, August, available from: www.gwu.edu/~nsarchiv/NSAEBB/NSAEBB328/II-Doc15.pdf.

Department of Defense (2003), 'Information Operations Roadmap', 30th October, Washington, DC: Department of Defense, in *National Security Archive Online*, available from: www.gwu.edu/~nsarchiv/NSAEBB/NSAEBB177/info_ops_roadmap. pdf.

Department of Defense (2007), *US Army Counterinsurgency Handbook*, New York: Skyhorse Publishing.

Department of Defense (2010), *Dictionary of Military and Associated Terms*, 8th November, available from: www.dtic.mil/doctrine/new_pubs/jp1_02.pdf.

Department of State (2004), 'Under Secretary for Public Diplomacy and Public Affairs', in *US Department of State Online*, Washington DC, available from: www.state.gov/r/.

Department of State (2007), 'Office of Private Sector Outreach' in *Department of State*, available from: www.state.gov/r/partnerships/.

Department of State (2011a), *Department Organisation*, available from: www.state.gov/r/pa/ei/rls/dos/436.htm.

Department of State (2011b), *Edited Transcript of the Public Meeting of the Advisory Commission on Public Diplomacy*, 29th November, Available from: www.state.gov/pdcommission/meetings/177317.htm.

Deputy Secretary of Defense (2006), *QDR Execution Roadmap for Strategic Communication*, available from: www.defense.gov/pubs/pdfs/QDRRoadmap20060925a.pdf.

Deputy Secretary of Defense (2007), *Memorandum: 'Policy for DoD Interactive Internet Activities'*, 8th June.

Deputy Secretary of Defense (2007) *Memorandum: 'Policy for Combatant Command Websites Tailored to Foreign Audiences'*, 3rd August.

De Toqueville, Alexis (1839), *Democracy in America – Vol. 1*, New York: Adlard and Saunders.

Deutch, J. (1997), 'Terrorism', in *Foreign Policy*, No. 108, pp. 10–22.

Development, Concepts and Doctrine Centre (2012) *Risk: The Implications of Current Attitudes to Risk for the Joint Operational Concept*, November, available from: http://s3.documentcloud.org/documents/799746/modstudy.pdf.

DeYoung, Karen and Pincus, Walter (2008), 'U.S. to Fund Pro-American Publicity in Iraqi Media', in *Washington Post*, 3rd October, available from: www.washingtonpost .com/wp-dyn/content/article/2008/10/02/AR2008100204223_pf.html.

Dillon, Jo (2001), 'ATTACK ON AFGHANISTAN: Coalition Leaders Kept in Line by Campbell's Spin Network', in *The Independent*, London, available from: http://findarticles.com/p/articles/mi_qn4158/is_20011111/ai_n14431847.

Djerejian, E.P. (ed.) (2003), *Changing Minds, Winning Peace: A New Strategic Direction for US Public Diplomacy in the Arab & Muslim World, Report of the Advisory Group on Public Diplomacy for the Arab & Muslim World*, 1st October, submitted to the Committee on Appropriations: US House of Representatives.

Dobbs, Michael (2003), 'Old Alliance, New Relevance' in *Washington Post*, 30th January.

DOD 26th July 1984, Directive S-3321.1, 26th July, *Overt Psychological Operations Conducted by the Military Services in Peacetime (U)*, available from: http://documents .theblackvault.com/documents/PSYOP/OvertPSYOP.pdf.

Doob, L.W. (1949), *Public Opinion and Propaganda*, London: Cresset Press.

Dorril, Stephen and Anonymous (2004), 'Restored Chapter Following Censorship', from *MI6: Inside the Covert World of Her Majesty's Secret Intelligence Service*, London: Simon & Schuster, available from: http://cryptome.org/mi6–sd36.htm.

Drumheller, Tyler (2008) *Interview with Peter Earnest – International Spy Museum Washington*, 1st February, available from: www.spymuseum.org/programs/spycast.php.

Dumbrell, John (2001), *A Special Relationship: Anglo-American Relations in the Cold War and After*, London: Macmillan.

Eden, Anthony (1965), *The Eden Memoirs: The Reckoning*, London: Cassell.

Eldridge, J. (ed.) (1995), *Glasgow Media Group Reader: Vol 1*, London: Routledge.

Ellul, Jacques (1973), *Propaganda: The Formation of Men's Attitudes*, New York: Vintage Books.

Erwin, Sandra (2009), 'U.S. Wants More Help From Allies? Not Really', in *National Defense Magazine* [Online], April, available from: www.nationaldefensemagazine.org/archive/2009/April/Pages/USWantsMoreHelpFromAlliesNotReally.aspx.

Erwin, Sandra (2010), 'Pentagon Contractors Souring on "Soft Power"', in *National Defense Magazine* [Online], August, available from: www.nationaldefensemagazine.org/archive/2010/August/Pages/PentagonContractorsSouringon'SoftPower'.aspx.

Executive Order S-12333 (2008) *United States Intelligence Activities* (Amended), 30th July, available from: www.fas.org/irp/offdocs/eo/eo-12333–2008.pdf.

Farrell, T. (2010), 'Improving in War: Military Adaptation and the British in Helmand, 2006–2009', in *The Journal of Strategic Studies*, Vol. 33, No. 4, pp. 2–33, available from: www.lifelong.ed.ac.uk/OAC2010/archive/Farrell 2010 Improving in War.pdf.

Farsetta, D. (2006), 'The Wages of Spin', in *Phil Taylor's Archive, University of Leeds*, available from: http://ics01.ds.leeds.ac.uk/papers/vp01.cfm?outfit=pmt&request-timeout=500&folder=2558&paper=2611.

Finney, N. (2008), *Human Terrain Team Handbook*, US Army, available from: http://wlstorage.net/file/human-terrain-handbook-2008.pdf.

Foot, M.R.D. (2002), 'OSS and SOE: An Equal Partnership?', in George C. Chalou, *The Secrets War: The Office of Strategic Services in World War II*, Washington: National Archives and Records Administration.

Foreign & Commonwealth Office (2004), *Departmental Report: 1 April 2003 – 31 March 2004, Presented to Parliament by the Secretary of State for Foreign & Commonwealth Affairs and the Chief Secretary to the Treasury by Command of Her Majesty*, also available from: www.fco.gov.uk/resources/en/pdf/pdf6/fco_pdf_deptreport2004foreword.

Foreign & Commonwealth Office (2006), 'Active Diplomacy for a Changing World', in *FCO Online*, March, available from: www.fco.gov.uk/resources/en/pdf/active-diplomacy.

Foreign & Commonwealth Office (2008), 'Coalition Information Centre', in *Freedom of Information Archive*, available from: http://foi.fco.gov.uk/content/en/foi-releases/2008a/10.1–digest.

Fox, Robert (2008), 'Promoting Petraeus', in *The Guardian*, 24th April, available from: www.guardian.co.uk/commentisfree/2008/apr/24/promotingpetraeus.

Fraser, L.M. (1957), *Propaganda*, London: Oxford University Press.

French, David (2011), *The British Way in Counterinsurgency 1945-67*, Oxford: Oxford University Press.

Frese, Michael (c.2009), 'Proactivity Research in Organisations: Michael Frese', in *University of Sheffield*, available from: www.proactivity.group.shef.ac.uk/index.php /sabine-sonnentag/17.html.

Frese, Michael, Kring, Wolfgang, Soose, Andrea and Zempell, Jeanette (1996), 'Personal Initiative at Work: Differences between East and West Germany', in *The Academy of Management Journal*, Vol. 39, No. 1, pp. 37–63.

Fromkin, David (1970), 'Entangling Alliances', in *Foreign Policy*, available from: www.foreignaffairs.com/articles/24183/david-fromkin/entangling-alliances.

Galula, David (2006), *Counterinsurgency Warfare: Theory and Practice*, Westport: Praeger Security International.

Gamble, A. and Wright, T. (2004), 'The Fallout from Iraq', in *Political Quarterly*, Vol. 75, No. 3, pp. 209–212.

GAO (2013), *Military Information Support Operations: Improved Coordination, Evaluations, and Training and Equipping Are Needed*, Report to the Committee on Armed Services, GAO-13–426SU.

Garratt, Bob (1994), *The Learning Organisation*, London: Harper-Collins.

Gellman, Barton (January 2005), 'Secret Unit Expands Rumsfeld's Domain: New Espionage Branch Delving Into CIA Territory', in *The Washington Post*, 23rd Januaray, p. A01, also available from: www.washingtonpost.com/wp-dyn/articles /A29414–2005Jan22.html.

Gerth, H. and Mills, C.W. (2005), *From Max Weber: Essays in Sociology*, Oxford: Routledge.

Gerth, Jeff (2005) 'Military's Information War Is Vast and Often Secretive', in *New York Times*, 11th December, available from: www.nytimes.com/2005/12/11/politics /11propaganda.html?_r=1.

Gerth, Jeff and Shane, Scott (2005), 'US is Said to Pay to Plant Articles in Iraq Papers', in *New York Times*, 1st December, available from: www.nytimes.com/2005/12/01 /politics/01propaganda.html?pagewanted=print.

Glaser, Charles L. (1994–95), 'Realists as Optimists: Cooperation as Self-Help', in *International Security*, Vol. 19, No. 3, pp. 50–90.

Goldberg, I. (2004), 'Definition of Information Warfare': Institute of Advanced Study of Information Warfare.

Goodin, R.E. (1980), *Manipulatory Politics*, New Haven and London: Yale University Press.

Goodman, A. (2003), 'Interview with Scott Ritter', *Democracy Now*, 30th December, available from: www.democracynow.org/2003/12/30/scott_ritter_how_the_british_spy.

Gorman, L. and MacLean, D. (2003), *Media and Society in the Twentieth Century: A Historical Introduction*, Oxford: Blackwell Publishers.

Government Accountability Office (2003), *US Public Diplomacy: State Department Expands Efforts but Faces Significant Challenges*, Report to the Committee on International Relations, House of Representatives, Government Accountability Office, Washington DC, September, also available from: www.gao.gov/new.items /d03951.pdf.

Gramsci, A. (1971), *Selections from Prison Notebooks*, London: Lawrence and Wishart.

Greenstock, Jeremy (2009), quoted in Sparrow, Andrew, 'Sir Jeremy Greenstock at the Iraq War Inquiry – Llive' in *The Guardian* [Online], available from:

www.guardian.co.uk/uk/2009/dec/15/iraq-war-inquiry-iraq.

Greenwald, Glenn, MacAskill, Ewen, Poitras, Laura, Ackerman, Spencer and Rushe, Dominic (2013), 'How Microsoft Handed the NSA Access to Encrypted Messages', in *The Guardian*, 12th July available from: www.guardian.co.uk/world/2013/jul/11 /microsoft-nsa-collaboration-user-data

Grey, Stephen (2003), 'Why No Questions About the CIA?', in *New Statesman*, 29th September, available from: www.newstatesman.com/200309290009.

Grey, S. (2009), *Operation Snake Bite*, London: Penguin.

Gross, Bertram (1990), *Friendly Fascism: The New Face of Power in America*, Montreal: Black Rose Books.

Guinsburg, Thomas (1982), *The Pursuit of Isolationism*, New York: Garland Publishing.

Hall, I. (2006), 'Power Politics and Appeasement: Political Realism in British International Thought, c. 1935–1955', in *The British Journal of Politics & International Relations*, Vol. 8, No. 2, pp. 174–192.

Hall, S. (1996), *Modernity: An Introduction to Modern Societies*, Oxford: Blackwell Publishing.

Halpern, Orly (2003), 'Iraqis gloat as North Americans suffer', in *Globe and Mail*, 16th August, available from: www.theglobeandmail.com/servlet/story/RTGAM .20030815.uiraq0816/BNStory/In%20ternational/.

Harding, Joel (2013), 'Information Recognised as a Catalyst for Change or Revolution in 1583', in *To Inform is to Influence*, 19th November, available from: http://toinformis-toinfluence.com/2013/11/19/information-recognized-as-catalyst-for-change-or -revolution-in-1583/.

Hastings, Max (2008), 'Forget Iraq, Afghanistan's Turning into a Disaster Too', in *The Daily Mail*, 22nd April, available from: www.dailymail.co.uk/debate/columnists /article-561183/Forget-Iraq-Afghanistans-turning-disaster-too.html#ixzz1BZbzRPYj.

Hastings, M. (2011), 'Another Runaway General: Army Deploys Psy-Ops on U.S. Senators', in *Rolling Stone*, 23rd February, available from: www.rollingstone .com/politics/news/another-runaway-general-army-deploys-psy-ops-on-u-s- senators-20110223?page=2.

Haynes, Deborah, Loyd, Anthony, Kiley, Sam and Coghlan, Tom (2010), 'Officers' Mess: Military Chiefs Blamed for Blundering into Helmand with "Eyes Shut and Fingers Crossed"', in *The Times*, 9th June, available from: www.timesonline.co.uk/tol /news/world/afghanistan/article7146449.ece.

Heath, Mike (Air Vice Marshall) (2004), quoted in House of Commons, 'Chapter 15', in *Select Committee on Defence Third Report*, 3rd March, available from: www .publications.parliament.uk/pa/cm200405/cmselect/cmdfence/63/6302.htm.

Hedges, S. (2005), 'Firm Helps U.S. Mold News Abroad', in *Chicago Tribune*, 13th November, available from: www.infowars.com/articles/media/propaganda /firm_helps_us_mold_news_abroad.html.

Heginbotham, E. (1996), *The British and American Armies in World War II: Explaining Variations in Organisational Learning Patterns*, Boston: MIT Defense and Arms Control Studies Program Working Paper.

Held, V. (2004), 'Terrorism and War', in *The Journal of Ethics*, Vol. 8, pp. 59–75.

Hennessy, P. and Anstey, C. (1990), 'Moneybags and Brains: The Anglo-American "Special Relationship" since 1945', in *Strathclyde Analysis Papers*, Vol. 1.

Herman, Edward S. and Chomsky, Noam (1988), *Manufacturing Consent: The Political Economy of the Mass Media*, New York: Pantheon Books.

Hersh, Seymour (2003), 'Who Lied to Whom', in *The New Yorker*, 31st March, available from: www.newyorker.com/archive/2003/03/31/030331fa_fact1?printable=true.

Hersh, Seymour M. (2004), *Chain of Command*, London: Penguin Books.

Hopkins, M.F.(1998), 'The Focus of a Changing Relationship: The Washington Embassy and Britain's World Role since 1945', in *Contemporary British History*, Vol. 12, pp. 103–114.

Hopkins, N. and Ackerman, S. (2013), 'Flexible Laws and Weak Oversight Give GCHQ Room for Manoeuvre', in *The Guardian*, 2nd August, available from: www.theguardian.com/uk-news/2013/aug/02/gchq-laws-oversight-nsa.

Hopkins, N. and Borger, J. (2013), 'Exclusive: NSA Pays £100m in Secret Funding for GCHQ', in *The Guardian*, 1st August, available from: www.theguardian.com/uk-news/2013/aug/01/nsa-paid-gchq-spying-edward-snowden.

Hopkins, N. and Taylor, M. (2013), 'Guardian Will not be Intimidated over NSA Leaks, Alan Rusbridger tells MPs', in *The Guardian*, 3rd December, available from: www.theguardian.com/world/2013/dec/03/guardian-not-intimidated-nsa-leaks-alan-rusbridger-surveillance.

Houghton, Kate (1996), 'Subverting Journalism: Reporters and the CIA', in the Committee to Protect Journalists, *SPECIAL REPORT: The United States Subverting Journalism*, available from: www.cpj.org/attacks96/sreports/cia.html.

House of Commons (2006) *Honorary Knighthoods*, available from: www.parliament.uk/deposits/depositedpapers/2009/DEP2009–2154.doc.

House of Representatives (2008) *MISLEADING INFORMATION FROM THE BATTLE-FIELD: THE TILLMAN AND LYNCH EPISODES*, Report to Congress, available from: www.gpo.gov/fdsys/pkg/CRPT-110hrpt858/html/CRPT-110hrpt858.htm).

Hutton, Lord (2004), 'Chapter 12', in *The Hutton Inquiry*, available from: www.the-hutton-inquiry.org.uk/content/report/chapter12.htm.

IMPACT-SE.ORG (2009), 'European Tour', available from: www.impact-se.org/docs/newsroom/euro-tour2009/Euro_Tour_II_report.pdf.

International Public Information (1999), *Presidential Decision Directive PDD 68*, 30th April, available from: www.fas.org/irp/offdocs/pdd/pdd-68.htm.

Iraq Inquiry (2010), *The Iraq Inquiry (Online)*, available from: www.iraqinquiry.org.uk/about.aspx.

Jackson, Roy (2005), *Writing the War on Terrorism*, Manchester: Manchester University Press.

Jeffrey, Keith (2010), *MI6: The History of the Secret Intelligence Service 1909–1949*, London: Bloomsbury.

Jenkins, Simon (2007), 'This Aerial Onslaught is War at its Most Stupid', in *The Guardian*, 7th February, available from: www.guardian.co.uk/commentisfree/2007/feb/07/comment.politics.

Johnson, Chalmers (2004), *The Sorrows of Empire: Militarism, Secrecy & the End of the Republic*, New York: Henry Holt & Co.

Joint Chiefs of Staff (1996), 'Doctrine for Joint Psychological Operations', in *IWAR: The Information Warfare Website*, available from: www.iwar.org.uk/PSYOP/resources/us/jp3_53.pdf.

Joint Chiefs of Staff (2003), *Joint Publication 3–53: Doctrine for Joint Psychological Operations*, Office of the Joint Chiefs of Staff, also available from: www.dtic.mil /doctrine/jel/new_pubs/jp3_53.pdf.

Jones, Jeffrey, B. (2005), 'Strategic Communication: A Mandate for the United States', in *Joint Force Quarterly*, Vol. 39, pp. 108–114, also available from: www.dtic.mil /doctrine/jel/jfq_pubs/1839.pdf.

Jones, Jeffrey B., Keuhl, Daniel T., Burgess, Daniel and Rodite, Russell (2009), 'Strategic Communication and the Combatant Commander', in *Joint Force Quarterly*, No. 55, pp. 104–108, also available from: www.ndu.edu/inss/Press/jfq_ pages/editions /i55/17.pdf.

Jones, Nicholas (2001a), *Personal Memo Regarding Alastair Campbell & Remembrance Sunday*, 15th November, London. (Provided by Jones during interview on 14th March 2006.)

Jones, Nicholas (2001b) *Email from N Jones, BBC Correspondent, to Richard Sambrook, BBC Director of News*, 30th November, London. (Provided by Jones during interview on 14th March 2006.)

Jones, Nicholas (2001c), *The Control Freaks*, London: Politico's.

Jowell, Tessa (2001), *Hansard: House of Commons*, Department of Culture Media and Sport, Volume 373, Column: 491W, also available from: www.publications .parliament.uk/pa/cm200102/cmhansrd/vo011029/text/11029w04.htm.

Jowett, Garth S. and O'Donnell, Victoria (1992), *Propaganda and Persuasion*, 2nd edition, Newbury Park: Sage Publications.

Jowett, Garth and O'Donnell, Victoria, (1999) *Propaganda and Persuasion*, 3rd edition, London: Sage Publications.

Just Foreign Policy (2013) *Iraq Deaths*, 21st July, available from: www.justforeignpolicy .org/.

Kambrod, Matthew (2007), *Lobbying for Defense: An Insider's View*, Annapolis, MD: Naval Institute Press.

Kean, T.H. and Hamilton, L.H. (2004), *The 9–11 Report: The National Commission on Terrorist Attacks upon the United States*, New York: St Martins Press.

Keane, J. (1991), *The Media and Democracy*, Cambridge: Polity.

Keeble, Richard (2008), 'Uncovered: British Reporters who are Spooks' in *The Latest.com*, 2nd July available from: www.the-latest.com/uncovered-british -journalists-who-are-spooks.

Keohane, Robert and Nye, Joseph (1998), 'Power and Interdependence in the Information Age', in *Foreign Affairs*, available from: www.foreignaffairs .com/articles/54395/robert-o-keohane-and-joseph-s-nye-jr/power-and-inter- dependence-in-the-information-age.

Kettl, D. (2002), *The Transformation of Governance: Public Administration for 21st Century America*, Baltimore: Johns Hopkins.

Kibbe, J.D. (2004), 'The Rise of the Shadow Warriors', in *Foreign Affairs*, Vol. 83 Issue 2, pp. 102–115.

Kier, Elizabeth (1995), 'Culture and Military Doctrine: France Between the Wars', in *International Security*, Vol. 19, No. 4, pp. 65–93.

Kilcullen, D (2004), 'Countering Global Insurgency', in *Small Wars Journal*, 30th

November, pp. 1–7, available from: http://smallwarsjournal.com/documents /kilcullen.pdf.

Kimball, Warren F. (1994), *The Juggler: Franklin Roosevelt as Wartime Statesman*, Princeton: Princeton University Press.

Kirby, D. (2000), 'Divinely Sanctioned: The Anglo-American Cold War Alliance and the Defence of Western Civilisation and Christianity, 1945–48', in *Journal of Contemporary History*, Vol. 35, No. 3, pp. 394–409.

Kirke, Charles (2010), 'Organisational Culture and Defence Acquisition: A Key Internal Factor for MoD', in *RUSI Defence Systems*, available from: www.rusi.org/downloads /assets/KirkeRDSSummer2010.pdf.

Koza, Frank (2003), 'Reflections of Iraq Debate/Votes at UN-RT Actions + Potential for Related Contributions', *Top Secret Email Sent to Recipients at GCHQ on 31st January 2003*, available from: www.guardian.co.uk/world/2003/mar/02/iraq.unitednations1.

Krauthammer, C. (2008), 'Charlie Gibson's Gaffe', in *The Washington Post*, 13th September, available from: www.washingtonpost.com/wp-dyn/content/article/2008 /09/12/AR2008091202457.html.

Lamb, C. (2005), *Review of Psychological Operations Lessons Learned from Recent Operational Experience*, Washington, DC: National Defense University Press.

Lasswell, H.D. (1934), 'Propaganda', in R. Jackall (ed.), *Propaganda*, 1995 edition, Basingstoke: Macmillan Press.

LeBaron, R. (2008), 'WILLIAM HAGUE SAYS "NEAR DEATH EXPERIENCE" HAS IMPROVED TORY CHANCES' *Leaked Cable in Wikileaks*, 1st April, available from: http://213.251.145.96/cable/2008/04/08LONDON930.html.

Le Gallo, Andre (2005), 'Covert Action: A Vital Option in US National Security Policy', in *International Journal of Intelligence and CounterIntelligence*, Vol. 18, Issue 2.

Leonard, M. and Alakeson, V. (2000), *Going Public: Diplomacy for the Information Society*, London: Foreign Policy Centre/Central Books.

Leppard, David (2000), 'Top Spy Chief Leads Drive to Gag Press', in *The Sunday Times –* Cryptome, 21st March, available from: http://cryptome.org/uk-spy-gag.htm.

Levi, W. (1965), 'The Relative Irrelevance of Moral Norms in International Politics', in *Social Forces*, Vol. 44, No. 2, pp. 226–233.

Lewis, J. (2004), 'At the Service of Politicians', in *The Guardian*, 4th August, p. 19.

Lichtblau, E. (2012), 'Saudi Arabia May Be Tied to 9/11, 2 Ex-Senators Say', in *New York Times*, 29th February, available from: www.nytimes.com/2012/03/01/us/graham-and-kerrey-see-possible-saudi-9–11–link.html?_r=1&.

Lippmann, W. (1954), *Public Opinion*, New York: Macmillan Company.

Lucas, W.S. and Morey, A. (2000), 'A Hidden Alliance: The CIA and MI6 Before and After Suez', in *Intelligence and National Security*, Vol. 15, No. 2, pp. 95–120.

Londoño, E. (2009), 'A High-Priced Media Campaign That Iraqis Aren't Buying', in *The Washington Post*, 7th June, available from: www.washingtonpost.com/wp-dyn /content/article/2009/06/06/AR2009060602144_pf.html.

Lukes, S. (2005), *Power: A Radical View*, London: Palgrave Macmillan.

Lundestad, Geir (2005), 'Toward Transatlantic Drift', in D.A. Andrews (ed.), *The Atlantic Alliance Under Stress: US-European Relations after Iraq*, Cambridge: Cambridge University Press.

Machiavelli, N. (1961), *The Prince* (trans. G. Bull), London: Penguin.

Macintyre, Donald (2002), 'American Spin Doctor in London', in *The Independent,* 19th March, available from: www.independent.co.uk/news/media/tucker-eskew -american-spin-doctor-in-london-654660.html.

Mackay, A. and Tatham, S. (2009a), 'Behavioural Conflict – From Generic to Strategic Corporal: Complexity, Adaptation and Influence', in *The Shrivenham Papers,* December, No. 9.

Mackay, A. and Tatham, S. (2009b), *Behavioural Conflict,* Saffron Waldon: Military Studies Press.

Mackenzie, Maj. Scott, (2001), 'Executing Joint Information Operations: Where Do We Go After Kosovo?', *Naval War College Paper, Defense Technical Information Center Online,* 5th February, available from: www.dtic.mil/cgi-bin/GetTRDoc?AD =ADA389521&Location=U2&doc=GetTRDoc.pdf.

Macmillan, Alan (1995), 'Strategic Culture and National Ways in Warfare: The British Case,' *RUSI Journal,* Vol. 140, No. 5, pp. 33–38.

Marrades, A. (2006–7), 'Anthropology and the "War on Terror": Analysis of a Complex Relationship', University of Sussex Thesis, available from: www.sussex.ac.uk /webteam/gateway/file.php?name=marrades.pdf&site=10.

McAskill, Ewan et al. (2013), 'GCHQ Taps Fibre-optic Cables for Secret Access to World's Communications', in *The Guardian,* 21st June, available from: www.theguardian .com/uk/2013/jun/21/gchq-cables-secret-world-communications-nsa.

McCarty, K. and Pfeifle, M. (2011), 'Strategic Communication: The Iraqi Surge Strategy', Conference Paper from: *Strategic Communications: The Cutting Edge* at King's College London, 9th–10th May, available from: www.kcl.ac.uk/sspp/departments /warstudies/research/groups/insurgency/events.aspx.

McChesney, Bob (2000), *Rich Media, Poor Democracy: Communication Politics in Dubious Times,* New York: The New Press.

McClam, E. (2013), 'Benghazi, IRS, AP: A Guide to the 3 Storms Confronting the White House', in *NBC News,* 16th May, available from: http://usnews.nbcnews.com /_news/2013/05/16/18298571-benghazi-irs-ap-a-guide-to-the-3-storms -confronting-the-white-house.

McFate, Montgomery (2005), 'Anthropology and Counterinsurgency: The Strange Story of their Curious Relationship', in *Military Review,* Vol. 3, pp. 24–38.

McKercher, B.J.C. (1999), *Transition of Power,* Cambridge: Cambridge University Press.

McKitrick, Jeffrey, Blackwell, James, Littlepage, Fred, Kraus, George, Blanchfield, Richard and Hill, Dale (1995), The Revolution in Military Affairs', in Air University, *The Battlefield of the Future – 21st Century Warfare Issues,* available from: www.airpower.maxwell.af.mil/airchronicles/battle/chp3.html.

McLellan, D. (1998), *Marxism After Marx,* London: Macmillan.

McNeill, William, Hardy (1970), *America, Britain, & Russia: Their Co-operation and Conflict, 1941–1946,* New York: Johnson Reprint Corp.

Meade, C. (2005), 'The War on Terrorism U.S. Public Diplomacy', in *U.S. Army War College,* 18th March, available from: www.dtic.mil/cgi-bin/GetTRDoc?Location =U2&doc=GetTRDoc.pdf&AD=ADA432489.

Meek, James (2010), 'Iraq War Logs: How Friendly Fire from US Troops Became Routine', in *The Guardian* (Online), 22nd October, available from:

www.guardian.co.uk/world/2010/oct/22/american-troops-friendly-fire-iraq.

Merton, R.K. (1995), 'Mass Persuasion: A Technical Problem and a Moral Dilemma', in R. Jackall (ed.), *Propaganda*, London: Macmillan.

Meyer, Christopher (2008), 'Christopher Meyer: Britain Must Start to Play Diplomatic Hardball', in *The Sunday Times* (Online), 18th October, available from: http://entertainment.timesonline.co.uk/tol/arts_and_entertainment/books/book_extracts/article6879258.ece.

Meyer, Christopher (2009), *Iraq Testimony in Chilcott Inquiry*, 26th November, available from: www.iraqinquiry.org.uk/media/40453/20091126am-final.pdf.

Midura, C. (2008), 'Testimony of Christopher Midura, Acting Director, Office of Policy, Planning and Resources, Under Secretary for Public Diplomacy and Public Affairs' *Senate Homeland Security and Governmental Affairs Subcommittee on Oversight of Government Management, the Federal Workforce, and the District of Columbia*, 23rd September, available from: http://hsgac.senate.gov/public/index.cfm?FuseAction =Files.View&FileStore_id=6d0ca93b-7d48–4a6b-914a-ff8a4c37a55e.

Miliband, David (2007), quoted in Black, Ian, 'US is our Most Important Ally Says Miliband in First Speech', in *The Guardian*, 20th July, p. 22.

Mill, J.S. (1989), 'On Liberty', in S.E. Collini (ed.), *On Liberty: With The Subjection of Women and Chapters on Socialism*, Cambridge: Cambridge University Press.

Miller, D. (1996), 'The Northern Ireland Information Service and the Media: Aims, Strategy, Tactics', in Bill Rolston and David Miller (eds), *War and Words: The Northern Ireland Media Reader*, Belfast: Beyond the Pale, http://www.dmiller. info/images/docs/Miller-Northern%20Ireland%20Information%20Service-Eldridge-Getting%20the%20Message%20–%201993.pdf

Miller, D. (2004a) 'Information Dominance: The Philosophy of Total Propaganda Control', in *Coldtype*, available from: www.coldtype.net.

Miller, D. and Mills, T. (2010), 'Producing and Communicating Terror Expertise', PSA Conference Paper, available from: www.academia.edu/attachments/30609277 /download_file?st=MTM5NDg4NzgyOCw3OC4xNDQuMTg5LjI1MCwzNDc5MT k3&ct=MTM5NDg4NzgzMSwzNDc5MTk3.

Miller, D. (ed.) (2004b), *Tell Me Lies: Media and Propaganda in theAattack on Iraq*, London: Pluto Press.

Miller, D. and Dinan, W. (2008), *A Century of Spin: How Public Relations Became the Cutting Edge of Corporate Power*, London: Pluto Press.

Miller, D. and Sabir, R. (2012), 'Counter-terrorism as Counterinsurgency in the UK "War on Terror"' in Scott Poynting and David Whyte, *Counter-terrorism and State Political Violence: The 'War on Terror' as Terror*, London: Routledge.

Ministry of Defence (2002), *Information Operations: Joint Warfare Publication 3–80*, Swindon: Joint Warfare and Concepts Centre.

Ministry of Defence (2003a), *Delivering Security in a Changing World: Defence White Paper*, Ministry of Defence, London: The Stationery Office.

Ministry of Defence (2003b), *Operations in Iraq: Lessons for the Future*, Ministry of Defence, London: Directorate of Corporate Communication.

Ministry of Defence (2004a), *Joint Operations Planning JWP 5–00*, available from: http://pksoi.army.mil/doctrine_concepts/documents/UK/jwp5_00.pdf.

Ministry of Defence (2004b), *MoD Internal Communications Survey*, London: Defence Analytical Services Agency.

Ministry of Defence (2012), 'The Implications of Current Attitudes to Risk for the Joint Operational Concept', *Development, Concepts and Doctrine Centre Report*, available from@ http://s3.documentcloud.org/documents/799746/modstudy.pdf.

Miracle, Tammy M. (Lt. Col.) (2003), 'The Army and Embedded Media', in *Military Review*, September–October, pp. 41–45.

Morgan, K.O. (2002), 'Labour and the Anglo-American Alliance', *CELCLA, Centre d'etudes en litterature et civilisation de langue anglaise*, France: L'universite de Rouen, pp. 169–184.

Morgenthau, Hans (2006), *Politics Among Nations*, Boston: McGraw-Hill.

Moser, J.E. (2003), 'The Decline of Anglophobia: Or, How Americans Stopped Worrying and Learned to Love the English', in CELCLA, *The 'Special Relationship'*, Textes rassembbles par Antoine Capet et Aïssatou Sy-Wonyu Actes du colloque organisé à l'université de Rouen les 8 et 9 Novembre 2002, France: Université de Rouen.

Mouffe, C. (1979), *Gramsci and Marxist Theory*, London: Routledge and Keegan-Paul.

Nagl, J. (2005), *Learning to Eat Soup with a Knife: Counterinsurgency Lessons from Malaya and Vietnam*, London: University of Chicago Press.

National Security Act of 1947 [50 U.S.C. 413b], Congressional modification to Section 503(e) adopted in 1991 in response to the findings of the Iran/Contra hearings of 1990.

Nelson, Daniel N. (2002), 'Transatlantic Transmutations', in *The Washington Quarterly*, Vol. 25, No. 4, pp. 51–66.

Nicholas, Herbert George (1963), *Britain and the United States*, London: Chatto & Windus.

Nichols, John and McChesney, Robert W. (2005), *Tragedy and Farce: How the American Media Sell Wars, Spin Elections, and Destroy Democracy*, New York: The New Press.

Norton-Taylor, Richard (2009), 'Foreign Office to Propose Self-Regulation for Private Military Firms', in *The Guardian* (Online), 24th April, available from: www.guardian.co.uk/world/2009/apr/24/private-military-firms-government.

NPR (2000), 'Army Media Intern Flap', in *All things Considered*, 10th April, available from: www.npr.org/templates/story/story.php?storyId=1072763.

Nugent, Brian (2008), *Orwellian Ireland*, Co. Meath: Brian Nugent, also available from: www.indymedia.ie/article/70223?userlanguage=ga&save_prefs=true.

Nye, J.S. (2002a), *The Paradox of American Power: Why the World's Only Superpower Can't Go It Alone*, Oxford and New York: Oxford University Press.

Nye, J.S. (2002b), 'The Information Revolution and American Soft Power', in *Asia-Pacific Review*, Vol. 9, No. 1, pp. 60–76.

Nye, J.S. (2004), 'The Decline of America's Soft Power', *Foreign Affairs*, 1 May, available from: www.foreignaffairs.com/articles/59888/joseph-s-nye-jr/the-decline-of-americas-soft-power.

Oates, Sarah (2007), 'The Framing of Terrorist Threat in British Elections: Full Research Report', *ESRC End of Award Report*, RES-228–25–0048, Swindon: ESRC.

Oates, S., Kaid, L. and Berry, M. (2009), *Terrorism, Elections, and Democracy: Political Campaigns in the United States, Great Britain, and Russia*, New York: Palgrave Macmillan.

O'Connell, M.E. (20th January 2012) 'Why Obama's "Targeted Killing" is worse than Bush's torture', available from: www.theguardian.com/commentisfree/cifamerica /2012/jan/20/why-obama-targeted-killing-is-like-bush-torture.

Office of the President of the United States (2002), *National Security Strategy*, available from: www.whitehouse.gov/nsc/nss.pdf.

Office of the Spokesperson (2013), DoS *Highlights of the Department of State and U.S. Agency for International Development Budget 2014*, available from: www.state.gov /r/pa/prs/ps/2013/04/207281.htm.

O'Hanlon, Michael E. (2000), *Technological Change and the Future of Warfare*, Washington, DC: Brookings Institution Press.

O'Hanlon, Michael and Pollack, Kenneth (2007), 'Stability in Iraq: A War We Just Might Win' in *Brookings*, 30th July, available from: www.brookings.edu/research /opinions/2007/07/30iraq-ohanlon

Paddock, Alfred H. (1982), 'Major General Robert Alexis McClure, Forgotten Father of US Army Special Warfare', in *PsyWarrior.com*, available from: www.psywarrior.com mcclure.html.

Page, C. (1996), *U.S. Propaganda During the Vietnam War 1965-1973: The Limits of Persuasion*, London: Leicester University Press.

Parker, M. (2000), *Organizational Culture and Identity*, London: Sage.

Parmar, Inderjeet (2008), 'Combatting Anti-Americanism: American Foundations and Public Diplomacy During the Cold War and the War on Terror', in Richard Higgott and Ivona Malbasic (eds), *The Political Consequences of Anti-Americanism*, Oxford: Polity Press, pp. 29–43.

Parry, Robert and Kornbluh, P. (1988), 'Iran-Contra's Untold Story', in *Foreign Policy*, No. 72, pp. 3–30.

Parsons, M. (2002), 'China, Korea and the Special Relationship: Between the United States and the United Kingdom 1945–1953', in CELCLA (ed.), *The 'Special Relationship'*, France: Université de Rouen.

Paton, Iain (2009), 'Planning a War, Badly', in *The Iraq Inquiry Digest*, 19th October, available from: www.iraqinquirydigest.org/?p=2355.

Paton, Iain (2010) 'My Submission to the Inquiry', in *The Iraq Inquiry Digest*, 11th March, available from: www.iraqinquirydigest.org/?p=8255.

Perkins, Richard and Neumayer, Eric (2010), 'The Organized Hypocrisy of Ethical Foreign Policy: Human Rights, Democracy and Western Arms Sales', *in Geoforum*, Vol. 41, No. 2, pp. 247–256.

Peterson, H.C. (1939), *Propaganda for War: The Campaign Against American Neutrality 1914–1917*, Norman: University of Oklahoma Press.

Philo, G. (2007), 'Can Discourse Analysis Successfully Explain the Content of Media and Journalistic Practise?', in *Journalism Studies*, Vol. 8, No. 2, pp. 175–196.

Philo, G. and Berry, M (2004) *Bad News from Israel*, London: Pluto Books.

Philo, G., Briant, E. and Donald, P. (2013), *Bad News for Refugees*, London: Pluto.

Phyllis, B. (2004), *An Independent Review of Government Communications*, Cabinet Office, available from: www.ppa.co.uk/legal-and-public-affairs/ppa-responses-and-evidence/~/media/Documents/Legal/Consultations/Lords%20Communications%2 0Committee/final_report.ashx.

Pierce, James G. (2010), 'Is the Organization of the US Army Congruent with the Professional Development of its Senior Officer Corps?', in *Strategic Studies Institute*, available from: www.strategicstudiesinstitute.army.mil/pubs/download.cfm?q=1015,

Pilon, J.G. (2007), *Why America is Such a Hard Sell: Beyond Pride and Prejudice*, New York: Rowman & Littlefield.

Pimlott, Ben (2002), 'Courting the President: Wilson and Johnson in the 1960's' – CELCLA, *Centre d'etudes en litterature et civilisation de langue anglaise*, France: L'universite de Rouen, 2003, pp. 185–191.

Pincus, Walter (2005), 'CIA, Pentagon Seek to Avoid Overlap', in *The Washington Post*, 4th July, available from: www.washingtonpost.com/wp-dyn/content/article/2005/07/03/AR2005070300885.html.

Posen, B. (2007), 'The Case for Restraint', in *The American Interest*, available from: www.the-american-interest.com/article.cfm?piece=331.

Powell, Jonathan (2002), *Email sent to Alastair Campbell Presented as Evidence during the Hutton Enquiry*, 5th September, available from: www.the-hutton-inquiry.org.uk/content/cab/cab_11_0017.pdf.

Pprune (2010), 'F15 Court Martial Updates', in *Professional Pilots Rumour Network*, available from: *www.pprune.org/atc-issues/81326–f15–court-martial-updates.html*.

Pugmire, Maj. Brian, (2002), 'Psychological Operations: Will the Real Approval Authority Please Stand Up?' in *Naval War College Paper, Defense Technical Information Center Online*, 4th February, available from: www.dtic.mil/cgi-bin/GetTRDoc?AD=ADA401091&Location=U2&doc=GetTRDoc.pdf.

Qualter, T.H. (1962), *Propaganda and asychological Warfare*, New York: Random House.

Quille, Gerrard (1998), 'The Revolution in Military Affairs and the UK', *International Security Information Service Briefing*, No. 73, December, available from: www.bu.edu/globalbeat/usdefense/Quille1298.html.

Quigley, Carroll (1981), *The Anglo-American Establishment*, New York: Books in Focus.

Quigley, John (2007), *The Ruses for War: American Intervention Since WWII*, New York: Prometheus Books.

Read, Chris (2010), *Letter Re. FOI Request – Directorate Media and Communications Ministry of Defence*, 23rd September.

Reith, John (2010), *Iraq Testimony in Chilcott Inquiry*, 15th January, available from: www.iraqinquiry.org.uk/media/42508/100115am-reith.pdf.

Reubner, J. (2011), 'Disincentives to Peace: US Weapons Sales to Israel', in *Counterpunch*, 22nd April, available from: www.informationclearinghouse.info/article27947.htm.

Reynolds, D. (2000), *Rich Relations: The American Occupation of Britain, 1942–1945*, London: Phoenix Press.

Reynolds, P. (2007), 'Declining Use of "War on Terror"', in *BBC News*, 17th April, available from: http://news.bbc.co.uk/1/hi/uk_politics/6562709.stm.

Ricks, Thomas (2004), 'Shift from Traditional War Seen at Pentagon', in *Washington Post*, 3rd September, pA01.

Riddell, Peter (2004), *Hug Them Close: Blair, Clinton, Bush and the 'Special Relationship'*, London: Politico.

Risen, James (2006), *State of War: The Secret History of the CIA and the Bush Administration*, London: Simon and Schuster.

Ritter, Scott (2005), *Iraq Confidential*, London: I B Tauris.

Robbins, J. (2008), 'Miliband's Apology over Rendition', in *BBC News*, 21st February, available from: http://news.bbc.co.uk/1/hi/uk_politics/7257574.stm.

Robins, K., Webster, F., and Pickering, M. (1987), 'Propaganda, Information and Social Control', in J. Hawthorn (ed.), *Propaganda, Persuasion and Polemic*, London: Edward Arnold.

Roff, Peter and Chapin, James (2001), 'Face-off: Bush's Foreign Policy Warriors', in *United Press International*, 18th July, available from: www.globalresearch.ca /articles/ROF111A.html.

Roosevelt, Franklin D. (1939), 'Fireside Chat', *The American Presidency Project*, 3rd September, available from: www.presidency.ucsb.edu/ws/index.php?pid=15801 #axzz1TyMznQ82.

Rose, David (2007), 'Spies and their Lies', in *New Statesman*, 27th September, available from: www.newstatesman.com/politics/2007/09/mi6–mi5–intelligence-briefings.

Rousseau, J. (1968), *The Social Contract*, Harmondsworth: Penguin Books.

Rowland, Lee and Tatham, S. (2010), *Strategic Communication & Influence Operations: Do We Really Get It?*, Shrivenham: Defence Academy of the United Kingdom.

Rufford, Nicholas (2003), 'Revealed: How MI6 Sold the Iraq War', in *The Times*, 28th December, available from: www.informationclearinghouse.info/article5433.htm.

Rumsfeld, Donald (2002), *Secretary Rumsfeld Media Availability En Route to Chile [Excerpt on DARPA'S Total Information Awareness Program]*, Federation of American Scientists, 18th November, available from: www.fas.org/sgp/news/2002/11 /dod111802.html.

Rumsfeld, Donald (2006), *Interview*, quoted in Tyson, A.S., 'Rumsfeld Urges Using Media to Fight Terror', in *The Washington Post*, 18th February, available from: www.washingtonpost.com/wp-dyn/content/article/2006/02/17 /AR2006021701980_pf.html.

Rycroft, Matthew (2002), 'IRAQ: PRIME MINISTER'S MEETING, 23 JULY', *Downing Street Memo to David Manning*, 23rd July, available from: http://en.wikisource .org/wiki/Downing_Street_memo.

Sawers, J. (2009), *Testimony to the Iraq Inquiry*, available from: www.iraqinquiry.org.uk /media/40668/20091210amsawers-final.pdf.

Scahill, Jeremy (2013), *Dirty Wars: The World Is a Battlefield*, New York: Nation Books.

Scarlett, J. (2009), quoted in Shipman, Tim 'We NEVER use Torture says UK's Top Spy, Real Life Bonds are Committed to Human Rights', in *The Daily Mail* (Online), 11th August, available from: www.dailymail.co.uk/news/article-1205696/Sir-John-Scarlett-UKs-spy-denies-use-torture-insists-real-life-Bonds-committed-human-rights.html.

Schaub, Gary (2008), 'SCHAUB: U.S. Shows that Soft Power can Work in a Hard War', in *The Washington Times*, 11th November, available from: www.washingtontimes.com /news/2008/nov/11/us-shows-that-soft-power-can-work-in-a-hard-war/print/

Scott, James (1990), *Domination and the Arts of Resistance*, New Haven: Yale University Press.

Scott, Len (2004), 'Secret Intelligence, Covert Action and Clandestine Diplomacy', in *Intelligence and National Security*, Vol. 19, No. 2, pp. 322–341.

Senate Joint Resolution 23 (2001), *Authorization for Use of Military Force*, 18th September, available from: http://foavc.org/file.php/1/Articles/Senate%20Joint%20 Resolution%2023.htm.

Shanker, Thom and Schmitt, Eric (2002), 'Pentagon Debates Propaganda Push in Allied Nations', in *New York Times*, 16th December, available from: www.nytimes.com /2002/12/16/international/16MILI.html.

Shadid, Anthony (2003), 'In Basra, Worst May Be Ahead: As Southern Iraq Bakes, British Also Frustrated by Shortages', in *Washington Post*, 12th August, available from: www.highbeam.com/doc/1P2-291990.html.

Sharp, J.M.O. (2003), 'Tony Blair, Iraq and the Special Relationship: Poodle or Partner?', in *International Journal*, Vol. LIX, No. 1, pp. 59–86.

Shaw, Martin (2005), 'Risk-Transfer Militarism and the Legitimacy of War after Iraq', in P. Eden and T. O'Donnel (eds), *The Problem of the Definition of Terrorism in International Law*, Ardsley, NY: Transnational.

Sheppard, Ben, Rubin, James G., Wardman, Jamie K. and Wesley, Simon (2006), 'Viewpoint: Terrorism and Dispelling the Myth of a Panic Prone Public', in *Journal of Public Health Policy*, Vol. 27, No. 3, pp. 219–245.

Shiffrin, Richard (2006), 'Restrictions on Influencing a Domestic Audience Applicable to the Department of Defense', from *MountainRunner Blog*, available from: http://mountainrunner.us/files/2012/05/DOD-legal-review-on-Restrictions-on-Influencing-Domestic-Audience.pdf.

Shipman, Tim (2009), 'Why the CIA has to spy on Britain', *The Spectator*, 28th February, pp. 20–21.

Shy, J. (1971), 'The American Military Experience: History and Learning', in *Journal of Interdisciplinary History*, Vol. 1, No. 2, pp. 205–228.

Silverberg, D. and Heimann, J. (2009), 'An Ever-Expanding War: Legal Aspects of Online Strategic Communication', in *Parameters*, pp. 77–93, available from: www.carlisle .army.mil/usawc/Parameters/Articles/09summer/silverberg%20and%20heimann.pdf.

Singer, P. (2005), 'Outsourcing War', in *Brookings Institution*, March/April: www.brookings.edu/research/articles/2005/03/01usdepartmentofdefense-singer.

SIPRI (2010), *SIPRI Military Expenditure Data 1988–2011*, available from: https://docs.google.com/spreadsheet/ccc?key=0AonYZs4MzlZbdDQyQWd3TDNM cXlLVU1abFRKVEh4WEE#gid=0.

SIPRI (2013), *Arms Transfers Database*, available from: http://armstrade.sipri.org /armstrade/page/values.php

Skidelsky, R. (2004), 'Imbalance of Power', in *Robert Skidelsky* (Online), available from: www.skidelskyr.com/site/article/imbalance-of-power/.

Smith-Mundt Act (1948), available from: http://us-code.vlex.com/source/us-code -foreign-relations-intercous-1021/toc/19.

Smith-Mundt Act (2012), available from: http://thomas.loc.gov/cgi-bin/query /z?c112:H.R.5736.

Smith, Bradley (1992), *The Ultra-Magic Deals and the Most Secret Special Relationship, 1940–1946*, Novato: Presidio.

Smith, Bradley (1995), 'The Road to the Anglo-American Intelligence Partnership', in *American Intelligence Journal*, No. 16, pp. 59–62.

Snow, Nancy (2003), *Information War: American Propaganda, Free Speech and Opinion Control Since 9-11*, New York: Seven Stories Press.

SourceWatch (2009), *Helle C Dale*, available from: www.sourcewatch.org/index .php/Helle_C._Dale.

Spinney, Franklin (2010), 'Can Obama, or Anyone Outmanouver the War Advocates?', blog entry by former military analyst for the Pentagon in *Fabius Maximus*, 2nd October, available from: http://fabiusmaximus.wordpress.com/2010/10/02/22109/.

Stanton, John (2010), 'Iraqi Insurgents Capture Human Terrain Team Member Issa T Salomi', in *Cryptome*, 7th February, available from: http://cryptome.org/0001/hts -salomi.htm.

START (2011), *Background Report: 9/11 Ten Years Later*, available from: www.start.umd .edu/start/announcements/BackgroundReport_10YearsSince9_11.pdf.

Stonor-Saunders, F. (2000), *Who Paid the Piper?* London: Granta.

Sumption, Jonathan (2010), quoted in Wheeler, Brian 'Post-it Notes and the End of Written History' in *BBC News*, 1st July, available from: http://news.bbc.co.uk /1/hi/politics/10338038.

Sunstein, Cass R. and Thaler, Richard H. (2003), 'Libertarian Paternalism is Not an Oxymoron', in *University of Chicago Law Review* Vol. 70, No. 4, pp. 1159–1202.

Susman, L. (2009), 'Shadow Defense Minister Fox Pledges Close US-UK Cooperation If Tories Gain Power', *Leaked cable in Wikileaks*, 10th December, available from: http://213.251.145.96/cable/2009/12/09LONDON2768.html.

Szoldra, P. (2012), 'Hagel was Right about Iraq Surge', in *Business Insider*, 31st January, available from: www.businessinsider.com/hagel-was-right-about-the-iraq-surge- 2013–1.

Tamm, Quinn (1945), *Foreign Relations of the United States, 1945–1950: Emergence of the Intelligence Establishment, Document 7*, 6th September, available from: http://history.state.gov/historicaldocuments/frus1945–50Intel/d7.

Tatham, Steve (2006), *Losing Arab Hearts and Minds: the Coalition, Al-Jazeera and Muslim Public Opinion*, London: Hurst.

Tatham, Steve (2008), 'Strategic Communication: A Primer', in *Advanced Research and Assessment Group*, Shrivenham: Defence Academy of the UK.

Taylor, P.M. (2003), *Munitions of the Mind: A History of Propaganda from the Ancient World to the Present Day*, 3rd edition, Manchester: Manchester University Press.

Taylor, Phil M. (2002), 'Debate: Strategic Communications or Democratic Propaganda?', in *Journalism Studies*, Vol. 3, No. 3, pp. 437–452.

Tempest, Matthew (2007), 'Beckett Welcomes US Troop Surge', in *The Guardian*, 11th January, available from: www.guardian.co.uk/politics/2007/jan/11/iraq.iraq.

The New Yorker (2002), 'The Rendon Group Got Almost $100M From CIA', 4th March, in *PR Watch* (21st April 2009), available from: www.prwatch.org/node/1067.

The White House (2003) 'Bush Establishes Office of Global Communications', *US Mission to Italy Online*, 21st January, available from: www.usembassy.it /viewer/article.asp?article=/file2003_01/alia/A3012105.htm.

Thiessen, M. (2010) 'Wikileaks must be stopped', in *The Washington Post*, 3rd August, available from: www.washingtonpost.com/wp-dyn/content/article/2010/08/02 /AR2010080202627.html.

Thomas, Gordon (2009), *Inside British Intelligence*, London: JR Books.

Thompson, E.P. (1991), *The Making of the English Working Class*, London: Penguin.

Thompson, Robert (1966), *Defeating Communist Insurgency: The Lessons of Malaya and Vietnam*, London: Chatto & Windus.

Thompson, Robert (1972), *Defeating Communist Insurgency: Experiences from Malaya and Vietnam*, London: Chatto & Windus.

Tomlinson, Richard (2001), *The Big Breach: From Top Secret to Maximum Security*, 192.com and Cutting Edge Press, also available from: http://cryptome.org/bigbreach-posts.htm.

Travis, A. (2001), 'Experts Back Startling Heroin Claims', in *The Guardian*, 3rd October, available from: www.opioids.com/afghanistan/heroin.html.

Triadafilopoulos, T. (1999), 'Politics, Speech, and the Art of Persuasion: Toward an Aristotelian Conception of the Public Sphere', in *The Journal of Politics* Vol. 61, No. 3, pp. 741–757.

Truman, H. (1945), *Correspondence with Kent Cooper*, 4th September. (Obtained at Interview from Matt Armstrong.)

Truman, H.S. (1947), 'Address of the President to Congress, Recommending Assistance to Greece and Turkey', 12th March, in *Truman Library Online*, available from: www.trumanlibrary.org/whistlestop/study_collections/doctrine/large/documents/pdfs/5–9.pdf#zoom=100.

Tumber, H. and Palmer, J. (2004), *Media at War*, London: Sage.

UNAMA (2013) 'Afghanistan/Civilian Casualties', in UNIFEED, 31st July, available from: www.unmultimedia.org/tv/unifeed/2013/07/afghanistan-civilian-casualties-3/.

UNHCR (2009), *Afghanistan*, available from: www.unhcr.org/474ac8e00.pdf.

US Advisory Commission on Public Diplomacy (2003), *Building America's Public Diplomacy Through a Reformed Structure and Additional Resources*, US Department of State, Washington DC, 21st January, available from: www.state.gov/documents/organization/13622.pdf.

US Army (2003), *Field Manual No. 3–05.301 Psychological Operations Tactics, Techniques, and Procedures, in Department of the Army*, available from: www.fas.org/irp/doddir/army/fm3–05–301.pdf.

US Army (2005a) *Psychological Operations Field Manual No. 3–05.30, Department of the Army*, available from: www.fas.org/irp/doddir/army/fm3–05–30.pdf.

US Army (2005b) 'Airborne Task Force Band of Brothers Public Affairs Guidance', *Wikileaks*, 11th November, available from: http://file.wikileaks.info/leak/us-101–pagthar-thar-investigation-2006.pdf.

US Embassy, Kabul (2008), 'Scenesetter For December 10–11, 2008 Visit To Afghanistan By SECDEF Robert M. Gates', in *The Guardian*, 2nd December 2010, available from: www.guardian.co.uk/world/us-embassy-cables-documents/181930.

US News (2005), 'How Rocket Scientists Got Into the Hearts and Minds Game', in *US News*, 17th April, available from: www.usnews.com/usnews/news/articles/050425/25roots.b1.htm.

US Senate (2006), *Congressional Record: Proceedings and Debates of the 109th Congress, Second Session*, Vol. 152, pt. 5: 5734.

US Strategic Command (2010), 'US Cyber Command Factsheet', in *US Strategic Command* (Online), available from: www.stratcom.mil/factsheets/cc.

Vanden Brook, T. (2012), 'US "Info Ops" Programs Dubious, Costly', in *USA Today*, 6th December, available from: http://usatoday30.usatoday.com/news/military/story/2012–02–29/afghanistan-iraq-military-information-operations-usa-today-investigation/53295472/1.

Van Dijk, T. (2000), 'New(s) Racism: A Discourse Analytical Approach' in S. Cottle,

Ethnic Minorities and the Media: Changing Cultural Boundaries, Maidenhead: Open University Press.

Vickers, R. (2004), 'The New Public Diplomacy: Britain and Canada Compared', in *The British Journal of Politics and International Relations*, Vol. 6, No. 2, pp. 182–194.

Waddell, R. (1993), 'The Army and Peacetime Low Intensity Conflict, 1961–1992: The Process of Peripheral and Fundamental Military Change', *Unpublished PhD Thesis*, Columbia University.

Waltz, Kenneth Neal (1979), *Theory of International Politics*, Boston, Mass. and London: McGraw Hill.

Warshaw, Shirley Anne (2009), *The Co-Presidency of Bush and Cheney*, Stanford: Stanford University Press.

Watson, Roland and Webster, Philip (2001), 'Campbell Helps to Bolster Alliance Support' in *The Times*, 27th October, p. 3.

Webster, F. (1995), 'Information Management and Manipulation: Jurgen Habermas and the Decline of the Public Sphere', in F. Webster (ed.), *Theories of the Information Society*, London: Routledge.

Weiner, Tim (2008) *Legacy of Ashes: History of the CIA*, London: Penguin.

Whitaker, Brian (2003), 'Poodle Power', in *The Guardian*, 17th February, available from: www.guardian.co.uk/world/2003/feb/17/worlddispatch.iraq.

Wilkerson, L. (2009), quoted in Worthington, A., 'An Interview with Col Lawrence Wilkerson', in *Future of Freedom Foundation Online*, 24th August, available from: www.fff.org/comment/com0908m.asp.

Williams, R. (1958), *Culture and Society: 1780–1950*, London: Chatto and Windus.

Williams, R. (1989), *Marxism and Literature*, Oxford: Oxford University Press.

Wilson, Clay (2006), 'Information Operations and Cyberwar: Capabilities and Related Policy Issues', *Congressional Research Report*, Library of Congress, Washington DC, 14th September, available from: www.fas.org/irp/crs/RL31787.pdf.

Wilson, James Q. (1989), *Bureaucracy: What Government Agencies Do and Why They Do It*, New York: Basic Books.

Wilton, Chris, Griffin, Jonathan and Fotheringham, Andrew (2002), *Changing Perceptions, Review of Public Diplomacy*, Foreign & Commonwealth Office, available from: www.fco.gov.uk/Files/kfile/PDWiltonReview_March2002.pdf.

Woodward, Bob (2004), *Plan of Attack*, London: Simon and Schuster.

Woodward, Bob (2007), *State of Denial*, London: Simon and Schuster, also available from: http://xa.yimg.com/kq/groups/4625512/827801246/name/Bob+Woodward+-+State+of+Denial+(America-911–WTC-Bush-Neocons-Terrorism-Fascism-Iraq).htm.

Woodward, E.L. (1947), 'The English at War', in E. Barker *The Character of England*, Oxford: Oxford University Press.

Worden, Simon (Brig. Gen.) (2005), 'How Rocket Scientists Got Into the Hearts and Minds Game' in *US News*, 17th April, available from: www.usnews.com/usnews/news/articles/050425/25roots.b1.htm.

Zakheim, D.S. (1996), 'Whither the Special Relationship', in *Round Table*, Vol. 337, pp. 73–82.

Zanini, Michelle and Edwards, Sean J.A. (2001), 'THE NETWORKING OF TERROR IN THE INFORMATION AGE', in J. Arquilla and D. Ronfeldt, *Networks and Netwars: The Future of Terror, Crime, and Militancy*, Santa Monica, CA: RAND.

Index

9/11 *see* September 11th 2001

academic involvement with the military
85–90
Adams, G. 111
Aegis (contractor) 119
Aftergood, Steven 83
Afghanistan
Helmand 136–137
Kabul 172–174
Taliban 101–102, 151, 209–210, 248
Al Iraqiya 229–231, 240
Al Jazeera 51, 105, 229–231, 238
Al Qaeda 25, 55, 84–87, 245
Aldrich, Richard 19
Anglo-American relationship 1, 16–24, 31,
185–189, 192–193, 207–220, 234–236,
244–246, 251
imbalance in 18–20, 22–24
Arendt, Hannah 8
Armitage, Richard 29, 27, 69, 72–74, 79,
84, 99, 101, 131–133, 149, 196–200,
203, 207, 235–237
Armstrong, Matt 20, 16, 41–42, 58–64,
95–99, 106, 108, 141–144, 160, 172,
217–219, 250
'Army 2020' doctrine 122
Arquilla, John 140
Arundell, Ralph 12, 14–15, 38–40, 48–51,

68, 79, 88, 116, 138–139, 175–176,
197, 212, 214, 218
asymmetric warfare 15
Ayers, Glenn 59–62, 87, 108, 111, 142, 154,
156–160, 211, 218, 239, 248

Baghdad 225, 236–238, 241
Baird, Brian 169
Barnett, Corelli 136
Basra 188, 203–204, 225–227, 231–232,
241
battalion system 134–136
Bauman, Zygmunt 80, 178
Baxter, Jeff 69
Baxter, Loy 69
Becket, Margaret 242
Beers, Charlotte 67, 96
behavioural approaches 64–66, 79–80,
136, 179, 249–250
Behavioural Dynamics Institute (BDI) 14,
80
Behavioural Insight Team 66
Bell Pottinger (contractor) 51, 78,
229–231, 240
Benbow, T. 141
Bentham, Jeremy 7
Berger, J. 85
Bernays, Edward 17, 86
Berry, M. 249

Billingslea, Marshall 83
bin Laden, Osama 85, 141
black propaganda 9, 15, 36, 39, 45, 247
Blackwill, Robert 187
Blair, Tony 23, 26, 90, 187–190, 206–210,
    232–234, 241–242
Bolton, Josh 170
Booz Allen Hamilton (contractor) 72, 241
Borger, J. 217
Branch, Austin 110, 112, 160–162, 241
Bremer, Paul ('Jerry') 227–232, 236–238,
    240
British Broadcasting Corporation (BBC)
    26, 40, 113–119, 167, 240
Brook, Paul 38, 63, 115, 137
Brooks, Rosa 110, 160
Brown, Gordon 189
BRUSA Agreement (1943) 18
bureaucratic momentum 132
Burnell, P. 4
Bush, George W. 22, 24–26, 68, 83, 96,
    163–164, 168, 178, 187–189, 206–207,
    210, 233–234
Byrnes, Jimmy 19

Cabayan, Doc 241
Cabinet Office, UK 120
Caldwell, Gen. William 58, 143, 162
Campbell, Alastair 112, 117, 208–211, 228
Card, Andy 178
Carlile, Lord 26
Carter, Lord 118
censorship 7–8, 119, 246–250
Central Command, US 82, 99–100
Central Intelligence Agency (CIA) 19,
    21–23, 43–47, 68–69, 75, 81–85, 95,
    98, 101–104, 165–166, 207–209,
    215–218, 220–221
  oversight of 46
Chalabi, Ahmed 165, 215
Charters, David 134
Cheney, Richard 72, 147–149, 164–165
'cherry-picking' intelligence 163

Chomsky, Noam 6–7, 131, 146
civilian casualties on the battlefield 54
Clarke, Torie 55, 66, 132, 145, 150–155,
    158, 192, 194, 232, 249
classification and overclassification of
    intelligence 8, 193–195, 249
Clinton, Bill 95–96, 188
Coalition Information Centres (CICs)
    99–100, 208–209, 224
Coalition Provisional Authority (CPA) 51,
    225
Cohen, E. 141
Cold War 4, 19–22, 25, 29
Combating Terrorism Research and
    Development Memorandum of
    Understanding 87
Consortium of Behavioural Scientists
    78–80
contracting 66–83, 199, 241; *see also*
    Bell Pottinger; Booz Allen Hamilton;
    Haliburton; Harris Corporation;
    Phase One; Rendon, John (and
    Rendon Group); Science Applications
    International Corp; Strategic
    Communication Laboratories
Cook, Robin 23
Cooper, Kent 17, 20
co-optation 81
coordination of propaganda 91–120; in
    the UK 112–119; in the US 95–103
Corcoran, Peter 64, 131, 139, 203, 231,
    240
Cordingley, Patrick 141
'corporate oligopoly' (Chomsky) 7
counter-insurgency 27–28, 65
covert operations 17, 38, 44, 48, 82–85, 91,
    102–103, 218–219
Creel Committee 17
Crocker, Ryan 167, 169, 171
Croft, Stuart 30, 128, 130
Curran, James 8
'Curveball' 164–165
cynicism 134

Dahrendorf, Ralf 133
Dale, Helle 89
Davis, Daniel 172
Dearlove, Richard 207–208
deception and propaganda 11, 38, 68, 83, 113, 159
Defense Intelligence Agency (DIA) 102
democracy and democratic values 2–7
'democratic' propaganda 3–7, 176–178, 247–249
De Rita, Larry 158
Deutch, John 218
Dillon, Jo 210
Dobbs, Michael 23
'dodgy dossier' 113–114, 128
Doob, L.W. 9
Dorril, Stephen 38, 44, 84, 215, 217, 220
Drogin, Bob 101–104, 142, 165–166, 215–216
drones, use of 83, 143, 248, 252
Drumheller, Tyler 163–166
Dugmore, Ian 116
Dumbrell, John 22

ECHELON system 22, 217
effectiveness of propaganda 6, 8, 15, 36, 40, 86–87, 91, 175, 200, 246–247
effects-based planning 53–54, 70, 114, 141, 191
Ellul, Jacques 3–6, 10, 36, 106, 177
embedding of journalists 115, 144, 150–151, 212
Erwin, Sandra 193
Eskew, Tucker 208–211
Etherington, Mark 182
ethics of propaganda *see* morality and ethics
European Union (EU) 187

Fallon, William 14, 28–29, 37, 68, 72–74, 76, 100, 129–130, 146, 156, 176–179, 182
Fallujah 100, 159, 224, 231, 232

Federal Bureau of Investigation (FBI) 104
First World War 2, 16–17, 18
Fitzpatrick, Sean 68, 76–77, 96, 113, 216
'flap potential' 104
Flohr, Linda 73
Fondacaro, Steve 171
Foreign [and Commonwealth] Office, UK (FCO) 19, 36, 66, 99, 114, 118, 212, 233, 235–236, 238–239
foreign policy, propaganda as a tool of 245
'4th generation warfare' 141, 191–192
Fox, Robert 203
Franks, Tommy 82, 149, 197, 225, 235
Fraser, L.M. 4
French, David 198
Frese, Michael 133
'friendly fire' incidents 134, 204
Fulbright, J. William 20
Furlong, Miles 239

Galula, David 27
Garratt, Bob 177
Gates, Robert 161
Gerth, Jeff 97
Glasgow University Media Group 249
Glassman, James 109
Goebbels, Joseph 3, 41
Goodin, R.E. 2–3, 8
Gorman, L. 200
Goss, Porter 103, 220
governmental cultures 130–132, 142–143
Graham, Bradley 49, 55, 57, 96, 147, 232
Gramsci, Antonio 4–5, 129
Greenstock, Jeremy 207, 237
grey propaganda 9–10, 15, 36, 55, 113
Guardian, the 246–247
Gulf War 187, 197, 215
Gutcher, Lianne 139, 173–175

Haass, Richard 218
Habermas, Jürgen 4
Hadley, Stephen 147, 163, 167–168
Hagel, Chuck 172

Haliburton (contractor) 72–73, 78
Hall, Stuart 197
Hamid, Tawfik 89–90
Hanasz, Paula 105, 127, 171–172, 173–175, 195
Harding, Joel 11–12, 42, 43, 52, 57, 65, 80, 85, 97, 109–112, 120, 154, 171, 194, 219
Harris Corporation (contractor) 239
Hayden, Michael 220
Heath, Mike 29, 63, 116
Heginbotham, E. 199
Heimann, J. 47–48, 61–62, 71
Held, V. 26
Helmand 136–137
Henoch, Margaret 166
Henry, Christopher ('Ryan') 141
'herd instinct' 141
Herman, Edward S. 6, 7, 131
Herring, Lee 86
Hersh, Seymour 82–83, 155, 164, 216, 232
Hoon, Geoff 188
Hoover, J. Edgar 19
Hopkins, M.F. 204
Hopkins, N. 217
'horizontal' propaganda 10, 19, 33, 50, 131, 197, 200, 204
Hughes, Karen 56, 208–209
Human Terrain System (HTS) 87–89, 171, 195, 202
Hurd, Douglas 187
Hussein, Saddam 213, 202
Hutton, Lord 113, 119

individualism 128, 144
Information Operations Roadmap (2003) 45, 57–59
Information Operations (IO) 11–13, 58–64, 154–157
information overload 8
Information Research Department, UK 21
information warfare 11
initiative, definition of 133

institutional cultures 123
institutional memory 135–136, 199
insurgency and counter-insurgency 27–28
intellectuals, 'traditional' and 'organic' 5
intelligence
  and 'cherry-picking' 165
  classification and overclassification of 193–195, 249
  Office of Strategic Services (OSS) 18
  see also Anglo-American relations;
    BRUSA Agreement; Central
    Intelligence Agency; 'Curveball';
    Defense Intelligence Agency; 'dodgy
    dossier'; ECHELON system; Federal
    Bureau of Investigation; Information
    Research Department; MI5; MI6;
    PRISM programme; TEMPORA
    programme
Interactive Internet Activities (IIA) 61
International Criminal Court 134
internet technology 55, 61
interoperability between armed forces 190–191
Iraq *see* Baghdad; Basra; Coalition
    Provisional Authority; Fallujah;
    Hussein, Saddam; 'surge' strategy
Iraqi Media Network (IMN) 229–231, 238
Irish Republican Army (IRA) 76

Jackson, Roy 181
Jefferson, Thomas 17
Jenkins, Jon 137
Jenkins, Roy 188
Johnson, Chalmers 22
Jolly, Stephen 39
Jones, Jeffrey 50, 68, 72, 85, 96–99, 105–107, 155, 194, 197, 235, 241
Jones, Nicholas 211
Jowell, Tessa 210
Jowett, Garth 94, 146

Kabul 171–173
Kambrod, Matthew 72, 148

Karsai, Hamid 69
Keane, J. 7
Keeble, Richard 44
Kelly, David 119
Kennan, George S. 146
Kennedy, John F. (JFK) 22, 178
Kerry, John 142
Kibbe, Jennifer 25, 83
Kier, Elizabeth 196
Kilcullen, D. 28
Kimball, Warren F. 23
Kirby, D. 17
Kirke, Charles 117, 135
Kissinger, Henry 146
Kitson, Sir Frank 133
Koza, Frank 234

Lamb, Christopher 106
Lamb, Graham 214
Lasswell, H.D. 3, 9, 176
League of Nations 17
LeBaron, Richard 110
Lee, Ian 115
Le Gallo, Andre 44, 82, 86
Lend-Lease 18–19
Levi, Werner 246
Lewis, J. 26
Libby, Scooter 148, 165
Lieberman, Joseph 142
Lincoln Group (contractor) 70, 74, 97
Lippmann, W. 3, 17, 132
Little, George 105, 110
Lloyd, Terry 116
Lloyd Owen, David 198
Lukes, Steven 248–250
Lundestad, Geir 24

McBride, Dennis 56–57, 69, 76, 85–86,
    100, 179–181, 216–217, 221
McCain, John 172
McCarty, Kevin 25, 40, 42, 50–52, 78–80,
    97, 108, 111, 142–143, 166–171, 218
McChrystal, Stanley 174

McClure, Robert 18
McCreary, Terry ('T') 12, 49, 56, 71, 115,
    128–129, 144, 150–154, 157, 159, 178
McDonough, Denis 172
McFadden, Charles 229
McFate, Montgomery 87–88, 141, 171, 199
McHale, Judith 109
Machiavelli, Nicolò 2
Mackay, A. 63–66, 87–89, 117–118,
    136–137, 144, 249
McKercher, B.J.C. 24
McLaughlin, John 164–166
MacLean, D. 200
McLellan, D. 5
Macmillan, Alan 201
Manley, Jim 169
Manning, David 207–208, 235–236
Manningham-Buller, Eliza 44
MANTECH International (contractor) 72
Marshall, Andrew 140
Marshall Plan 20
Media Operations 63–64, 144
    definition of 12
Merton, R.K. 4
Meyer, Chris 112, 187, 197, 235–236
MI5 44–45, 113, 216
MI6 13, 44–45, 113, 208, 215–216, 220
Miliband, David 190
military culture 133
Mill, John Stuart 4
Miller, David 7, 11, 22, 89
Miller, Franklin 36, 50, 56, 58, 98, 100,
    103, 147–151, 163–166, 177, 192–199,
    207–208, 217–219, 224, 233–236
Mills, Tom 11, 89
Milner Group 17, 19
Miracle, Tammy 115
morality and ethics of propaganda
    2, 6, 7–8, 16, 36–38, 73,
    80, 85, 154–155, 180, 217, 246
Military Information Support Operations
    (MISO) 12, 46, 48–49
Moxham, Jody 73, 77

Myers, Gen. Richard 56, 82, 128–129, 152, 155, 214

Nagl, John 27, 53, 94, 122–123, 130–136, 140, 145, 182, 186, 200, 203
Negroponte, John 103
neo-Conservatives in politics and the military 128, 146, 206
neo-liberalism 187
North Atlantic Treaty Organisation (NATO) 20, 189–191, 205
Northern Ireland 199, 203
'nudging' people 136
Nye, Joseph 27, 79

Oakes, Nigel 14, 64–65, 80, 240–241
Obama, Barack 22, 80, 84, 205
O'Connell, M.E. 83
O'Donnell, Victoria 94, 146
O'Hanlon, Michael 140, 169
Omar, Mullah 214
openness, principles of 36
organisational culture 95
organisational learning 123
'otherness' 25, 26, 182
outsourcing of propaganda work 68, 72–74, 79
Overt Peacetime Psychological Operations Program 57

Pakenham, Michael 113
Palmer, Chris 137
Panetta, Leon 161
paternalism 176–179, 182, 202, 245, 249–250
Paton, Iain 193
Pavitt, Jim 68, 163, 166
Pennett, Miles 72, 238–243
Pentagon, the *see* United States Department of Defense
perception management 84
Percival, Alan 209
Peterson, H.C. 17

Petraeus, David 58, 167–171, 195, 203
Pfeifle, Mark 97, 108–109, 156, 168–170, 219
PhaseOne (contractor) 69–78
Philo, G. 26, 248
Phyllis Report (2004) 63
Picard, Iain 238
Pierce, James G. 98, 141
Pimlott, Ben 189
Pincus, Walter 102–103
Plame Wilson, Valerie 102, 129, 148, 165–166
Plato 2
politicisation 144
Pollack, Kenneth 169
Ponsonby, Lord 2
Posen, Barry 145
Potomac Institute for Policy Studies 56–57, 70, 72, 76
Powell, Colin (and Powell Doctrine) 25, 133, 149, 164–166, 200, 210, 233–234
pre-propaganda 106
PRISM programme 217
propaganda
American and British perceptions of 'rules' 38–43
audiences for 36–38
black 9, 36, 39, 45, 247
categories of 9–10
coordination of 91, 94–120
covert and overt 36
and deception 10, 38, 68, 83, 113, 159
definition of 9
as 'democratic' 2–7, 176–178, 247–249
domestic authorities' rules and restrictions 41–43, 45–46, 60, 70, 247
effectiveness of 6, 8, 15, 36, 40, 86–87, 91, 175, 200, 246–247
evolution of 53
grey 9–10, 15, 36, 55, 113
history of 6, 16–24
horizontal 10, 19, 33, 50, 131, 197, 200, 204

indirect forms of 20
inevitability of 14
intentions and goals of 5, 249
internal and external 10, 247–248
morality and ethics of 2, 6, 7–8, 16,
  36–38, 73, 80, 85, 154–155, 180, 217,
  246
and social media 91, 143, 176
'spin' and 'spin doctors' 9
and 'sponsorship' of media 57
and truth 2, 9, 37, 39
vertical 10
white 9, 36, 37, 181
see also behavioural approaches;
  Information Operations; information
  warfare; Media Operations;
  perception management;
  psychological operations; Public
  Affairs; Public Diplomacy
proportionality 46–47
Psychological Operations (PSYOP) 11–15,
  39–44, 56, 107, 131
Psychological Warfare Division 18
Public Affairs 12–13, 36, 42, 49–50, 55–63,
  66–67, 70, 96, 99, 102, 108–110,
  153–162, 213, 246, 248
Public Diplomacy (PD) 12, 20, 40, 48–49,
  52, 57, 62, 66, 114, 142–143, 153, 211
  definition of 13
public interest and the public good 8,
  132–133, 245–246, 250
public opinion 3–4, 6, 167, 247
'public service' concept 127–134
Pugmire, Brian 95

Qualter, T.H. 4
Quille, Gerard 141

redundancies in the armed forces 122
Reeve, A. 4
regimental system 135
Reith, Sir John 197, 235
Rendition 216, 221

Rendon, John and Rendon Group
  (contractor) 68–70, 73, 97
Reuters 17
Revolution in Military Affairs (RMA)
  140–141, 192
Reynolds, D. 18
rhetoric 2, 25–26, 28
Rhodes, Ben 97, 172
Rice, Condoleezza 57, 147–148, 163, 189,
  207, 235
Riddell, Peter 22, 24
Riedel, Bruce 22
Risen, James 207–208, 213
Ritter, Scott 45
Rogan, Janet 238
Roosevelt, F.D. 17–18
Rose, David 45
Rove, Karl 207
Rowland, Lee 14, 64, 80, 137
Rowlands, Kirsteen 115–122, 191
Rowlands, Tony 239
rules of propaganda
  American perceptions of 40–41
  British perceptions of 38–40
Rumsfeld, Donald 50, 55–57, 68–72,
  81–84, 96, 99–104, 107, 122, 145–155,
  158, 164, 214, 224–227, 232–234
Rusbridger, Alan 247
Russia 19

Sada-e Azadi (newspaper) 139, 174–175
al-Sadr, Muqtada 232
Sambrook, Richard 210
Sanchez, Ricardo 98, 225
Sattler, John 192
Sawers, Sir John 228, 236
Scahill, Jeremy 83
Scarlett, John 113, 220
Science Applications International
  Corp (SAIC) (contractor) 70,
  238–239
Scott, Len 47, 113, 221
Second World War 6, 18–19, 23–24

Secret Intelligence Service (SIS) *see* MI6
security, concept of 27
September 11th 2001 1, 26, 90,
    130, 188, 210–211, 245, 248
Sforza, Scott 228
Sharon, Ariel 90
Shaw, Martin 248
Sheinwald, Nigel 235
Sheriff, Vickie 66, 116–117, 137–138, 209
Shiffrin, Richard 245–247
Shiner, Phil 202
Shipman, Tim 190
Shy, J. 200
Silverberg, D. 47–48, 61–62, 71
Skidelsky, R. 24
'SMART power' concept 79, 131
Smith, Bradley 18
Smith, Dorrance 51, 155, 157–158, 227,
    233, 237–238
Smith-Thornberry Amendment (2009)
    109
Snowden, Edward 22, 194, 217–219
social class in British military 201
'special relationship' between US and UK
    see Anglo-American relationship
Spicer, Tim 199
'spin' and 'spin doctors' 9
Spinney, Franklin 148
'sponsorship' of media 57
Stanton, John 88
Stelloh, Ren 43–44, 46, 67–78, 163
Stonor-Saunders, F. 21
'stovepipes' 132
Strategic Communication 48–49, 55, 59,
    80, 107–112, 119–122, 150, 159, 172,
    205, 224
  definition of 105–112
Strategic Communication Laboratories
    (contractor) 80, 240
Sunstein, Cass R. 136
'surge' strategy 100–101, 108, 111,
    167–172, 241
Synnott, Hilary 232

Taliban 101–102, 151, 209–210, 248
Tatham, Steve 14, 63–66, 80, 87–89, 105,
    117–122, 127, 136, 144, 249
Taverner, Angus 39, 51, 63–64, 78,
    112–119, 127–128, 134, 137–139, 144,
    192, 194–195, 208–209, 212
Taylor, Phil 5, 11, 25, 105, 176, 249
TEMPORA programme 217
Tenet, George 68, 103, 207–208
'terrologists' 11, 89
terrorism 8, 25, 84, 188, 245
  definition of 25–29
Thaler, Richard H. 136
Thatcher, Gary 240
Thiessen, Marc 84
think tanks 85–89; *see also* Potomac
    Institute for Policy Studies
Thomas, Gordon 44, 104, 220
Thompson, E.P. 177–178
Thompson, Robert 27, 85
Thorp, Frank 29, 37, 54, 56, 59–60, 67, 70,
    74–76, 81, 96–99, 107–108, 154–160,
    205, 212–213, 220, 224
Tomlinson, Richard 44
torture and abuse of detainees 134, 152,
    180–181, 216, 220
  Abu Ghraib 15, 59, 88–93, 152–153
  definition of 134
Treadwell, Jim 61
Truman, Harry 19
Tunnicliffe, Ian 38, 47, 53–54, 137,
    225–229, 238

United Kingdom
  10 Downing Street 112, 209–211
  Behavioural Insight Team 66
  Cabinet Office 120
  Defence Crisis Management Centre
    114–115
  Defence Media Operations Centre 138,
    192
  Defence Science Technology Laboratory
    137

Department for International
  Development 114
Foreign and Commonwealth Office
  (FCO) 19, 36, 66, 99, 114, 118, 212,
  233, 235–236, 238–239
Government Communication Network
  (GCN) 63
Government Communications
  Headquarters (GCHQ) 22, 194, 217
Human Rights Act 134
Information Research Department 21
Joint Intelligence Committee 23, 113
MI5 44–45, 113, 216
MI6 13, 44–45, 113, 208, 215–216,
  220
Ministry of Defence (MoD) 53, 78,
  113–120, 135–136, 195
Official Secrets Act (1911) 8
Phyllis Report (2004) 63
Special Air Service (SAS) 214
Security Assistance Group (SAG) 122
Special Operations Executive (SOE) 18,
  19
Targeting and Information Operations
  Director[ate] 114, 116–117
Terrorism Act (2000) 8
United Nations (UN) 17, 128, 234
  Security Council 22
United States
  Central Command 82, 99
  Centre for Strategic Counterterrorism
    Communications 109, 241
  Congress 17, 41–42, 46, 71, 140
  Counter Terrorism Information
    Strategy Policy Coordinating
    Committee 97
  Cyber Command 84
  Defense Intelligence Agency (DIA) 102
  Defense Science Board 80
  Department of Defense (DOD) 42–43,
    47–48, 61–62, 71, 75, 77, 81–83,
    98–111, 141–145, 149–150, 154, 156,
    193–194

Government Accountability Office
  (GAO) 96
Human Terrain System (HTS) 87–89,
  171, 199, 202
Information Agency (USIA) 20, 22
Information Operations Roadmap
  (2003) 45, 57–59
International Public Information Core
  Group 95–96
National Clandestine Service (NCS) 43
National Security Act (1947) 41
National Security Agency (NSA) 22,
  194, 217, 219
National Security Council (NSC) 47,
  97–98, 101, 111, 119, 163, 227,
  250–251
Neutrality Act (1939) 17
Office of Global Communications 56
Office of Strategic Influence (OSI)
  55–58, 70, 153–155
Office of Strategic Services (OSS) 18
Smith-Mundt Act (1948) 20, 42
Smith-Thornberry Amendment (2009)
  109
Special Operations Command 81–83,
  214
Special Operations Military
  Information Support Teams 99
State Department 20, 36, 41, 48–49,
  56–57, 67, 71–72, 77, 95–99, 109–112,
  120, 142–143, 156, 196
Stategic Communication Information
  Group (SCIG) 108
US Code 41–42
White House 95–97, 110–112, 120–121,
  155, 167–172, 209–212, 227–228,
  234–237
  see also Central Intelligence Agency;
    Federal Bureau of Investigation

van Dijk, T. 26
Vanden Brook, T. 49
Vanity Fair 239

Vaz, Keith 247
'vertical' propaganda 10
Vietnam War 20, 100
Voice of America 41, 52, 245

Waltz, Kenneth Neal 146
'War on Terror' 25, 35, 84, 96, 128,
     141, 144, 181, 185, 191, 198, 245,
     250–251
Washington, George 16
Waziristan 74–75
Weale, Adrian 133, 135, 139, 152,
     179, 182, 202–205, 214, 220–221, 225,
     228–229, 232, 252
Weiner, Tim 21
whistleblowers 152, 246
white propaganda 9, 36, 37, 181
Wilkerson, Lawrence 25, 37, 50, 56, 71–72,
     81, 98–99, 101–103, 148–149,

     152, 154, 164–165, 178, 182, 235
Wilkerson, Paul 89
Williams, Raymond 127–129, 176–179,
     200, 249
Wilson, Doug 48–49, 101–102, 105,
     108, 109–110, 142–143, 153, 155,
     160–161, 172
Wilson, Woodrow 17
Wingfield, Thomas 40–47, 217, 219
Woodward, Bob 148, 189, 207–208
Worden, Simon ('Pete') 70, 153–154
Wright, Graham 5, 22, 36, 40, 63–69, 74,
     87, 91, 100, 112–119, 206–207,
     211, 218, 241–242

Zinni, Tony 71, 78
Zorinsky, Edward 20